Beyond the Case

Recent Titles in

Global and Comparative Ethnography
Edited by Javier Auyero

Violence at the Urban Margins
Edited by Javier Auyero, Philippe Bourgois, and Nancy Scheper-Hughes

Concrete Jungles
By Rivke Jaffe

Soybeans and Power
By Pablo Lapegna

Occupying Schools, Occupying Land
By Rebecca Tarlau

Privilege at Play
By Hugo Cerón-Anaya

Narrow Fairways
By Patrick Inglis

Lives on the Line
By Jeffrey J. Sallaz

The Ambivalent State
By Javier Auyero and Katherine Sobering

Beyond the Case

The Logics and Practices of Comparative Ethnography

Edited by

COREY M. ABRAMSON AND NEIL GONG

OXFORD
UNIVERSITY PRESS

OXFORD
UNIVERSITY PRESS

Oxford University Press is a department of the University of Oxford. It furthers the University's objective of excellence in research, scholarship, and education by publishing worldwide. Oxford is a registered trade mark of Oxford University Press in the UK and certain other countries.

Published in the United States of America by Oxford University Press
198 Madison Avenue, New York, NY 10016, United States of America.

Library of Congress Cataloging-in-Publication Data
ISBN 978–0–19–060849–1 (pbk.)
ISBN 978–0–19–060848–4 (hbk.)

Contents

Acknowledgments

This volume has benefited tremendously from the contributions, commentary, and opportunities for dialog offered by scholars who work on the theory and practice of comparative social science. First and foremost, we would like to acknowledge each of our contributors, without whom this volume would quite literally not exist. Each has provided important methodological contributions that we are extremely grateful to be able to share. We would also like to thank Martín Sánchez-Jankowski, Stefan Timmermans, Aaron Cicourel, Hannah Landecker, Dan Dohan, Loic Wacquant, Rogers Brubaker, and George Marcus for thoughtful comments and conversations over the course of this project. In addition, Martín Sánchez-Jankowski provided detailed comments that helped improve the content of our introductory and concluding chapters. We would also like to acknowledge the members of the Center for Ethnographic Research at UC Berkeley and the participants of the Beyond Positivism Conference in Montreal organized by George Steinmetz, Phil Gorski, and Douglas Porpora for comments that helped in conceptualizing this volume early in the process. The Udall Center at the University of Arizona provided support during Abramson's sabbatical year (2019). The Michigan Society of Fellows provided support during Gong's tenure as a junior fellow (2019). Although the standards of peer review preclude naming them directly, numerous anonymous reviewers helped improve the scholarship throughout this volume through their detailed commentary on each of the included chapters. We would like to acknowledge Erin Murphy Heinz, who provided research assistance as well as substantive commentary on our introduction and conclusion. Finally, we would like to thank Oxford University Press and our editor, James Cook, for their patience and support for this volume.

Contributor Biographies

Editors

Corey M. Abramson is Associate Professor of Sociology at the University of Arizona. His research uses a combination of quantitative, qualitative, and hybrid methods to understand how persistent social inequalities structure everyday life and are reproduced over time. His recent ethnography on this topic, *The End Game: How Inequality Shapes Our Final Years* was published by Harvard University Press in 2015 and released in paperback in 2017. Since its release, *The End Game* has been awarded the 2016 Outstanding Publication Award by the American Sociological Association Section (ASA) on Aging and the Life Course, selected for an Author Meets Critic Session at the ASA, featured in national media outlets including the *New York Times* and *The Atlantic*, and translated into Korean. Abramson's recent methodological works, including pieces in *Sociological Methodology* and *Ethnography*, focus on integrating computational techniques to improve the scalability, replicability, and transparency of large multisite comparative ethnographic projects conducted in accordance with realist principles. His current book project deploys these techniques to examine how the biological, institutional, interpersonal, and economic implications of terminal cancer shape the lives and deaths of people from different backgrounds.

Neil Gong is Assistant Professor of Sociology at the University of California, San Diego and is currently a Junior Fellow at the University of Michigan Society of Fellows. His research uses diverse empirical cases to study power and social control in modernity, with a specific focus on understanding liberal social order. Neil's book project, is a comparative ethnography of public safety net and elite private psychiatric services in community settings, and he has previously researched a no-rules libertarian fight club. His articles have appeared in *The American Sociological Review; Social Problems; Theory and Society*; and *Ethnography*.

Contributors

Alissa Bernstein is a medical anthropologist and research fellow at the Philip R. Lee Institute for Health Policy Studies at the University of California San Francisco (UCSF) and a Senior Atlantic Fellow at the Global Brain Health Institute. Her research focuses on improving access to social services for caregivers of people with dementia, and on building and implementing tools to assist primary care providers in the assessment and management of dementia in the primary care setting. She is a qualitative researcher on a number of studies through the UCSF Memory and Aging Center and the Global Brain Health Institute.

Lynn S. Chancer is Professor of Sociology at Hunter College and the Graduate Center of the City University of New York. She is the author and coeditor of seven books, including *Sadomasochism in Everyday Life: Dynamics of Power and Powerlessness* (Rutgers 1992); *Reconcilable Differences: Confronting Beauty, Pornography and the Future of Feminism* (University of California Press 1998); *High Profile Crimes: When Legal Cases Become Social Causes* (University of Chicago Press 2005); *The Unhappy Divorce of Sociology and Psychoanalysis* (coedited with John Andrews, London Palgrave Macmillan 2014); and most recently *Youth, Jobs and the Future: Problems and Prospects* (coedited with Martín Sánchez-Jankowski and Christine Trost, Oxford 2018) and *After the Rise and Stall of American Feminism: Taking Back a Revolution* (Stanford University Press 2019). She is also the author of articles on varied subjects from criminology, gender, sex, and sex work through social and feminist theory.

Aaron V. Cicourel is Professor Emeritus of Sociology, Cognitive Science, and Pediatrics at the University of California, San Diego. Cicourel has been a practicing ethnographer for over six decades and was a central figure in the emergence and international development of both ethnomethodology and cognitive sociology. He has written myriad papers and books on diverse topics such as sociolinguistics, medical communication, decision-making, juvenile justice, and child socialization. In addition to his empirical works, Cicourel has produced important methodological works, including his now classic book *Method and Measurement in Sociology* (Free Press of Glencoe 1964). Cicourel has won various international awards and honorary doctorates and was elected to the American Academy of Arts and Sciences in 1992.

Claire Laurier Decoteau is Associate Professor of Sociology at the University of Illinois at Chicago. Her research focuses on the social construction of health and disease, the politics of knowledge production, and peoples' grounded experiences with healing and healthcare systems. Her first book, *Ancestors and Antiretrovirals: The Biopolitics of HIV/AIDS in Post-Apartheid South Africa* (University of Chicago Press 2013) was awarded three honorable mentions for outstanding book awards from ASA sections: Medical Sociology; Science, Knowledge and Technology; and the Theory Section. Decoteau has articles published in journals such as *Sociological Theory; Political Power and Social Theory; European Journal of Social Theory; BioSocieties; Social Science & Medicine*; and *Social Studies of Science*. Decoteau is currently writing her second book, *The "Western Disease": Epistemic Contestations over Autism in the Somali Diaspora*, which is under contract with the University of Chicago Press.

Thomas DeGloma is Associate Professor of Sociology at Hunter College and the Graduate Center, City University of New York. His research interests fall within the intersecting areas of cultural sociology and symbolic interaction, and include explorations of cognition, memory, time, knowledge, autobiography, identity, and trauma. DeGloma's book *Seeing the Light: The Social Logic of Personal Discovery* (University of Chicago Press 2014) explores the stories people tell about life-changing discoveries of "truth" and illuminates the ways that individuals and communities use autobiographical stories to weigh in on salient moral and political controversies. This book received the 2015 Charles Horton Cooley Book Award from the Society for the Study of Symbolic Interaction. DeGloma has also published articles in *Social Psychology Quarterly; Symbolic Interaction; Sociological Forum*; and the *American Journal of Cultural Sociology*, along with several chapters in various edited volumes. He is currently working on his second book, which explores the phenomenon of anonymity and the impact of anonymous actors in various social situations and interactions. He recently served as president of the Society for the Study of Symbolic Interaction (2017–2018) and Secretary of the Eastern Sociological Society (2016–2019).

Daniel Dohan is Professor of Health Policy and Social Medicine at the University of California, San Francisco (UCSF), where he works on understanding and enhancing the culture of medicine. Current projects examine research participation, novel neurotechnologies, and provision of surgery to frail older adults. He teaches medical students and postdoctoral trainees and coleads the UCSF/UC Hastings MS degree program in Health Policy and Law.

Ching Kwan Lee is Professor of Sociology at the University of California, Los Angeles. Her research interests include labor, political sociology, globalization, development, China, Hong Kong, the Global South, and comparative ethnography. She is the author of three award-winning monographs on China's turn to capitalism through the lens of labor: *Gender and the South China Miracle: Two Worlds of Factory Women* (University of California Press 1998), *Against the Law: Labor Protests in China's Rustbelt and Sunbelt* (University of California Press 2007), and *The Specter of Global China: Politics, Labor and Foreign Investment in Africa* (University of Chicago Press 2017). Her articles have appeared in the *American Journal of Sociology; American Sociological Review; Theory and Society; New Left Review*; the *China Quarterly*; and *Journal of Asian Studies*. Her most recent coedited volumes include *The Social Question in the 21st Century: A Global View* (University of California Press 2019) and *Take Back Our Future: An Eventful Political Sociology of the Hong Kong Umbrella Movement* (Cornell University Press 2019).

Max Papadantonakis is a PhD candidate in Sociology at the City University of New York, the Graduate Center and Graduate Teaching Fellow at Queens College, where he teaches classical and contemporary sociological theory. His interests are in the areas of social theory, culture, sociology of work, and ethnography. Recently he published a chapter (with Sharon Zukin) in *Precarious Work*, an edited volume of the series Research in the Sociology of Work (Emerald Publishing Limited 2017). Max also recently carried out an ethnography in seven hackathons in New York City and looked at the different ways workers' consent is manufactured in the "new" economy.

His dissertation research focuses on the social formation of the tech workforce in New York City with emphasis on the cultural differences between engineers and entrepreneurs.

Martín Sánchez-Jankowski is Professor of Sociology and Director of the Institute for the Study of Societal Issues at the University of California, Berkeley. His research has focused on the sociology of poverty and violence. He has conducted long-term participant-observation field research for 42 years. He has published a number of books and research papers, among them *Islands in the Street: Gangs and American Urban Society* (University of California Press 1991); *Cracks in the Pavement: Social Change and Resilience in Poor Neighborhoods* (University of California Press 2008); and *Burning Dislike: Ethnic Violence in High Schools* (University of California Press 2016). His current field research focuses on the poverty conditions of rural indigenous people in the United States, Fiji, and India.

Iddo Tavory is Associate Professor of Sociology at New York University. A sociologist of culture and an ethnographer, he is broadly interested in the interactional patterns through which people come to construct and understand their lives across situations. His book *Abductive Analysis* (with Stefan Timmermans, University of Chicago Press 2014) provides a pragmatist account that allows researchers to make the most of the surprises that emerge in the process of research. His second book, *Summoned* (University of Chicago Press 2016), is an ethnography of a Jewish neighborhood in Los Angeles as well as a treatise on the coconstitution of interaction, identity, and social worlds. He is currently working on an ethnography of an advertising agency in New York, and coauthoring a book on pro bono work and notions of worth in the advertising world. Among other awards, Iddo has received the Lewis A. Coser Award for theoretical agenda setting in sociology.

Stefan Timmermans is Professor of Sociology at the University of California, Los Angeles. His research interests include medical sociology and science studies. He has conducted research on medical technologies, health professions, death and dying, and population health. He is the author, most recently, of *Postmortem: How Medical Examiners Explain Suspicious Deaths* (University of Chicago Press 2006); *Saving Babies? The Consequences of Newborn Genetic Screening* (with Mara Buchbinder, University of Chicago Press 2013); and *Abductive Analysis: Theorizing Qualitative Research* (with Iddo Tavory, University of Chicago Press 2014). He is also senior editor of medical sociology for the journal *Social Science and Medicine*.

Beyond the Case

Introduction

The Promise, Pitfalls, and Practicalities of Comparative Ethnography

Corey M. Abramson and Neil Gong

> Thinking without comparison is unthinkable. And in the absence of comparison, so is all scientific thought.
>
> —Guy Swanson

> There is only one method . . . the comparative method. And that is impossible.
>
> —E. E. Pritchard

The social sciences have seen an increase in comparative and multi-sited ethnographic projects over the last three decades. This growth calls for a careful consideration of methodological practices. Field research methods have traditionally been associated with small-scale, in-depth, and singular case studies, yet contemporary approaches are often much broader. Further, comparative ethnography encompasses very different methodological traditions with divergent approaches toward comparative social science. Practitioners have reflected on *multi-sited* approaches within particular traditions,[1] yet the act of *comparison*, and the practical and analytical moves that this entails, requires elaboration and reflection. At present researchers seeking to design comparative field projects have studies to emulate, but few scholarly works detailing how comparison is actually conducted in different ethnographic traditions. Just as comparative historical researchers advanced their methodological toolkit with reflections on why and how to compare, ethnographers

[1] For examples see Falzon 2016 and Burawoy 2007.

Corey M. Abramson and Neil Gong, *Introduction* In: *Beyond the Case*. Edited by: Corey M. Abramson and Neil Gong, Oxford University Press (2020).
DOI: 10.1093/oso/9780190608484.003.0001

can benefit from examining our varied approaches to comparison and their analytic consequences.

Beyond the Case addresses these issues by showing how practitioners employ comparison in a variety of ethnographic traditions such as phenomenology, grounded theory, behavioralism, and interpretivism. It aims to connect the long history of comparative (and anti-comparative) ethnographic approaches to their contemporary uses. Each chapter allows influential scholars from their respective traditions to: (1) unpack the methodological logics that shape how they use comparison, (2) connect these precepts to the concrete techniques they employ in their work, and (3) articulate the utility of their approach. By honing in on how ethnographers render sites, groups, or cases analytically commensurable and comparable, these contributions offer a new lens for examining the assumptions, payoffs, and potential drawbacks of different approaches so that readers can critically evaluate their intellectual merits. For those new to comparative ethnography, this will aid in selecting and applying an approach that maps on to their research goals. For those already committed to an existing approach or tradition, engagement with alternatives may provide insights into the strengths, weaknesses, and potential avenues for improving their own work.

The remainder of this introductory chapter provides important background information about the methodological and practical challenges that comparative ethnographers face. We begin by considering discussions of both the utility and difficulty of comparative field research. We then consider how ethnography's unusually diverse set of traditions provides both unique challenges and possibilities for comparative social science. Next, we turn to the ways in which this diversity translates into divergent approaches to comparison. This is followed with an overview of the structure of the volume explaining how the chapters that follow advance comparative ethnographic methods. We conclude with a discussion of why acknowledging, maintaining, and utilizing ethnographic pluralism, rather than pushing for a single catch-all approach, can benefit both individual scholars and the field of ethnographic methodology.

The Promise of Comparison in Ethnography

Ethnographers have long reflected on the simultaneous appeal and difficulty of engaging in comparison in field research. The promise of comparative ethnography is that it provides analytical possibilities that are challenging or impossible in traditional single-case studies—for instance, enrichening interpretation through contrast, aiding in causal inference, showing how different contexts shape ostensibly similar phenomena, or revealing similarities across seemingly different objects. Yet such comparison is also fraught with methodological questions. Are the sites, cases, or people under study truly comparable? Does such an approach require the reduction of fine-grained detail and narrative to render objects similar enough for side-by-side examination? If so, is such a reduction useful or does it compromise the purpose of in-depth fieldwork? As this volume will demonstrate, positions on these questions vary substantially among contemporary ethnographers. The following discussion of ongoing debates about the value and pitfalls of ethnographic comparison provides useful context.

In previous eras, scholars have argued that the comparison of ethnographic materials is either indispensable or infeasible. Sometimes, they argued both at the same time. The social anthropologist E. E. Evans-Pritchard reportedly quipped, "There is only one method . . . the comparative method. And that is impossible."[2] In his influential vision of a comparative anthropology that encompassed the globe, a fieldworker "compares the structures his analysis has revealed in a wide-range of societies" (1950, 122). This was the logic driving the development of massive comparative archives like the Human Relation Area Files (HRAF) that aimed to document cultural practices around the world and facilitate a general science of human culture. Yet Evans-Pritchard saw immense analytical difficulty in reducing cases for comparative analysis. Regarding his own studies of the Nilotic peoples of South Sudan, he wrote, "I have found that even they are too heterogeneous a group for intensive comparison, with regard to environment, culture, and history" (1965, 20). If mid-century anthropologists were frustrated by the ethnological comparison of whole peoples, some later anthropologists after the post-structural turn rejected it outright—deconstructing "societies" as distinct units, critiquing the normative evaluations associated with comparing "primitive" to "modern" cultures, and seeing radical incommensurability between contexts (Jensen et al. 2011).

Contemporary sociological ethnographers, on the other hand, have been more apt to design comparative studies. This may derive from the strong

[2] As with many such aphorisms, it is unclear whether Evans Pritchard actually said this. It never appeared in his published writings, but was relayed by colleagues (see Needham 1975).

position of comparative approaches in the discipline found in both survey research and historical analyses. Furthermore, rather than comparing at the level of "peoples," sociological fieldworkers have typically sought to compare and contrast more delimited objects of study. For instance, sociologists have engaged in comparisons of how parents from different class backgrounds engage in childrearing (Lareau 2011), how gangs in different parts of the United States operate (Sánchez-Jankowski 1991), how factories owned by the same company yet sitting on different sides of a national border treat workers (Lee 1995), how scientists reason in physics versus biology labs (Knorr-Cetina 1999), and how organizations fail in settings ranging from romance to space shuttle launches (Vaughan 2014).

Yet some sociologists have questioned even this more tempered comparative approach. Consider the recent methodological debate between, and divergent positions of, two prominent sociologists: Michael Burawoy and Matt Desmond. In his 2014 call for a "relational ethnography," Desmond identifies the comparative work of Michael Burawoy and his students, who often compare organizations in different macro contexts, as an especially problematic approach to be avoided. In selecting objects to compare based on prior theoretical assumptions, Desmond contends, these researchers reify places, assume the existence of groups, and impose other pre-existing theoretical categories in ways that do not map on to the flow of everyday life. Desmond sees these analytic impositions as a failure to break with harmful preconceptions and suggests instead following flows and associations in a multi-sited rather than comparative frame (e.g., Marcus 1995; Tsing 2011).

In his rebuttal, Burawoy (2017) responds that it is Desmond who fails to move beyond everyday categories to substantive sociological analysis precisely because he does not frame his objects as theoretical cases to be compared. Burawoy contends that Desmond's ostensibly relational research on home eviction, with its focus on transactions between landlords, tenants, and street-level bureaucrats, misses the crucial "structural relations" with larger markets and the state because Desmond does not situate the eviction process of a single city in a comparative frame that allows for broader statements. According to Burawoy, the lack of comparative thinking further prevents Desmond from offering a causal account of the patterns of variation seen in his data, and his lack of theoretical engagement (with Marxism in particular) means his take on "exploitation" leads only to bland and insufficiently "structural" policy proposals. Burawoy ultimately suggests that Desmond is engaged in a rehashing of empiricist micro-interaction that never moves beyond the accounts of his research subjects.[3]

In the terms set by these authors, it becomes apparent that case comparison remains both highly consequential and contested. It can either trap ethnographers by reifying inappropriate objects with preconceived notions (Desmond's concern), or it is precisely the process that allows ethnographers to break with common sense, generate knowledge, and unmask the operation of social processes (Burawoy's position). Yet this debate, and the long and fraught history of comparing peoples in sociology and anthropology, can present an opportunity instead of an impasse. Rather than embrace a singular mode of comparison or anti-comparison a priori, this volume examines how ethnographers from a variety of perspectives have grappled with such issues and complicated the division. A useful parallel can be drawn with comparative historical researchers, who found themselves at a similar crossroads in the mid-twentieth century. Positioned between quantitative researchers who questioned the scientific value of "small-n" studies and interpretivists who rejected the ability to compare radically unique historical events (see Steinmetz 2004), they used the opportunity to reflect on why and how they engaged in comparison, and their position vis-à-vis the sciences and humanities.

It was a moment of both intellectual advancement and consolidation, with some scholars worried that a singular comparative method would edge out a pluralistic variety of comparative strategies. For our purposes, the development of historical sociology offers a complementary case pointing to the need for rigorous self-reflection and the possibility of pluralism. Box I.1 provides background for readers interested in the ways these issues have manifested in comparative historical debates, and how engaging with them has strengthened the field.

Box I.1 Lessons from Comparative Historical Sociology

Reacting to seemingly ahistorical social theory that perceived societies as relatively static wholes, mid-twentieth-century historical sociologists aimed to show how social systems developed over time. Most prominently

[3] Burawoy (2019) also revisits this position on the dangers of empiricism in his response to Lubet's critique of ethnography (Lubet 2017).

in the United States were thinkers like Barrington Moore and his students Charles Tilly and Theda Skocpol, in what has been called the "second wave" after the classical thinkers like Marx, Weber, Durkheim, de Tocqueville, and Dubois. It was an enormously productive moment, with such classics as Moore's (1966) *Social Origins of Dictatorship and Democracy* reviving interest in, to paraphrase Tilly (1989), huge comparisons and the "big" questions. It was also marked by tension between these approaches and more quantitative models of sociology.

Beginning in the early 1980s, a group of historical sociologists and political scientists attempted to scientifically ground and justify their practice relative to hostile critics. One tactic was to view rigorous *case comparison* as the key distinction from purely narrative history and the humanities, as it might allow for theoretical generalization of explicitly causal processes. Widely cited pieces like Skocpol and Somers (1980) typologized varieties of historical comparison, and a series of edited volumes linked these new works to the foundational ambitions of classical social theorists. Consider Skocpol's identification of three main types of comparative historical work (1984). First, sociologists may attempt to apply an ostensibly universal theory to multiple cases to show how it does and does not fit. A second strategy, used by "interpretivists" in historical work as well as field research, is to use comparisons to clarify particularities through contrasts. For instance, Geertz compares Islam in Indonesia and Morocco, the poles of the Muslim worlds, so "they form a kind of commentary on one another's character." Finally, a third strategy is to explain variation in causal regularities in history, such as Skocpol's own work on revolutions in France, Russia, and China.[4]

The productivity of this moment was matched by criticism from multiple directions, and new debates. Quantitative researchers (e.g., Lieberson 1991) in turn criticized the "small-n" research as unscientific. This prompted further responses, including the notion that qualitative comparative research that drew on variable logics might attain scientific status in relation to idiographic or descriptive history (e.g., King, Keohane, and Verba 1994; Brady and Collier 2004), as well as elaborations of case-based approaches (Ragin 2004). Prominent comparativists worked to create a new subfield—drawing sociology and political science together with

[4] Of course, each position has spawned a dialog that includes critiques, responses, and counter-responses that have implications for methodological comparison more broadly (cf. Burawoy 1989; Gorski 2004).

historians, and creating conferences, awards, and other institutional infrastructure. Mahoney and Rueschemeyer's (2003) celebrated volume helped brand a "comparative historical research" that was interdisciplinary, institutionally viable, and scientifically respectable. Noticeably, the interdisciplinarity extended to political science and history, but generally rejected postmodern and literary approaches. That is, in the formation of what would be scientifically respectable, there were clear forms of boundary work to exclude specific "cultural" approaches.

What should ethnographers interested in the potential of comparative research learn from the evolution of comparative historical methods as they grapple with these challenges to their works' scientific status? On the one hand, there were significant developments in knowledge and method. The period saw extended debates on whether and how to compare units, the utility of variable logics versus case logics, and where the comparative historical fit in with humanistic or social scientific strains of social analysis. Mahoney and Rueschemeyer's volume further clarified different logics of comparison, and how these did and did not align with quantitative research. Some of these distinctions—causal versus interpretive, hypothesis testing versus narrative—may seem overly simplistic now. Yet for a generation of researchers, both the substantive works and methodological reflections offered models for how to produce rigorous, creative scholarship.

On the other hand, there was reason for caution. Even in the immediate years after Mahoney and Rueschemeyer, scholars cautioned that these battles over legitimation had drawbacks. As Rogers Brubaker argued in 2003, one could read the emergence of comparative historical research as a useful and even necessary act that was, by then, already stifling creativity. He wrote,

> At a particular moment—what one might call the Skocpolian moment—it was useful to represent comparative historical sociology as a distinctive enterprise, founded on a distinct method. In retrospect, this can be seen as a strategy of academic legitimation and institution building . . . One token of its success, however—about which one can be ambivalent—is that today we see a routinization of comparative work, sometimes involving a rather mechanical and intellectually dubious application of a Millian "method of difference," or some other method. (Brubaker 2003, 4)

Titling his essay "Beyond Comparativism," Brubaker was troubled that creative modes of comparison were being superseded by the institutionalization of dogmatic methods toward "truth." The point was not that institution-building is somehow illegitimate or that methodological papers positioning a distinct comparative method were purely acts of scientific "boundary work," but rather that the mechanical application of methods without reflection could produce mechanical and unreflexive scholarship. Still, the growth of comparative historical research as a sociological subfield and area of interdisciplinary inquiry stimulated important reflection on how to produce good comparative research as well as the limits of comparison. That is what we hope to offer in this volume.

This volume takes cues from the lessons of historical scholarships' examinations of comparative methods to chart different approaches to ethnographic comparison and what each might yield. Doing so, however, requires that we first outline the diverse set of approaches subsumed under the label of "ethnography."

The Meanings of Ethnography and Ethnographic Comparison

Any discussion of ethnographic comparison must begin with a simple but important acknowledgment: ethnography is not a single method. For the last five decades the term has been used by scholars in disciplines such as anthropology and sociology to refer to vastly different approaches for understanding the social world—from the direct extension of conventional scientific concerns with producing valid behavioral data, on the one hand (Cicourel 1982; Sánchez-Jankowski 2002), to philosophical reflection and skepticism of the very possibility of empirical social science, on the other (Clifford and Marcus 1986).[5] Consequently, ethnographic approaches lack a unified model of inquiry, let alone comparison. In an influential article from 1999 titled "Participant Observation in the Era of Ethnography,"

[5] The use of the term "ethnography," and the deployment of ethnographic methods, goes back much further (cf. Atkinson et al. 2001). Our point here is simply to acknowledge that in the period between World War II and the present, the term has been used to refer to drastically different traditions that frequently coexist in both time and professional space (Abramson and Dohan 2015; Atkinson 2001; Jerolmack and Kahn 2017).

Columbia sociologist Herbert Gans noted that ethnography had become divorced from its anthropological and sociological roots in participant observation. He quipped that in contrast to participant observation, "empirical ethnography is now a synonym for virtually all qualitative research except surveys and polls" (Gans 1999, 541).[6] What Gans's commentary minimizes, however, is that even social scientific approaches that employ participant observation fieldwork vary widely. If we hope to facilitate understanding different approaches to ethnographic comparison, and learn from both their contributions and mistakes, we must begin by acknowledging substantial contrasts in underlying assumptions about the social world and how to study it.

Divergent Logics and Languages

In the two decades since Gans's "Participant Observation in the Era of Ethnography" was published, the bounds of both participant observation and ethnography have continued to expand. In sociology, there is renewed attention to the potential of multi-researcher collaborations and scaled observational projects for both science and policy (Abramson et al. 2018; Bernstein and Dohan, this volume). The quantitative–qualitative fissures that led to assiduous battles in mid-twentieth-century social science have been eclipsed by a recognition that different methodological approaches can contribute to understanding the social world (cf. Brady and Collier 2004; Lamont and White 2008; Porpora 2015; Ragin 1994; Small 2009). Mixed-methods approaches that explicitly integrate and compare aspects of participant observation data with data from surveys, interviews, and historical analysis have assumed a new prominence and growing legitimacy in both academic disciplines and applied research (Small 2011).[7] Diachronic studies

[6] Gans's piece laments the proliferation of approaches that moved away from traditional fieldwork in the wake of the postmodern turn—literary deconstructionism (e.g., Clifford and Marcus 1986; Marcus and Fischer 1986), analyses of historical data (Biernacki 1995), textual dialogs with theorists, and biographic "autoethnographies" (Lochlann Jain 2013). Gans's hope was that a more traditional form of participant observation would once again become the coin of the social-scientific realm, even as he acknowledges that the new forms of contemporary ethnography are here to stay. While Gans critiques the current state of affairs, he concludes his piece by acknowledging that while he finds the rise of these forms unfortunate, he is confident that participant observation will always have a place in social science because it is one of the most useful ways to understand how and why people behave the way they do.

[7] For a critique and discussion of the potential dangers of mixed-method tokenism, see Hancock et al. 2018.

and revisits have made their way back into a method that was at times defined by immersion and exit (cf. Burawoy 2007; Collier 1997). Anthropology has witnessed an expansion of approaches in response to its ostensible postmodern turn, ranging from a revival of immersive fieldwork and collaboration with indigenous peoples to understand radically different "ontologies" (e.g. Kohn 2013) to the fictionalization of field research in comic book form (Hamdy and Nye 2017).

While the bounds of ethnography remain contested in disciplines like sociology and anthropology (Abramson and Dohan 2015), postwar traditions such as grounded theory (Glaser and Strauss 1967), ethnomethodology (Garfinkel 1967), symbolic interactionism (Blumer 1969), interpretivism (Geertz 2000 [1973]), the Chicago School of Ethnography (Deegan 2001), and positivism (Gans 1999; Sánchez-Jankowski 2002) continue to exist alongside slightly more contemporary alternatives such as postmodernism and poststructuralism (Tyler 1986), relational sociology (Desmond 2014), analytic ethnography (Lofland and Lofland 1984; Vaughn 2004), carnal sociology (Wacquant 2015), the extended case method (ECM) (Burawoy 1998), and feminist institutional ethnography (Smith 2005).[8] Finally, of particular importance for this volume, comparative ethnographic approaches have continued to grow and evolve within and across traditions.

Understanding why ethnography can take on such different forms requires understanding the role of divergent approaches to examining the social world, and the comparisons we make in trying to understand it. Rather than representing a unified qualitative block, ethnographers from different traditions rely upon radically different, and sometimes incompatible, philosophical logics and practices. Put simply, ethnographers may appear to overlap in *basic procedures* (e.g., participation in, observation of, and documentation of human social action) but differ in *what they aim to do* (e.g., describe, explain, critique) and *how they approach it* (e.g., through the deployment of conventional scientific logic or alternatives drawn from humanistic inquiry). The underlying philosophical differences in ethnographic approaches can be tremendously consequential for how research is conducted, the comparisons ethnographers make, and how their work is evaluated.

Often, those who are not directly involved in these debates underestimate these divides. Consider the following example. Several years ago, one of the

[8] For a more in-depth review of various traditions see Atkinson et al. 2001.

authors of this chapter (Abramson) was discussing the state of ethnography with a well-known survey methodologist in sociology. The methodologist was genuinely puzzled by the level of disagreement and in-fighting in ethnography, since it is all "qualitative" research. That individual noted that quantitative scholars do have heated disagreements about measurement and model specification, but the dialog rarely regresses into direct public attacks or claims about illegitimate methodological philosophy. Such talk, according to this person, was largely a waste of time that could be spent working on measurement. Abramson responded that while ethnographers should certainly avoid ad hominem attacks, they actually do not have the luxury of sidestepping discussions on the philosophy of method. In survey research it is possible to disagree heatedly on the deployment of the conventional scientific approach without invoking ontology or epistemology. However, that is because such a disagreement around surveys presupposes shared understandings about the research enterprise—such as that there are real social phenomenon, social scientists measure these in the most objective way possible, and their claims are evaluated based on how well they correspond to data.[9] Survey researchers have a shared language that uses agreed upon terms such as validity, reliability, generalizability, and replicability. Ethnographers do not.

The Challenge and Potential of Ethnographic Diversity

The fact is that ethnographers from different traditions lack consensus on the shared aims and common language quantitative scholars take for granted. Participant observers operating in realist approaches descendant from positivism often use the same general criteria and terms as quantitative scholars, and evaluate work according to those measures. For them validity, reliability, and generalizability are central concerns for all research, and participant observation's value is its ability to provide contextualized data other methods cannot (Cicourel 1982; Sánchez-Jankowski 2002). Others reject social science in a positivist vein as a fantasy, preferring humanistic traditions of

[9] Philosophical differences affect other forms of research as well, but the effect is often less stark and central. Of course, there are growing debates about whether this ought be the case. In recent years, scholars have argued for the need to return to a more philosophically grounded form of social sciences and that researchers might benefit from grappling more directly with meta-theoretical questions shaping their consensus (cf. Gorski 2013).

hermeneutics and interpretation (Clifford and Marcus 1986). These methodological critiques often dovetail with longstanding political critiques, from postcolonial theorists who note anthropology's historical complicity in the colonial project (e.g., Said 1991), to neo-Foucaultians who see the human sciences as integral parts of modern systems of power (e.g., Rose 1998). Many approaches operate in the space somewhere in between an embrace of conventional science and a radical critique (e.g., Burawoy 1998; Desmond 2014; Tavory and Timmermans 2014).

Ethnographers' differences extend to their core assumptions about social research. Practitioners disagree about the fundamental nature of the social world (*ontology*), how to best understand or study it (*epistemology*), and how to relate to human values and politics in social research (*axiology*). Recognizing the variation in these positions is more than methodological navel-gazing; it can shape all aspects of the research process including if and how ethnographers use comparisons. While this variation allows the method to speak to numerous disciplinary audiences, the variation can create immense challenges and frustrations when goals and criteria of ethnographic scholarship are unclear or misinterpreted. This is true for both ethnographers who are frustrated with their work being evaluated using classical positivist criteria they reject as misguided (e.g., Burawoy 1998) and those who are frustrated with being evaluated with the literary or political criteria they see as irrelevant to science (e.g., Abramson and Sánchez-Jankowski, this volume).

These disagreements have implications for public work and standards of evidence that reach beyond academic debates (Lubet 2017; Burawoy 2019). While some might hope ethnographers would collectively acknowledge that there is utility (and an opportunity for dialog) in maintaining their pluralism, in practice we often talk past each other.[10] Box I.2 provides additional

[10] Sociology provides an ironic case study in pluralism and reification. Sociologists have long recognized the utility of methodological pluralism. The underlying notion, hegemonic to much contemporary "post-positivist" social science, is that while approaches such as survey research, comparative historical analyses, and participant observation produce different types of findings, each can fruitfully contribute to understanding the social world. That diverse methods can coexist under a newfound pluralism is near consensus in contemporary sociological discourse (cf. Lamont and White 2009; Porpora 2015; Small 2009; Singleton and Straights 2005). This newfound coexistence, which provided an alternative to the assiduous quantitative–qualitative divide of mid-century American sociology, frequently relies on a distinction between case-oriented (often qualitative) and variable oriented (often quantitative) approaches (Goertz and Mahoney 2012; Ragin 1994; Small 2009). The comforting thought that quantitative and qualitative research can coexist because they employ fundamentally different and complementary logics appeals because it purports to offer a way out of a once impassible quantitative–qualitative. However, an unintended consequence is a heightened methodological "tribalism" on the "qualitative" side (Lamont and Swidler 2014), where those who

background information on how key philosophical differences translate into sometimes irreconcilable forms of social science and how this relates to the confusion and contestation in contemporary ethnography.

Box I.2 Divergent Philosophies of Social Science

Being knowledgeable about (or at least aware) of the different philosophies that shape various ethnographic traditions is necessary for representing different approaches accurately. At minimum, it is necessary to look at interconnected aspects of "meta-theory" that guide inquiry (e.g., ontology, epistemology, axiology), and the relationship of various traditions to dominant models of quantitative social science.

It can be helpful to think of the philosophical and practical responses to the challenges of studying social life in contemporary social science traditions as part of a set of continuums. Ontological positions about the nature of the social world range from an embrace of realism (i.e., the notion there is a real, observable, extra-individual social world that exists outside the mind) to forms of anti-realism (postmodernism, phenomenological subjectivism, and other approaches that take their rejection of realism as a starting point). Epistemological positions on how to understand or explain the social world, and how to evaluate attempts to do so, vary similarly. On one side of the spectrum is a focus on correspondence and validity (the notion that explanations are evaluated by virtue of how well they map onto the world). On the other side is a rejection of such criteria, favoring evocative and coherent narratives, aesthetics, or usefulness for critiquing the status quo in a society. Positions about how to relate to human values (i.e., axiology) vary in parallel ways. Some embrace value neutrality, the notion that while values affect what social scientists study they should not drive (or even affect) their findings (Weber 1949 [1917]). This stands in contrast to explicitly political projects, which often reject such assumptions as both unrealistic and complicit in domination and advocate for explicitly political work (de Beauvoir 1949). Finally, approaches vary in what they consider a good explanation, model, or representation. For instance, even among realists there are debates about whether

claim to pursue a particular approach to a method jostle to have their model legitimated as the appropriate contribution by "big tent" methodological pluralists.

explanations ought to be causal or whether description is enough (King, Keohane, and Verba 1994). Some of these key axes of philosophical variation are represented visually in Figure I.1.

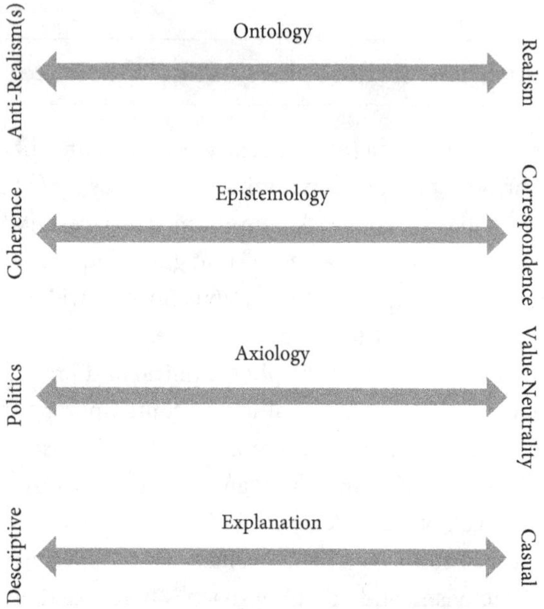

Figure I.1 Key Axes of Philosophical Variation in Social Science Research

Where traditions are positioned on these scales have wide-reaching consequences for their approach to comparative social science. On one side of the spectrum is Durkheim and his notion of social facts. Social facts are real, discernable, extra-individual phenomena that vary from other types of facts (e.g., physical, biological), primarily because they would not exist without people (Durkheim 2014 [1895]). For Durkheim, sociology is a positive science that examines a substantive domain (society) that other sciences cannot. Durkheim is both a realist and an objectivist, even in his examinations of mental phenomena. His epistemic approach focuses on correspondence (i.e., models are evaluated by how they map onto facts). Explanation for him is causal. According to Durkheim, when sociology is done properly it can produce covering laws similar to those in the physical and biological sciences. These laws reflect the objective nature of social reality, and as such should emerge regardless of the values of individual researchers. Comparison serves this purpose by using variation (e.g., difference in suicide rates) to get at invariant principles (the importance of social connection and solidarity). He represents social scientific positivism in the extreme.

On the other end of the spectrum are forms of anti-realism. Postmodern anthropology often rejects the principles central to Durkheim's positivism (Tyler 1986; Clifford and Marcus 1986; Reed 2010). Drawing on subjectivism and the egoism of strong phenomenology (i.e., Husserl 2015 [1931]), some question the notion of a real, or at least objectively knowable, external world (Husserl 2015 [1931]; Bunge 1993). They are less concerned with correspondence or causal explanation. They find greater value in literary or aesthetic merits and deconstruction of the taken-for-granted (Clifford and Marcus 1986). This is often, though not always, tied explicitly to political projects, with a belief that analysis is intimately entangled with a scholar's position (de Beauvoir 1949). In anthropology, this is tied to reckoning with their colonial legacy (Said 1991), and the Foucaultian analysis of the human sciences as key components of modern power (Rose 1998). In sociology, this is tied to a longstanding concern with inequality and domination (Collins 1990). Many eschew explanation as a chief goal or a goal at all.

Weber's neo-Kantian interpretivism, Simmel's work, and Bourdieu's attempt to connect the first and second order objectivities of the mental and external social world lie somewhere between.[11] Furthermore, intellectual traditions are often diverse, and combine positions in various ways. For instance, feminist standpoint epistemology was often painted as relativist, but ranged from the general privileging of women's claims to knowledge about gender, to post-structural rejections of the category "woman," to empirically based claims that certain women do have special knowledge, such as the intimate observation many black women gained of white families via relegation to family service roles (Collins 1990). The former are philosophical axioms, and the latter is empirically observable. Likewise, realist traditions concerned with causality, such as analytical sociology and critical realism, diverge sharply in the way they deal with human values and causality (Little 2012; Porpora 2015; Hedstrom and

[11] In the modern era, philosophical positions have loosely mapped on to disciplinary responses to the challenges to conventional positivism. While some social sciences (e.g., economics and psychology) have largely embraced a model of normal science, sociocultural anthropology has largely rejected this model— particularly after the postmodern turn while physical anthropology had embraced it, and sociologists remain split (Steinmetz 2005). It is not entirely surprising that ethnographers, who are most typically sociologists or anthropologists, operate in the most contested philosophical spaces.

Ylikoski 2010). Many veins of critical realism lean toward the right side of the spectrums discussed here, with the exception of their axiological position, which views values as a central to the research enterprise and places "human flourishing" as an explicit goal (Gorski 2013).

The differences described in this section are not surface issues nor are their effects abstract. Different ethnographic approaches can have irreconcilable philosophies that have an "elective affinity" with particular approaches to social science, which are often contested even within academic fields with pluralist inclinations.[12] Abramson and colleagues (2018) explain that ethnographic diversity and contestation translate into persistent definitional challenges and confusion:

> While ethnography's epistemic diversity can be a strength, it also creates definitional and positional challenges, particularly for those taking the NST [Normal Scientific Tradition] approach (Abramson and Dohan, 2015). The label "ethnography" is used to describe a variety of approaches (Gans, 1999; Atkinson et al., 2001) that are often premised on incompatible meta-theories and postures towards NST research. For instance, those who embrace a broad NST tradition argue that ethnography or, more precisely, participant observation, can make substantial scientific contributions within the logic of that approach (Cicourel, 1982; Gans, 1999; Jerolmack and Kahn, 2014; King et al., 1994; Sánchez-Jankowski, 2002; Sánchez-Jankowski and Abramson, forthcoming). In contrast, a second camp rejects these propositions and argues ethnography's role is to be a critical corrective, and alternative to, the problems of positivist science (Burawoy, 1998; Decoteau, 2016; Glaser and Strauss, 1967; Tavory and Timmermans, 2014). A third group posits that ethnography can, and should, have a fundamentally different, but potentially complementary, case logic (Ragin, 1994; Lofland, 1995; Small, 2009). A fourth group rejects the notion of scientific inquiry in general and positions ethnography as a humanist enterprise within the general field of cultural

[12] For instance, in recent years, rather than being seen as an umbrella term that encompasses diverse approaches, some scholars have framed sociological ethnography as a broadly (and inherently) interpretive method, the strength of which lies in descriptive depth and connection to the understandings of subjects (cf. Lareau and Rao 2016; Katz 2004; Cobb and Huang 2015; Desmond 2014). This sort of interpretation is problematic in that it 1) Conflates analytically distinct ethnographic approaches; 2) limits vibrant ethnographic epistemic diversity; and 3) legitimates one approach at the cost of others. As the discussions of traditions in this volume suggest, this is not the result of any intrinsic characteristic of ethnography's history or tools, but the result of historical and professional processes.

> production (Clifford and Marcus, 1986; see also Hartblay, 2018). The theoretical foundations, research practices and evaluation criteria of these approaches are in many cases fundamentally incompatible with one another. (Abramson et al. 2018, 257)

A key takeaway is that this historical and philosophical variation profoundly shapes what ethnographers do, how they relate to one another, and how audiences of non-ethnographers both within and outside of the academy interpret the value of ethnographic work (Burawoy 2019; Goldthorpe 2000; Lubet 2017).

Shared Challenges in Ethnography

Yet for all the differences described in the previous section, there are shared methodological issues that all approaches to ethnographic fieldwork must address (Abramson and Dohan 2015). The major ethnographic traditions in social science each have models (implicit or explicit) of how to address the following practical and scientific dilemmas:

(1) how researchers position themselves in the various social settings they encounter;
(2) how to handle the effect of their presence on a site or in a situation;
(3) how to manage long-term relationships with their subjects;
(4) how to use or attempt to bracket prior knowledge that affect experiences and observations in the field;
(5) how to relate to theory;
(6) what to record and formalize as data;
(7) how to analyze their observations;
(8) how to represent their findings to a broader audience;
(9) how to position themselves vis-à-vis quantitative social science; and
(10) if, and how, to engage in comparison.

In the day-to-day practices of actual research, ethnographers with different positions may converge. Furthermore, our contributors show nuanced responses to challenges and critiques from other traditions. Nonetheless, it is revealing to examine the strong differences in how ethnographers' approach shared challenges.

Consider the following examples of responses to shared challenges:

Field Presence

Positivists and behavioralists view the presence of the researcher as both necessary to observing behavior outside the lab and a potential source of bias. Consequently, they advocate for extended immersion and other strategies that minimize the long-term impact of the researcher on the patterns of behavior they are trying to understand (Sánchez-Jankowski and Abramson, this volume). In contrast, many symbolic interactionists view the presence of the researcher as a central aspect of the situations they are studying. Rather than minimize presence, interactionists and ethnomethodologists often use the researcher's presence as a tool to disrupt and understand the microdynamics of social situations (Garfinkel 1967).

Prior Knowledge and Theory

Those who employ the ECM see their task as using ethnographic data to extend and modify existing theories, such as Marxian models for explaining the dynamics of global capitalism (Burawoy 1998; Sallaz 2009). They enter the field with a specific theory in mind and reflexively use it to explain what they are seeing, modifying and extending the theory in the process. Traditional grounded theorists, on the other hand, try to eschew entering the field with any strong prior analytical frameworks. They see doing so as an imposition of their own biases and overdetermined social scientific models on the lives of the people they are studying (Glaser and Strauss 1967). Cognitive sociologists and behavioralists believe that using prior knowledge (including both folk and formal theories of social action) is an unavoidable aspect of being human. They see the strong grounded theory position as impossible and the ECM as unnecessarily overdetermined in the selection of a single theory (cf. Sánchez-Jankowski 2002; Cicourel, this volume). Abductive researchers similarly chart a middle ground, drawing on grounded theory's coding procedures but encouraging wide-ranging theoretical engagement (Tavory and Timmermans 2014).

Explanation and Evaluation

Interpretivists following in the tradition of Clifford Geertz view coherence and "thick descriptions" of social life as the central ethnographic goal, eschewing causal statements or predictions (Geertz 2000 [1973]). Theoretical coherence and evocative writing are central criteria for how these ethnographers evaluate work (Geertz 2000 [1973]; Lareau and Rao 2016). In contrast, critical realists, behavioralists, and cognitive sociologists are fundamentally concerned with producing explanations that chart causal mechanisms and typically judge explanation by their correspondence with observable patterns of social life (Decoteau this volume; Sánchez-Jankowski and Abramson this volume).

Extension and Generalization

Different approaches vary in the scope of their statements and how they extend their explanations. Behavioral approaches focus on generating a sample that represents and can be generalized to a large population of a given unit of analysis such as people, organizations, or neighborhoods, in order to evaluate existing theories and generate new ones. The ECM uses specific cases to extend and contribute to social theory. Ethnomethodologists focus on the organization of experience and cognition and aim to uncover (sometimes hidden) rules. And again, there is diversity even within traditions. For instance, some symbolic interactionists eschew generalization beyond the construction of meaning in a given situation. Others, however, may seek to uncover transposable interactional structures that share general features across a variety of situations.

These differences are paralleled in, and directly connected to, the way ethnographers from different traditions compare.

Approaches to Ethnographic Comparison and Volume Structure

Contemporary ethnographers vary substantially in how they use comparison. They vary on *what they compare*—such as people, cases, variables, mechanisms, understandings, sites, or situations. They vary in their *mode of comparison*—such as using similarity and dissimilarity, focusing on case boundaries, or identifying invariance. Finally, they vary in the *goals of comparison*—establishing generalizable patterns of behavior, showing variation in sociohistorical contexts, uncovering causal mechanisms, or allowing more imaginative theorizing. In each chapter, this volume's contributors clarify their positions and how they translate into different forms of inquiry.

The first section of the volume begins by examining the evolution of classic behavioral and phenomenological approaches to ethnographic comparison.

In chapter 1, "Foundations of the Behavioralist Approach to Comparative Participant Observation," Sánchez-Jankowski and Abramson argue that while ethnography is often pitched as a critical alternative to the (typically) quantitative, variable-based approaches associated with the conventional scientific tradition (CST), this is not inherent in the method. Comparative participant observation actually provides an irreducible tool for those operating in the CST framework by allowing the observation of situated causal processes that other methods are ill-suited to capture. Chapter 2, "Conducting Comparative Participant Observation: Behavioralist Procedures and Techniques," builds on the methodological scaffolding outlined in the previous chapter to show how behavioralist principles translate to procedures and techniques for charting causal mechanisms—specifically, a variable-centered approach to multilevel sampling, pattern observation, and replicable comparative analyses that leverage both variance and invariance in field data to produce generalizable explanations.

Chapter 3 turns to a contemporary approach drawing on phenomenological traditions. In "The Thematic Lens: A Formal and Cultural Framework for Comparative Ethnographic Analysis," DeGloma and Papadantonakis outline a comparative framework for ethnographic analysis that uses insights from Simmel's formalism, social pattern analysis, symbolic interaction, and the strong program in cultural sociology. They advocate the identification of key interactional dynamics or meanings from one case and use it as a thematic lens through which to view other cases, revealing connections across ostensibly different phenomena. Chapter 4 turns to Cicourel's approach to cognitive sociology, which has long aimed to link the micro and macro, phenomenological and behavioral. In "Comparative Ethnographic Views of Social Structure: The Challenge of Linking Micro and Macro Levels of Analysis," Cicourel revisits divergent concepts of social structure and their application to ethnographic comparison, arguing for the need to uncover often overlooked connections between micro-structure, macro-structure, and forms of representing social reality.

The volume continues by turning to contemporary variants of critical approaches including the ECM, critical realism, and an abductive approach descendent from grounded theory and pragmatism. In chapter 5, "An Ethnography of Comparative Ethnography: Pathways to Three Logics of Comparison," Lee reflects on the comparative use of the ECM to show that there are several forms of comparison used by practitioners, each of which contributes to the central aim of extending theory. She describes her initial attempts at controlled "variable" comparison of similar organizations in different nation-states, as well as her later works that reveal the interconnection between cases, or leverage different responses to historical events. In chapter 6, "Critical Realism and Contrastive Ethnography: The Curious Case of Autism in Somali Refugee Communities," Decoteau outlines a critical realist approach to ethnographic comparison that aims to examine both agency and conjunctural causality. Building on the ECM's comparative approach, it advocates for comparison not only of actual empirical events, but also seemingly different cases that reveal the real mechanisms lying behind those actualities. In chapter 7, "Sequential Comparisons and the Comparative Imagination," Tavory and Timmermans expand their approach to abduction that draws its lineage from grounded theory and an open-ended form of inquiry. Rather than prescribe the need for comparison at the outset or a particular type of comparative logic, they suggest that researchers only reach for a second case when the initial study presents surprises that call for contrasting material.

The final section introduces a set of chapters that situate these practices in the world of academia and policy. In chapter 8, "Using Computational Tools to Enhance Comparative Ethnography: Lessons from Scaling Ethnography for Biomedicine," Bernstein and Dohan describe how comparative ethnographic work provides necessary insights into culture, narrative, and practice for the field of biomedicine. They introduce two specific techniques for addressing issues of scaling ethnography to generate the wider data demanded by their projects in this field: interactive heat maps, or "ethnoarrays," and the deployment of geospatial data about ethnographic subjects. In chapter 9, "Elite Ethnography: Studying Up or Down in US and French Sociology," Chancer turns to the question of not just how, but who ethnographers study and compare. She offers explanations for the disproportionate focus of American ethnographers on the downtrodden in the United States, and outlines an argument for the importance of studying populations across the class spectrum. Chapter 10 features "A Dialog with Aaron Cicourel on Comparative Ethnography." In this chapter, eminent ethnographer and cognitive sociologist Cicourel shares insights gleaned from using ethnographic methods for the past six decades. In conversation with Corey Abramson, Cicourel addresses a number of important issues about both the practice of comparative ethnography and the academic contexts in which it takes place. The volume closes with a discussion of the implications of these contributions for the theory and practice of ethnographic comparison.

Toward Productive Pluralism in Comparative Ethnography

The contributions presented in this volume serve a dual purpose. Most directly, they offer guidelines for students and researchers who aim to design a comparative research project, and alternative techniques for those who already engage in such work. Additionally, the self-reflection on logic of comparison pushes scholars to clarify areas not always articulated in descriptions of single studies. In examining issues of casing, variable and case logics, and even the possibility of commensurability and comparability of social phenomena, scholars show both what is distinct about their traditions and areas of overlap or synergy with other approaches.

It is important to note that this volume does not advocate for any particular school of ethnography or approach to comparison. We see the collective contributions of our authors as modeling how pluralism in ethnography can allow practitioners the opportunity to refine their positions and improve practices. We use the term *productive pluralism* to emphasize that the coexistence of different ethnographic approaches can contribute to and enrich the human sciences, and that there is value in this coexistence even when the work being produced cannot be easily integrated within a single philosophy of science. What makes this productive, rather than live-and-let-live pluralism, is that practitioners are expected to at minimum acknowledge and ideally engage the alternatives and critiques of peers to hone their own approaches (a theme in many of our contributors' chapters). Even established traditions can grow through engagement with the techniques, methods, and vocabularies of others.[13] Furthermore, an acknowledgment of diverse forms of contribution is directly connected to the issues of misinterpretation, misrepresentation, and confusion about evaluation described here. Participant observation conducted according to the principles of normal science (Gans 1999; Sánchez-Jankowski 2002), critical alternatives (Burawoy 1998; Tavory and Timmermans 2014), and humanistic critique (Clifford and Marcus 1986) aim to do different things. Evaluations of the contributions of ethnography would benefit from an acknowledgment of this, and painting

[13] Although he may underestimate the potential for this phenomenon in "critical" and "policy" approaches, Burawoy's (2005) warning is relevant. Traditions and disciplines may stagnate when ideas go unchallenged and assume the status of a professional common sense, reproduced uncritically in self-referential exchanges of the likeminded.

all with the same terminological brush may miss precisely what different approaches offer.

In this vein, we aim neither to decide for the reader which of these approaches is right, nor to convince them that all are equally reasonable. We expect that readers will make their own decisions about which approaches are better suited to which tasks, and we predict that scholars will continue to disagree on these issues even after reading the contributions contained herein. Yet by engaging with critiques and alternative approaches to comparison, they will have the opportunity to expand on or improve their own approaches. The authors in this volume have taken on this task by clarifying how and why they compare, and the way in which their positions align with or diverge from alternatives. Our hope is that readers can both better understand positions that may differ from their own, and critically compare the merits of various approaches themselves.

References

Abramson, Corey M., and Daniel Dohan. 2015. "Beyond Text: Using Arrays to Represent and Analyze Ethnographic Data." *Sociological Methodology*, 45, no. 1: 272–319.

Abramson, Corey M., Jacqueline Joslyn, Katharine A. Rendle, Sarah B. Garrett, and Daniel Dohan. 2018. "The Promises of Computational Ethnography: Improving Transparency, Replicability, and Validity for Realist Approaches to Ethnographic Analysis." *Ethnography* 19, no. 2: 254–284.

Atkinson, Paul, Amanda Coffey, Sara Delamont, John Lofland, and Lyn H. Lofland, eds. 2001. *Handbook of Ethnography*. Los Angeles: SAGE Publications.

Biernacki, Richard. 1995. *The Fabrication of Labor: Germany and Britain, 1640–1914*. Berkeley: University of California Press.

Blumer, Herbert. 1969. *Symbolic Interactionism; Perspective and Method*. Englewood Cliffs, NJ: Prentice Hall.

Brady, Henry E., and David Collier. 2004. *Rethinking Social Inquiry: Diverse Tools, Shared Standards*. Lanham, MD: Rowman & Littlefield.

Brubaker, Rogers. 2003. Unpublished manuscript. "Beyond Comparativism?" https://works.bepress.com/wrb/1/.

Bunge, Mario. 1993. "Realism and Antirealism in Social Science." *Theory and Decision* 35, no. 3: 207–235.

Burawoy, Michael. 1998. "The Extended Case Method." *Sociological Theory* 16, no. 1: 4–33.

Burawoy, Michael. 2005. "For Public Sociology." *American Sociological Review* 70, no. 1: 4–28.

Burawoy, Michael. 2007. *The Extended Case Method: Four Countries, Four Decades, Four Great Transformations, and One Theoretical Tradition*. Berkeley: University of California Press.

Burawoy, Michael. 2017. "On Desmond: The Limits of Spontaneous Sociology." *Theory and Society* 46, no. 4: 261–284.

Burawoy, Michael. 2019. "Empiricism and Its Fallacies." *Contexts* 18, no. 1: 47–53.

Cicourel, Aaron V. 1964. *Method and Measurement in Sociology*. Glencoe, IL: Free Press of Glencoe.

Cicourel, Aaron V. 1982. "Interviews, Surveys, and the Problem of Ecological Validity." *The American Sociologist* 17, no. 1: 11–20.

Clifford, James, and George E. Marcus. 1986. *Writing Culture: The Poetics and Politics of Ethnography*. Berkeley: University of California Press.

Cobb, Jessica, and Kimberly Kay Hoang. 2015. "Protagonist-Driven Urban Ethnography." *City and Community* 14, no. 4: 348–351.

Collier, Jane Fishburne. 1997. *From Duty to Desire: Remaking Families in a Spanish Village*. Princeton, NJ: Princeton University Press.

Collins, Patricia Hill. 1990. *Black Feminist Thought: Knowledge, Consciousness, and the Politics of Empowerment*. New York: Routledge.

de Beauvoir, Simone. 1949. *The Second Sex*. Harmondsworth, UK: Penguin.

Deegan, Mary Jo. 2001. "The Chicago School of Ethnography." In *Handbook of Ethnography*, edited by Paul Atkinson, Amanda Coffey, Sara Delamont, John Lofland, and Lyn H. Lofland, 11–25. Los Angeles: SAGE Publications.

Desmond, Matthew. 2014. "Relational Ethnography." *Theory and Society* 43, no. 5: 547–579.

Durkheim, Émile. 2014 [1895]. *The Rules of Sociological Method: And Selected Texts on Sociology and Its Method*. Edited by Steven Lukes. Translated by W. D. Halls. New York: Free Press.

Evans-Pritchard, Edward Evan. 1950. "Social Anthropology: Past and Present; the Marett Lecture." *Man* 198, no. 5: 118–124.

Evans-Pritchard, Edward Evan. 1965. *The Position of Women in Primitive Societies: And Other Essays in Social Anthropology*. New York: Free Press.

Falzon, Mark-Anthony. 2016. "Introduction: Multi-Sited Ethnography: Theory, Praxis and Locality in Contemporary Research. In *Multi-Sited Ethnography*, 15–38. New York: Routledge.

Gans, Herbert J. 1999. "Participant Observation in the Era of 'Ethnography.'" *Journal of Contemporary Ethnography* 28, no. 5: 540–548.

Garfinkel, Harold. 1967. *Studies in Ethnomethodology*. London: Blackwell.

Geertz, Clifford. 1971. *Islam Observed: Religious Development in Morocco and Indonesia*. Chicago: University of Chicago Press.

Geertz, Clifford. 2000 [1973]. "Thick Description: Towards an Interpretive Theory of Culture." In *The Interpretation of Cultures: Selected Essays*, 3–30. New York: Basic Books.

Glaser, Barney G., and Anselm L Strauss. 1967. *The Discovery of Grounded Theory: Strategies for Qualitative Research*. New York: Aldine Publishing Company.

Goertz, Gary, and James Mahoney. 2012. *A Tale of Two Cultures: Qualitative and Quantitative Research in the Social Sciences*. Princeton, NJ: Princeton University Press.

Goldthorpe, John H. 2000. *On Sociology: Numbers, Narratives, and the Integration of Research and Theory*. Oxford: Oxford University Press.

Gorski, Philip S. 2013. "What Is Critical Realism? And Why Should You Care?" *Contemporary Sociology: A Journal of Reviews* 42, no. 5: 658–670.

Hamdy, Sherine, and Coleman Nye. 2017. *Lissa: A Story about Medical Promise, Friendship, and Revolution*. Vol. 1. Toronto: University of Toronto Press.

Hancock, Black Hawk, Bryan L. Sykes, and Anjuli Verma. 2018. "The Problem of 'Cameo Appearances' in Mixed-Methods Research: Implications for Twenty-First-Century Ethnography." *Sociological Perspectives* 61, no. 2: 314–334.

Hartblay, Cassandra. 2018. "This Is Not Thick Description: Conceptual Art Installation as Ethnographic Process." *Ethnography* 19, no. 2: 153–182.

Hedstrom, Peter, and Petri Ylikoski. 2010. "Causal Mechanisms in the Social Sciences." *Annual Review of Sociology* 36: 49–67.

Heritage, John. 1984. *Garfinkel and Ethnomethodology*. Cambridge, MA: Polity Press.

Husserl, Edmund. 2015 [1931]. *Idea: General Introduction to Pure Phenomenology*. New York: Routledge.

Jensen, Casper Bruun, Barbara Herrnstein Smith, G. E. R. Lloyd, Martin Holbraad, Andreas Roepstorff, Isabelle Stengers, Helen Verran, et al. 2011. "Introduction: Contexts for a Comparative Relativism." *Common Knowledge* 17, no. 2: 1–12.

Jerolmack, Colin, and Shamus Khan. 2014. "Talk Is Cheap: Ethnography and the Attitudinal Fallacy." *Sociological Methods & Research* 43, no. 2: 178–209.

Jerolmack, Colin, and Shamus Khan. 2017. *Approaches to Ethnography: Analysis and Representation in Participant Observation*. New York: Oxford University Press.

Katz, Jack. 2004. "On the Rhetoric and Politics of Ethnographic Methodology." *Annals of the American Academy of Political and Social Science* 595: 280–308.

King, Gary, Robert O. Keohane, and Sidney Verba. 1994. *Designing Social Inquiry: Scientific Inference in Qualitative Research*. Princeton, NJ: Princeton University Press.

Knorr Cetina, Karin. 1999. *Epistemic Cultures: How the Sciences Make Knowledge*. Cambridge, MA: Harvard University Press.

Kohn, Eduardo. 2013. *How Forests Think: Toward an Anthropology beyond the Human*. Berkeley: University of California Press.

Lareau, Annette. 2011. *Unequal Childhoods: Class, Race, and Family life*. Berkeley: University of California Press.

Lareau, Annette, and Aliya Hamid Rao. 2016. "It's About the Depth of Your Data—Contexts." *Contexts*. https://contexts.org/blog/its-about-the-depth-of-your-data/.

Lamont, Michèle, and Ann Swidler. 2014. "Methodological Pluralism and the Possibilities and Limits of Interviewing." *Qualitative Sociology* 37, no. 2: 153–171.

Lamont, Michèle, and Patricia White. 2008. Workshop on Interdisciplinary Standards for Systematic Qualitative Research. Arlington, VA: National Science Foundation.

Lee, Ching Kwan. 1995. "Engendering the Worlds of Labor: Women Workers, Labor Markets, and Production Politics in the South China Economic Miracle." *American Sociological Review* 60, no. 3: 378–397.

Lieberson, Stanley. 1991. "Small N's and Big Conclusions: An Examination of the Reasoning in Comparative Studies Based on a Small Number of Cases', *Social Forces* 70, no. 2: 307–320.

Little, Daniel. 2012. "Symposium / On Analytical Sociology: Critique, Advocacy, and Prospects Analytical Sociology and The Rest of Sociology." https://doi.org/10.2383/36894.

Lofland, John. 1995. "Analytic Ethnography." *Journal of Contemporary Ethnography* 24, no. 1: 30–67.

Lofland, John., and Lyn H. Lofland. 1984. *Analyzing Social Settings: A Guide to Qualitative Observation and Analysis*. Belmont, CA: Wadsworth.

Lochlann Jain, Sarah S. 2013. *Malignant: How Cancer Becomes Us*. Berkeley: University of California Press.

Lubet, Steven. 2017. *Interrogating Ethnography: Why Evidence Matters*. Oxford: Oxford University Press.

Mahoney, James, and Dietrich Rueschemeyer, eds. 2003. *Comparative Historical Analysis in the Social Sciences*. Cambridge: Cambridge University Press.

Marcus, George E., and Michael Fischer. 1986. *Anthropology as Cultural Critique: An Experimental Moment in the Human Sciences*. Chicago: University of Chicago Press.

Marcus, George E. 1995. "Ethnography In/of the World System: The Emergence of Multi-Sited Ethnography." *Annual Review of Anthropology* 24: 95–117.

Moore, Barrington. 1966. *Social Origins of Dictatorship and Democracy: Lord and Peasant in the Making of the Modern World*. Boston, MA: Beacon Press.

Needham, Rodney. 1975. "Polythetic Classification: Convergence and Consequences." *Man* 10, no. 3: 349–369.

Porpora, Douglas V. 2015. *Reconstructing Sociology: The Critical Realist Approach*. Cambridge: Cambridge University Press.

Ragin, Charles C. 1994. *Constructing Social Research: The Unity and Diversity of Method*. Thousand Oaks, CA: Pine Forge Press.

Ragin, Charles C. 2004. "Turning the Tables: How Case-Oriented Research Challenges Variable-Oriented Research." In edited by Henry E. Brady and David Collier, 123–138. Lanham, MD: Rowman & Littlefield.

Reed, Isaac. 2010. "Epistemology Contextualized: Social-Scientific Knowledge in a Post Positivist Era." *Sociological Theory* 28, no. 1: 20–39.

Rose, Nikolas. 1998. *Inventing Our Selves: Psychology, Power, and Personhood*. Cambridge: Cambridge University Press.

Said, Edward W. 1991. *Orientalism: Western Conceptions of the Orient*. New York: Penguin.

Sallaz, Jeffrey J. 2009. *The Labor of Luck : Casino Capitalism in the United States and South Africa*. Berkeley: University of California Press.

Sánchez-Jankowski, Martín. 1991. *Islands in the Street: Gangs and American Urban Society*. Berkeley: University of California Press.

Sánchez-Jankowski. 2002. "Representation, Responsibility and Reliability in Participant Observation." In *Qualitative Research in Action*, edited by Tim May, 144–160. London: SAGE Publications.

Skocpol, Theda. 1984. "Emerging Agendas and Recurrent Strategies in Historical Sociology." In *Vision and Method in Historical Sociology*, edited by Theda Skocpol, 356–391. Cambridge: Cambridge University Press.

Skocpol, Theda and Margaret Somers. 1980. "The Uses of Comparative History in Macrosocial Inquiry." *Comparative Studies in Society and History* 22: 174–197.

Singleton, Royce A., and Bruce C. Straights. 2005. *Approaches to Social Research*, 4th ed. New York: Oxford University Press.

Small, Mario Luis. 2009. "'How Many Cases Do I Need?' On Science and the Logic of Case Selection in Field-Based Research." *Ethnography* 10, no. 1: 5–38.

Small, Mario Luis. 2011. "How to Conduct a Mixed Methods Study: Recent Trends in a Rapidly Growing Literature." *Annual Review of Sociology* 37: 57–86.

Smith, Dorothy E. 2005. *Institutional Ethnography: A Sociology for People*. Lanham, MD: Altamira.

Steinmetz, George. 2004. "Odious Comparisons: Incommensurability, the Case Study, and 'Small N's' in Sociology." *Sociological Theory* 22, no. 3: 371–400.

Steinmetz, George. 2005. "Introduction: Positivism and Its Others in the Social Sciences." In *The Politics of Method in the Human Sciences*, 1–59. Duke University Press.

Tavory, Iddo, and Stefan Timmermans. 2014. *Abductive Analysis: Theorizing Qualitative Research*. Chicago: University of Chicago Press.

Tilly, Charles. 1989. *Big Structures, Large Processes, Huge Comparisons*. New York: Russell Sage Foundation.

Tsing, Anna Lowenhaupt. 2011. *Friction: An Ethnography of Global Connection*. Princeton, NJ: Princeton University Press.

Tyler, Stephen. 1986. "Post-Modern Ethnography." In *Writing Culture: The Poetics and Politics of Ethnography*, edited by James Clifford and George E Marcus, 122–149. School of American Research Advanced Seminar Series. Berkeley: University of California Press.

Vaughn, Diane. 1986. *Uncoupling*. New York: Oxford University Press.

Vaughn, Diane. 2004. *The Challenger Launch: Risky Technology, Culture, and Deviance at NASA*. Chicago: University of Chicago Press.

Vaughn, Diane. 2014. "Theorizing: Analogy, Cases, and Comparative Social Organization." In *Theorizing in Social Science: The Context of Discovery*, edited by Richard Swedberg, 61–84. Stanford, CA: Stanford University Press.

Wacquant, Loïc. 2015. "For a Sociology of Flesh and Blood." *Qualitative Sociology* 38, no. 2: 1–11.

Weber, Max. 1949 [1917]. "Meaning of 'Ethical Neutrality' [Wertfreiheit] in Sociology and Economics." In *The Methodology of the Social Sciences*.

SECTION I

THE EVOLUTION OF CLASSIC APPROACHES TO COMPARISON

1

Foundations of the Behavioralist Approach to Comparative Participant Observation

Martín Sánchez-Jankowski and Corey M. Abramson

Introduction

Although the specter of positivism and its concerns with measurement, representation, causal inference, and generalization linger large in both the discussion and the practice of sociological research (Steinmetz 2005), many contemporary responses have emphasized how ethnographic inquiry provides a critical alternative or corrective to the *conventional scientific tradition* (CST) (e.g., Becker 2009; Blumer 1969; Burawoy 1998; Clifford 1988; Geertz 2000 [1973]; Glaser and Strauss 1967; Stacey 1988; Tavory and Timmermans 2014).[1] Ethnography is frequently contrasted to CST approaches in general and deductive, counterfactual, "theory testing," and generalizing approaches of large-N variable-centered statistical methods in particular (Small 2009). In various traditions, sociological ethnography is framed as a means of inductive theory-building (Corbin and Strauss 2008; Glaser and Strauss 1967), reflexive theory extension (Burawoy 1998), thick description (Geertz 2000 [1973]; Lareau and Rao 2016), criticism (Clifford 1988; Crapanzano 1986), and radical mode of accessing interactional meaning (Blumer 1969).[2] Even those responses that have advocated for the complementary character of qualitative and quantitative methodologies have generally argued that the two differ substantially on a host of factors that include various epistemic logics and goals with regards to

[1] We would like to thank Claude Fischer, Aaron Cicourel, Frédéric Vandenberghe, Neil Gong, and the anonymous reviewers for helpful comments on previous versions of this manuscript.

[2] For important and contentious exceptions see the 2008 National Science Foundation report on systematic qualitative research edited by Lamont and White (2008), as well as King et al. (1994).

Martín Sánchez-Jankowski and Corey M. Abramson, *Foundations of the Behavioralist Approach to Comparative Participant Observation* In: *Beyond the Case*. Edited by: Corey M. Abramson and Neil Gong, Oxford University Press (2020).
DOI: 10.1093/oso/9780190608484.003.0002

sampling, generalization, and the role of theory (Abramson and Dohan 2015; Goertz and Mahoney 2012; Roth and Mehta 2002; Small 2009). While recognizing the immense importance of having diverse approaches for social scientific inquiry as well as the methodological refinements spurred by past criticisms and "post-positivist" methodologies (Abramson et al. 2018; Reed 2010; Steinmetz 2005), we argue that within the logic and parameters of the broadly realist approaches that are descendent from the CST in sociology[3] and other variable-driven social science disciplines,[4] the longstanding behavioralist approach to participant observation research can, and must, play a renewed role in attempts to document real-world causal mechanisms (Sánchez-Jankowski 2002; Gans 1999).

This task is complicated by the fact that how and why participant observation is conducted within the behavioralist tradition is often misunderstood or misrepresented. To address this issue, we offer a formal statement of this method including its logic, practice, and connection to CST approaches. This chapter presents understandings of causality and inference underlying participant observation done in the behavioralist tradition. In particular, we argue that comparative participant observation serves a necessary role in behavioralist research by providing essential techniques for observing causal processes in real-world contexts and reducing inferential error in new and existing models of human behavior. We explain how behavioralist participant observation is a key tool in explicating the association between antecedent and intermediary factors in causal chains as well as producing robust models that link micro-, meso-, and macro-level social processes. The complementary following chapter examines what comparative participant-observation research using the behavioral tradition entails in practice.[5]

[3] By "broader tradition," we include those responses to the philosophical criticisms of positivism that maintain significant continuity with key goals of this tradition, most prominently, analytical sociology and critical realism. The role of these philosophical traditions in the model of participant observation we espouse is discussed throughout the text.

[4] As Steinmetz notes, although the politics of method sometimes dictate that the term "positivism" is left out, the assumptions and forms of the larger positivist-behavioral tradition underlie many of the debates at elite journals, presses, and universities (Steinmetz 2005).

[5] Some of the more quantitatively oriented language used in this chapter may seem alien or even antagonistic to many of those who are committed to certain critical forms of ethnography. However it is our hope that even researchers operating in alternative traditions might focus on the substantive discussions in each section to better understand how the behavioralist form of participant observation is used for understanding social phenomena and developing social policies to improve social life. It is not the language, but what the method is attempting to provide researchers that is the focus of this chapter. Further, this clarifies CST criteria for examining the accuracy and generalizability of claims about the social world and clarifies the essential role of participant observation. Each of these topics serves as necessary background for the procedures and techniques discussed in the following chapter.

The Philosophical Priors

This section states common philosophical priors that underlie the discussions that follow. These priors are commonly shared in quantitative CST approaches, but are contested in in ethnography (Abramson and Gong, this volume; Abramson et al. 2018), so it is worth stating them here. The first prior is the position that there is a social world which exists independently from the researcher's mind or language used to describe or explain it. That is to say, our extension of this tradition is based in a realist ontology. The second prior is the axiological position that researchers are human actors who in practice cannot be value neutral and choose projects accordingly, but should aim to mitigate the potential for their values to bias data collection and analysis.[6] The third prior is the epistemological position that knowledge is produced through the accumulation of corresponding findings that provide an evidentiary basis for moving toward, but never completely establishing, explanations concerning the operations of the social world. While this position provides room for accepting the imperfection of data, the theory-infused nature of observation, and the fallibility of the research enterprise (Fay 1996), the method is still based on a directional model of collective and non-relativist knowledge accumulation that judges claims based on how well they "correspond" to the real world being studied (Russell 1994 [1905]).

Defining Participant Observation

Although the label ethnography has become common in sociology, anthropology, and related social science disciplines, in practice this term is applied to a panoply of methods including those that may or may not include the direct observation of human behavior in real world social contexts (Gans

[6] There exists in every human a set of morals and values that have developed over time concerning a wide range of social life, but researchers would benefit from both acknowledging that they exist and working to neutralize them while gathering data and engaging in scientific analyses. Max Weber (1949 [1917]), in his "Ethical Neutrality," comments that it is best for teachers (and by extension researchers) to acknowledge to their audience that they have values concerning the topics being discussed and then proceed to offer analysis. This allows the students (or readers) to know that values are important to the researcher and to be on the lookout for where they may have influenced the analysis in a manner that distorts the results. This is most clear when the researcher observes values, beliefs, attitudes, or opinions that she finds either morally or politically objectionable or counterproductive to an espoused goal that she holds. In this tradition, the researcher deals with this potential ethical issue by reporting a finding as truthfully as possible along with an objective analysis of what produced that finding and the effect it had on the research question.

1999). Although the term "ethnography" has certain appealing aspects, such as the implication of deep immersion in a social world (Geertz 1973; Lofland 1995), its imprecision makes it unsuitable for our task in the present paper. Consequently, we use the term "participant observation" to describe the method we are concerned with here. A reasonable starting description of what participant observation entails is offered by Becker in his classic article on the topic:

> The participant observer gathers data by participating in the daily life of the group or organization he studies. He watches the people he is studying to see what situations they ordinarily meet and how they behave in them. He enters into conversation with some or all of the participants in these situations and discovers their interpretation of the events he has observed. (Becker 1958)

This definition is broad enough to include a number of types of ethnographic research practiced by social scientists, including symbolic interactionism (Blumer 1969), ethnomethodology (Garfinkel 1967), analytic ethnography (Lofland 1995), the extended case method (Burawoy 1998), positivist-behavioral approaches (Sánchez-Jankowski 2002), interpretivism (Geertz 2000 [1973]), carnal sociology (Wacquant 2009), and grounded theory (Glaser and Strauss 1967). However, Becker's definition is also narrow enough to exclude ethnographic methods that do not involve at least one researcher observing social interaction between *live* participants in real-world settings.[7]

The level to which the researcher participates with the people and social settings in question varies according to the methodology and the goals of a given project (Woodward 2008). However, even in the most hands-off observational studies, the researcher participates with the social system in question by being present to record behavior over time and acquire a deep enough immersion in the social settings involved to understand the meanings attached to behavior. As Geertz classically noted (in his invocation of Ryle), this is necessary to discern, whether the contraction of an eyelid signals a

[7] The definition excludes audit studies of video (Katz 1999), qualitative content analysis without the direct observation of behavior (Altheide 1987), and comparative historical inquiries (Biernacki 1995) that are sometimes called ethnographic. Our point is not that these methods are without merit, but rather they are substantively different from participant observation. Further, although lab experiments involve the direct observation of human behavior, we exclude these studies from our definition, as the notion of constructing interactions in a lab environment differs in important ways from observing social life in pre-existing everyday settings.

socially meaningful wink or simply an involuntary twitch to the actors involved (Geertz 2000 [1973]; Geertz 1974). The contemporary behavioralist approach to participant observation likewise proceeds under the premise that explaining behavior generally requires understanding the meanings attached to subjects, actions, and contexts by people.

The Aims of Participant Observation

Although the behavioralist mode of participant observation has key practical and philosophical overlaps with the focus on meaning found in various interpretivist traditions (e.g., Geertz 2000 [1973]; Weber 1978), the primary goal of this attention differs from the strong focus on "thick description" found in some veins of contemporary interpretivism. The behavioralist researcher seeks not just a greater understanding of the systems of meaning that underlie and are produced by social action, or an evocative description that conveys a sense of immersion to a reader, but the production of more general scientific models of human behavior for which these meanings are but a part. Although in sociology the concern with producing generalizable models is often associated with Durkheim's writings on charting social facts (Durkheim 1982 [1895]), participant observation in the behavioralist tradition also draws from Weber's understandings about the production of explanations. As Weber notes, "Sociology is a science concerning itself with the interpretive understanding of social action and thereby with a causal explanation of its course and consequences" (Weber 1978). Participant observation is a method that facilitates this. It is in the tensions and intersections between the Weberian and Durkheimian approaches to explaining the social world that participant observation in the behavioralist tradition derives its three aims:

1) Observing meaningful human behavior in real-world contexts;
2) Using these observations to illuminate how causal mechanisms linking antecedent factors to observable outcomes operate in and across social contexts;
3) Producing more general explanations outside the samples or cases from which observations are drawn.[8]

[8] See also King, Keohane, and Verba (1994).

Thus the core function of participant-observation in the behavioralist tradition is to observe, identify, and generalize about mechanisms.

Illuniating Causal Mechanisms through Field Observations

It is generally acknowledged that one of the fundamental differences between survey research and participant observation has to do with the total number of observed people constituting the data set to be analyzed. As a method that generally involves lower numbers of individuals in a sample (i.e., "Small-N's"), participant observation is not well-suited to adequately addressing questions about population distributions. Questions that ask *what proportion* of a large population reports thinking or acting in a certain way, or to a lesser degree, the *extent* to which they think or act in a particular way, cannot be answered with any degree of confidence using participant observation. Instead, the questions for participant observation to address are what, where, when, how, and why thoughts and behaviors are developed, related, and instanced in everyday life.[9] Participant observers can directly observe behavior in social settings that provides a useful lens for examining how, when, and why things happen the way they do. The longitudinal nature of ethnographic research allows the observer to see how one set of factors (i.e., independent variables) works to affect another (i.e., dependent variable). Thus, when researchers move from what factors exist to how they work (i.e., mechanisms), the research project incorporates the necessary properties to satisfy the requirements for "understanding" in the phenomenological sense. Additionally, when the analysis moves from *how* factors work to produce an outcome to *why* they work to produce an outcome (Katz 2004), then it has evolved into "explanation" and the potential for prediction, in the sense of relative likelihoods given necessary conditions.[10] There is a good deal at stake

[9] Lofland's (1995) article makes an overlapping point in noting that in general, the participant-observation framework does not—and by extension, should not—address the macro-distributional questions of frequency and magnitude (e.g., "how many" and "how much" type questions) that are more easily answered using methods like survey research that can draw on a larger sample of individuals. He also correctly notes that qualitative methods broadly construed can provide a contribution to questions of type, structure, process, and agency. However, following the inferential logic we will outline here, we differ from Lofland in our assertion that statements of conditional cause and consequence directly benefit from participant-observation data.

[10] This notion is closely related to Bayesian principles about approaching specific hypotheses. It is also related to more general questions about using data to speak to the "relative plausibility of models" (e.g., Ragin 2004).

in correctly specifying the question to be addressed and making sure that participant-observation methodology is the most appropriate to answer it.

Given these strengths and limitations, participant observation in the behavioralist tradition places a great deal of weight on identifying the mechanisms involved in producing various social outcomes. The term "mechanisms" refers to social actions and interactions that link antecedent factors to observable outcomes (Hedström and Ylikoski 2010). Mechanisms are the elements and processes that combine to produce various outcomes in social life. It is the identification and description of the mechanisms needed to answer research questions of theoretical, human and policy significance, that is the primary empirical task for the participant observers working in the behavioralist tradition. The observer's physical location to the people being researched is what provides her or him the opportunity to see the intersection of social forces and human behaviors in the concrete contexts of everyday life (Gans 1999; Sánchez-Jankowski 2002; Small 2002).

One of the participant observer's primary objectives is determining which social behaviors constitute a mechanism. It is the recording and analysis of myriad interactions that provides the basis for identifying mechanisms. This effort to identify mechanisms involves some level of quantification, as the claims offered about mechanisms within or among populations will be based on the number of observances ranging from $N_0 \ldots N_\infty$. It is important to emphasize that the small "N" characterizing participant observation research is generally associated with the number of individuals in the study. This is not only misleading but inaccurate. Participant-observation research normally, though not always, involves small numbers of individuals. However, it is conventionally based on large numbers of observed interactions.[11] It is specifically the number of times that an observation has occurred that forms the basis for making empirical claims about patterns and is directly related to the confidence level in evaluating their validity. Within the behavioralist tradition it is not possible for any researcher to avoid issues of validity and reliability if they wish their results to be either evaluations of existing theories or used in the effort to construct new ones.[12]

[11] Participant observation has small N's of individuals for practical reasons. It is difficult for a single researcher, or even a team of researchers, to observe large numbers of independent individuals for an extended period of time. Still, the real difference between participant observation and survey research is not the size of N but the mode of collecting and analyzing data.

[12] Behavioralist research presupposes adequate time in the field to see relevant variation in those behaviors and patterns which can be identified as mechanisms.

Mechanisms in participant-observation research are technically identified and represented through inductive and deductive processes of concept formation. Concepts are defined as ideas, or idealized components, used to think about some aspect of the real world (Kaplan 1964). Concepts are used in all types of research, but in behavioralist participant observation the process is as much, or more, dependent on the inductive production of categories based in observed patterns than on the application and testing of existing theories. In brief, the use of concepts raises important issues concerning the validity of what is being represented, and this is dependent on whether the categories used to represent patterns of behavior correspond to 1) the observations (i.e., observational validity); 2) the literature (i.e., external validity); and 3) the rest of the data set (i.e., internal validity). The validity of an observation refers to its correspondence, or likely correspondence, to the discernable features in the real world. The validity of any representation related to mechanisms rests on whether it is speaking to the same phenomena that previous research has been speaking to and thereby achieving the external validity required to relate it to existing literatures. If the concepts used in the representation are differently defined, but used with appropriate rational justifications and used consistently enough to establish internal validity, then they warrant confidence that apples were compared to apples and not to oranges.

Representation can be understood as having three constituent processes. The first comprises identifying the mechanisms existing in the social environment under study, which involves some form of interpretation and analysis. There are two levels of interpretation here: the first is the researcher's interpretation of their subject's interpretations, that is, the researcher's understanding of the subjects' understandings (Geertz 2000 [1973]);[13] and the second is the researcher's understandings of the broader context in which these interpretations are occurring. That is to say, the researcher looks at the way individuals understand their actions, but also constructs their own analytical models of the actions in the social system under study. The two are related, but the latter is not strictly bound by the former—i.e., the researcher's models take into account, but are not limited to, subjects' understandings and interpretations.

[13] We invoke Geertz here because he is associated with, and clearly articulates, this element of interpretation. It should be stated, however, that Geertz has been rightfully criticized for conflating this with an artificial coherence and holism in his conceptualization of worldviews (c.f. Abramson 2012; Swidler 2001). The two are not necessarily inexorably intertwined.

Consider the following hypothetical example of a disconnect between a subject's interpretation of an event and its broader sociological significance: A researcher observes that a soldier in combat left a strategic position that they and two other members of their unit occupied. Their intent was to get a cup of coffee, and that was all the soldier thought he/she was doing or did. However, in the soldier's absence, the researcher observed that the position was left exposed, and the occupied area was subsequently overrun by opposing forces.

There are two interpretations here: (1) the soldier's initial interpretation of what they did (get coffee) and (2) the researcher's interpretation that the soldier's search for coffee led to the strategic position held at one time by all three soldiers being compromised and overrun. Focusing only on the subject's understanding, here that of the coffee-seeking soldier, would miss the broader social significance of the behavior and focusing only on the broader social significance risks missing or imputing motive (Roth and Mehta 2002). Similarly, using the accounts of interviewed subjects as a direct proxy for behavior that was not directly observed leaves researchers vulnerable to missing the social significance of behaviors in their real world contexts and introduces other risks related to accepting self-reports about behavior at face value (Gans 1999; Jerolmack and Khan 2014; Sanchez-Jankowski 2002).

The second process in representation is establishing what mechanisms are involved in answering the research question and organizing them into associational correspondence or causal sequences in the form of recursive or nonrecursive models. This assumes the creation of variables that can be defined as analytic constructs for capturing aspects of the world. The analyst explains not merely the association between variables, but begins to stage the variables, or sets of variables, into a temporal sequence that is unidirectional in the nonrecursive model or as in the recursive model, multidirectional with reciprocal associations. In other words, the researcher represents how social factors affect one another over time to produce an observable outcome or phenomenon. The mechanisms themselves may involve two factors. The first are verbal behaviors (i.e., prompted or unprompted speech) that help to capture the strategic use of language in interaction, as well as the psychological/cognitive/cultural morals, values, beliefs, attitudes, and opinions that underlie behavior. The second are physical nonverbal behaviors involving bodily movements (including gestures) that affect social interaction. The establishment of a mechanism comes from direct and/or indirect observation. Direct observation includes the first-hand use of the researcher's eyes and ears to record both physical and verbal behavior, as well as the meanings assigned by the social actors to them (Warren 2011). Indirect observation consists of information collected partially from observing the behavior of interest and validating the accuracy of the observation and the interpretation assigned to it through the corroborative recall of independent observers of the same behavior. For example, suppose subject S says she is working at a particular occupation in a factory and the researcher follows the person to the factory, but is barred access. The researcher never directly observes the subject working at the job and so asks independent observers whether the subject works at that particular occupation in the factory, and they affirm that subject S does work in the factory at that occupation. Although S's work at the factory is never directly observed, assuming that the other respondents have little incentive to fabricate their statements, the researcher can infer with a reasonable degree of confidence that S does work in the factory at that occupation.

At this point it is worth noting that the potential for misrepresentation is directly associated with what is unique about participant observation. Participant observation, regardless of its methodological tradition, carries with it the unique condition that while the researcher is participating in the life of those under study, she or he is the instrument of data gathering and of analysis. As such, decisions of what to record in notes, as well as the meaning of what was recorded, integrates data gathering with some elements of analysis and presents increased possibilities of misrepresentation by introducing susceptibility to error in both. The behavioralist response to this methodological issue, as compared to other traditions, is discussed in more depth in the next chapter.

Mechanisms documented in the analysis stage of participant observation research connect identified factors (i.e., variables) by determining the patterns of association, and the direction of the association. A pattern involves the observation of multiple occurrences of something over time, and cannot be ascertained without some minimal level of implicit or explicit quantification (i.e., counting). Thus, a pattern can be established by 1) the sum of observations of an occurrence ($\Sigma_n ob$); or 2) the number of observations of an occurrence during periods in which the same social or physical conditions are present ($\Sigma_n ob_{ij}$, i.e., the total number of observations of "i" under conditions "j"). If there were no deviations—that is, every time "i" was observed, it was under "j" conditions—then that pattern can be noted with a degree of confidence, but if "i" occurred under, say, "j, k, l" conditions, it will require that comparisons be made with each to see which of the "j," "k," or "l" conditions, if any, have the strength of evidence. This could be calculated as $\frac{\sum_n ob_{ij}}{\sum_n ob_{ij\ldots z}}$ which is to take the total number of observations of "i" occurring under "j" conditions divided by the total number of observations of "i" in all conditions, thereby establishing a ratio that could allow for a comparison between conditions of "j," "k," and "l" as to relative strength of "i" occurring under each condition. However, ultimately after noting this pattern in each, an examination would need to occur as to what was shared within conditions "j," "k," and "l" that produced a similar result and what it was about condition "j" (or any of the others) that was different to produce more occurrences of "i."

This exercise is neither frivolous nor window dressing, for it produces two analytic advantages: the first is to examine the likelihood that "i" will occur in a certain condition; and the second to examine whether "i" can occur within other conditions because it shares certain identified properties with the caveat that the absence of *all* the properties produces a weaker likelihood of occurrence. However, while it is not necessary for participant observers using the behavioralist method to present their findings using the relatively formal procedures just discussed, it would provide important leverage for these researchers if they employed them during the analysis stage (e.g., Abramson 2015; Sánchez-Jankowski 1991, 2008, 2016).

The use of mechanisms within participant-observation research involves a philosophical tension between understanding and explaining social life. This is the same tension that underlies Weberian and Durkheimian approaches to the social world (Ragin and Zaret 1983). Although understanding and explanation are sometimes mistakenly framed as incompatible, they need not be, and many times they are combined in participant-observation research. It is worth noting that the potential for misrepresentation is directly associated with what is unique about participant observation. Participant observation, regardless of its methodological tradition, carries with it a unique condition: the researcher participating in the life of those under study assumes the position of being both the instrument of data gathering and of analysis. As such, decisions of what to record in notes, as well as the meaning of what was recorded, increases the possibility of representational error in both. The behavioralist oriented participant observational response, as compared to the other ethnographic traditions, to this methodological issue, is offered in the next chapter.

The interpretivist focus on understanding social behavior in a contingent reciprocal relationship that establishes both meaning and the concomitant behavioral responses, and the CST focus on formulating explanations for prediction both must first understand how, when, and where factors operate the way they do. Descriptive approaches can stop with understanding how, when, and where the factors operate the way they do, but the researcher who wants to state *why* factors operate the way they do become involved in the project of explanation—a key aspect the of CST and behavioralist approaches.

Finally, once explanation has been embarked upon, the process of creating causal models exists in either an explicit or latent form. In the behavioralist approach to participant observation research, the process of explicitly establishing causality begins with identifying factors (i.e., independent variables) that are operative in affecting other factors, and then specifying how they operate to form a sequence of interactions producing a particular outcome or change in a social object of interest (i.e., a dependent variable).

Inference and Causality

The effort to establish understanding or explanation involves the act of interpretation. The common notion that participant observers are engaged in interpretation whereas survey and experimental research is involved in measurement and inference is misguided (Bevir and Rhodes 2005; Cicourel, this volume). Both involve collecting information from the world, categorizing that information, and making statements based upon it. Weber's explication of interpretation's role for the social sciences is applicable to most, if not all, methods utilized in sociology. Other than simply reporting what the subjects of an investigation said and the meaning they provided, it is hard to conceive of how raw data can be used in explanations without the use of interpretation. However, contrary to some attempts to implement a phenomenological approach to ethnography (Katz and Csordas 2003), participant observers in the behavioralist tradition record the meanings of micro social interaction but do not stop with the meaning subjects assign to their own and other's actions. The behavioralist participant observer's goal is to relate the subjects' meanings to patterned actions within the micro-, meso-, and macro-level structures of a society and its various contexts (Weber 1949 [1917]). In this way, researchers in the behavioralist tradition position themselves to utilize the sort of triangulation that is necessary to see the larger social mechanisms and their meaning for individual, community, and society, mechanisms that may be outside the realm of the subject's awareness (see the preceding example of the soldier, as well as Roth and Mehta 2002).

Deductive reasoning is most often associated with positivist approaches, especially statistical analyses of theoretical propositions in the form of variable-centered hypothesis testing, while participant observation and other qualitative research are often connected to more inductive case-centered reasoning (Ragin 1994, 2004). Although theories of induction and general approaches towards moving beyond the case or observation vary in accordance with the deployment of sampling versus case logics (i.e., analytic vs. probabilistic induction), using data to make some form of larger statement (i.e., a generalization) is key to both (Freedman 2010a; Lieberson 1991). An integral part of inductive reasoning involves using data to draw conclusions about how the world works, or, in the case of causal inference, why something occurred. Participant observers in the behavioralist tradition need to be attentive to the fact that inference refers to the size of two analytical gaps connected to the potential for error: 1) the disconnect between behavior and how it is recorded—that is directly, via accounts, or standardized measures (cf. Cicourel 1964; Jerolmack and Kahn 2014; Sánchez-Jankowski 2002); and 2) between a sample or case and the population or category to which generalizations are drawn. For participant observation the level of inference varies depending on whether the behavior was directly or indirectly observed. That is, inference is involved regardless of whether direct or indirect observation is involved, but when trying to establish understanding or explanation, the level of inference for a claim increases as the observation moves from direct to indirect. There is an additional proposition concerning inference as it relates to participant-observation research in the behavioralist tradition, and it can be stated as follows: the chance of error decreases as the sample of valid observed situations where the event can potentially occur increases (Freedman 2010a).

The level of inference in a model and the ability to establish convincing causal links are closely related. Even in its most nuanced forms (see Barringer, Eliason, and Leahey 2013), the concept of causality as commonly used in social science is rooted in the establishment of cause–effect relationships that can be simplified to: the occurrence of a particular event (x) produces another event (y). This is represented formally as X►Y. There are two basic positions on causation operating within the general behavioralist tradition. The first, associated with traditional positivist principles, would maintain that the establishment of causal associations in the social world needs to be treated as generalizable without qualification like those made by the physical sciences. Such statements might include the sorts of covering laws made in the natural sciences (e.g., aggression is part of animal biology) or economics (markets function based on supply and demand relationships). The second would understand the establishment of causal associations to be situation specific and based on inference that includes the use of some level of probability theory (Porter 2002). In other words, this second position would understand the social world to be extremely complicated, limiting generalizations about the causal associations to be based on the conditional probabilities of imperfect models. Thus, the first posits universal generalizability and the second posits conditional generalizability rooted in likelihoods, but both assume that causality exists and is observable over time. For the behavioralist researcher two related questions for the basis for thinking causally are *1) When Y occurred, how did the various existing elements work to make it happen? and 2) Under what conditions (i.e., when) did those elements work the way they did?*

Causal assertions X►Y are maintained when the level of inference involved is low, and errors are minimized, though always possible—that is, when there is little or no variance in the direct observation of a particular agent's actions influencing the actions or properties of another agent or group of agents. For the researcher using survey data, causality may be stated as a particular event that produces changes in another event and is usually inferred when a numerically specified variable produces a measured change in another variable (Heise 1975).[14] However, for the researcher using participant-observational data within the behavioralist model, causality is usually restated as "under condition X, you will get Y." This is because the focus is on the *manifestation* of mechanisms that produced the observed behavioral association rather than a quantitative measure of the degree to which one variable affects another. Parenthetically, for researchers using statistical operations the construction of precisely measured variables is done in part—and the emphasis here is *in part*—because the degree of the effect (i.e., statistically determined amount) is a proxy for not being able to observe and assess the impacts of thinking and behaving in real-world settings and times, whereas participant observation does have this capability (cf. Cicourel 1964). Thus, within the behavioralist

[14] For a review of the various models of causality in quantitative research see Barringer, Eliason and Leahey (2013).

participant-observation framework the construction of causal statements involves inferring the relationship between two or more variables that are linked temporally within specific circumstances, because the participant observer cannot be omnipresent to observe all the behaviors that have taken place in everyday life or the potential manifestation of previously unobserved counterfactuals (Morgan and Winship 2007). Consequently, behavioralist participant observers employ a qualified and probabilistic principle of causation that emphasizes the observed verbal and physical behaviors have a high probability of occurring under like conditions.

When framed as "under conditions 'X' there is *high(er) probability* you will get 'Y'," as opposed to the stricter proposition that "under conditions 'X' you *will* get 'Y' " (Pearl 2000), the behavioralist approach to participant observation typically incorporates some of the tenets advanced by traditions like critical realism and analytical sociology, which employ causal statements that are delivered as generalizable across situations or circumstances, but accepts the more prudent position that cause and effect are often predicated on conditional circumstances and potential path dependencies (Barringer, Eliason, and Leahey 2013; Gorski 2013; Hedström and Bearman 2009; Porpora 2015). Still, the notion differs from classic interactionist approaches (symbolic interaction and ethnomethodology) in that these statements are made with the expectation that there is high probability of observing them again in similar situations (Collier 2005). Veins of symbolic interaction, postmodernism, and even ethnomethodology often assume that situations and conditions are temporary because human life is too complicated to produce the very same factors, conditions, and situations in social life. What the researcher sees is real, but not capable of being reproduced. In contrast, participant observation in the behavioralist tradition maintains an interest in parsing causality by identifying event patterns where sequencing establishes a hierarchical order related to action–reaction dyads between events. Participant observation is particularly suited to charting the following four causal forms (shown in Figures 1.1–1.4):

1. Singular Causality [variable X causes variable Y to exist or change in some way through mechanism "M"].

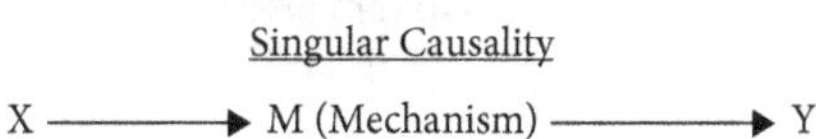

Figure 1.1 Causal Mechanism: Singular Causality

2. Multiple Independent Causality [multiple variables work independently to cause *Y* to exist or to change in some way].

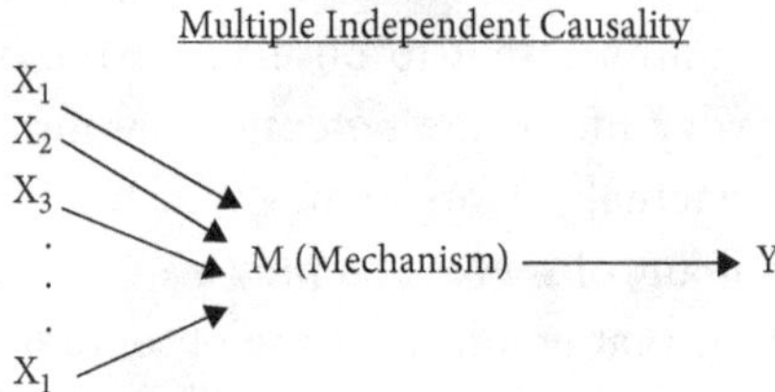

Figure 1.2 Causal Mechanism: Multiple Independent Causality

3. Multiple Interactive Causality [variables interact with any other number of variables to produce a combined effect (interaction of X_1, X_2 and interactions of X_3, $X_4 \ldots X_n$) causing *Y* to exist or to change in some way].

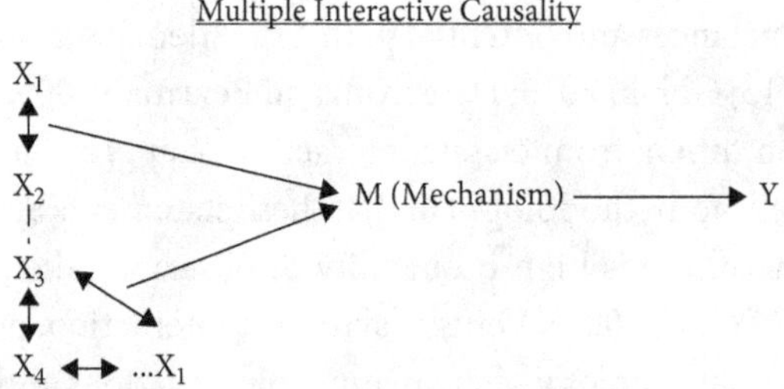

Figure 1.3 Causal Mechanism: Multiple Interactive Causality

4. Sequential Causality [variable X1 affects X2 which affects X3 to cause Y to exist or change in some way].

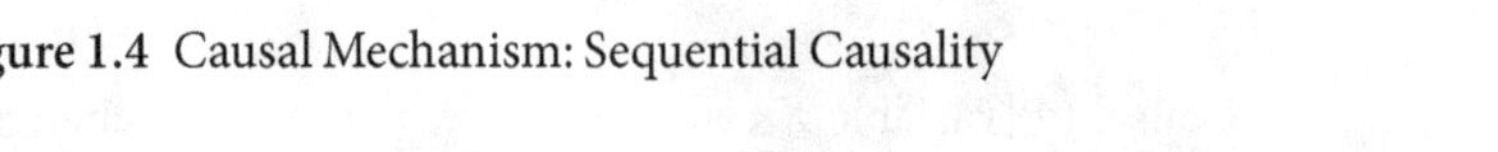

Sequential Causality

X_1 → M (Mechanism) → X_1 → M (Mechanism) → X_1 → M (Mechanism) → Y

Figure 1.4 Causal Mechanism: Sequential Causality

This method is key for engaging in what methodologists in other social science fields call causal process observation (CPO) (Brady, Collier, and Seawright 2004; Freedman 2010b). Participant observation shows both how variables manifest in daily life, as well as how the process indicated by arrows operates in interactional sequences. Although other CST methods can make similar causal claims, participant observation shows *how causal processes operate in real-world settings* in ways impossible for other methods to observe.[15]

Generalization

Generalizability is one of the fundamental tenets of positivist-oriented science and its CST descendants. Generalizability refers to the extent to which a relation, causal or otherwise, can be extended to a larger population beyond the sample of data. The ability to generalize is dependent on the population, research design, and sample used to represent it. Participant-observation research will generally experience a disadvantage in the raw number of individuals sampled per unit time, but it has the advantage of observing much larger and varied numbers of longitudinal interactions than survey research, experiments, or in-depth interviewing (Abramson and Dohan 2015; Sánchez-Jankowski 2002). Thus, one of the fundamental differences is that surveys using sampling frames that include large numbers of randomly selected individuals are better able to establish the breadth of their findings among the targeted population than a participant-observation study. Survey researchers may also be more strategically placed to identify the relevant factors that are involved in explaining the answer to distributional questions about how many or how strongly events or attitudes occur, and how these are associated with other factors. However, these methods do not directly demonstrate how these factors are connected to behavioral responses in everyday life, or the forms these responses take in practice (Cicourel 1964; Cicourel, this volume; Gans 1999; Sánchez-Jankowski 2002). *Here participant observation provides an important contribution to social scientific generalization, but this contribution must focus on when, where, and how the identified factors (either identified by the observer or past researchers) behave, either alone or interactively, to produce an observed outcome.* Thus, for participant-observation methodology the sole focus is not on maximizing the number of individuals observed, but the number of observed events among a number

[15] This focus on how mechanisms manifest is not necessarily at odds with the counterfactual model of causality articulated by Morgan and Winship (2007). For an examination of the relationship between ethnography and counterfactual causality see Smith (2012).

of individuals. Although this method suffers an "inferential disadvantage" in going from sample to population due to its depth, it has an "inferential advantage" in observing rather than imputing behavior and in linking broader mechanisms to their operations in daily life (Cicourel 1982). In contrast to the distribution claims of statistical data sets, the focus of the behavioralist is on "causal process observations" (Brady, Collier, and Seawright 2004; Freedman 2010b).

Validity and Reliability

Most participant-observation researchers would like to have their generalizations considered useful and used by others interested in the same or related substantive areas. For this to occur within the CST framework, the issues of validity (analytical correspondence) and reliability (observational consistency) are central. Assuming the criteria of analytical correspondence are met (i.e., the type of data relates to the type of claims being made), the issue becomes how valid the data are as representations of the world. There is considerable disagreement among participant observers regarding the importance of validity and reliability. At one end of the spectrum, generally seen in anti-CST approaches, there are two related positions. The first is that direct observation of behavior has face validity and concomitant reliability; the second is that validity is not a concern and reliability is not possible because the events observed, being time and circumstance dependent, are temporary, making them incapable of existing and being seen in exactly the same way again (Blumer 1969). At the other end of the spectrum, those employing behavioralist approaches accept the position that all the behaviors they observe are subject to potential errors, but that this does not necessitate abandoning the CST. It is only through careful empirics (that maximize validity and reliability), and the replication of results, that social scientific explanations can be improved over time. Both validity and reliability are predicated on the ability of researchers to place themselves in a position to 1) observe their subjects' verbal and physical behaviors; 2) assess the accuracy of the type of events reported (i.e., were the same events observed); and 3) evaluate the analyses of the events presented (i.e., why and under what conditions they continued to occur), vis-à-vis previous studies. For those using the behavioralist approach science is a cumulative effort, in which there is a dependency on a community of scholars committed to producing shared and objective knowledge

(Bevir and Rhodes 2005), supported by the replication and reanalysis of results. Most acknowledge that while the scientific method is imperfect, such an approach still has the greatest potential for understanding and improving the social world.[16]

For the participant observer in the behavioralist tradition, replication must occur for reliability to be established and validity to be assessed. This can only be done when previous research provides the necessary information about the population or site studied so that future researchers can restudy a population or site that approximates the same population/site conditions reported in the earlier studies (Burawoy 2007; Lewis 1972). If there are differences in what is observed in both studies, then what is found to be the same is given more explanatory strength. However, if differences are found and these differences are accompanied by reasoned explanations for the differences, there exists an empirical puzzle that can only be adjudicated by the weight of evidence provided by subsequent independent studies examining these and plausible alternative explanations.

Conclusions

We have argued that participant observation conducted according to behavioralist principles serves a necessary role in the realist variable-based approach that has succeeded positivism as the standard for mainline social science. However, addressing concerns about validity, generalization, and replication endemic to the CST involves more than a symbolic gesture toward these issues, or critiques of other methods that predictably end in assertions of the superiority of ethnography. The sections in this chapter have endeavored to provide this, through an outline of the fundamental positions of the contemporary behavioralist approach to participant observation.

[16] Although not all traditions of participant observation argue replication is possible or needed, at least two from the phenomenological tradition would be amenable to it. Ethnomethodologists would agree to the position that circumstances are constantly changing and generalizations concerning them are not possible, but the identified rules that individuals use to negotiate their constantly changing conditions do exist and these rules are capable of being observed from one time to another (Garfinkel 1967; Goffman 1986). Likewise, some symbolic interactionists generalize about the acts of interpretation and definition used to construct interactions that are constantly changing. For ethnomethodology it would be possible to observe whether or not rules were operative in social life, and for symbolic interaction it would be possible to observe individuals interpreting the meanings of others and defining how others are to act (Blumer 1969). In brief, although validity is emphasized, reliability is an issue for these two methods and supports their understanding that they are engaged in science as well.

Table 1.1 Observational Strengths of Common Social Scientific Methods

	OVB	OVB-E	OPB	OPB-E
Experimental	X		X	
Survey	X			
In-Depth Interviewing	X			
Participant Observation		X		X

OVB = Observes Verbal Behavior, which involves both what is being said and how it is said.

OVB-E = Observes Verbal Behavior, which involves both what is being said and how it is said, and does it in the subject's everyday life environment

OPB = Observes the Physical Behavior of the subject

OPB-E = Observes the Physical Behavior of the subject, and does it in the subject's everyday environment

Before moving on to the specific techniques participant observers can deploy in the next chapter, we briefly examine what this form of participant observation provides vis-à-vis the other methods in the CST repertoire.

There are numerous methods that provide evidence about social life even within the broad framework of the behavioralist tradition, none of which can be considered perfect for explaining the world. This section is an effort to briefly look at where participant observation provides the most analytical leverage within the CST tradition. Table 1.1 summarizes the various differences between common methods employed by social science for studying human subjects, and their relative inferential advantages and disadvantages from the behavioralist perspective. It is important to point out that all methodological techniques involving living human subjects focus on verbal and physical behavior, but not all of them do this in the same way, and it is these differences that present advantages and disadvantages for each.[17] There are four primary methods of social science that involve living people as their primary subjects: 1) experimental methods, 2) survey research, 3) in-depth interviewing, and 4) participant observation. In each case a researcher collects and analyzes both verbal and physical behavior.

Survey research and in-depth interviewing are often concerned with verbal and physical behavior but rely on subjects to tell researchers about

[17] Of course, the shortcoming of any given method can be addressed in part by complementing the research with other methods either within or across studies.

those behaviors, what happened before and after the behaviors, and what they think about various aspects of life that may have influenced their behaviors. Both methods have the strength of using systematic questioning to ascertain thoughts, but because they do not observe any behavior other than that of the subjects answering the question, they must accept accounts of their subjects' behavior as a proxy for that behavior. This can lead to inaccurate or misleading representations of the behavior being measured (Becker 1958; Cicourel 1982; Gans 1999; Sánchez-Jankowski 2002). The lack of behavioral observation allows for these research methods to build inferential explanations about large populations, but they have the disadvantage of not being able to demonstrate how the variables operate in concrete real-world contexts to explain the observed outcome. Further, if the outcome in question is a behavior that is recorded on the basis of a respondent's recollection, or willingness to share, there is an increased chance of error. In other words, these methods contribute by specifying that $X_1, X_2, X_3 \ldots X_n$ make S behave in Y manner, but they must exercise increased inference as to how $X_1, X_2, X_3 \ldots X_n$ work either independently or interactively to produce S's behavior Y because of the lack of observation of the behavior and its predictors in context C.

Experimental research is able to directly observe both verbal and physical behavior. The controlled environment where manipulation is possible makes this form of research theoretically able to isolate what independent variables explain the behavior associated with the dependent variable. Experimental research is able to connect verbal to physical behavior, but its strength in isolating what variables are causing behavior becomes its weakness because the controlled laboratory environment does not approximate the complexity of the outside world. This has often been conceptualized in terms of related challenges of external and ecological validity (Cicourel 1982). Whether the universal effect produced in a lab after controlling out all variation (e.g., race, class, gender, age) is actually universal, or alternatively artificial and contingent on the laboratory context, is ultimately an empirical question that can only be answered in comparison with behavioral data from the world outside the laboratory.

Participant-observation research typically has the disadvantage of having small numbers of observed individuals compared to surveys or even large interview studies. This makes it harder to make distributional claims about the extent to which people think or act in a particular way in a population. Likewise, participant observation does not have the advantage of the experiment because it lacks the ability to control through manipulation of independent variables and therefore specify with certainty what factors act alone or in combinational sequence to influence behavior. However, it has the advantage of being able to both more thoroughly understand and accurately explain the conditions and complexity of everyday life in existing social contexts.

As Herbert Gans notes, participant observation's power lies in the fact that it "allows researchers to observe what people do, while all the other empirical methods are limited to reporting what people say about what they do" (Gans 1999, 540). Ultimately, the strength of participant observation in the behavioralist tradition is derived from the method's ability to identify the way subjects think about real-world objects before acting, how they behave toward these objects when action is decided upon, and how they made sense of their behavior afterward.[18] In brief, participant observation provides techniques to map the relationship between action, motivation, and justification (Sánchez-Jankowski 2002; Vaisey 2009).[19]

By way of conclusion, although confronted by the complexity of factors that interact to influence how subjects behave, participant observation has the unique ability to directly observe the challenges the real world presents to subjects as they go about their everyday lives, how these subjects negotiate the challenges, and to what effect (Becker 1958). It is a method that provides vital data and analysis about the micro foundations operating within society's meso and macro processes because it is done within the life worlds of the subjects under study with the least amount of disruptive intrusion to their natural rhythms.

[18] Often people assume that participant-observation research is concerned only with how people behave. Participant-observation research does attempt to account for behavior, but in doing so it needs to determine which factors—antecedent and intervening variables—affect other aspects of social life and how. These factors include the way people think, what influenced them to think this way, and how this led to behaving in a certain manner and context.

[19] Within survey analysis, a technique is often used whereby verbal reports are cross-checked with behavior, and while this can produce consistencies, it involves considerable inference as to how the thought reported by the subject produced the behavior in question. The mechanism may well involve something extra to the original thought, and this could not be determined by such a method. In contrast, participant-observation done within the behavioralist tradition is not only capable of identifying the mechanism, but would confine its findings to what was observed, linking thought directly or indirectly through some other variable to behavior.

References

Abramson, Corey M. 2012. "From 'Either-Or' to 'When and How': A Context-Dependent Model of Culture in Action." *Journal for the Theory of Social Behaviour* 42, no. 2: 155–180.

Abramson, Corey M. 2015. *The End Game: How Inequality Shapes Our Final Years.* Cambridge, MA: Harvard University Press.

Abramson, Corey M., and Daniel Dohan. 2015. "Beyond Text: Using Arrays to Represent and Analyze Ethnographic Data." *Sociological Methodology* 45, no. 1: 272–319. https://doi.org/10.1177/0081175015578740.

Abramson, Corey M., Jacqueline Joslyn, Katharine A. Rendle, Sarah B. Garrett, and Daniel Dohan. 2018. "The Promises of Computational Ethnography: Improving Transparency, Replicability, and Validity for Realist Approaches to Ethnographic Analysis." *Ethnography* 19, no. 2: 254–284. https://doi.org/10.1177/1466138117725340.

Altheide, David L. 1987. "Ethnographic Content Analysis." *Qualitative Sociology* 10, no. 1: 65–77.

Barringer, Sondra N., Scott R. Eliason, and Erin Leahey. 2013. "A History of Causal Analysis." In *Handbook of Causal Analysis for Social Research*, edited by L. Stephen Morgan, 9–26. Dordrecht: Springer Netherlands. https://doi.org/10.1007/978-94-007-6094-3_2.

Becker, Howard. 1958. "Problems of Inference and Proof in Participant Observation." *American Sociological Review* 23, no. 6: 652–660.

Becker, Howard S. 2009. "How To Find Out How To Do Qualitative Research." *International Journal of Communication* 3 (March): 545–553.

Bevir, Mark, and R. A. W. Rhodes. 2005. "Interpretation and Its Others." *Australian Journal of Political Science* 40, no. 2: 169–187.

Biernacki, Richard. 1995. *The Fabrication of Labor: Germany and Britain, 1640–1914.* Berkeley: University of California Press.

Blumer, Herbert. 1969. *Symbolic Interactionism: Perspective and Method.* Englewood Cliffs, NJ: Prentice Hall.

Brady, Henry E., David Collier, and Jason Seawright. 2004. "Refocusing the Discussion of Methodology." In *Rethinking Social Inquiry: Diverse Tools, Shared Standards*, edited by Henry E. Brady and David Collier, 1–18. Berkeley, CA: Rowman & Littlefield.

Burawoy, Michael. 1998. "The Extended Case Method." *Sociological Theory* 16, no. 1: 4–33.

Burawoy, Michael. 2007. *The Extended Case Method: Four Countries, Four Decades, Four Great Transformations, and One Theoretical Tradition*. Berkeley: University of California Press.

Cicourel, Aaron V. 1964. *Method and Measurement in Sociology*. Glencoe, IL: Free Press of Glencoe.

Cicourel, Aaron V. 1982. "Interviews, Surveys, and the Problem of Ecological Validity." *The American Sociologist* 17, no. 1): 11–20.

Clifford, James. 1988. *The Predicament of Culture: Twentieth-Century Ethnography, Literature, and Art.* Cambridge, MA: Harvard University Press.

Collier, Andrew. 2005. "Philosophy and Critical Realism." In *The Politics of Method in the Human Sciences: Positivism and Its Epistemological Others*, edited by George Steinmetz, 327–345. Durham, NC: Duke University Press.

Corbin, Juliet M. M., and Anselm L. Strauss. 2008. *Basics of Qualitative Research: Techniques and Procedures for Developing Grounded Theory*, 3rd ed. Thousand Oaks, CA: SAGE Publications.

Crapanzano, Vincent. 1986. "Hermes' Dilemma: The Masking of Subversion in Ethnographic Description." In *Writing Culture: The Poetics and Politics of Ethnography*, edited by George E. Marcus and James Clifford, 51–76. Berkeley: University of California Press.

Durkheim, Emile. 1982 [1895]. *The Rules of Sociological Method*. New York: The Free Press.

Fay, Brian. 1996. *Contemporary Philosophy of Social Science: A Multicultural Approach*. Oxford: Blackwell.

Freedman, David A. 2010a. "Black Ravens, White Shoes and Case Selection: Inference with Categorical Variables." In *Statistical Methods and Causal Inference: A Dialogue with the Social Sciences*, edited by David Collier, Jasjeet S. Sekhon, and Philip B. Stark, 105–114. Cambridge: Cambridge University Press.

Freedman, David A. 2010b. "On Types of Scientific Inquiry: The Role of Qualitative Reasoning." In *Statistical Methods and Causal Inference: A Dialogue with the Social Sciences*, edited by David Collier, Jasjeet S. Sekhon, and Philip B. Stark, 337–356. Cambridge: Cambridge University Press.

Gans, Herbert J. 1999. "Participant Observation in the Era of Ethnography." *Journal of Contemporary Ethnography* 28, no. 5: 540–548.

Garfinkel, Harold. 1967. *Studies in Ethnomethodology*. London: Blackwell.

Geertz, Clifford. 1974. "'From the Native's Point of View': On the Nature of Anthropological Understanding." *Bulletin of the American Academy of Arts and Sciences* 28, no. 1: 26–45.

Geertz, Clifford. 2000 [1973]. "Thick Description: Towards an Interpretive Theory of Culture." In *The Interpretation of Cultures: Selected Essays*, 3–30. New York: Basic Books.

Glaser, Barney G., and Anselm L. Strauss. 1967. *The Discovery of Grounded Theory: Strategies for Qualitative Research*. New York: Aldine Publishing Company.

Goertz, Gary, and James Mahoney. 2012. *A Tale of Two Cultures: Qualitative and Quantitative Research in the Social Sciences*. Princeton, NJ: Princeton University Press.

Gorski, Philip. 2013. "What Is Critical Realism and Why Should You Care?" *Contemporary Sociology* 42, no. 5: 658–670. https://doi.org/10.1177009430611 3499533.

Goffman, Erving. 1986. *Frame Analysis: An Essay on The Organization of Experience*. Boston: Northeastern University Press.

Hedström, Peter, and Peter Bearman. 2009. "What Is Analytical Sociology All About?: An Introductory Essay." In *The Oxford Handbook of Analytical Sociology*. edited by Peter Hedström, Paul Bearman, 3–24. New York: Oxford University Press.

Hedström, Peter, and Petri Ylikoski. 2010. "Causal Mechanisms in the Social Sciences." *Annual Review of Sociology* 36: 49–67.

Heise, R. David. 1975. *Causal Analysis*. New York: John Wiley & Sons.

Jerolmack, Colin, and Shamus Khan. 2014. "Talk Is Cheap: Ethnography and the Attitudinal Fallacy." *Sociological Methods & Research* 43, no. 2: 178–209. https://doi.org/10.1177/0049124114523396.

Kaplan, Abraham. 1964. *Conduct of Inquiry: Methodology of the Behavioral Sciences*. San Francisco, CA: Chandler Publishing.

Katz, Jack. 1999. *How Emotions Work*. Chicago: University of Chicago Press.

Katz, Jack. 2004. "On the Rhetoric and Politics of Ethnographic Methodology." *Annals of the American Academy of Political and Social Science* 595: 280–308.

Katz, Jack, and Thomas J. Csordas. 2003. "Phenomenological Ethnography in Sociology and Anthropology." *Ethnography* 4, no. 3: 275–288.

King, Gary, Robert O. Keohane, and Sidney. Verba. 1994. *Designing Social Inquiry: Scientific Inference in Qualitative Research*. Princeton, NJ: Princeton University Press.

Lamont, Michèle, and Patricia White. 2008. Workshop on Interdisciplinary Standards for Systematic Qualitative Research. Arlington, VA: National Science Foundation.

Lareau, Annetta, and Aliya Hamid Rao. 2016. "It's About the Depth of Your Data." *Contexts* (blog), March 19. https://contexts.org/blog/its-about-the-depth-of-your-data/.

Lewis, Oscar. 1972. *Life in a Mexican Village: Tepoztlán Restudied*. New York: Peter Smith Publishing, Inc.

Lieberson, Stanley. 1991. "Small N's and Big Conclusions: An Examination of the Reasoning in Comparative Studies Based on a Small Number of Cases." *Social Forces* 70, no. 2: 307–320.

Lofland, John. 1995. "Analytic Ethnography." *Journal of Contemporary Ethnography* 24, no. 1: 30–67.

Morgan, Stephen L., and Christopher Winship. 2007. *Counterfactuals and Causal Inference: Methods and Principles for Social Research* New York: Cambridge University Press.

Pearl, Judea. 2000. *Causality: Models, Reasoning, Inference*. Cambridge: Cambridge University Press.

Porpora, Douglas V. 2015. *Reconstructing Sociology: The Critical Realist Approach*. Cambridge: Cambridge University Press.

Porter, Sam. 2002. "Critical Realist Ethnography." In *Qualitative Research In Action*, edited by Tim May, 53–72. Thousand Oaks, CA: SAGE Publications.

Ragin, Charles C. 1994. *Constructing Social Research: The Unity and Diversity of Method*. Thousand Oaks, CA: Pine Forge Press.

Ragin, Charles C. 2004. "Turning the Tables: How Case-Oriented Research Challenges Variable-Oriented Research." In *Rethinking Social Inquiry: Diverse Tools, Shared Standards*, edited by Henry E. Brady and David Collier, 123–138. Lanham, MD: Rowman & Littlefield.

Ragin, Charles, and David Zaret. 1983. "Theory and Method in Comparative Research: Two Strategies." *Social Forces* 61, no. 3: 731–754.

Reed, Isaac A. 2010. "Epistemology Contextualized: Social-Scientific Knowledge in a Postpositivist Era." *Sociological Theory* 28, no. 1: 20–39.

Roth, Wendy D., and Jal D. Mehta. 2002. "The Rashomon Effect: Combining Positivist and Interpretive Approaches in the Analysis of Contested Events." *Sociological Methods and Research* 31, no. 2: 131–173.

Russell, Bertrand. 1994 [1905]. "The Nature of Truth." In *The Collected Works of Bertrand Russell*, edited by A. Urquhaut, 492–506. London: Routledge.

Sánchez-Jankowski, Martín. 1991. *Islands in the Street: Gangs and American Urban Society*. Berkeley: University of California Press.

Sánchez-Jankowski, Martín. 2002. "Representation, Responsibility and Reliability in Participant Observation." In *Qualitative Research in Action*, edited by Tim May, 144–160. London: SAGE Publications.

Sánchez-Jankowski, Martín. 2008. *Cracks in the Pavement: Social Change and Resilience in Poor Neighborhoods*. Berkeley: University of California Press.

Sánchez-Jankowski, Martín. 2016. *Burning Dislike: Ethnic Violence in High Schools*. Oakland: University of California Press.

Small, Mario Luis. 2002. "Culture, Cohorts, and Social Organization Theory: Understanding Local Participation in a Latino Housing Project." *American Journal of Sociology* 108, no. 1: 1–54.

Small, Mario Luis. 2009. "How Many Cases Do I Need?" *Ethnography* 10, no. 1: 5–38.

Smith, Robert Courtney. 2012. "How Did You Pick That School?: Ethnography, Epistemology, and Counterfactual Causality." In *American Journal of Sociology Conference on Causal Thinking and Ethnographic Research*, March 8. Chicago: University of Chicago Press.

Stacey, Judith. 1988. Can there be a feminist ethnography? *Women's Studies International Forum* 11:21–27.

Steinmetz, George. 2005. "Scientific Authority and the Transition to Post-Fordism: The Plausibility of Positivism in U.S. Sociology Since 1945." In *The Politics of Method in the Human Sciences: Positivism and its Epistemological Others*. edited by George Steinmetz, 275–326. Durham, NC: Duke University Press.

Swidler, Ann. 2001. *Talk of Love: How Culture Matters*. Chicago: University of Chicago Press.

Tavory, Iddo, and Stefan Timmermans. 2014. *Abductive Analysis: Theorizing Qualitative Research*. Chicago: University of Chicago Press.

Vaisey, Stephen. 2009. "Motivation and Justification: Towards a Dual-Process Theory of Culture in Action." *American Journal of Sociology* 114, no. 6: 1975–1715.

Wacquant, Loïc. 2009. "Habitus as Topic and Tool: Reflections on Becoming a Prizefighter." In *Ethnographies Revisited*, edited by William Shaffir, Antony Puddephatt, and Steven Kleinknecht, 137–151. New York: Routledge.

Warren, Carol, A. B. 2011. "The Eyes Have It." *Ethnography* 12, no. 4: 543–555.

Weber, Max. 1949 [1917]. "Meaning of 'Ethical Neutrality' [Wertfreiheit] in Sociology and Economics." In *The Methodology of the Social Sciences*. Translated by Edward Shils and Henry A. Finch. Glencoe: Free Press.

Weber, Max. 1978. *Economy and Society*. Berkeley: University of California Press.

Woodward, Kath. 2008. "Hanging Out and Hanging About: Insider/Outsider Research in the Sport of Boxing." *Ethnography* 9, no. 4: 536–560.

2

Conducting Comparative Participant Observation

Behavioralist Procedures and Techniques

Corey M. Abramson and Martín Sánchez-Jankowski

Introduction

Following the argument for the importance of comparative participant observation for approaches descendent from the conventional scientific tradition (CST), this chapter outlines how the behavioralist foundations summarized in chapter 1 translate to procedures and techniques for charting causal mechanisms in comparative ethnographic research. The chapter begins by examining the practices and techniques of the behavioralist approach in detail and describes the mode of research design, sampling, data collection, analysis, and explanation associated with this approach, giving examples from prior empirical works. The chapter then turns to longstanding concerns about ethnographic reliability and replication and explains how this approach addresses them. In doing so, it shows how behavioralist criteria align with, and diverge from, other methodological approaches to the collection, analysis, and extension of ethnographic data. The chapter concludes by explaining the contributions that can be made by repositioning participant observation within the spectrum of approaches to understanding causal processes in the social sciences.

Research Design and Sampling

Participant observers operating in the behavioralist tradition begin designing their research by generating an empirical question, with an uncertain answer, that can be adjudicated by data (King, Keohane, and Verba

Corey M. Abramson and Martín Sánchez-Jankowski, *Conducting Comparative Participant Observation* In: *Beyond the Case*. Edited by: Corey M. Abramson and Neil Gong, Oxford University Press (2020).
DOI: 10.1093/oso/9780190608484.003.0003

1994).[1] Research questions for participant observers typically entail an inquiry into which factors present in real-world settings operate to produce outcomes and how they do so (Lamont and White 2008; Lofland 1995).[2] In generating such a question, researchers in the behavioralist tradition examine existing theoretical and empirical literatures to identify areas in which empirical answers as to how factors involved in a particular social setting have produced the outcome of interest. Contrary to the approach associated with classical grounded theory, neither the substantive area of interest nor the research question is left to be decided while one is formally in the field gathering data. Research questions are selected on the basis of both empirical and theoretical importance in providing data on a topic and their potential to contribute to knowledge about the social world (King, Keohane, and Verba 1994). Any theoretical priors, hypotheses, and relevant researcher characteristics that influence the collection of data are integrated into the research design and made explicit for review.[3]

The manner in which participant observers in the behavioralist tradition manage the question of theoretical priors and existing categories is by being, to the extent possible, explicit about what those categories are and careful in explaining how they influence the collection and analysis of data. In this sense, participant observation in the behavioralist framework is 1) similar to the extended case method and other approaches that encourage transparency and reflexivity as central to the research enterprise (e.g., Bourdieu and Wacquant 1992; Burawoy 1998; King, Keohane, and Verba 1994; Tavory and Timmermans 2014); and 2) divergent from classic grounded theory's attempts to set aside prior categories and

[1] We would like to thank Claude Fischer, Aaron Cicourel, Frédéric Vandenberghe, Neil Gong, and the anonymous reviewers for helpful comments on previous versions of this manuscript.

[2] As noted in our chapter "Foundations of the Behavioralist Approach to Comparative Participant Observation" in this volume, in line with other contemporary approaches, our use of behavioralism does not invoke the hardline model of absolute confirmation or refutation characteristics of early positivism, but rather the use of imperfect data to make claims of relative plausibility (Fay 1996). In this understanding, although the null hypothesis provides an important counterfactual, like all truth claims it can never be absolutely refuted. Following philosophical turns to Bayesianism, the idea is to "update probabilities [of a proposition or hypothesis] in light of the evidence" (Godfrey-Smith 2003). The key distinction is that although inquiry is fallible, all solutions are not equally plausible given the evidence (Fay 1996).

[3] Unfortunately, the practices that allow transparency in reporting on the research process and data are often constrained by the page limitations imposed by journals and book publishers. New technologies for data sharing and the growth of online supplements to printed publications, however, may move us toward at least a partial solution (see Abramson and Dohan 2015; Abramson et al. 2018).

focus only on what "emerges" from the data (Glaser and Strauss 1967).[4] However, unlike these methods, the question being researched within the behavioralist tradition remains the same over the course of the project, even though at the various stages of investigation the understandings and explanations evolve.

In comparative participant observation conducted according to CST principles, the research question must stay consistent for the duration of the project because it is carefully chosen to address important issues in the current state of knowledge by leveraging the strengths of the method. Consequently, switching topics necessitates redesigning the entire project with a clear statement of the new question to be addressed, a corresponding sampling frame, and appropriate observational strategies. Switching questions mid-project based on findings that are interesting (but tangential to the original research question) risks generating a biased sample with inconsistent observations across the life of a project. Put otherwise, there is a high risk of methodological misspecifications that increases the likelihood of producing errors in data collection, analysis and generalization. This does not mean that comparative behavioralist researchers do not read new literatures or take observed patterns seriously in generating inductive explanations. Both of these are a necessary and intrinsic part of the method. However, rather than a commitment to a theory (Burawoy 2007), a setting (Glaser and Strauss 1967), or the idea of identifying emerging puzzles (Tavory and Timmermans, this volume), the behavioralist is committed to systematically answering a question chosen because of its scientific and (often) policy significance—for example, why gangs continue to exist in poor urban areas despite persistent attempts to eradicate them (Sánchez-Jankowski 1991), how inequality shapes the lives of older Americans (Abramson 2015), or how cultural repertoires shape responses to poverty (Dohan 2003). While new findings may shape answers and lead to future projects, they do not change the importance of the underlying research question or the researcher's commitment to answering it.

Once a question has been determined, an initial unit of analysis (individuals, organizations, community, etc.) is selected as central to the question and appropriate to sample upon. Although this can be done in random or

[4] Although grounded theory has provided important methodological advances in systematizing categorization and induction, the notion of bracketing theoretical priors to inductively generate more organic data is cognitively implausible and has been criticized on numerous accounts. See for instance Burawoy (1998), Reed (2010), and Goldthorpe (2000).

nonrandom ways, the selection of the specific units to observe in the sample is consciously done in a way to represent the larger universe of such units (e.g., poverty neighborhoods, gangs, terminal cancer patients). What constitutes the sample is a function of the question being asked and the central unit of analysis for the study. For instance, a study of organizations would involve the construction of a sample of organizations, a study of communities would construct a sample of communities, and a study of individuals would involve the selection of individuals.

Behavioralists acknowledge the irreducible duality between individuals and groups (Breiger 1974; Giddens 1984; Marx 1852) and account for this in their research design. Since larger social groupings like communities and organizations include, shape and are constituted by the actions of individuals and smaller social groupings, the researcher needs to develop a strategy for sampling the various actors nested within larger social units. These subsamples are constructed to maximize variance in the observation of factors that are likely to influence outcomes. For instance, a study of communities could include key community organizations identified in previous literature, or a diverse array of individuals within each of those organizations or communities. Likewise, a sample of individuals must account for the fact that people are part of larger order groupings such as neighborhoods, churches, cliques, and so on, and build that variation into the sample (e.g., Abramson 2015). The sample may also expand beyond the initially selected groups to include other organizations not identified a priori when this is necessary to answer the question. For instance, in his examination of how older adults navigate American inequality, Abramson (2015) did not initially plan to spend time in bars. As local bars emerged as a major locus of sociability in his observations of and conversations with seniors, he identified bars to observe and integrated them into his sample of public spaces in which seniors congregate. Yet, the goal of the study did not change. In his study of gangs, when specific gangs Sánchez-Jankowski (1991) was observing ceased to exist as groupings (i.e., the organizations died), he randomly selected new gangs from a pre-established list to be added into his sampling pool.

While acknowledging the connection between individuals, groups, and levels of social reality more broadly (Cicourel, this volume), identifying a primary unit to design a sample that best lines up with the questions and eventual answers proposed by the researcher is a methodological necessity. More specifically there must be congruence between the sample and eventual analytical claims involving 1) *comparison*, 2) *levels of analysis*, and 3) *representation*.

The first point about congruence in comparison seems simple but is often neglected in participant-observation research. Making a methodologically reasonable comparative claim requires comparative observation across multiple sites or cases. For instance, comparing the poor to the middle class without observing the middle-classes (Duneier 1999) produces comparisons that are loose, speculative, and often driven by political or theoretical commitments rather than data. Comparative claims that go beyond a case should not be made on the basis of a single case. Thus, the behavioralist approach is not about the in-depth study of a case, but rather the creation of a comparative multilevel sample that includes variation on the parameter being compared (e.g., socioeconomic background, geographic location, organizational type) in order to draw broader generalizations. In this regard, the comparative behavioralist approach differs from the single case-based approaches found in both historical methods and other ethnographic traditions.[5] Even multi-case approaches to ethnography typically differ in their logic and execution from the approaches and model of generalization in the conventional scientific tradition (CST).

The behavioralist approach to participant observation follows CST principles of sampling on subjects or conditions that represent larger populations of individuals and socioeconomic, political, and geographic conditions. Generalizations are drawn in a probabilistic way rather than using a formal logic of similarity and difference. Here the concern for participant observers is the same as for other methods, minimizing error and addressing the unavoidable specters of reliability and validity (internal, external, and ecological). From the behavioralist approach, the case study method is seen as introducing vulnerabilities that are discordant with its underlying variable based-framework. In particular, it risks oversampling on the dependent variable, introduces the seduction of selecting a case with ideal conditions that creates problems of generalizations outside of that particular case, and often relies on a modes of drawing larger conclusions via formal comparisons of similarity and difference (e.g., analytic induction) that understate the

[5] There is some parallel concern with congruent comparison in traditions using case-logics. This is because a focus on cases as real phenomena necessitates the selection of a research site that represents the subjects and conditions that are of empirical and theoretical interest, even if the efforts to generalize are using a form of analytic induction based in logical similarity and difference rather than the probabilistic style of generalization found in variable-based social science (Ragin 2004; Ragin and Becker 1992).

probability of error.[6] Purposefully selecting cases that are conservative or representative, and employing hybrid analytical techniques like qualitative comparative analysis (QCA), might help mitigate these risks if adopted by participant observers. Still, the risks and fundamental incompatibility of case studies with the variable-centered logic of a CST approaches makes case-studies suboptimal for participant observation conducted in the behavioralist tradition.[7]

Second, concerning levels of analysis, there needs to be congruence between the object of study and the level of analysis indicated in the question (Cicourel 2011). Macro-historical questions, such as what constitutes the nature of capitalism (Marx 1867), cannot be answered by observing micro-interactions in any one element of the capitalist system (e.g., a particular market, firm, factory). Nonetheless, specifics aspects of this question could be addressed, for instance: How do various aspects of this system work out in everyday life within different elements (i.e., market, firm, factory), and why? The answer to this question advances the larger question of charting capitalism's character. However, and importantly, in the behavioralist tradition the eventual truth claim must be moderated so it relates back, and corresponds, to the data. The extent to which data are extended to macro-theoretical phenomena is much more constricted than in approaches such as the extended case method.

Finally, on issues of representation, claims should be based on samples that represent the object in question in the ways specified here. For instance, claims about the social organization of poor communities in urban society should be based on a sample of poor communities, or a comparative study of poor and nonpoor communities, rather than poor people in a single middle-class community (e.g., Duneier 1999). That is to say, the object of study must be *represented* in the pool of observed interactions as directly as possible. Further, samples should be representative of the group

[6] For a classic parallel of this argument with respect to historical research, see Lieberson (1991).

[7] See Ragin (2004), who attempts to show that case studies can overcome the apparent problem identified by Freedman (2010a), but in our judgment, he is not able to move beyond the statement that a case study may find causal associations because generalizing outside the case remains extremely problematic without an adequate number of cases that do not exhibit the same properties or results. Participant observation in the behavioralist tradition does, however, share the concern with the plausibility of explanation, causal heterogeneity, iterative acquisition of data in constructing a social object, and accounting for, rather than discarding, "causal specks" or outliers (Ragin 2004; Small 2009). Further, advances in methodologies using case-logics may lead to new hybrid approaches like QCA that help address some of these issues (Thiem and Baumgartner 2016). Still, these approaches are rarely employed by ethnographers using case-based approaches, although that may change in the near future.

or phenomenon being studied in so far as this is possible (e.g., Sánchez-Jankowski 2002) rather than reflecting convenience or a personal connection to a site (e.g., Contreras 2013; Moon 2004; Kahn 2012), even if that site is related to important questions.

The notion of representativeness raises an important question addressed by Small (2009) regarding the demands of answering the quantitative query of how many cases are necessary to make larger claims in participant-observation research. As elaborated here, participant observation using behavioralist techniques is based on a variable based logic rather than case logic, and always involves comparative samples. Unlike the response of Small and others who argue for ethnographers to use an alternative logic drawing on case-centered approaches, we have previously argued that participant observation is both compatible with, and necessary for, CST variable-based approaches (Sánchez-Jankowski and Abramson, this volume). Consequently, the question for researchers in the behavioralist tradition is not just how many cases to include but how many observations, in which settings, are sufficient to make generalizations with confidence. In some projects, this will simply be the raw number of times the researcher has observed a particular physical or verbal behavior, while at others it will be the number of times that a particular physical or verbal behavior has occurred under the same conditions. Therefore, while the question of how many cases parallels behavioralist concerns with issues of comparison, sampling breadth, levels of analysis, and representativeness, the language, execution, and underlying rationale governing generalizability differ.

Participant observation in the behavioralist tradition requires two categories from which samples of individuals, organizations, communities, or other units of analysis are drawn to address representativeness: one category where specific characteristics are expected to be exhibited, and a second where they are not. For instance, a study of how poverty neighborhoods function needs to include a control category of nonpoverty neighborhoods or a neighborhood where all the characteristics seen in the poverty neighborhoods chosen do not exist fully in the one to be used as quasi-control (Sánchez-Jankowski 2016, 2008).[8] Ideally, studies should include other categories that provide variation in potential explanatory factors. For instance, Abramson selected urban neighborhoods that vary with respect to socioeconomic status and

[8] Jack Katz, in his review of the book *Cracks in the Pavement* for the *American Journal of Sociology*, argues that "He [the author] does not grasp that the uncontrolled acquisition of field data in five sites vitiates the creative sampling and experimental logics he has involved." This statement misinforms

levels of racial segregation to help in understanding how variation both within and across social contexts shaped the lives of seniors from different backgrounds.[9] Dohan and team sampled a diverse group of stage IV cancer patients in two states to see why some individuals entered into early-phase clinical trials while others did not (Abramson and Dohan 2015; Dohan et al. 2016; Garrett et al. 2017). Broader topics, such as understanding the social organization of poverty (e.g., Sánchez-Jankowski 2002), require both more variation in a sample and more time in a field than narrower topics such as how group violence unfolds in high-schools (Sánchez-Jankowski 2016).

This touches on an important and frequently misunderstood point about how controls function for sample selection in qualitative research. If one is to use statistical theory to generalize from nonexperimental data, it is also necessary to have sampling categories where an outcome can be, but is not expected to be, exhibited (Freedman 2010a). This avoids sampling on the dependent variable, that is to say picking sites, people, organizations, and so on, that are more likely to produce a particular outcome that is more in line with what the researcher hoped or wanted to observe. For instance, a study of school violence should not include only high-violence schools, but should also include schools where there has been no history of observed violence.

the reader by introducing two faulty propositions: 1) that in designing a sample in which one of the investigative elements (in this case neighborhoods) has some of the attributes of the others (i.e., sites in this case) but not all of them is meaningless because field studies involving the everyday world lack the ability to control all the behaviors of the subjects they are studying in a manner commensurate with those studies utilizing a classic experimental design, where it is possible to intervene and manipulate the independent variables to determine and measure the importance of each; and 2) that observations within everyday life are too varied and thus what is recorded is predicated on the prejudgment of the research which lacks the observational precision that is part of an experimental design.

As to the first point, Professor Katz was either ill-informed, or in an effort to maintain a negative review of the book, chose to ignore that there are at least two ways in which the use of a control group sampling strategy can, and is, used effectively. One is used by researchers operating within an experimental design where manipulation of the independent variables can be invoked at any time, and the other is used by researchers in nonexperimental "observational" designs, usually those involving aggregate data, in which units—people, neighborhoods, organizations, firms, etc.—have some of the characteristic elements of the primary sample but not all of them. Here a "quasi control" is used in an effort to determine which factors are important in creating observed deviations in behavior between groups and which ones do not. Such a sampling frame and analytical approach is consistent with the "Stratified Sampling Technique," (Sudman 1976) and widely used in various quantitative analyses.

In regards to Katz's second point, it is true that there is a great deal of variation in behaviors observed in the everyday lives of individuals, and as a result exact precision in recording every behavior is incomplete. This is something to which most every ethnographic tradition has a response (Abramson and Gong, this volume). For the behavioralist approach, observations of meaningful deviations between the sites are not only possible to observe, but central to understanding (1) which factors were involved in creating patterns and deviations, (2) how these factors shaped behavior, and (3) which factors were invariant in the subsamples (i.e. did not explain variation), and (4) why this was the case.

[9] See Smith (2012) for an example using a counterfactual framework.

Even though it is statistically less likely that these schools will provide observations of violence, if they do, this observation can provide powerful data about how and why violence functions in a larger population of schools (Freedman 2010a, 2010b; Taleb 2007).[10]

In participant observation, the goal of including a control case is to allow comparisons between observations and to allow for the possibility that unexpected or rare alternatives to exhibit themselves in ways that do not map onto the researcher's prior theories or expectations. This is very different from the tactic of removing variation to isolate causality in a controlled laboratory setting.[11] Deploying the experimental model of sequentially introducing treatments does not adequately allow for important observations of on-the-ground variation in behavior, causal heterogeneity, and the rare but potentially crucial events that occur in real life (Cicourel 1982; Freedman 2010a; Taleb 2007). Further, as both Small (2002, 2009) and Burawoy (1998) note, it is essential that participant observation includes a temporal component and accounts for the possibility of change over time rather than accepting observations (in the lab or in the field) to reveal time invariant laws. *However, the possibility of change over time does not imply that change in the phenomena of interest is inevitable.* Whether and to what extent social formations transform over the period of research is an empirical question, but the likelihood of historical change requires that it be considered in research design. While the ability to create an ideal sample is constrained by social circumstance (e.g. time, money, access), researchers operating within the behavioralist framework, and who commit to their study over a significant period of time, aim to leverage temporal and substantive variation in order to determine causal mechanisms among a sample that represents the population being studied.

A related question is often asked of those who employ this form of participant observation: What happens when a research site that initially seems suitable on paper does not allow the observation of necessary phenomena or function as a meaningful control? The answer is straightforward: if the research site is not able to help answer the research question, then another site must be drawn from the larger number of sampling sites that have been

[10] This also allows for the potential observation of what statisticians refer to as "black swans" and "white ravens"; that is, low-likelihood but high-impact observations (i.e., meaningful outliers) that can powerfully contribute to an explanation of some social phenomena (Taleb 2007).

[11] A long-standing critique, often leveraged by ethnographers, is that the use of the experimental designs produces artificial results that compromise not only external validity but the ecological validity (provided by observing humans in their real-world settings) that is a central strength of the method (Cicourel 1982).

accumulated for that purpose, or if there is a problem with a number of sites in the accumulated pool, then more research on potential sites for the sampling pool that meet the criteria necessary for the study is required. What the behavioralist method avoids is having the researcher simply go to a site that seemed capable to them for addressing the research question and sticking to that site out of a misplaced commitment to it, or alternatively that the researcher simply found interesting. Preliminary investigation of sites to determine whether they embody the criteria to answer the question is necessary, but the researcher must be open to going back to the pool they systematically created if a site does not meet the criteria of the sample. What absolutely needs to be avoided is going to a convenient or seemingly "exotic" field site as if one were on a fishing expedition, hoping to catch an interesting question. This strategy, often associated with classical grounded theory and still practiced, is incompatible with the purposeful preselection of a meaningful social scientific question that can be answered using comparative participant observation.

Data Collection

Participant observation presents concrete dilemmas to which researchers operating within each of the major philosophical traditions must provide a response (Abramson and Dohan 2015). The two most fundamental for the behavioralist approach involve 1) the impact of the researcher's intrusion into the everyday routines of the people being studied; and 2) the manner in which a human researcher, studying other human beings, is able to collect and process the overwhelming pool of potential data in the field.[12]

The Effect of Observation on Behavior

Whenever a new person enters an existing environment, something has changed socially. This effect is often amplified in participant observation,

[12] The term "potential data" is used to highlight that the natural social world is filled with innumerable elements that could be data for a specific research topic or data for some subsequent or alternative research project. The issue for researchers when they are in the field is determining what will be considered relevant data for the current project, what might be relevant data for some subsequent project, and what is interesting but not related to the current project.

as the researcher (typically an outsider) necessarily becomes an actor in the settings being studied. Each major tradition of participant observation provides a response to this problem. Symbolic interactionism deals with the issue by making the social construction of meaning in interaction, including that between the researcher and subjects, the focus of inquiry (Blumer 1969; Goffman 1959). In a similar vein, those employing the extended case method focus on "context effects," interactions and power dynamics between the researcher and subjects, as a way to generate data and extend theory (Burawoy 1998). Interpretivists like Geertz (2000 [1973]) are apt to consider researcher presence as necessary for facilitating cultural immersion that allows access to a deeper web of meanings, which the researcher makes comprehensible. Researchers in the behavioralist tradition go a step further, and seek to minimize and manage the biases introduced by the presence of the participant observer. They do so in part by spending a tremendous amount of time among the subjects of their study so as to both understand the context and get observations farther removed from the disruption that their initial presence may have initiated. Time allows them opportunities to observe and determine relevant behaviors that characterize their research settings, and to make claims about patterns with greater confidence (Becker 1958; Gans 1999; Sánchez-Jankowski 2002).

Like other approaches to field work, the behavioralist tradition recognizes that the participant observer can never simply be a fly on the wall. The same is true of all science—observation introduces the possibility of changing that which is observed. *However, the fact that the researcher has a potential influence on the field of her or his study does not logically, or practically, imply that their presence need be a (or the) central object of inquiry* (an existing premise of the extended case method and symbolic interactionist approaches), nor, as the postmodern anthropological approach suggests, force her or him to abandon science for humanistic critique. The overriding argument is that given enough time and strategic field placement, it is unlikely the subjects will continue to adopt patterns of daily life that fundamentally differ from those normally employed in that setting because the cost and effort is too great to make altering entire patterns of life over years a sustainable practice for the research subjects. (Becker 1958; Sánchez-Jankowski 2002). Thus, any potential error being introduced by the researcher's presence diminishes over time as they become a fixture at field sites. The extent to which this involves participation, role assumption, or distancing varies between cases as well as characteristics of the observer (which may affect the reaction of other actors). Finding a role which allows minimum disruption given the observer's demographics, such as working as a janitor in a school (Sánchez-Jankowski 2008) or a volunteer in a senior center (Abramson 2015), often helps.[13] This is further facilitated by the fact that time in the field allows the observer to gain the trust of the subjects being studied, making subjects less likely to hide activities that are illegal or stigmatized (which some do in the early months of field work). Researchers are morally obligated to honor this trust by protecting them from potential legal, financial, and social harm even if it comes at the cost of the researcher's personal well-being.[14]

The Observer as Research Instrument

Data collection is complicated by the fact that the participant observer is the primary instrument of data collection. As in all research, the data collected is influenced by analytical priors as well as corporeal-cognitive processes that affect how humans experience and make sense of the world (Bourdieu 1990; Wacquant 2009; Wacquant 2004). The behavioralist methodological response again attempts to deal with this issue through techniques designed to minimize researcher bias. Theorists recognize that what can be observed during fieldwork is based on the individual researcher's filtering system, which contains a library of social cues, prior theories, and cognitive intuitive resources (Sánchez-Jankowski 2002; Wacquant 2009).[15] This filtering system necessarily has an impact on what is seen and considered data for the current research project. Having too thick a filtering system in the way of an overcommitment by researchers to a particular theory can lead to the misinterpretation of behavior, and as a result fail to observe or misclassify behaviors that are relevant data in addressing the current research question. Having too thin a filtering system, as in the classical grounded theory approach of letting findings simply emerge, can also lead to misinterpretation because the researcher is not able to discern what is relevant to the question at hand and falls back on, and thus reproduces, her or his own latent commonsense theories. The behavioralist researcher maintains an awareness of

[13] A complete discussion of how researchers might endeavor to minimize bias by adopting various field postures is beyond the scope of this article.

[14] Further, protecting research subjects is essential to ensuring access for future researchers as well as protecting the reputation of both their discipline and social science more broadly.

[15] How those participant observers in the behavioralist tradition deal with this epistemic issue has more in common with the practices of phenomenological and cognitive sociology (Bourdieu 1990; Cicourel 2006) than with those of postmodern deconstructionism and strong relativism found in Clifford (1988) or Ellis (2004).

this issue and remains vigilant to record observations that reflect potential answers to when, where, and how things are working in the everyday world that relates to their primary research question. In this regard, as time in the field expands, so too does the participant observer's library of meaningful cues as they relate to the thoughts and behaviors of their subjects. This helps the researcher produce work that speaks to the plausibility of new and existing explanations for the question being researched.

These data collection issues reinforce the imperative to spend substantial time in the field in order to expand beyond both a narrow focus on prior theory and an overemphasis on the folk understandings of the researcher or their subjects (Sánchez-Jankowski 2002). Although increased field time does not remove all the problems associated with cultural bias and variation in intuition, it does furnish the opportunity to observe interactions that can be seen by future researchers as well as provide a data resource that other researchers can use in their attempts to understand the meanings attached to the social interactions of like agents. This allows readers and future researchers some ability to evaluate the adequacy of the current researcher's filtering system and if interested, replicate the observations on which general propositions are made. Obviously, this is a key element of the transparency issue discussed here and to which we return later in this chapter.

Data Analysis

The purpose of research in the behavioralist tradition is to evaluate and improve social scientific explanations. Under this perspective, participant observation is not simply a theory-building or theory-extending method that complements theory-testing quantitative methods, as others have suggested (cf. Burawoy 2007; Small 2009). Likewise, although all methods vary in the relative extent to which they use emergent analysis and deduction to arrive at empirical statements, in practice, most involve both deductive and inductive moments (e.g., researchers use new and existing information to both build new explanations and rule out or modify existing ones). Consequently, participant observation is best understood as a specific technique that has inferential advantages and disadvantages in examining aspects of the social world and speaking to the plausibility of competing explanations for observed patterns. As discussed in the previous chapter, it is useful for understanding the micro-dynamics (in situ interactions) and mechanisms other methods have difficulty uncovering and measuring. It contributes to answering questions that require the observation of behaviors in real-world settings in ways other methods cannot (e.g., is crime higher in poor areas because they are disorganized or because rational actors pursue the limited range of lucrative activities in their neighborhoods even if they are considered illicit by the state?). As described in the previous chapter, the advantages of participant observation make it well-suited to charting the operation of causal mechanisms within and across social contexts even though constraints on sampling may limit generalizations.

At the most basic level, the analysis of participant observation data involves identifying patterns of behaviors (both physical and verbal), categorizing them, and situating them according to when and how they produce particular social outcomes. Thus, the first step is to identify patterns of behavior. We have discussed what constitutes a pattern in the previous chapter. At the most basic level, behavioralist researchers may refer to the raw number of times one observes a behavior in a particular context, under certain conditions. Although the numbers may vary for different behaviors, contexts, and conditions, the researcher's analysis is dependent on accessing whether the number of recorded behaviors is sufficient for them to be confident that a pattern exists and whether another researcher would be able to observe this same pattern in similar contexts and conditions at another time—that is, whether they are confident in the reliability of their observed pattern. Further, it is important that researchers within the behavioralist tradition report idiosyncratic behaviors that deviate from the pattern and explain why these occurred. This provides other researchers with additional information and strengthens claims about the validity and limits of patterns.

Data analysis involves both deductive and inductive components, which are deployed iteratively and in dialog with one another over the course of a project.[16] On the deductive side, researchers use new data to evaluate, modify, or rule out existing models. Prior to entering the field, participant observers in the behavioralist tradition generate questions based on problems in new or existing fields, generate hypotheses and counterfactual explanations that are often, but not always, based in existing scholarship, and design a sampling scheme that allows them to transform observable social

[16] Seizing upon a renewed interest in pragmatism, recent methodological pieces have labeled this combination as "abduction" (Tavory and Timmermans 2014). While many of the practices are similar (e.g. iteratively dealing with both prior writings and emerging findings), such approaches add in various political and ontological premises that are incompatible with CST approaches.

phenomena into data capable of speaking to the plausibility of hypotheses about when, why, and under what conditions outcomes of interest occur. In the analysis phase, data is categorized or referenced according to existing theoretical and practical categories, and the way in which these categories map onto or fit the new data is assessed. This is neither mechanical nor especially quantitative, particularly as the technologies for doing sensitive quantitative analysis of this sort are at present underdeveloped for field data (Abramson et al. 2018). However, the idea of speaking to the relative plausibility of a model is conceptually the same as what one finds in quantitative methods. If a hypothesis posits that under circumstances X, Y occurs for Z interactive reasons, and this is not substantiated in patterned observations that meet the conditions for that proposition to be realized, the relative plausibility of that hypothesis declines.[17]

On the inductive side, comparative participant observation, like other methods classified as "qualitative," necessarily includes strategies for analyzing emergent patterns and concepts as well. As mentioned earlier, researchers conducting participant observation in the behavioralist tradition differ from grounded theorists in their treatment of deductive propositions and theoretical priors. Nonetheless, the notion in grounded theory of systematically clustering data and building models based on potentially surprising observations (e.g., Glaser and Strauss 1967) has much in common with participant observation in the behavioralist tradition. Unlike a survey where the range of responses to a verbal prompt is preset, participant observation allows the possibility of seeing variation in speech and behavior that was not recorded in prior inquiries (Cicourel 1964). Consequently, this sort of research must involve techniques for dealing with emergent patterns that may lead to new explanations. These emergent patterns within the behavioralist branch of participant observation are used to create new hypotheses and models for answering the research questions that guide the project. These are then compared to existing and subsequent data for fit, as just described. In this sense, as with grounded theory and the extended case method, analysis of observational data within the behavioralist tradition is always iterative and mutually self-informing.

[17] For a review of how this plays out with Bayesian logic and subjective probability, as well as criticisms of this approach, see our chapter "Foundations of the Behavioralist Approach to Comparative Participant Observation" in this volume.

Although cohesion and parsimony may be culturally desirable in models of human action, the overarching concern in the analysis of data for behavioralists more generally, is minimizing errors of association and correspondence (King, Keohane, and Verba 1994). Ultimately, models are assessed by how well they correspond to the social world. Choosing the correct method for a particular question helps to minimize errors in the correspondence between phenomena and their recording by decreasing the inferential leaps required to support a proposition. In the data analysis stage, the issue shifts to examining and developing understanding of the associations between factors while working toward explaining sequential relationships. This happens first with the internal workings of these factors that clarify when (i.e., the sequential relationship) and how they work to produce a particular outcome in like conditions—the behavioralist participant observer's primary form of a causal model (Sánchez-Jankowski and Abramson, this volume). Of course, it is here that the chance of a type 1 (false positive) or type 2 (false negative) error in correspondence between factors emerges as an overriding issue for the behavioralist researcher. Computer assisted qualitative data analysis software (CAQDAS) is often used to help see what patterns exist and whether they fit existing models. This can minimize the impact of human memory (limitations that challenge any participant observation researcher), reduce the corresponding tendency to skew analysis towards recent or disturbing events, and indicate how data clusters around like properties in ways that reveal new patterns that may have escaped notice (Abramson et al. 2018; Dohan and Sánchez-Jankowski 1998). However, the use of software is merely a tool and cannot substitute for rigorous analysis that aims to minimize error.

Explanation and Understanding

Generating explanations for the participant observer operating in the behavioralist tradition involves bringing rigorous data collection and analysis procedures to bear on developing understandings concerning *when, how*, and *why* factors in everyday life work to produce outcomes of interest. This work can help produce new models concerning which factors are involved and the manner in which they work to produce social outcomes under specified conditions. Through this exercise, it contributes to existing theoretical evaluation, extension, and construction, and in the process diverges from other participant observation traditions such as some forms of phenomenology or postmodernism, where behaviors are often considered nonreplicable by default; the extended case method, where the goal is to modify rather than speak to the plausibility of theory; and forms of hermeneutic interpretivism that privilege coherence over correspondence.[18]

From these characteristics, and our prior discussions of statistical induction and generalization, we can derive a few general principles for expanding models beyond the sample in question. These principles correspond to those currently practiced by researchers using other methods within the CST approach.

> First, procedures and analysis should be public and transparent. In that regard, the methods of observation, the logic of site selection, and the modes of analysis have to be explicit and cannot simply be subsumed into a narrative (King, Keohane, and Verba 1994).
>
> Second, while explanations and conclusions are always uncertain, they should be internally consistent and engage with prior knowledge to the extent possible (King, Keohane, and Verba 1994).
>
> Third, explanations should have visible implications and be subject to subsequent evaluation and replication insofar as this is possible (Abramson et al. 2018; King, Keohane, and Verba 1994; Sánchez-Jankowski 2002). Therefore, researchers must expect to answer counterfactual questions such as "What would this look like if you were wrong?" (Duneier 2011; Lamont and White 2008).
>
> Fourth, the scientific value of a work depends in part on the methods employed (King, Keohane, and Verba 1994). For example, novels, poetry, and art can provide insights to the human condition, but they are not science because a scientific approach requires systematically using all of the

[18] When the behavioralist strategy of participant observation is utilized in evaluating and extending existing theories it shares much with grounded theory and analytic ethnography, although the role of theoretical priors as well as the strategies of data collection vary. As discussed in the previous chapter, and in the first section in this one, participant observation in the behavioralist tradition provides a useful tool for charting how antecedent factors link to observable outcomes in and across social contexts in existing causal models. The goal is to aid in the evaluation and production of models of social behavior that can explain larger social phenomena and processes beyond the sample the researcher employs. When existing theories fit, we use them. When they require modifications, we modify them. When they require abandonment because they are at odds with the data, we identify this mismatch. In this sense, explanation is pragmatic and question centered.

available evidence and taking the issues of site selection, bias, and sampling seriously.

It is necessary to remind the reader of a few key divergences from the mode of participant observation in the behavioralist model that we advance here and the stronger claims of classical positivist epistemology. First, contemporary research in this tradition is concerned with producing more generalizable assertions about mechanisms, but there is no assumption that this will lead to the discovery of covering laws or even law like properties. Second, research in this tradition acknowledges, as well as attempts to deal with, the theory-infused nature of observation and the role of researcher presence. Finally, research in this tradition recognizes the fallibility of the research enterprise: the potential to get it wrong, despite all attempts to get it right. No data about human behavior collected by epistemically limited humans (Goldman 1988) is strong enough to unequivocally confirm or falsify a model. However, data that is collected in a systematic way speaks to the relative plausibility of a model or explanation and should not be ignored for reasons of inconvenience or politics (professional or otherwise).

Reliability and Replication

Few arenas of sociological research feature the level of vitriol found in the discussions around urban ethnography, where accusations of lies and misrepresentation abound (Lubet 2017; Duneier 2011; Katz 2010; Wacquant 2002). This points to a fundamental methodological problem: there are divergent and competing standards for producing, evaluating, and representing models of the social world in the social sciences.[19] Even within sociology, different epistemic and methodological traditions of sociology disagree about what constitutes evidence and how research should be judged (Abramson and Gong, this volume; Goertz and Mahoney 2012). From the behavioralist perspective espoused in both the previous and present chapter, the issue is that even within the CST research (i.e., an approach concerned with producing valid, reliable, and replicable data) there are contested standards

[19] How to understand this is an empirical question. Sociological explanations for the peculiar professional practices of ethnographic critique might focus on the often-political nature of the subject matter, the small, insular, and competitive culture of the field, or the dispositions, traits, and organizational commitments of the researchers who select into this arena. The point here is simply that regardless of which factors drive this process, there is still an underlying methodological issue to be addressed.

and safeguards to check the validity and reliability of qualitative research findings. For those employing behavioralist principles, the established standard of replicable procedures that reliably produce a match between data and explanation apply to comparative participant observation. Replication of analytical procedures should produce the same results. Collecting new observations under similar circumstances should reveal similar patterns or explainable deviations.

As this volume demonstrates, however, these are not standards agreed to by all ethnographers. Even within sociology, ethnographers vehemently disagree about 1) whether social science is possible; 2) whether reliability and validity are meaningful standards for ethnography; 3) how to evaluate ethnographic work; 4) how to approach representation; and 5) how this relates to political commitments (Abramson and Gong, this volume; Duneier 2011; Katz 2004; Sánchez-Jankowski 2002; Small 2009). Many ethnographic traditions explicitly reject the notion of replication as an imposition of naïve positivist assumptions, and even those who use this terminology use it in an inconsistent way that frequently conflates ex-post facto interviews of prior subjects with re-observing in situ behavior. The fact that it is important methodologically to discuss "how not to lie" epitomizes the current state of affairs (Duneier 2011; Lubet 2017). In practice, it is not uncommon for ethnographers and critics to suggest (typically without providing any substantial evidence) that the data produced by a scholar with whom they disagree are not real (cf. Duneier 2006; Katz 2010; Sullivan 1994). The importance of recognizing inconvenient phenomena, including those that are inconvenient politically to specific researchers (Wacquant 2002; Duneier 2011), is an essential starting point. So too is incentivizing academics to act as honest brokers by not taking legitimate points of disagreement and sensationalizing them for professional visibility. However, there are real issues related to ethnography's lack of transparency (Abramson et al. 2018). While solving these issues is beyond the scope of this chapter, we briefly turn to accusations of lying and how those concerned with deploying participant observation within the pantheon of CST approach these issues.

The term "lying" is a rhetorical rather than scientific term. It has a deeply moral connotation that personalizes attacks while simultaneously conflating various distinct errors that produce false claims—for example, fabrication or censorship of findings. A more technical term in the CST framework is *representational error*. Here, representations do not adequately correspond to the population being studied for *any* reason. There are two common categories of representational error that can occur in participant observational research: 1) those based in fabrication, such as having not been in the field or observed what was reported; and 2) those based in a partial or complete *misrepresentation* of what was observed.

Representational errors resulting from fabrication involve producing fictions about the world, then representing them as fact. Historically, scientific hoaxes and fraudulent data have been an issue particularly in the medical, physical, and biological sciences, where tremendous resources are involved and funders demand tangible "deliverables."[20] Although it may take time, these fabrications are eventually exposed when subsequent researchers are unable to replicate the results and show the data to be in error. The problem in the physical sciences is the immense startup cost that is necessary to replicate research. In participant observation, on the other hand, replication requires comparatively little overhead. Any research that relies on outright fabrication should be shown false or questionable in future inquiries, and research based in genuine observation should subsequently be supported by corroborating evidence.

A case in point involves the debate around the research findings reported by Sánchez-Jankowski in his book *Islands in the Street* (1991), a comparative participant-observation study of gangs. The notion that gangs act as organizations in a coordinated manner to rationally pursue goals in the communities in which they are situated was at odds with the criminological orthodoxy of the time. One author (Sullivan 1994) suggested that the evidence presented was "too good" to be true, accusing Sánchez-Jankowski of fabrication. While such assaults on a researcher's character can be damaging professionally and personally, the broader issue is one of producing scientific explanations. No study is an actual island, and explanations need to be verified, disproven, or modified in light of new data. For those in the behavioralist tradition, the only way for claims of lying or representational error to be resolved is through the replication of the findings. In this case, such replications have been conducted using both participant observation and survey methodology. They provide supporting evidence on most of the highly contested findings reported by Sánchez-Jankowski—on the concept of "defiant individualism" (Jensen 1996; Vigil 1988); that members rationally enter a gang to get material benefits (Padilla 1992; Venkatesh 2000b); on

[20] Well-known recent examples include the Lancet article linking vaccines and autism (Rao and Andrade 2011), the Heart Stem-Cell studies associated with Harvard Medical School (Johnson 2018), and Anil Potti's cancer research at Duke (office of research integrity 2018).

organizational traits (Venkatesh 1997); and on the nature of the gangs' community relations (Brotherton 2007; Padilla 1992; Venkatesh 2000a). Such replications create confidence in earlier findings and build cumulative knowledge, in this instance regarding aspects of Sánchez-Jankowski's 1991 study.[21] Where there is an absence of corroboration, it is incumbent on the part of the authors of the new study to offer why there is a difference in findings. For without this it is impossible for subsequent research to adjudicate between different findings and offer additional explanations.

The possibility of fabrication is troublesome, but outright fabrications can and will be subsequently overturned by future research. Partial representations or misrepresentations, which involve the researcher observing certain outcomes and then reporting them in a way that has some elements of truth but neutralizes statements that are seen as politically undesirable, or potentially so, are harder to account for. This can happen when the researcher did not want to observe particular behaviors or outcomes, because they wanted to help the people they were studying, feared that a larger constituency would disapprove of them reporting findings that would add to existing patterns of marginalization or were afraid of the results being misappropriated or used by those with different political leanings (e.g. as in the case of "The Culture of Poverty"). Researchers employing this category of misrepresentation choose to either not report all relevant findings or to report only a few, leaving the most damaging out, or at minimum try to counterbalance the negatives with justifications for the negatives or even with positives.[22] From the behavioralist perspective, partial representations are more insidious than total fabrications because they contain grains of truth and therefore have some face validity. What is more, elements can show up in replications since the data were censored, but not fabricated. These sorts of misrepresentations are further complicated by the fact that they are often related to goals sociologists may be amenable to—such as to avoid producing models that place additional stigma on the downtrodden. Reviewers and publics are often less suspicious of misrepresentations, usually because they

[21] Although scholarly review and replication involve social actors and are subject to error, the point is that the system should be adequately robust to produce data that can overturn outright fabrications.

[22] An illustrative example is found in the Lareau's (2011) preface description of her interactions with a colleague in anthropology who suggested that she should censor findings that could potentially be politically appropriated and used against the poor families she included in her study. Lareau reports that she did not censor her data, but did make an effort to highlight the potential upsides of lower-class parenting styles.

tell a story that holds cache within a community. Still, partial representations contribute to producing inaccurate models of the world, undermine the legitimacy of social science disciplines and can unintentionally thwart potential interventions (through policy, activism, etc.) by pushing interventions away from the best available evidence. Although these sorts of misrepresentations are likely to be both more common and more difficult to eradicate, the solution offered by the behavioralist tradition once again lies in replication, review, and the development of new tools for sharing behavioral data among researchers, such as producing de-identified data repositories that allow analyses of the claims made by participant observers (Abramson et al. 2018).

Without access to the experiences of the participant observer, misrepresentations are also harder to pick up. It has been argued that including lengthy quotes that allow telling alternative stories about data provides an option to reduce misrepresentation (Katz 2004). Yet, field notes are not unmediated observations but a selective representation of experiences and observations, albeit optimally those of a systematic variety, collected by a researcher (Cicourel 2006). Including a "thick" five-page description of an observation, carefully selected from thousands of pages of possible notes to make a point, does little to address the problem. Similarly, novelists can produce lengthy and convincing accounts of social life without systematic observations as well. Consequently, there is often the temptation on the part of ethnographers to follow suit by giving additional details the author feels will enhance narrative scope. Often these circumstances degenerate into ethnography being evaluated on its literary rather than scientific merits, with evocative writing substituting for analytical rigor and claims grounded in the longitudinal observation of robust patterns. This risks not only encouraging error through unnecessary embellishment, but also potential harm to the scientific status of observational approaches.

It is also periodically argued that sharing the names of respondents and neighborhoods within a particular study allows an important scientific safeguard by allowing the interview of past subjects (cf. Jerolmack and Murphy 2015; Lubet 2017; Katz 2010).[23] Such approaches are neither an adequate safeguard for science nor an ethical approach to human-subjects research. Compromising the confidentiality of subjects and their communities carries with it the placing of research subjects at risk of direct or indirect consequences even if the ethnographer is trying to represent them favorably (e.g., Duneier

[23] see also Reyes (2018) on naming and transparency.

1999), which is itself a problem of representation from the CST perspective. Further, presenting names, neighborhoods, and notes of behaviors, situations, and conditions does not capture all the elements that the researcher used to make sense of the situations she or he analyzed, nor does this provide access to the pool of observed behaviors on which broader claims are made. Further, the site in question may have changed substantially in the time elapsed.[24]

It has been argued that shared and transparent data sets in repositories that contain both quantitative summaries and linked de-identified interactional data would seem to be the ideal for participant observers in the behavioralist tradition (Abramson and Dohan 2015; Abramson et al. 2018). However, this is not a panacea. In the future, these data sets could enable reanalysis of participant observation data without identifying subjects, as well as limited, though not total, replication of behavioral patterns while protecting confidentiality of the people being studied (Abramson and Dohan 2015; Abramson et al. 2018). Yet even if this removes some of the problems with outing research subjects (the problem with naming names) and allows the sharing and visualization of a broader set of data points, the idea of shared ethnographic data sets has substantial limitations for behavioralists. Behavioralists recognize that results emanating from participant observation are the result of observing and recording behavior in real world settings. This is why the data from participant-observation research is different from that gathered using a survey where repositories are most common.

Thus, making de-identified or quantified field observations available to the public may allow *partial replication* of analytical claims (e.g., testing whether claimed patterns in the data are indeed patterns in the data as can be done with surveys), but can also introduce errors in the misinterpretation of data. While this is an issue in quantitative research as well (e.g., researchers misusing variables in a data set), the challenge is magnified with multilayered field data. Repositories cannot simply overcome longstanding questions about 1) the recording of data in which the researcher needs to decide what to record, and this would be the case even if video or audio recording is used; 2) lost *verstehen* (interpretive understanding) in which there can be a gap in understanding between someone who has spent substantial time in a setting and a reader who is attempting a reanalysis, which would remain a problem even with access to underlying fieldnotes which incompletely capture experiences; 3) ethical concerns about indirectly compromising the

[24] This is issue is treated in more detail below.

anonymity of those being studied (this is true with micro-use data in general); and 4) legal and bureaucratic problems associated with statutes on the protection of human subjects.[25] Providing a way to reanalyze data (i.e. procedural replication) is important for transparency, but it falls short of full replication.

This begs the question, what is full replication in participant-observation research and why is it the gold standard safeguard against misrepresentation for CST approaches? Replication in this sense is a process whereby future research uses new data to reproduce a specific study, or parts of it, and reports the results that support, question, or leave open findings from the previous study. It is only through full replication with new data that adequate adjustments can be made to the general knowledge base of various subjects or subject areas. Within the behavioralist tradition there is no substitute for replication in moving toward cumulative knowledge-building. Unfortunately, researchers often confuse laboratory models of replication, or journalistic re-interviewing, with behavioral models of replication in social context.

In participant observation, replication does not mean that a researcher necessarily restudies the same geographic area, institution, or organization of a previous study. While this may be reasonable in some cases, typically as time elapses social change occurs; the area may not have the same sociological characteristics in degree or kind that it had during the original study. Neighborhoods gentrify, schools change leadership, subcultures evolve, regulatory environments and economies shift. The fact that the study is in the same physical place does not make it the same social object. This is a central reason why ethnographers leverage the value of a revisit to examine change over time (cf. Burawoy 2007; Collier 1997). The key point is this—*the same space is not necessarily sociological equivalent in future years or decades*. For a well-known example of this misunderstanding being used to critique important ethnographic work while unproblematically accepting the attitudes of a previous study's subjects decades after the observations took place, one need only read the criticisms of William Foot Whyte's *Street Corner Society* offered by W. A. Marianne Boelen (1992). For a more recent example see Mitchell

[25] Further, such data sets risk the imposition of a rigid and inappropriate structure, best seen in the failures of anthropology's Human Relations Area Files (Abramson and Dohan 2015). At best, even the proponents of de-identified data sets and the development of computer assisted analyses argue there are limits in using these developing approaches beyond the replication of analytical procedures, and the verification of basic typological and distributional claims in the data (Abramson et al. 2018). In short, such approaches are in their infancy and even when developed will provide resources for procedural replication, but will not be a substitute for full replication

Duneier's critique of Eric Klinenberg's sociological study of the heatwave that occurred in Chicago and Klinenberg's response (Duneier 2006; Klinenberg 2006). In each case, selective ex-post facto interviews under different circumstances are used as a proxy for replication.

In the behavioralist model, replication is more than talking to prior subjects—it requires observing behavior. Replications need not necessarily be done in the same physical space, because as discussed above, time may have changed the conditions which produced the causal mechanisms that are the focus of the original and subsequent replication inquiries. Rather, replication needs to be done on a comparable social space. Such a space includes the same substantive object of study experiencing similar conditions to those originally studied. For instance, replication of behavioralist analysis of the microdynamics of the 1967 Detroit riots would not involve (a) going to Detroit when there is not a riot or (b) talking to people about their interpretation of the ethnographer's book in 2018. It would involve observing riots in other cities. Since for the behavioralist participant observer causal explanations are most often in the form of factor "X" *affects mechanism "M" to produce outcome* "Y," *under "C" contexts*, it is therefore necessary that C_2 approximates C_1.

There has been a long tradition in anthropology—and some elements of this are present in sociology—of avoiding replication and reporting findings that contradict previous participant-observation research for fear of antagonizing colleagues. However, it is essential for establishing reliable evidence on a subject that replications state clearly when results converged with previous research and when they differed, along with an explanation of why the researcher believes their results differed with previous research. Burawoy (2007) provides this in relation to his study of the same factory that was previously studied by Roy (1952, 1953, 1954), emphasizing the temporal dimension that those who confuse fact-checking with replication miss. Sánchez-Jankowski (2008) does this as it relates to a number of other studies done on urban poverty neighborhoods, including showing the value of Whyte's observations. Explanation of contradictions and convergences provides researchers with additional information to re-evaluate and adjudicate between conflicting findings, as well as providing a point of reference for further replication. It is only the accumulation of replication studies that provide the evidence for remaining more confident regarding what is known about a particular subject.[26]

[26] It should be added that the probability of succumbing to type 1 or 2 errors increases when researchers accept the findings from a single replication study, emphasizing the importance of seeing replication as a cumulative and collective project.

Conclusions

The previous chapter explained how participant observation conducted in accordance with behavioralist principles provides distinct analytical tools and inferential advantages for the observation, understanding, and explanation of causal mechanisms for social scientists operating in the CST (conventional scientific tradition). This chapter has shown how this method can and should be conducted in order to fulfill this promise, as well as how the contemporary behavioralist approach to comparative participant observation varies from existing ethnographic approaches with respect to the collection, analysis, and extension of data.

The contribution of this pair of chapters is simple but important. Together they clarify what comparative participant observation in the behavioralist framework actually entails. Within ethnography the term "positivism," and often the larger behavioralist tradition, are much derided but often ill-defined. Various ethnographic approaches to social research have argued that participant observation is fundamentally incompatible with CST inquiry (e.g., Burawoy 1998; Clifford 1988). While these approaches provide important criticisms that we addressed in these chapters, they incorrectly characterize both the theory and practice of comparative participant observation as practiced by contemporary proponents of the CST. In fairness, this is due at least in part to the failure of researchers in the behavioralist tradition to provide a clear outline of how they conduct participant observation in accordance with CST principles. By providing such an outline, including a candid acknowledgment of important contemporary deviations from traditional positivist models, the two chapters together clarify the behavioralist approach to participant observation research. It is our intention that the propositions and examples provided in these two chapters will aid the dialog occurring between different approaches with the hope of refining both the behavioralist approach and its alternatives.

By relating the method of comparative participant observation back to the shared CST language and concerns of inference, mechanisms, and causality, this chapter identifies where this tool fits within the larger repertoire of social science methods. Instead of placing participant observation as a critique of the CST framework, we have argued that behavioralist participant observation is well situated for observing causal mechanisms within and across social contexts. We have provided an explicit alternative to approaches that place ethnography as a means for producing thick descriptions or telling sociological stories. We have explained how participant observation in the behavioralist tradition is not only amenable to, but also dependent upon, the ideas of validity, representativeness, generalizability, and replication. We explained how this translates into practices across the life course of a project from the selection of a research question to the presentation of findings.

Finally, while acknowledging the practical and analytical difficulties involved in questions of how to reproduce and replicate this form of research exist, the present chapter identifies a number of analytical and technical solutions for sharing data, reproducing findings, and evaluating evidence. In examining these tools, we advance a framework for evaluating sociological evidence in a way that will allow scholarly discourse to move beyond simply making claims of data falsification whenever a disagreeable finding is presented. In doing so, we advance a model of how CST approaches to comparative participant observation can, and should, move beyond rich but ultimately limited stories, narratives, and anecdotes toward the pursuit of a systematic and comparative form of causal process observation that can advance social scientific knowledge.

References

Abramson, Corey M. 2015. *The End Game: How Inequality Shapes Our Final Years.* Cambridge, MA: Harvard University Press.

Abramson, Corey M., and Daniel Dohan. 2015. "Beyond Text: Using Arrays to Represent and Analyze Ethnographic Data." *Sociological Methodology* 45, no. 1: 272–319. https://doi.org/10.1177/0081175015578740.

Abramson, Corey M., Jacqueline Joslyn, Katharine A. Rendle, Sarah B. Garrett, and Daniel Dohan. 2018. "The Promises of Computational Ethnography: Improving Transparency, Replicability, and Validity for Realist Approaches to Ethnographic Analysis." *Ethnography* 19, no. 2: 254–284. https://doi.org/10.1177/1466138117725340.

Boelen, W. A. Marianne. 1992. "Street Corner Society: Cornerville Revisited." *Journal of Contemporary Ethnography* 21, no. 1: 11–51.

Becker, Howard. 1958. "Problems of Inference and Proof in Participant Observation." *American Sociological Review* 23, no. 6: 652–660.

Blumer, Herbert. 1969. *Symbolic Interactionism: Perspective and Method.* Englewood Cliffs, NJ: Prentice Hall.

Bourdieu, Pierre. 1990. *In Other Words: Essays Toward a Reflexive Sociology* Stanford, CA: Stanford University Press.

Bourdieu, Pierre, and Loïc J. D. Wacquant. 1992. *An Invitation to Reflexive Sociology.* Chicago: University of Chicago Press.

Breiger, Ronald L. 1974. "The Duality of Persons and Groups." *Social Forces* 53, no. 2: 181–190.

Brotherton, David. 2007. "Towards the Gang as a Social Movement." In *Gangs in the Global City*, edited by John Hagedorn, 251–272. Urbana: University of Illinois Press.

Burawoy, Michael. 1998. "The Extended Case Method." *Sociological Theory* 16, no. 1: 4–33.

Burawoy, Michael. 2007. *The Extended Case Method: Four Countries, Four Decades, Four Great Transformations, and One Theoretical Tradition*. Berkeley: University of California Press.

Cicourel, Aaron V. 1964. *Method and Measurement in Sociology*. Glencoe, IL: Free Press of Glencoe.

Cicourel, Aaron V. 1982. "Interviews, Surveys, and the Problem of Ecological Validity." *The American Sociologist* 17, no. 1: 11–20.

Cicourel, Aaron V. 2006. "Cognitive/Affective Processes, Social Interaction, and Social Structure as Representational Re-Descriptions: Their Contrastive Bandwidths and Spatio-Temporal Foci." *Mind and Society* 5, no. 1: 39–70.

Cicourel, Aaron V. 2011. "Evidence in Macro-Level and Micro-Level Healthcare Studies." In *Handbook of Communication in Organizations and Professions*, edited by Christopher N. Candlin and Srikant Sarangi, 61–82. Berlin/Boston: De Gruyter Mouton.

Clifford, James. 1988. *The Predicament of Culture: Twentieth-Century Ethnography, Literature, and Art*. Cambridge, MA: Harvard University Press.

Collier, Jane Fishburne. 1997. *From Duty to Desire: Remaking Families in a Spanish Village*. Princeton, NJ: Princeton University Press.

Contreras Randol. 2013. *The Stickup Kids: Race, Drugs, Violence, and the American Dream*. Berkeley: University of California Press.

Dohan, Daniel. 2003. *The Price of Poverty: Money, Work, and Culture in the Mexican American Barrio*. Berkeley: University of California Press.

Dohan, Daniel, and Martín Sánchez-Jankowski. 1998. "Using Computers to Analyze Ethnographic Field Data: Theoretical and Practical Considerations." *Annual Review of Sociology* 24: 477–498.

Dohan, Daniel, Sarah B. Garrett, Katharine A. Rendle, Meghan Halley, and Corey Abramson. 2016. "The Importance Of Integrating Narrative Into Health Care Decision Making." *Health Affairs* 35, no. 4, 720–725.

Duneier, Mitchell. 1999. *Sidewalk*. New York: FSG.

Duneier, Mitchell. 2006. "Ethnography, the Ecological Fallacy, and the 1995 Chicago Heat Wave." *American Sociological Review* 71, no. 4: 679–688.

Duneier, Mitchell. 2011. "How Not to Lie with Ethnography." *Sociological Methodology* 41, no. 1: 1–11.

Ellis, Carolyn. 2004. *The Ethnographic I: A Methodological Novel About Autoethnography*. Walnut Creek, CA: AltaMira Press.

Fay, Brian. 1996. *Contemporary Philosophy of Social Science: A Multicultural Approach*. Oxford: Blackwell.

Freedman, David A. 2010a. "Black Ravens, White Shoes and Case Selection: Inference with Categorical Variables." In *Statistical Methods and Causal Inference: A Dialogue with the Social Sciences*, edited by David Collier, Jasjeet S. Sekhon, and Philip B. Stark, 105–114. Cambridge: Cambridge University Press.

Freedman, David A. 2010b. "On Types of Scientific Inquiry: The Role of Qualitative Reasoning." In *Statistical Methods and Causal Inference: A Dialogue with the Social Sciences*, edited by David Collier, Jasjeet S. Sekhon, and Philip B. Stark, 337–356. Cambridge: Cambridge University Press.

Gans, Herbert J. 1999. "Participant Observation in the Era of Ethnography." *Journal of Contemporary Ethnography* 28, no. 5: 540–548.

Garrett, S. B., C. J. Koenig, L. Trupin, F. J. Hlubocky, C. K. Daugherty, A. Reinert, P. Munster, and D. Dohan. 2017. "What Advanced Cancer Patients with Limited Treatment Options Know About Clinical Research: A Qualitative Study." *Support Care Cancer* 25, no. 10: 3235–3242. PMID: 28488050.

Geertz, Clifford. 2000 [1973]. "Thick Description: Towards an Interpretive Theory of Culture." *The Interpretation of Cultures: Selected Essays*, 3–30. New York: Basic Books.

Giddens, A. 1984. *The Constitution of Society: Outline of the Theory of Structuration*. Berkeley: University of California Press.

Glaser, Barney G., and Anselm L. Strauss. 1967. *The Discovery of Grounded Theory: Strategies for Qualitative Research*. New York: Aldine Publishing Company.

Godfrey-Smith, Peter. 2003. *Theory and Reality: An Introduction to the Philosophy of Science*. Chicago: University of Chicago Press.

Goertz, Gary, and James Mahoney. 2012. *A Tale of Two Cultures: Qualitative and Quantitative Research in the Social Sciences*. Princeton, NJ: Princeton University Press.

Goffman, Erving. 1959. *Presentation of Self in Everyday Life*. New York: Anchor.

Goldman, Alvin I. 1988. *Epistemology and Cognition*. Cambridge, MA: Harvard University Press.

Goldthorpe, John H. 2000. *On Sociology: Numbers, Narratives, and the Integration of Research and Theory*. Oxford: Oxford University Press.

Jensen, Gary, F. 1996. "Defiance and Gang Identity: Quantitative Test of Qualitative Hypotheses." *Journal of Gang Research* 3, no. 4:13–29.

Jerolmack, Colin, and Shamus Khan. 2014. "Talk Is Cheap: Ethnography and the Attitudinal Fallacy." *Sociological Methods & Research* 43, no. 2: 178–209. https://doi.org/10.1177/0049124114523396.

Johnson, Carolyn. 2018. "Scientists Argue Heart Stem Cell Trial Should Be Paused." *Washington Post*, October 18.

Kahn, Seamus Rahman. 2012. *Privilege: The Making of an Adolescent Elite at St. Paul's School*. Princeton, NJ: Princeton University Press.

Katz, Jack. 2002. "From How to Why: On Luminous Description and Causal Inference in Ethnography; Part 2." *Ethnography* 3, no. 1: 63–90.

Katz, Jack. 2004. "On the Rhetoric and Politics of Ethnographic Methodology." *Annals of the American Academy of Political and Social Science* 595: 280–308.

Katz, Jack. 2010. "Review of Cracks in the Pavement." *American Journal of Sociology* 115, no. 6: 1950–1952.

King, Gary, Robert O. Keohane, and Sidney. Verba. 1994. *Designing Social Inquiry: Scientific Inference in Qualitative Research*. Princeton, NJ: Princeton University Press.

Klinenberg, Eric. 2006. "Blaming the Victim: Hearsay, Labelling, and the Hazards of Quick Hit Disaster Ethnography." *American Sociological Review* 71, no. 4: 693–702.

Lamont, Michèle, and Patricia White. 2008. Workshop on Interdisciplinary Standards for Systematic Qualitative Research. Arlington, VA: National Science Foundation.

Lareau, Annette. 2011. *Unequal Childhoods: Class, Race, and Family life*. Berkeley: University of California Press.

Lieberson, Stanley. 1991. "Small N's and Big Conclusions: An Examination of the Reasoning in Comparative Studies Based on a Small Number of Cases." *Social Forces* 70, no. 2: 307–320.

Lofland, John. 1995. "Analytic Ethnography." *Journal of Contemporary Ethnography* 24, no. 1: 30–67.

Lubet, Steven. 2017. *Interrogating Ethnography: Why Evidence Matters*. New York: Oxford University Press.

Marx, Karl. 1852. "The Eighteenth Brumaire of Louis Bonapart." In *Die Revolution*, no. 1.

Marx, Karl. 1867. *Das Capital: Kritik der politischen Oekonomie*. Hamburg: Verlag von Otto Meissner.

Moon, Dawn. 2004. *God, Sex, and Politics: Homosexuality and Everyday Theologies*. Chicago: University of Chicago Press.

Padilla, Felix. 1992. *The Gang as American Enterprise*. New Brunswick, NJ: Rutgers University Press.

Ragin, Charles C. 2004. "Turning the Tables: How Case-Oriented Research Challenges Variable-Oriented Research." In *Rethinking Social Inquiry: Diverse Tools, Shared Standards*, edited by Henry E. Brady and David Collier, 123–138. Lanham, MD: Rowman & Littlefield.

Ragin, Charles C., and Howard Saul Becker. 1992. *What is a Case?: Exploring the Foundations of Social Inquiry*. New York: Cambridge University Press.

Rao, T. S. Sathyanarayana, and Chittaranjan Andrade. 2011. "The MMR Vaccine and Autism: Sensation, Refutation, Retraction, and Fraud." *Indian Journal of Psychiatry* 53, no. 2: 95–96. https://doi.org/10.4103/0019-5545.82529.

Reed, Isaac A. 2010. "Epistemology Contextualized: Social-Scientific Knowledge in a Postpositivist Era." *Sociological Theory* 28, no. 1: 20–39.

Reyes, Victoria. 2018. "Three Models of Transparency in Ethnographic Research: Naming Places, Naming People, and Sharing Data." *Ethnography* 19, no. 2 (June): 204–226.

Roy, Donald. 1952. "Quota Restrictions and Goldbricking in a Machine Shop." *American Journal of Sociology* 57, no. 5: 427–442.

Roy, Donald. 1953. "Work Satisfaction and Social Reward in Quota Achievement: An Analysis of Piecework Incentive." *American Sociological Review* 18, no. 5: 507–514.

Roy, Donald. 1954. "Efficiency and the 'Fix': Informal Intergroup Relations in a Piece-Work Machine Shop." *American Journal of Sociology* 60, no. 3: 255–266.

Sánchez-Jankowski, Martín. 1991. *Islands in the Street: Gangs and American Urban Society*. Berkeley: University of California Press.

Sánchez-Jankowski, Martín. 2002. "Representation, Responsibility and Reliability in Participant Observation." In *Qualitative Research in Action*, edited by Tim May, 144–160. London: SAGE Publications.

Sánchez-Jankowski, Martín. 2008. *Cracks in the Pavement: Social Change and Resilience in Poor Neighborhoods*. Berkeley: University of California Press.

Sánchez-Jankowski, Martín. 2016. *Burning Dislike: Ethnic Violence in High Schools*. Oakland: University of California Press.

Small, Mario Luis. 2002. "Culture, Cohorts, and Social Organization Theory: Understanding Local Participation in a Latino Housing Project." *American Journal of Sociology* 108: 1–54.

Small, Mario Luis. 2002. "Culture, Cohorts, and Social Organization Theory: Understanding Local Participation in a Latino Housing Project." *American Journal of Sociology* 108, no. 1: 1–54.

Smith, Robert Courtney. 2012. "How Did You Pick That School?: Ethnography, Epistemology, and Counterfactual Causality." In *American Journal of Sociology*

Conference on Causal Thinking and Ethnographic Research, March 8. Chicago: University of Chicago Press.
Sudman, Seymour. 1976. *Applied Sampling*. New York: Academic Press.
Sullivan, Mercer L. 1994. "Review of Islands in the Street: Gangs and American Urban Society." *American Journal of Sociology* 99, no. 6: 1640–1642.
Taleb, Nassim Nicholas. 2007. *The Black Swan: The Impact of the Highly Improbable*. New York: Random House.
Tavory, Iddo, and Stefan Timmermans. 2014. *Abductive Analysis: Theorizing Qualitative Research*. Chicago: University of Chicago Press.
Thiem, Alrik and Michael Baumgartner. 2016. "Modeling Causal Irrelevance in Evaluations of Configurational Comparative Methods." *Sociological Methodology* 46, no. 1: 345–357. https://doi.org/10.1177/0081175016654736.
Venkatesh, Sudhir. 1997. "The Social Organization of Street Gang Activity in an Urban Ghetto." *American Journal of Sociology* 103, no. 1: 82–111.
Venkatesh, Sudhir. 2000a. *American Project: The Rise and Fall of a Modern Ghetto*. Cambridge, MA: Harvard University Press.
Venkatesh, Sudhir. 2000b. "'Are We a Family or a Business?': History and Disjuncture in the American Street Gang." *Theory and Society* 29, no. 4: 427–462.
Vigil, James, Diego. 1988. *A Rainbow of Gangs*. Austin: University of Texas Press.
Wacquant, Loïc. 2002. "Scrutinizing the Street: Poverty, Morality, and the Pitfalls of Urban Ethnography." *American Journal of Sociology* 107, no. 6: 1468–1532.
Wacquant, Loïc. 2004. *Body & Soul: Notebooks of an Apprentice Boxer*. New York: Oxford University Press.
Wacquant, Loïc. 2009. "Habitus As Topic And Tool: Reflections on Becoming a Prizefighter." In *Ethnographies Revisited*, edited by William Shaffir, Antony Puddephatt, and Steven Kleinknecht, 137–151. New York: Routledge.

3

The Thematic Lens

A Formal and Cultural Framework for Comparative Ethnographic Analysis

Thomas DeGloma and Max Papadantonakis

Introduction: Comparative Analysis Through a Thematic Lens

Left-wing guerilla resistance movements, like the Ejército Zapatista de Liberación Nacional (EZLN) or Zapatista Army of National Liberation, and right-wing reactionary racist movements, like the American Ku Klux Klan (KKK), have radically different (even oppositional) political ideologies and agendas. These particular movements are rooted in different national contexts and span different periods of time. Their respective participants have different cultural backgrounds and most likely speak different languages. Yet despite these very significant differences, both groups use anonymity to subvert the normative social and political orders of their environments in ways that share important characteristics.[1] Both perform their political activities behind masks, and, like the modern hacktivist network known as Anonymous, their masks have become symbolic icons of their political ideologies and practices. Further, such divergent groups and networks use their masks to evoke some meaningful scene and political disposition associated with the past which is now performed as rising from suppression (in the case of the EZLN, the early twentieth-century agrarian revolutionary movement led by Emiliano Zapata in Mexico; in the case of the KKK, the antebellum South and the Confederacy in the United States). Moreover, while using different symbols and pursuing different objectives, such variant

[1] All discussions of anonymity in this chapter stem from DeGloma's book in progress, currently titled *Anonymous: The Performance and Impact of Hidden Identities*. Subversive anonymity is only one of several generic dimensions of anonymity explored in this project.

Thomas DeGloma and Max Papadantonakis, *The Thematic Lens* In: *Beyond the Case*. Edited by: Corey M. Abramson and Neil Gong, Oxford University Press (2020). © Oxford University Press.
DOI: 10.1093/oso/9780190608484.003.0004

subversive agents use anonymity to deprecate the individual ego and accentuate the collective character of their oppositional standpoints.

As this brief example suggests, a sociology of subversive anonymity will look much different than a sociology of the EZLN, the KKK, the hacker network Anonymous, or any other particular social movement or organization. Rather than relying solely on a case-based logic limited to ethnographic immersion in a particular demarcated field site, such an approach involves being guided by a socially and culturally significant theme that is relevant to a number of otherwise different cases (Zerubavel 2007, 133, 140). Using such a *thematic lens* allows ethnographers to transcend the conventionally circumscribed character of their analytic concerns and consider multiple cases in order to develop a much greater and more complex understanding of the broadly relevant phenomenon at hand. However, rather than engaging in comparison to focus on the differences between cases and contexts (or that which makes any particular case unique), this theme-guided approach to comparative research and theory development first views otherwise variant cases as constituent examples tied together by a common "social pattern" (Zerubavel 2007). In the preceding example, it allows us to hone our interpretive lens on *anonymity*, which DeGloma views as a generic mode of social performance and form of interaction, in order to gain insight into the practices and implications of a variety of very different groups and situations.[2] Only by focusing on a theme such as anonymity would we be able to see common practices shared by the KKK, the EZLN, and modern hacktivists. Only by comparing such a multiplicity of different cases can we start to see the more general significance of ego-deprecation and subversive commemoration in the political performances of anonymity. Using a thematic lens thereby enables us to ask questions such as: How might divergent social situations—despite being seen as different due to context-related values, behaviors, beliefs, languages, and histories—involve fundamentally similar interactive processes, structures of meaning, or performative features, and how can we understand the general implications of these multicontextual properties? Moreover, how do actors creatively use these patterned social and cultural formulae to accomplish their particular goals in different social settings?

In this chapter, we explore the benefits of adopting a thematic lens as a foundation for comparative ethnographic research and other modes of

[2] See also Thompson (1974, 398–400) and Scott (1990, 140–152), who were among the first to discuss anonymity as a means of performing resistance to domination.

comparative qualitative analysis. Synthesizing previous work that outlines the general tenets of formal sociology (Simmel 1909, 1950a) and social pattern analysis (Zerubavel 1980, 2007; Brekhus 2007), generalized symbolic interaction (Prus 1987a) and formal grounded theory (Glaser and Strauss 2008 [1967]), and the strong program in cultural sociology (Alexander and Smith 1993, 2003), we explicitly consider how a "theme-driven" (Zerubavel 2007, 140; Brekhus 2007, 458) approach to social analysis provides a compelling impetus to compare different cases and contexts. We seek to bridge the concerns of these various programs while considering how together they can help us to hone the interpretive and descriptive strengths traditionally associated with ethnography on the underlying formal and generic dimensions that tie otherwise distinct cases together.

Using a thematic lens to engage in comparative analysis invites us to explore how *social* forms of interaction and *cultural* structures of meaning mutually sustain and inform one another across multiple cases and levels of analysis. Therefore, we can elucidate the links between these interactionist and cultural dimensions. As the concept of a lens implies, this approach involves a particular way of *focusing* (Zerubavel 1980, 2007, 139–141; cf. Burawoy 2009, 205) in order to reveal multicontextual social and cultural structures that drive the dynamics of the cases, contexts, and issues we study. When individuals act locally, they often creatively deploy a "situated version" of a formulaic interactive dynamic and meaning structure (DeGloma 2014, 22) that is relevant beyond their particular situation. As actors in various settings cooperate with others to bring their concerns to life, they act in patterned ways. By adopting a thematic lens and engaging in comparative analysis, we can reveal these deep foundations of social life and, consequently, gain richer insight into the particular contexts and cases we explore.

Ethnographic Generalization and Modes of Comparison

While addressing the implications of ethnographic methods for theory development, scholars have advanced various approaches suited to comparison in ethnographic research. Some of the most notable include (a) the grounded theory approach, (b) the extended case method, and (c) the abductive analysis/pragmatic approach. We briefly address these methodological programs here to acknowledge some of their important contributions. We also stress that our discussion of what we call a thematic lens is not meant to provide an alternative. In fact, one of the strengths of thematic analysis is that it can serve as a complement to different methodological strategies (see also Brekhus 2007, 459). We contend that researchers working within different traditions might benefit from focusing their analyses to see the deep social forms and cultural structures that underlie the cases they study and then building comparative sets around the general themes that such structures reveal.

In their call for a grounded approach to the construction of "multi-area formal theory," Barney G. Glaser and Anselm L. Strauss (2008 [1967], 82) argue that one of the most fruitful ways that scholars can develop multicontextual theory is to isolate formal properties from "a substantive theory" that stems from the focused analysis of a single case or particular area of study. Ethnographic immersion can provide a basis for such a substantive theory and thus "an initial direction in developing relevant categories and properties" (79), which can then be generalized and explored further via a "comparative investigation of different substantive areas" (81) or a "systematic study of multiple comparison groups and substantive theories" (97). Likewise, John Lofland (1995, 30) outlines a method of "analytic ethnography" that in part "attempts to provide generic propositional answers to questions about social life and organization" (30) and requires the researcher "to search out patterns and regularities in the context of close-up depiction" (Lofland 1972, 3; 1995, 34). Like Glaser and Strauss, when Lofland (echoing Goffman) encourages researchers "to conceive their answers as more abstract generic propositions rather than as historically particular information" (1995, 39), he posits an inductive and case-transcendent process of generalization, though he is less clear on the details of multicase formal comparison.[3] Though these scholars argue that ethnographers should extract the general (formal and generic) from the particular to provide a basis for identifying similar processes in other contexts, they are less clear about how a formal or thematic lens can lead to unique (and otherwise unseen) insights about our particular cases. Moreover, they do not adequately address culture or, therefore, the relation between social forms and cultural structures of meaning.

Michael Burawoy (1998, 2009) also develops his extended case method "in order to extract the general from the unique" and "justify... extravagant leaps

[3] Lofland (1995, 40) writes, "In this upward categorization, generic propositional framing strives to find fundamental human themes and concerns in obscure and sometimes seemingly trivial social doings."

across space and time, from the singular to the general" (1998, 5). However, for Burawoy, comparative research is about using ethnographic cases to explore the slightly different local manifestations of widespread social forces (1998, 18–19) (specifically, the economic and political forces of global capitalism and imperialism) and, indeed, his approach is well-suited to this objective. From a critical Marxist perspective, he is guided by a theoretical framework through which the past (origins and motives), present (relations and conditions), and future (objectives and orientations) are interpreted. His intention has been to connect "large-scale historical transformation" and observable "microprocesses" (2009, 6) and "to demonstrate that Marxism and ethnography can indeed be partners" (8).[4] We share Burawoy's commitment to exposing the links between micro and macro levels of analysis while comparing different cases. However, our notion of thematic analysis allows for the consideration of more generally applicable and formal social processes and structured cultural forces. Our thematic lens, therefore, allows for a wider degree of variation among cases of a comparative set that despite being united by a theme, are often otherwise very different in most regards. Whereas Burawoy speaks of generalization and patterns, he also argues that cases are "rooted in their broader political and economic context" (2009, 203). While he suggests we should "see . . . microprocesses as an expression of macrostructures" (203), he is primarily focused on the social forces that are central to his theoretical frame, not the broadly relevant social forms and cultural structures we address here.

Moving beyond the inductive/deductive divide, Iddo Tavory and Stefan Timmermans (2014; see also Timmermans and Tavory 2012), building on the work of Charles Sanders Peirce, propose a process of abductive analysis in which a theoretically informed researcher (2014, 41–44) remains committed to developing new theory by "fitting unexpected or unusual findings" that emerge from meticulous fieldwork "into an interpretive framework" that is "aimed at theoretical generalizations" (123). Tavory and Timmermans's abductive program strikes a careful balance between theoretical flexibility, focused empirical observations, and theory development. Their approach to comparison stems from their imperative to study "how iterations of meaning-making emerge in different cases, over time, or across situations"

[4] For an important critique, see Tavory and Timmermans (2014, 18–19), who argue that this approach "tethers researchers to the theoretical framework they began with" (19) and "is mostly compatible with theories that tie observations in the field to larger, usually unobservable patterns of control and macrostructures of domination" (18).

(72) so that the researcher may refine her understanding of those phenomena (and learn from surprises and variations among a set of occurrences and observations) (67–86, 122–124). For these scholars, new understandings emerge when, via this process, "a researcher is led away from old to new theoretical insights" (Timmermans and Tavory 2012, 170). Taking a position we believe to be consistent with this approach, we argue that a researcher's "disposition to perceive the world and its surprises in certain ways" (Tavory and Timmermans 2014, 41) can and should include a sensitivity to the kinds of deep case-transcendent social forms and cultural structures we highlight here (see 2014, 78–80, on different degrees of "intersituational variation" where "seemingly unrelated actions make sense as a single set under the researcher's theoretical description" (79)). Further, the puzzles and surprises that provide the "innovative potential" (Timmermans and Tavory 2012, 171) that Tavory and Timmermans are right to centralize in the process of theory development can and do also arise from the comparison of otherwise very different cases that come together as variants of a common social theme. In our view, such a comparative set of cases—in which underlying formal commonalities are pondered next to variations of locally situated content—can propel the development of rich and new theory, especially deep cultural theory, that elucidates phenomena more broadly relevant than any one case. New insights derived from such a comparative analysis then allow the researcher to revisit each case with the thematic generalities in mind, seeing it now from a broader perspective.

Developing a program for "analytical field research," Eviatar Zerubavel (1980, see also 2007) was perhaps the first to systematically outline methodological guidelines for the type of thematic focus we endorse and develop here. Building on Simmel's (1909, 297–298) emphasis on interactive "forms of socialization,"[5] Zerubavel encourages researchers to "view specific sociohistorical configurations as mere instantiations of" more broadly relevant "generic social patterns" and, in extracting social themes from such patterns, to "thereby [make] their essentially decontextualized findings more generalizable" (Zerubavel 2007, 131; see also Backhaus 1998, 272). He encourages us to bracket our analytic attention ("focus") and consider how these basic structural characteristics of group life might be relevant to multiple settings and cases.[6] After a researcher identifies a formal

[5] See also Simmel (1950a).

[6] See also Brekhus (2007, 458) on the analyst's attempt "to isolate thematic highlights from the data" that stem from multiple and variant cases.

property, the form becomes the "sensitizing concept" (Blumer 1954, 7–10; see also Zerubavel 1980, 26, 28–31) from which one seeks out cases to fill a comparative set (see also Glaser and Strauss [2008 (1967), 45–77] on "theoretical sampling," Vaughan [1992] on "theory elaboration," and Snow et al. [2003] on "theoretical extension"). As soon as the formal theme is observed, the single case is put on hold as the primary basis of analysis (permanently or temporarily) and the researcher starts to *see* the world (and other cases) through the lens of the theme itself. Building on this tradition, Snow, Morrill, and Anderson (2003) note "the relative dearth of systematic procedures for analyzing field data in a fashion that facilitates theoretical elaboration across sites" and argue for a "theoretically-engaged ethnography" (182) that "extends preexisting theoretical or conceptual formulations to other groups or aggregations, to other bounded contexts or places, or to other sociocultural domains" (187). As Brekhus (2007, 458–459) notes, one of the core strengths of such a theme-driven sociological analysis is that ethnographers and other researchers can use it to cultivate an intellectually "nomadic perspective" (459) as, when guided by an analytic theme, we are drawn into unexplored empirical territory to find connections between cases and areas of study that are not typically thought to have anything in common.[7] We seek to advance these prior efforts.

Engaging a thematic lens leads to a particular kind of study—perhaps outside of the ethnographic comfort zone for some—but one that is rewarding in that it will allow the researcher to understand both the general phenomenon and particular cases in new and fruitful ways. Notably, researchers can build their comparisons with a multiethnographic research design, but comparative elaborations can also be accomplished with a variety of other data and methods, including secondary and historical case analyses (see also Glaser and Strauss 2008 [1967], 65–69; Vaughan 1992, 185, 199; DeGloma 2014). The point, most generally, is that a thematically focused, empirically grounded comparative elaboration of ethnographic analysis can broaden our

[7] See also Simmel (1950a, 14), Glaser and Strauss (2008 [1967], 94–99), Denzin (1978, 18), and Prus (1987a, 263–264). This approach can be contrasted with the trend of single-case analysis in ethnography with its emphasis on in-depth storytelling (which often involves the publishing of extended excerpts from the researcher's field notes). Such a more conventional ethnography—producing what Prus (1987a, 253) refers to as "isolated accounts of community life" and Strauss (1970, 53) refers to as "respected little islands of knowledge"—has its strengths in analytic depth and literary detail, but often also has weaknesses in breadth of analysis and conceptual/theory development. On this point, see also Brekhus (2007, 457–458).

understanding of the robust foundations of social life while also helping us to deepen our analysis of the particular cases in our comparative set. We are left with an interpretive analysis that is honed on a theme, not just any one case, and an intellectual process that promotes scholarly innovation and theory development.

Patterned Dynamics and Formal Symbolic Interaction

Because symbolic interactionists are typically focused on the interactive dynamics and emergent meanings grounded in observable social situations, many confine themselves to the analysis of one social setting or case. However, as is evident (in different ways) in the work of Erving Goffman (1959, 1961), Norman Denzin (1978), Robert Prus (1987a, 1987b), and others, the analysis of a particular social setting can reveal "generic social processes" (Prus 1987a) that serve to (a) provide a framework for a researcher to engage in multicontextual comparative analysis, and (b) connect the empirical work of multiple researchers who are concerned with different cases and contexts (providing a framework for cooperation and dialog among researchers). With particular regard to emergent symbolic interactive dynamics, Prus writes:

> The phrase *generic social processes* refers to the transsituational elements of interaction, to the abstracted formulations of social behavior. Denoting parallel sequences of activity across diverse contexts, generic social processes highlight the emergent, interpretive features of association; they focus on the activities involved in the "doing" or accomplishment of group life. (Prus 1987a, 251)

Thus, Prus calls on interactionist-oriented researchers and ethnographers to think beyond their cases and consider how patterned interactive dynamics tie otherwise divergent cases and settings together.[8]

In this tradition, several interactionist-oriented researchers have advanced comparative analyses guided by generalizable social patterns. Such scholars have revealed formal patterns pertaining to interactive dynamics

[8] Prus (1987a, 256) argues that the Chicago School roots of symbolic interaction involved "a strong underlying appreciation of generic interactional sociology." See also Tavory and Timmermans (2014, 15).

and interpersonal relations, performances, the construction of self and narrative identity, modes of communication and reality maintenance, and a range of other phenomena. However, the level of abstraction varies among these studies. Some comparative interactionist researchers identify patterns across multiple cases within a particular substantive domain.[9] These include studies of trauma (DeGloma 2009), "patterns of [family] disruption that stemmed from having a child with problems" (Francis 2015, 15),[10] and "the general process of establishing professional status and control over clients" in sales settings (Corrado 2002, 35). Others advance broadly relevant theories rooted in patterns of interaction that span multiple substantive spheres. For example, Gubrium and Holstein (2000) build on their previous ethnographic research to elaborate the "relatively stable, routinized, ongoing patterns of action and interaction" (2000, 102) common to a "ubiquity and variety of venues" (104) in order to elucidate the common ways different groups and organizations guide the construction of the self and "shape the discursive contours of subjectivity" (95). In this latter example, comparative analysis provides for a general theoretical framework and elucidates patterns that are not restricted to any one realm of social life.

Taking a formal narrative perspective, DeGloma illustrates how his interest in the generalized theme of "awakenings" (significant personal discoveries and self-transformations) grew from research originally grounded in a particular substantive area. He writes,

> I first took interest in awakenings while studying trauma narratives. In particular, as I was researching "recovered" memories of child sexual abuse, I began to notice that the process of recovering memories involves a formulaic discovery of "truth" (in this case, the memory of abuse) and a consequent formulaic account of the narrator's "false" belief (the prior, mistaken perception that the abuse wasn't there). Such self-identified survivors of child sexual abuse tell scripted stories about awakening to the truth about their lives. . . . At a transcontextual level, such stories are formally similar to stories told in other settings about different topics. . . . By focusing on the formal properties shared by these . . . stories at the expense of their

[9] Compare with Glaser and Strauss (2008 [1967], 79–99) on the distinctions between "substantive theory," "one-area formal theory," and "multi-area formal theory."

[10] See also Gengler (2015) on general processes of "emotional threat management" in families when children have been diagnosed with life-threatening illnesses.

> otherwise significant differences, we can begin to see how this story formula has a generic social logic. (DeGloma 2014, 10–11)

While developing his study of such personal discoveries, DeGloma intentionally backgrounds "the nuances that set [multiple] topics [and cases] apart from one another and intentionally" foregrounds "the underlying patterns that tie them together" in order to expose the formal and cultural similarities shared by "a variety of political, religious, sexual, psychological, scientific, and philosophical stories from various times and places" (2014, 5). As opposed to treating any one case or substantive domain as the primary or bounded focus of study, the thematic character of the story *plot* (a shared structural foundation) becomes the primary analytic lens though which cases are selected, compared, and analyzed.[11] Moreover, this thematic and comparative focus allows us to see that very different individuals use the same story formula to ascribe various meanings to their lives and to weigh in on various moral-political controversies. From this comparative perspective, autobiography can be seen as an articulation of one's relational standpoint in a contentious field. The formal comparison and simultaneous interpretation of otherwise different cases allows us to see a more comprehensive cultural picture. In other words, comparison yields new and novel insight (and raises new questions) that would not necessarily be possible with a single case study.

Max Papadantonakis's ongoing research shows how a thematic lens can shape ethnographic focus and provide an empirical basis for abstraction and generalization to other cases of potential comparative value. Closely observing everyday interactions in an urban street market in Athens, Papadantonakis (2014) shows how discriminatory myths are constructed in daily conversations among local vendors and native residents. These locals stigmatize immigrant workers, large groups of whom typically cohabitate in the small dilapidated basements of the neighborhood, by declaring that such living arrangements mean that they inevitably engage in homosexual activity. This discriminating claim was reinforced through the shared misconception of an everyday gesture—the *long handshake*. When shaking hands upon

[11] We can also consider how studies developed by different scholars can reveal a common narrative pattern that ties otherwise divergent cases together. For example, see Mason-Schrock (1996) on pre-operative transsexuals, Johnston (2013) on Pagan practitioners, and Winchester (2015) on Eastern Orthodox Christians. While focused on very different cases and populations, each of these scholars shows how individuals adopt a similar narrative of continuity to define their changing selves. See also Zerubavel (2003) on the plot structure of historical continuity more generally.

greeting one another, some immigrant workers casually drop their clasped hands to their waists and continue to hold onto each other while talking. Locals used this banal gesture as a weapon to ridicule a large segment of immigrant workers, with many Greek vendors and neighborhood residents being utterly convinced that these men all engaged in sexual activity of which they disapproved. Papadantonakis's analysis of othering through the interactive and discriminatory (mis)interpretation of gesture arose from the ethnographic observation of a very specific and bounded context—he examines the construction of the "deviant and homosexual immigrant" in an urban Greek street market at the time of the recent economic and migrant crisis. However, the general interactive theme can be abstracted and investigated across a range of different contexts (with regard to the imputation of sexuality via the interpretation of gesture) and cases (with regard to other acts of classification based on gesture), such as policing (to consider how police officers interpret some gestures or bodies as indicative of criminality) and psychological diagnosis (to consider how psychological practitioners interpret the gestures and body language of their clients as indicative of pathology), for example. As Papadantonakis is demonstrating, formal interactive dynamics and interpretive patterns with regard to physical gesture sustain acts of stigmatization/discrimination/othering that create or reproduce meaningful cultural distinctions and structural inequalities across a variety of otherwise different cases.

In addition to interactive dynamics, formulaic narratives, and interpretive patterns, interactionist researchers have also developed Simmel's (1950a, 1950b) notion of the social type as a thematic lens through which to study and compare multiple cases and contexts (see also Snow, Morrill, and Anderson 2003, 190). The key to understanding social types is to grasp that an individual's experiences and socially defined characteristics can (in many ways) stem from one's generic structural location (one's situated position in relation to others) regardless of one's personality or the particular venue in which one is situated (like Simmel's "stranger"). In other words, others in different venues or settings can act in similar ways and have similar experiences given that they share a common, patterned structural location and, consequently, patterned interactions with their interlocutors (see also Coser 1971, 182).

We can use social types as thematic lenses to explore patterns in human experiences and motivations to act across different cases and settings. One of the best examples of this type of comparative analysis is Jamie L. Mullaney's

(2006) study of abstinence as "a chosen identity path" (67), where she identifies "abstainers" as a social type. Whether individuals choose to abstain from a particular food, sexual intercourse, alcohol, caffeine, or something else is of secondary concern for Mullaney, who reveals the common characteristics all such individuals share by virtue of their chosen abstinence in general. The formal and comparative analysis of abstinence, Mullaney (2006, 13) argues, provides important information that the substantive investigation of any single case or situation does not. Similarly, DeGloma (2014, 18–20) identifies awakeners "as a social type of storyteller" given their shared "dialogical orientations" despite their different concerns and particular social affiliations. Likewise, Chancer (1992) treats the sadist and the masochist as generic positions that take form vis-à-vis one another in a formal dynamic that is relevant to multiple social contexts and institutions. In all of these examples, the researcher uses a social type (whether strangers, abstainers, awakeners, or sadists/masochists) as a thematic lens to focus on the general characteristics shared by a variety of different actors in the same structural position.

Cultural Patterns, Structures of Meaning, and Formulaic Modes of Performance

While symbolic interactionists are typically concerned with reciprocal action and emergent meanings, strong program cultural sociologists are generally concerned with underlying structures of meaning—including durable cultural codes (such as good and evil, sacred and profane, true and false, for example) and background symbolism (Alexander and Smith 1993, 2003).[12] Cultural sociologists seek to expose these "deeper generative principles" (Alexander and Smith 2003, 11) and argue that "every action, no matter how instrumental, reflexive, or coerced . . . is embedded to some extent in a horizon of affect and meaning" (12). While focused on the durable underlying structures of culture, strong program researchers often then analyze how actors use them to give rise to the character of a class or type of event or experience (Alexander 2004a; Smith 2005; DeGloma 2014) and make the meanings of particular issues and historical occurrences (e.g., Wagner-Pacifici and Schwartz 1991; Wagner-Pacifici 1994; Eyerman 2001; Alexander 2004b). Their work invites us to explore "the relationship between the foundational

[12] See also Rambo and Chan (1990).

and contextual levels of culture—between culture as a durable" underlying transcontextual phenomenon and culture as emergent and performed in more local situations (DeGloma 2014, 22). Thus, we can compare such local situations or particular events, experiences, and issues by virtue of their shared cultural-structural foundations. We can also consider how formulaic structures of meaning underlie the patterned interactive dynamics and formulaic plot structures that recur in various cases across time and space.

Two concepts that are central to the strong program in cultural sociology—structural hermeneutics (Alexander and Smith 2003) and cultural pragmatics (Alexander 2006; Alexander and Mast 2006)—can help us to develop our thematic lens and deepen our analytic insights while comparing multiple cases that adhere to the same foundational properties.

The concept of structural hermeneutics calls our attention to two important and related points. First, binary cultural and emotion codes (Alexander and Smith 1993, 2003; Loseke 2009; DeGloma 2014) (like good and evil, fair and biased, hope and despair, for example) often serve as foundational building blocks of the formal and structural frameworks underlying interactions and relationships, and our narrative accounts pertaining to institutions, events, experiences, and the motivations of the actors involved (see also Smith 2005). As people define aspects of the world around them (for example, the character of different parties in a conflict, or the nature of a social movement or policy), they do so by coding them in relation to one another (the hero/protagonist versus the villain/antagonist, for example, or the liberating versus the oppressive social movement). As Smith (2005, 38–39, emphasis added) demonstrates, "cultural sociology . . . enables us to speak of *repeated instantiations* of particular culture structures rather than of unique conjunctions and unrepeatable, locally situated meanings" (see also Reed 2006, 159). In other words, different actors mobilize the same broadly relevant cultural and emotion codes (structured cultural resources) as they enact the rituals and construct the narratives with which they make sense of their particular events and experience specific situations, contexts, and circumstances.

Second, a focus on widely relevant coded structures of meaning not only provides a basis for comparison, but also (and consequently) allows for a deeper understanding of each particular case in our comparative set. By focusing our hermeneutic analysis of each case through the lens of the shared cultural codes at hand (see, e.g., Alexander and Smith 1993), we can consider how different actors mobilize these foundational cultural structures to achieve *situated* meanings and objectives. As with the situated claims, events, and experiences defined as phenomena of trauma (Alexander 2004a; DeGloma 2009), for example, different contexts and cases can be seen as separated "instantiations" of the same underlying coded structure of meaning, yet such coded structures only come to life *in* and *as* the circumstantial interactions and narratives that give meaning to those seperated events and experiences (Smith 2005; DeGloma 2014). As Rambo and Chan (1990, 640) point out, "to explain concrete occurrences in the world, [a cultural] code has to be represented with reference to the way people experience the code. Otherwise action is portrayed as a crude caricature." We maintain that the specific details of multiple particular cases, when taken together as a formal comparative set, remain crucial to our ability to more fully understand the underlying cultural codes, and in turn our grasp of the general cultural codes allows us to better understand each concrete case. In other words, general theme and particular cases are complementary aspects (complementary ways of looking) that allow us to deepen our understanding of our topic and develop widely relevant theory (see also Backhaus 1998, 268–270; Tavory and Timmermans 2014).

Using such an approach, DeGloma explores "the ways individuals and communities draw on shared sociomental norms and deep-seated cultural and emotion codes to frame the relationship between the 'true' and the 'false' as they tell their seemingly personal awakening stories" (DeGloma 2014, 4). Unpacking the semiotic structure and coding of awakenings (14–18), he shows how such accounts draw on a common stock of metaphoric contrasts ("asleep versus awake, darkness versus light, blindness versus sight, and lost versus found") as well as shared emotion codes ("betrayal, hurt, anger, and fear" versus "hope, salvation, pride, and love") and a general "vertical organization of enlightenment" despite pertaining to a wide range of different subject matters rooted in different social contexts and historical periods. The study of particular cases elucidates the general theme and vice-versa as DeGloma works "to illuminate broadly relevant and durable aspects of culture and show how they serve as meaning-making resources for individuals who are constructing [different] identities and" characterizing different events while "situating themselves" in various contexts and communities in the world around us (29).

Enhancing this perspective, the concept of cultural pragmatics (Alexander 2006; Alexander and Mast 2006) calls our attention to the fact that actors in different settings (with different objectives) draw on collectively rooted "background representations" (entrenched symbols and meanings) in an attempt to win the hearts and minds of others. In the process, "abstract categories" and codes, along with "general narrative structures . . . are made concrete and particular via walking and talking performers" in their specific situations (Reed 2006, 153). Thus, actors engage in social performances that often share background or foundational characteristics that transcend the particularities of any one performative act. This notion allows us to further develop our cultural framework for comparison. On the one hand, different actors of the same broad cultural milieu draw on the same stock of background cultural resources to accomplish different objectives. On the other hand, we can use this insight into the cultural foundations of performance to explore how actors in significantly different cultural environments (fundamentally different times and contexts) engage in their performances in ways that tie different cases together via a general *performative theme*.

Taking an example that illustrates the latter dimension, when subversive actors mask themselves to act anonymously, they often draw on deep-seated cultural symbolism (via the appearance of their masks, for example) and basic cultural codes (such as obscurity versus transparency or genericity versus distinction, for example) to perform anonymity according to the meanings they wish to convey and the particular objectives they wish to achieve. While the study of such subversive performances of anonymity illuminates the meanings central to various particular cases, the performative accomplishment of anonymity is also a general phenomenon that provides a framework for comparative analysis across different environments. The cases of the EZLN and the KKK, cited at the start of this chapter, serve to illustrate this point. While the Zapatistas mask themselves to raise the spirit of Emiliano Zapata, Klan radicals don hoods and cloaks to raise the specters of fallen Confederate soldiers. While their particular symbolism and meanings are quite different (and, ideologically speaking, perhaps even antithetical), they share general performative features (such as the performative accomplishment of mass resistance steeped in nostalgia for a bygone era) that stem from their common anonymous posture. These cases, taken together, help us to see the more general meaning and manifestation of anonymous acts as forms of performance serving to subvert dominant social and political norms.[13] They also help us to see how anonymous performances

[13] Cf. Thompson (1974, 398–400) and Scott (1990, 140–142) on anonymity as a performative tactic of mass social resitance.

subsume individual actors (who become devoid of personal characteristics) under broader critical-cultural standpoints. In this project, DeGloma uses the theme of anonymity as his analytic focal point and guide as he works to link the situational dynamics of anonymous acts to their foundational cultural environments while also comparing cases rooted in fundamentally different performative arenas.

Typological Frameworks and the Analysis of Variations on a Theme

While the "deep structural patterns" (Brekhus 2007, 457) that underlie social life transcend context, time, and level of analysis, they also provide an analytic basis with which to consider how variations of such patterns occur and lead to different subtypes of cases (see also Brekhus 2007, 456–457). After all, "speaking generally does not preclude taking account of difference" (Francis 2015, 15). We can use the variations we observe on the theme of focus, both within and among our cases, to build analytic frameworks with which to focus additional observations and develop our theoretical accounts.[14]

Building on Max Weber's (1949 [1903–1917], 90) notion of ideal types, many scholars have developed *formal typologies* that serve as analytic instruments with which to interpret variations among cases. For example, in his study of the identity management strategies of "gay suburbanites," Wayne Brekhus (2003) distinguishes between "identity peacocks" (those who view gayness as "the essential defining feature of who one is and how one lives" [2003, 35]), "identity chameleons" (48) (those who emphasize different aspects of their identities depending on where they are), and "identity centaurs" (74) (those who always view themselves as a complex combination of integrated identity characteristics). However, while Brekhus's empirical research is focused on variations among gay suburbanites, his ideal typology of identity management strategies is formal and generalizable; it can be applied to a wide variety of otherwise different cases. Likewise, Eviatar Zerubavel (1991) distinguishes between rigid, flexible, and fuzzy sociomental styles of classification. As his eclectic array of examples suggests, Zerubavel's typology of classification styles might be applied to a study of religious sects, political

[14] Glaser and Strauss (2008 [1967]) stress that a grounded formal theory can reveal both unseen similarities and variations among cases. See also Denzin (1978, 48–49) on "ad hoc classificatory systems" and "categorical systems or taxonomies."

parties, academic schools, or a wide variety of other cases. In his study of the erotic dimension of social life, Murray Davis (1983) distinguishes between Jehovanists (who view sex as taboo and have strict rules governing sexual activity), Naturalists (who view sex as natural rather than something dirty or taboo), and Gnostics (who worship sex and seek to violate Jehovanist rules as a part of erotic experience). Davis outlines these ideal types to elucidate the variant sociomental styles of approaching sex and sexuality. However, his typological framework would be equally useful for approaching other morally charged subject matters, such as "explicit" lyrics in commercial music or the legalization of marijuana, for example. All of these scholars develop formal typologies that are applicable well beyond any one empirical case or context.

Such ideal typologies can also tune our attention to the ways that interactive relations often take form as variants (subtypes) of a broader patterned dynamic. For example, when DeGloma (2015) studied the ways that "subversive" and "reactive" agents dispute the past, he emphasized different patterned ways that dueling agents in such mnemonic disputes raise oppositional narrative claims that "take form in dynamic relation to one another" (164). With this approach, he identifies "key distinctions" between different cases and "develop[s] an ideal typology of mnemonic conflict" (164) that distinguishes between disputes over the "existence of the past," the "nature of the past," and the "relevance of the past." Each of these types of mnemonic conflict, he argues, is "more broadly relevant than any of the particular cases" he analyzes (165).[15] Disputes over the existence of the past, the primary mode of dispute relevant to debates over recovered memories of child sexual abuse, also occur with regard to the Armenian Genocide and The Nanking Massacre (168–169). Disputes over the nature of that past, the primary mode of dispute relevant to the conflict over the Vietnam War, also occur with regard to "Bloody Sunday" in Northern Ireland and the establishment of Israeli statehood (174–175). Finally, disputes over the relevance of the past, the mode of dispute that most accurately captures the dynamic tensions over American slavery, also occur with regard to the colonization of the Americas and the criminal convictions of job seekers (179–180). Thus, DeGloma presents "a typology of mnemonic battles that can be used as a framework for comparative analysis and an analytic instrument . . . to guide various empirical studies of conflict over the past" (165).

[15] They are also "equally useful for interpreting cases . . . spanning different . . . levels of analysis—from micro to macro arenas of contestation" (DeGloma 2015, 165).

Taking another example, Reed (2006) develops Alexander's (2006) notion of cultural pragmatics by examining "three classic accounts of culture-in-action from symbolic and structural anthropology: Victor Turner on the Henry II–Thomas Becket social drama, Marshall Sahlins on the arrival of Captain Cook to the Hawaiian Islands, and Clifford Geertz on the Balinese Cockfight" (147). He uses these as exemplary cases illustrating "ideal types of social performance" (147) "whose empirical properties are generalizable in a way useful for further research" (150). Reed refers to the case concerning the conflict between Henry II and Thomas Becket as a "serious social drama" (150) that "exemplifies complicity-in-conflict" in which all parties to the drama "work from within the same deeply felt set of collective representations" (149) and "opposing actors share the same discursive frameworks and value-orientations" (154). Alternatively, Reed argues, the case of Captain Cook's shipwreck shows how "cognitive dissonance" (159) can be the principal aspect of a conflict. Here, opposing parties are rooted in completely different cognitive and moral frameworks. "There is *conflict without complicity*" (160, emphasis in original) and tensions stem from the fact that the dueling actors understand their scenes and actions, as well as the actions of the other party, completely differently. Finally, with regard to Geertz's famous depiction of the Balinese cockfight, we have "a liminoid activity" that "relates *metaphorically* to Balinese society" (164, emphasis in original). With this work, Reed shows us three patterned ways that social contention is performed, and he thereby provides three ideal typical models with which we can examine, interpret, and compare cases of conflict or competition in other arenas and contexts.

Discussion: Honing the Thematic Lens

The strength of using a thematic lens lies in the fact that it can lead to valuable analytic breadth (a basis for fruitful comparisons of otherwise different cases and settings) as well as an alternative footing from which to achieve analytic depth (new insights into the particular cases of a formal comparative set). Moreover, thematic analysis illuminates the complementary character of recurrent social forms and cultural structures that, together, are "fundamental to our meaning-making enterprises" (DeGloma 2015, 183), allowing us to develop a richer understanding of the cases we study. By tuning into such broadly relevant phenomena that tie multiple cases together, ethnographers who use a thematic lens can expose the deep foundations of the interactions, thoughts, feelings, and performances going on in various times and places. Such an approach serves to "demystify individual substantive areas" by revealing their common foundational dynamics (Prus 1987a, 264; see also Corrado 2002, 63). It also allows us to see how patterns are replicated in micro, meso, and macro contexts, helping us to understand the relationship between these levels of analysis (Vaughan 1992, 174, 182–184; Zerubavel 2007, 134–141; DeGloma 2015). Without this perspective, "people involved in the study of social life within any particular specialty," as Prus (1987a, 263) warns, "may be greatly shortchanged theoretically should they neglect research on parallel *processes* in other settings."

By developing a thematic perspective, ethnographers can go into the field and, when exploring particular contexts and cases, actually observe general social forms and processes, social types, and cultural structures (see also Zerubavel 1980). Indeed, such a method of focus invites "a conscious and explicit comparative agenda" (Snow, Morrill, and Anderson 2003, 194; see also Zerubavel 2007; Brekhus 2007, 457). However, despite primarily focusing on a broadly relevant theme, researchers should continue to tell the stories of each main case in the comparative set with enough analytic sophistication to bring them to life for their readers. In addition to respecting local details, combining a thematic focus with such attention to the character of the cases being compared allows us to accomplish three things. First, it shows the strength and durability of the thematic pattern as it holds across multiple dimensions of social life *despite variations* that inevitably become more evident when we attend to the particularities of each case. Second, it allows us to refine our understanding of the social theme at hand and to develop a more robust general theory in the process. Third, it allows us to avoid the mistake of "forcing fit" (Vaughan 1992, 195–197) by bringing the particularities of each case to light and showing exactly how their differences enhance the durability of the thematic pattern. While this process is inherently interpretive at both levels (theme and cases), the researcher remains focused on the theme first and the particular cases second, although she weaves back and forth between these analytic dimensions. Interpretation, in this sense, is focused through the thematic lens to become a means to illuminate the general and particular aspects of the topic at hand.

Finally, such an approach compels us to reflect on the pedagogical value of thematic thinking. As many of us know from experience, using multiple case examples to illustrate the same concept in the classroom often helps students to become more comfortable using those concepts (cf. Becker 1998, 4–5). While Prus (1987a, 267) encourages us to "develop courses focusing on one or more generic processes," such a pedagogical model might not only reflect the strengths of thematic research and analysis, but might also provide the most fruitful path forward in the contemporary drive to structure colleges and universities in terms of interdisciplinarity. In other words, while the thematic lens "provides a unique analytic literacy that cuts across the various subfields of contemporary sociology" (Brekhus 2007, 448), it also provides a technique for developing more complex academic visions that traverse conventional substantive and disciplinary divides. It helps students and researchers to hone in on the analytic utility of the conceptual theme, moving beyond its applicability to any one area or case of substantive concern (trying not to get stuck in one particular application) to be able to think creatively with the concept and apply it elsewhere—to other cases that despite their significant differences, are equally relevant to the thematic focus at hand.

References

Alexander, Jeffrey C. 2004a. "Toward a Theory of Cultural Trauma." In *Cultural Trauma and Collective Identity*, edited by Jeffrey C. Alexander, Ron Eyerman, Bernhard Giesen, Neil J. Smelser, and Piotr Sztompka, 1–30. Berkeley: University of California Press.

Alexander, Jeffrey C. 2004b. "On the Social Construction of Moral Universals: The 'Holocaust' from War Crime to Trauma Drama." In *Cultural Trauma and Collective Identity*, edited by Jeffrey C. Alexander, Ron Eyerman, Bernhard Giesen, Neil J. Smelser, and Piotr Sztompka, 196–263. Berkeley, California: University of California Press.

Alexander, Jeffrey C. 2006. "Cultural Pragmatics: Social Performance Between Ritual and Strategy." In *Social Performance: Symbolic Action, Cultural Pragmatics, and Ritual*, edited by Jeffrey C. Alexander, Bernhard Giesen, and Jason L. Mast, 29–90. Cambridge: Cambridge University Press.

Alexander, Jeffrey C., and Jason L. Mast. 2006. "Introduction: Symbolic Action in Theory and Practice: The Cultural Pragmatics of Symbolic Action." In *Social Performance: Symbolic Action, Cultural Pragmatics, and Ritual*, edited by Jeffrey C. Alexander, Bernhard Giesen, and Jason L. Mast, 1–28. Cambridge: Cambridge University Press.

Alexander, Jeffrey C., and Philip Smith. 1993. "The Discourse of American Civil Society: A New Proposal for Cultural Studies." *Theory and Society* 22, no. 2: 151–207.

Alexander, Jeffrey C., and Philip Smith. 2003. "The Strong Program in Cultural Sociology: Elements of a Structural Hermeneutics." In *The Meanings of Social Life: A Cultural Sociology*, 11–26. Oxford: Oxford University Press.

Backhaus, Gary. 1998. "Georg Simmel as an Eidetic Social Scientist." *Sociological Theory* 16, no. 3: 260–281.

Becker, Howard S. 1998. *Tricks of the Trade: How to Think about Your Research While Doing It*. Chicago: University of Chicago Press.

Blumer, Herbert. 1954. "What Is Wrong with Social Theory?" *American Sociological Review* 19, no. 1: 3–10.

Brekhus, Wayne. 2003. *Peacocks, Chameleons, Centaurs: Gay Suburbia and the Grammar of Social Identity*. Chicago: University of Chicago Press.

Brekhus, Wayne. 2007. "The Rutgers School: A Zerubavelian Culturalist Cognitive Sociology." *European Journal of Social Theory* 10, no. 3: 448–464.

Burawoy, Michael. 1998. "The Extended Case Method." *Sociological Theory* 16, no. 1: 4–33.

Burawoy, Michael. 2009. *The Extended Case Method: Four Countries, Four Decades, Four Great Transformations, and One Theoretical Tradition*. Berkeley: University of California Press.

Chancer, Lynn S. 1992. *Sadomasochism in Everyday Life: The Dynamics of Power and Powerlessness*. New Brunswick, NJ: Rutgers University Press.

Corrado, Marisa. 2002. "Teaching Wedding Rules: How Bridal Workers Negotiate Control Over Their Customers." *Journal of Contemporary Ethnography* 31, no. 1: 33–67.

Coser, Lewis A. 1971. *Masters of Sociological Thought: Ideas in Historical and Social Context*. New York: Harcourt Brace Jovanovich.

Davis, Murray S. 1983. *Smut: Erotic Reality/Obscene Ideology*. Chicago: University of Chicago Press.

DeGloma, Thomas. 2009. "Expanding Trauma Through Space and Time: Mapping the Rhetorical Strategies of Trauma Carrier Groups." *Social Psychology Quarterly* 72, no. 2: 105–122.

DeGloma, Thomas. 2014. *Seeing the Light: The Social Logic of Personal Discovery*. Chicago: University of Chicago Press.

DeGloma, Thomas. 2015. "The Strategies of Mnemonic Battle: On the Alignment of Autobiographical and Collective Memories in Conflicts Over the Past." *American Journal of Cultural Sociology* 3, no. 1: 156–190.

Denzin, Norman K. 1978. *The Research Act: A Theoretical Introduction to Sociological Methods*. New York: McGraw-Hill Book Company.

Eyerman, Ron. 2001. *Cultural Trauma: Slavery and the Formation of African American Identity*. Cambridge: Cambridge University Press.

Francis, Ara. 2015. *Family Trouble: Middle-Class Parents, Children's Problems, and the Disruption of Everyday Life*. New Brunswick, NJ: Rutgers University Press.

Gengler, Amanda M. 2015. "'He's Doing Fine': Hope Work and Emotional Threat Management Among Families of Seriously Ill Children." *Symbolic Interaction* 38, no. 4: 611–630.

Glaser, Barney G., and Anselm L. Strauss. 2008 [1967]. *The Discovery of Grounded Theory: Strategies for Qualitative Research*. New Brunswick, NJ: AldineTransaction.

Goffman, Erving. 1959. *The Presentation of Self in Everyday Life*. New York: Anchor Books, Doubleday.

Goffman, Erving. 1961. *Asylums: Essays on the Social Situation of Mental Patients and Other Inmates*. New York: Anchor Books.

Gubrium, Jaber F., and James A. Holstein. 2000. "The Self in a World of Going Concerns." *Symbolic Interaction* 23, no. 2: 95–115.

Johnston, Erin F. 2013. "'I Was Always This Way . . .': Rhetorics of Continuity in Narratives of Conversion." *Sociological Forum* 28, no. 3: 549–573.

Lofland, John. 1972. Editorial Introduction. *Urban Life and Culture* 1, no. 1: 3–5.

Lofland, John. 1995. "Analytic Ethnography: Features, Failings, and Futures." *Journal of Contemporary Ethnography* 24, no. 1: 30–67.

Loseke, Donileen R. 2009. "Examining Emotion as Discourse: Emotion Codes and Presidential Speeches Justifying War." *Sociological Quarterly* 50, no. 3: 497–524.
Mason-Schrock, Douglas. 1996. "Transsexuals' Narrative Construction of the 'True Self.'" *Social Psychology Quarterly* 59, no. 3: 176–192.
Mullaney, Jamie L. 2006. *Everyone Is NOT Doing It: Abstinence and Personal Identity.* Chicago: University of Chicago Press.
Papadantonakis, Max. 2014. *Coexistence and Conflict: An Ethnography of Street Market Workers in Athens, Greece.* Master's thesis, Department of Cultural Anthropology, Utrecht University.
Prus, Robert. 1987a. "Generic Social Processes: Maximizing Conceptual Development in Ethnographic Research." *Journal of Contemporary Ethnography* 16, no. 3: 250–293.
Prus, Robert. 1987b. "Generic Social Processes: Implications of a Processual Theory of Action for Research on Marketplace Exchanges." *Advances in Consumer Research* 14, no. 1: 66–70.
Rambo, Eric, and Chan, Elaine. 1990. "Text, Structure, and Action in Cultural Sociology." *Theory and Society* 19, no. 5: 635–648.
Reed, Isaac. 2006. "Social Dramas, Shipwrecks, and Cockfights: Conflict and Complicity in Social Performance." In *Social Performance: Symbolic Action, Cultural Pragmatics, and Ritual*, edited by Jeffrey C. Alexander, Bernhard Giesen, and Jason L. Mast, 146–168. Cambridge: Cambridge University Press.
Scott, James C. 1990. *Domination and the Arts of Resistance: Hidden Transcripts.* New Haven: Yale University Press.
Simmel, Georg. 1909. "The Problem of Sociology." *American Journal of Sociology* 15, no. 3: 289–320.
Simmel, Georg. 1950a. "The Field of Sociology". In *The Sociology of Georg Simmel*, edited by Kurt H. Wolff, 3–25. New York: The Free Press.
Simmel, Georg. 1950b. "The Stranger." In *The Sociology of Georg Simmel*, edited by Kurt H. Wolff, 402–408. New York: The Free Press.
Smith, Philip. 2005. *Why War? The Cultural Logic of Iraq, the Gulf War, and Suez.* Chicago: University of Chicago Press.
Snow, David A., Calvin Morrill, and Leon Anderson. 2003. "Elaborating Analytic Ethnography: Linking Fieldwork and Theory." *Ethnography* 4, no. 2: 181–200.
Strauss, Anselm. 1970. "Discovering New Theory from Previous Theory." In *Human Nature and Collective Behavior: Papers in Honor or Herbert Blumer*, edited by Tamotsu Shibutani, 46–53. New Brunswick, NJ: Transaction Books.
Tavory, Iddo, and Stefan Timmermans. 2014. *Abductive Analysis: Theorizing Qualitative Research.* Chicago: University of Chicago Press.
Thompson, E. P. 1974. "Patrician Society, Plebeian Culture." *Journal of Social History* 7, no. 4: 382–405.
Timmermans, Stefan, and Iddo Tavory. 2012. "Theory Construction in Qualitative Research: From Grounded Theory to Abductive Analysis." *Sociological Theory* 30, no. 3: 167–186.
Vaughan, Diane. 1992. "Theory Elaboration: The Heuristics of Case Analysis." In *What is a Case? Exploring the Foundations of Social Inquiry*, edited by Charles C. Ragin and Howard S. Becker, 173–202. Cambridge: Cambridge University Press.
Wagner-Pacifici, Robin. 1994. *Discourse and Destruction: The City of Philadelphia versus MOVE.* Chicago: University of Chicago Press.

Wagner-Pacifici, Robin, and Barry Schwartz. 1991. "The Vietnam Veterans Memorial: Commemorating a Difficult Past." *American Journal of Sociology* 97, no. 2: 376–420.

Weber, Max. 1949 [1903–1917]. *The Methodology of the Social Sciences.* Glencoe, Illinois: The Free Press.

Winchester, Daniel. 2015. "Converting to Continuity: Temporality and Self in Eastern Orthodox Conversion Narratives." *Journal for the Scientific Study of Religion* 54, no. 3: 439–460.

Zerubavel, Eviatar. 1980. "If Simmel Were a Fieldworker: On Formal Sociological Theory and Analytical Field Research." *Symbolic Interaction* 3, no. 2: 25–34.

Zerubavel, Eviatar. 1991. *The Fine Line: Making Distinctions in Everyday Life.* Chicago: University of Chicago Press.

Zerubavel, Eviatar. 2003. *Time Maps: Collective Memory and the Social Shape of the Past.* Chicago: University of Chicago Press.

Zerubavel, Eviatar. 2007. "Generally Speaking: The Logic and Mechanics of Social Pattern Analysis." *Sociological Forum* 22, no. 2: 1–15.

4

Comparative Ethnographic Views of Social Structure

The Challenge of Linking Micro and Macro Levels of Analysis

Aaron V. Cicourel

> Cellular functions arise from an intricate network of macromolecular interactions. Hence it is of fundamental importance to decipher this "molecular sociology" of cells ideally by direct visualization (1). Cryo-electron tomography (cryo-ET) provides three-dimensional (3D) images of cellular landscapes at increasingly higher resolutions; with cellular fractionations, subnanometer resolutions have been attained (2,3) (969). . . . . In conclusion (972), the volumes reconstructed from these data reveal that many macromolecular complexes can be visually recognized without the need for computerized averaging approaches and provide insight into structural variations at the level of individual complexes. Assisted by the synergistic application of recent technical developments, cryo-ET holds promise for revealing the molecular organization giving rise to cellular function in unperturbed environments.
>
> —Mahamid et al., "Visualizing the Molecular Sociology at the HeLa Cell Nuclear Periphery" (2016)

Introduction

In the introductory part of this chapter, we provide a brief case study of institutionalized organizational problems necessary for synchronizing specialty

Aaron V. Cicourel, *Comparative Ethnographic Views of Social Structure* In: *Beyond the Case.* Edited by: Corey M. Abramson and Neil Gong, Oxford University Press (2020). © Oxford University Press.
DOI: 10.1093/oso/9780190608484.003.0005

clinical scheduling.[1] The chapter compares what are often called "micro" and "macro" levels of social structure. The micro level refers to social cognition, linguistic anthropology/sociolinguistics, cognitive linguistics, and the use of recorded, moment-to-moment analogical, thinking, relational reasoning (Holyoak 2012; Lombrozo 2012) and vocal explanations achieved "by iteratively re-representing in different representation formats what its internal representations represent" (Karmiloff-Smith 1992, 15).

Karmiloff-Smith's concept of "representational re-description" refers to the human capacity to synthesize, compress, and summarize our emergent conscious and unconscious experiences by going beyond the limitations of human sensory capacities.

Macro "social structure," therefore, relies on compressed, summarized accounts of perceived, written depictions of verbal reports of socially organized institutionalized activities such as creating demographic, census, sample survey, and open-ended interview accounts. In practice, the latter reference to "interview accounts" masks essential micro, moment-to-moment, behavioral, daily, real-time, real-life, tacit, and descriptive organizational achievements.

Micro research requires time-consuming, negotiated, ethnographic entry into communal real-time, real-life, verbal, nonverbal, cognitive, emotional, moment-to-moment daily life; recorded, situated language use.

Macro theories of social structure rely on methods contingent on presumed uniform standardized language use and elicitation procedures inherent in dictionary definitions whose compositionally based summaries make possible the creation of normatively "structured" information about attitudes, opinions, and belief systems, and correlating the latter with comparative demographic changes.

Macro theory and data, therefore, are useful for addressing global or national generalizations, abstract policy issues contingent on normatively enabled, standardized forms of reasoning and quantitative outcomes; that is, concepts presumed to be simulating real-time, real-life decisions, but which fail to satisfy Egon Brunswik's (1957) concept of "ecological validity" and "behavioral ecological" research by biologists described in the following sections. Brunswik notes his discipline, cognitive experimental psychology, is often labeled as "a science of the organism" rather than the more appropriate study of the organism's "contact and interaction with the environment" (1957, 6).

[1] The chapter has benefited from Corey Abramson's thoughtful and useful editorial suggestions.

Ecological validity, therefore, requires comparison of laboratory (psychometric, sample survey) controlled memory retrieval of testing tasks, with real-time, real-life ecological conditions whereby patients (test subjects) are asked to explain their understanding of each test item.

The "environment" refers to "objective surroundings as the 'ecology' of an individual or species" (Brunswick 1957, 6); that is, actual daily life conditions of communal language use and living, in contrast to such details about the experimental environment itself and the subject's comprehension of the experimental task, all of which are unexamined situated, moment-to-moment antecedent behavioral details presumed to be self-evident.

The Importance of Moving Beyond Nonsituated Macro Structure

By necessity, macro theory and methods eschew the study of real-time, real-life, metaphoric, metonymic speech and nonverbal communication, essential for the creation and understanding of structural phenomena.

Macro research, therefore, ignores invariant, socially organized, cognitive, analogical, relational reasoning, language use, episodic, conscious, and procedural unconscious memory (Squire and Kandel 1999) enabling "concepts" presupposed in fixed-choice, sample survey questions. Macro research is contingent on standardized, fixed-choice questionnaires, and normatively guided coding rules insuring the choices given to respondents justify the assignment of digital outcomes. Coding standardized dictionary language using denumerable digital measures remains a serious theoretical and methodological conundrum; the compositional language mappings do not satisfy real-time, daily, real-life attributions of metaphorical, metonymical meanings constructed enabled by mundane communal life.

While contemporary theories often attempt to move beyond these divides, the reliance on sample-survey methods and the professional publishing contexts in which empirical social science is evaluated reifies these dualisms.

Integrating Ethnography and Experimental Insights of Language and Cognition

Rumelhart and Abramson (1973, 1–2) refer to experimental research necessary for retrieval of "*structure*, as opposed to the *content* of organized memory." Achieving macro methods requires standardized, factual, compositional, normative, episodic memory "to answer a question. . . . [that] might be called remembering" (1–2). Experimental tasks (similar to controlled psychometric tests, sample surveys, demographic data), therefore, create normative, daily life structural tasks subjects can resolve by immediate conscious remembrance. In other words, they can contribute to our understanding of micro structures (with important caveats to be discussed).

Retrieval of memory content necessary for analogical "reasoning" with "words," note Rumelhart and Abramson (1973, 2), only occurs if "specific information is not available [to answer a structural question and assumes] one can consult the stored semantic meaning of the words in question and one's knowledge of history to derive a plausible answer."

However, Rumelhart and Abramson underscore a *key issue* vis-à-vis remembering and reasoning analogically:

> In conclusion then it should be clear that we are not proposing that this [mathematical] model of analogical reasoning is completely general. It seems rather that the semantic relationships among certain sets of concepts can be represented by a multidimensional structure. (1973, 27–28)

Rumelhart and Abramson thus firmly acknowledge that when "relations among words . . . are not well represented in a multidimensional space," we must view processing "multidimensional representation space as a special case" of daily life analogical, relational cognitive processing (1973, 27).

Rumelhart and Abramson's truncated reference to "relations among words" can be clarified by two metonymical expressions. The first is well-known to cognitive linguists (Langacker 1986, 1988; Fillmore 1982; Fauconnier and Turner 2002, Lakoff and Johnson 1980, among many others) and presuppose qualitative, daily life, ecological, ethnographic settings. For example:

> The ham sandwich walked out without paying.

Readers are assumed to be capable of activating a cultural social context known as a restaurant in which two servers were discussing an occasion in which a client had ordered a ham sandwich and subsequently walked out without paying one of the servers. As suggested by Rumelhart and Abramson, "relations among words" (1973, 27) require participants to activate knowledge about local practices and historical activities.

A second metonym was discerned by the author while engaged in research on diagnostic reasoning in a University of California, San Diego (UCSD) clinic. At a meeting pathological and pediatric faculty and pathologist residents discussing patients with infectious diseases, a pathologist was reviewing conditions of existing patients in the infectious disease ward and stated:

> I see that the pseudomonas in 8B went home yesterday.

The pathologist was referring to a patient discharged from room 8B at one of UCSD's hospitals. The "relations among words" is again exemplified by a metonym not readily amenable to algorithmic reasoning (Rumelhart and Abramson 1973, 27).

Both metonyms reflect the use of lexical items, "words," constitutive of everyday language noted by Rumelhart and Abramson (27).

Rumelhart and Abramson clarified the limitations and advantages of a multidimensional, Euclidian model of algorithmic remembrance viewed as a special case of analogical reasoning, but not readily generalizable to ethnographic, real-time, real-life metaphorical, metonymical reasoning constitutive of communal life.

Classic Attempts to Integrate Micro and Macro Structure with Sociological Ethnography

MacIver states that "social structure is for the most part created. Unlike the physical nexus," the social causal nexus "does not exist apart from the objectives and motives of social beings" and requires a methodological strategy that fits the distinctiveness of social events (MacIver 1942, 20–21).

MacIver's cogent remarks presuppose that

> the theoretical presuppositions of method and measurement in sociology cannot be viewed apart from the language that sociologists use in their theorizing and research . . . because linguistic structure and use affects the way people interpret and describe the world to themselves, others, and especially to research social scientists. (Cicourel 1964, 1)

The meanings attributed to language use during the application of research methods presuppose a "theory of instrumentation" and "a theory of data" representative of observed, real-time, real-life, day-to-day communal life.

The way different ethnographic traditions have responded to this challenge is suggestive for integrating micro-level phenomena into macro-level explanation.

The Chicago School and Beyond

During the early part of the twentieth century, a form of micro-level sociological theory and research emerged and often called "urban ethnography." In contrast, earlier and more extensive anthropological research observed, and sometimes recorded, non-Western peoples' day-to-day life during participant observation. Anthropologists engaged in open-ended interviews and informal, moment-to-moment social interaction in different specified and unspecified settings, attempted forms of language use, along with extensive field notes, to represent "interior" and exterior reasoning associated with informants' activities and personal beliefs. The participants thus negotiated perceived practical and normative aspects and constraints of non-Western communal life.

Social philosophical theorists such as pragmatists John Dewey and George Herbert Mead, among others, underscored the centrality of individuals' reflexive "self-conceptions" or sense of "agency"; associated with a sense of "community" derived from face-to-face collaboration, conflict and other forms of interpersonal relationships among neighbors, ethnic, religious loyalties, local commerce, work, and governance. Mead's (1934) social psychological concepts of the "I," the "me," "generalized other," and "taking the role of the other" became essential conceptual resources. Rather than being part of a monolithic Chicago School, mid-twentieth-century approaches to ethnography could be varied in theory and substantively.

Pioneering symbolic interaction research at Indiana University included Edwin Sutherland's (1949) study of white-collar crime, Alfred Lindesmith (1964) on sociological social psychological theory of drug addiction, and Donald Cressey (1971) on incarcerated white-collar criminals. The Indiana group did not refer to "grounded theory" nor "theoretical sampling." A fairly standardized group at the University of Iowa pursed a form of experimental social psychology.

Subsequent symbolic interaction research was notably influenced by B. G. Glaser and Anselm Strauss (1968) and Howard Becker (1963), and included methodologically innovative suggestions on interviewing, proposed the notion of "theoretical sampling" and the concept of "grounded theory," and often became an "insider" of the activity or group being studied. An early study of day-to-day practices in an informally organized setting was pursued by William Foote Whyte in a neighborhood gang in Boston (Whyte 1943).

Socially organized insider decisions were a focus of research by Melville Dalton's doctoral dissertation at the University of Chicago (1959) and employed a convincing methodological strategy during his normal occupational work. Dalton's position as industrial chemist consultant enabled him to observe formal organizational, insider, real-time, moment-to-moment decisions. Although unable to take extensive field notes, there were occasions when Dalton could take substantive notes during lunch breaks, visits to toilet facilities, in his automobile, and evenings at home, all while pursuing his graduate studies.

Dalton states: "In the process of reconstructing interviews, I noted down emphasis made, facial expressions, marks of concern and relief, and other gestures—aware they could mislead—as possible clues to more basic things" (1959, 277).

Sociological field research, therefore, has been reliant on tacit insider folk knowledge, subjective descriptive reports of "native members" *within selective ethnographic settings and practices.*

Early anthropological field research varied according to the focus of a particular person; some sought to acquire information about tacit use of gestures, facial expressions, and prosody while others focused on daily life routinized, communal survival practices, learning and creating an explicit grammar for one or more languages or dialects, relations among enemies and friends, food resources and consumption, living conditions, local kinship structure and practice, and demographic data about a given community.

A Classic of Chicago Symbolic Interaction Field Research

Glaser and Strauss (1968, 1965) on dying is often viewed as a classic example of symbolic interaction field research of the Chicago School. Two following summary statements by the researchers are clear and informative:

> Like *Awareness of Dying*, this book is based on intensive field work involving a combination of observation and interviewing at six hospitals located in the Bay Area of San Francisco. This field work was supplemented with rapid "check-out" or "pinpointing" field work at approximately ten hospitals in Italy, Greece, and Scotland. . . . We choose a number of medical services at

> each [San Francisco] Bay Area Hospital, selected to give us a maximum exposure to different aspects of dying—localess where death was sometimes speedy, sometimes slow; sometimes expected, sometimes unexpected; sometimes anticipated by the patients, sometimes unanticipated, and so on. (Glaser and Strauss 1965, xi–xii)

Glaser and Straus present a convincing account of their work and raise essential research issues (xi–xii and 232–233 in Glaser and Strauss 1965).

> As we said in *Awareness of Dying*, the reader who is unacquainted with this style field research need only imagine the sociologist moving rather freely within each medical service, having announced to the personnel his intention of "studying terminal patients and what happens around them." He trails personnel around the service, watching them at work, sometimes questioning them about details. He sits at the nursing station. He listens to conversations. Occasionally he queries the staff members, either about events he has seen or about events someone has described to him. Sometimes he interviews personnel at considerable length, announcing "an interview," perhaps even using a tape recorder. He sits in on staff meetings. He follows, day to day, the progress of various patients, observing staff interactions with them and conversation about them. He talks with patients, telling them only that he is "studying the hospital." (Glaser and Strauss, 232–233)

The two summary statements by Glaser and Strauss are clear and informative. A few readers (the present author included) might hope for further details, such as recording a given date by each field researcher, detailed excerpts from a recorded staff meeting, and at least one doctor–patient interview, to provide the reader with details about the patient's clinician's reasoning, apparent knowledge of medical issues as they emerged, and how different staff members informally reacted to impending death.

Glaser and Strauss provide a suggestive *summary* of how different actors become aware of local institutional practices vis-à-vis dying.

> Entering a hospital and being admitted to a ward entail a maze of social conditions and processes that give the various concerned persons varying states of awareness of the initial dying trajectory. The definitions become the basis of their ensuing behavior toward each other. These conditions

> and processes result in patient and family awareness of initial definitions, whether or not doctors decide to state them explicitly. (Most doctors hedge and do not clearly disclose "certain" dying.) They give rise to constant debate among the staff as to whether the patient "really knows" when he has not been told. (1965, 50)

The language and reasoning employed by different actors is not pursued, but the breadth and depth of the authors' descriptive vocabulary is convincing in ways not achieved by digital summaries using survey and demographic data. The authors, however, do not probe subtleties of actual connected speech acts suggesting pending death, nor the way "most doctors hedge." Thus, an artifact and limitation of this approach is that it does not succeed in going beyond truncated, descriptive materials, and does not include sufficient details of actual language use and reasoning, and is a drawback of their approach.

But they did succeed in going beyond the dominant quantitative aggregations of their era, which missed in situ opportunities entirely. The work, however, still represents a missed opportunity of being attentive to language use that is indicative of problems in most sociological approaches (including ethnographic traditions).

One of the few quoted statements by staff occurs in a section on *Dying at Home*:

> "So often we don't get in on terminal cases until close to the end. It would be much better to start when they are still in the hospital. . . . It's so much better if, before the family faces the pressures and emotion of the patient home from the hospital. I can tell them about the disease, and what they will be able to do to work with us." She concluded her remarks with, "They need more preparation when they know it's going to be a long thing, chronic or terminal." So, to some extent, the nurse coaches a responsible family member about what to expect in the way of bodily deterioration and worsening symptoms, and the change of work that probably will be entailed by the patient's decline: "We talk to them about the nature of the disease and what to expect and how to take care of it." (Glaser and Strauss 1965, 77)

The descriptive narrative attributed to a nurse by Glaser and Strauss appears to be a response to a question by a member of their research team. The question is not included, and additional details are absent. The nurse implies that terminally ill patients are often seen at home rather than in the hospital.

No case is presented on how the nurse spoke with family members before leaving the hospital. The reader cannot follow a verbatim transcript of interaction between hospital staff and family members. Nor is there a recording of how members of the hospital staff or the attending physician spoke to a terminally ill patient.

The authors then refer to death as a complete surprise:

> In general, the greatest surprise impact from an expected quick trajectory occurs in the case of a patient who was not expected to die, but who was indeed, expected to make a complete recovery. The essence of the complete surprise when a patient goes into a quick dying trajectory is the low probability of such a reversal, although, as one nurse said, "... Everyone knows that this could happen, but it only happens once in umpteen times. This kind of death is very upsetting to everybody." Her statement referred to the explosion of the anesthetic in a patient's chest, but it could just as well apply to any other source of unexpected quick dying in hospitals—suicide, drug effects, heart arrest, hospital accident, respiration difficulties, etc. As we saw in Chapter II, if the patient has been on several wards, a good portion of hospital staff can become distressed over the sudden death of a patient on the mend. (Glazer and Strauss 1986, 132)

Additional selective cases might have clarified how families differed across economic, ethnic, religious, and educational levels of the six California hospitals. An attentiveness to detailed speech acts, such as conversations inherent in all ethnographic comparisons, how they emerge and operate in different contexts, would have advanced and helped refine Glaser and Strauss's insights.

Parallel Biological, Nonhuman, Field, and Experimental Research

Behavioral biological ecologists (Davies, Krebs, and West 2012) rely on recorded, moment-to-moment, ethnographic observation of nonhuman ecological evolution; day-to-day behavioral survival skills in the wild, and subsequently under controlled laboratory conditions. Behavioral ecologists rely on human theories of micro social structure to frame their research in the wild and in laboratory settings. The following passage provides a useful introductory summary:

> Our aim was to understand how behaviour evolves in the natural world. This requires links between studies of behaviour, evolution and ecology. The link with evolution is central because we expect natural selection to favour those behaviour patterns which maximize an individual's chances of surviving and passing copies of its genes on to future generations. The link with ecology comes in because ecology sets the stage on which individuals play their behavior, so the best way to behave depends on ecological selection pressures, such as the distribution in space and time of food, enemies and places to live. The social environment will be important too, because individuals will often have to compete for scarce resources. So we need to consider how behavior evolves when there are social interactions with the potential for both conflict and cooperation. (Davies et al. 2012, x–xii)

The quotation, in contrast to macro demographic, economic, and sociological theory and research, seeks a direct link between the moment-to-moment details of molecular, behavioral, and social levels of social interaction and explanation.

Collective evolutionary survival requires adaptive forms of living constrained and fostered by social conflict, cooperation, and individual competition for scarce resources. The latter conditions can only be speculatively inferred in macro sociological research because it eschews the study of real-time, real-life behavioral activities.

Davies and colleagues continue:

> Clayton's second study investigated "social cognition": the ability of a bird to behave as though it could [attribute and] interpret the knowledge of another individual. Dally et al. (2006) found that when a scrub jay had been observed by another individual whilst catching food, it would later on in private, move its caches to new locations, as though it were aware of the fact that it had been observed and that the observer might pilfer the caches. Furthermore, the jays re-cached more of their food items when they had been observed by a dominant bird, than when they have been observed by their partner or by a subordinate bird. There is also an intriguing hint that birds that have pilfered themselves are more likely to move their caches when they have been observed, a case of "it takes a thief to know a thief" (Emery and Clayton 2001). (Davies et al. 2012, 71–72)

Davies et al. have presented a convincing "relationship between ecology, behavior, and the brain."

The case of humans described next, and Brunswik's concept of ecology, include the cultural invention of local, normative, and situated social ties; uses of complex artifacts; the activation of extensive conversational encounters; and that these are sustained by different memory resources essential for real-life, moment-to-moment remembrance and reasoning.

The Everyday Presentation of Self

Erving Goffman's (1953) unpublished PhD dissertation at the University of Chicago is an example of selective descriptive scenarios of daily life on a Shetland Island. While not ethnographic in the sense described earlier (he does not provide the reader with recordings of actual real-time, real-life details), Goffman's well-known works have received considerable praise for his unusual simulation of elements of ethnographic field research, and curiously have convinced some readers they represent actual, real-time, real-life settings.

For example, the first paragraph of Goffman's book states:

> When an individual enters the presence of others, they commonly seek to acquire information about him or to bring into play information about him already possessed. They will be interested in his general socio-economic status, his conception of self, his attitude toward them, his competence, trustworthiness, etc. Although some of this information seems to be sought almost as an end in itself, there are usually quite practical reasons for acquiring it. Information about the individual helps to define the situation, enabling others to know in advance what he will expect of them and what they may expect of him. Informed in these ways, the others will know how best to act in order to call forth a desired response from him. (1956, 1)

Goffman's succinct opening remarks is a clever summarization of micro sociology or what was often called "sociological social psychology."

Goffman's view of everyday social interaction is unique in the sense that no discussion of sampling, or what counts as evidence and received theory, much less methodology, are required. Goffman's style, though impressive, is difficult to describe, and not readily integrated with sociological ethnography.

My work has attempted to show an alternative perspective, that at best comparative ethnography can employ rigorous observation of language use in comparative contexts to show both contextual variation and micro-invariances to enable a comprehensible social world (Cicourel, 2011). I provide a brief example of the conditions necessary for enabling an important, taken-for-granted practice—the scheduling of appointments at a specialty medical clinic.

I observed, for over several months, the daily work activities of "Sari," a patient coordinator in a university hospital medical specialty clinic. Brief excerpts are presented of the social interaction between Sari and an attending physician to illustrate ethnographic aspects of organizational constraints inherent in healthcare delivery. The brief exchange is part of a larger study (Cicourel 2002) of Sari's often hectic daily life interaction with attending, board-certified clinicians.

Sari, like all participants in institutionally organized settings, must cope with "cognitive overload" consisting of simultaneous demands on one's attention (e.g., simultaneous telephone calls, computer work, and face-to-face messages from physicians, nurses, patients, and other clinic personnel). Essential for Sari's ability to cope with continuous cognitive overload was the use of compressed brief summaries about her work, such as handwritten annotative marks on slips of paper, and truncated remarks on documents necessary to complete organizational reports.

Sara's annotative attempts to recover the gist of activities before, during, and after frequent interruptions—sustained, daily structural accounts of "what happened"—are continually absent from administrative and demographic records. Daily clinic exchanges with and about a patient's condition and future are a selective part of what is reported as "objective" information about a patient's clinical record.

Interruptions always have the potential to shift the professional and client/patient's attention away from ongoing information processing, thereby "erasing" or modifying the patient and clinical personnel's working memory.

Sari's work required giving patients instructions about a liquid food diet the day before a procedure, and no medications containing aspirin. She had to verify that the clinical procedures were available (such as suites containing apparatuses for endoscopies, flexible sigmoidoscopies, colonoscopies, and pulmonary procedures). Sari's daily workload included parallel processing obstacles: phone calls, email, patients coming to her workstation, and visits of a variety of clinical healthcare personnel.

The following brief, recorded fragments of longer speech events were recorded by me (Cicourel 2002) sitting nearby.

The speech event began when a physician and patient approached Sari (Box 4.1, while she was busily scheduling procedures for other physicians' patients. The approaching physician, accompanied by a new patient, contributed to her cognitive overload when the physician asked, with a very brief salutation, for Sari's help to enable the patient to receive an unexpected medical procedure (in what sounded like a firm, authoritative voice).

Box 4.1 Paper7_Cicourel_Levels

Figure 1: Exchange with physician at Sari's workstation while she continued to work on two prior scheduling tasks as the physician began speaking to her.

1: Sari—Hi.
2: Dr—Uhh, I was wondering if you could
3: do an endoscopy on her today?
4: Sari—Today? (rising voice intonation and also a troubled facial expression)
5: Dr—Yeah
6: Sari—I don't think there's any more room today,
7: 'cause I was doing good
8: to get the two that I got.
9: Dr—Okay. Well, just check on it (?)
10: (Sari—okay) (not clear)

Lines 6–8 suggest Sari is engaged in mental simulation, described by Rumelhart (1989); for example, imagining some action and the consequences that might follow in order to resolve a problem.

Redescription (Karmiloff-Smith 1992) by Sari was necessary to process a complex but unlikely solution, which activated her experiences with bureaucratic obstacles associated with the problem at hand (colloquially described in lines 6–8).

The physician's request Box 4.1, in lines 2–3 and 9–10, is characteristic of interruptions Sari experienced daily in the specialty clinic.

Sari did not tell the clinician to wait before he began speaking, but he observed her hurried actions at the computer, and suddenly did not continue speaking for a few moments while she completed entering information for two new scheduling tasks. Sari then turned slightly to her right and looked in the direction of where the physician was standing.

The physician's question in lines 2–3 could be viewed metaphorically as "saying" Sari would be "doing" the procedure instead of the physician.

I perceived Sari as expressing an apparent, diminished drop of a few decibels in her intonation, signaling discomfort, but she did not look into the physician's eyes, and her facial expression appeared firmer than usual.

The latter subjective redescriptive observations would have been more convincing had I been allowed to videotape elements of silent differences and collaboration noted earlier.

The physician's request for another endoscopy during an already crowded clinic schedule appeared stressful for Sari based on her subsequent guarded remarks to me, and my subjective assessment of her facial expressions and voice intonation.

Sari's subsequent suggestion that the physician alter *his* schedule and not give his patient an endoscopy that same day would have challenged the physician's professional relationship with Sari, and his subsequent personal plans.

The "hedge" or linguistic speech markers by Sari ("wondering," lines 2–3), and the physician's subsequent metaphorical request (line 9, "Okay. Well, just check on it") can be viewed as an indirect order in response to Sari's metaphorical remarks in lines 6–8 ("I don't think there's any more room today, 'cause I was doing good to get the two that I got").

Sari's voice intonation suggested anxiety (which she subsequently reported), unless the physician assured her that he would allow his clinic personnel to go beyond the usual bureaucratically scheduled time period. The attending would have had to agree to go beyond the authorized organized scheduled time period, or else she could not schedule an endoscopy for the patient standing to her right.

The example of Sari's conundrum illustrates what the work of Glaser and Strauss, Goffman, and the Chicago School miss vis-à-vis comparative ethnography: the inherent role of recorded, moment-to-moment, complex redescriptive nonverbal and speech acts that are foundational of communal life.

Methodological Concerns in Linking Micro and Macro Structure

Sociologist Charles Tilly (1998) describes useful, plausible elements of micro and macro theories of social structure, but not how to proceed empirically. For example: "Structural theorizing" (Tilly 1998), a meta-level theoretical frame of reference, refers to structural representational measures of a population, or "ontologies" and "standard stories." Tilly (1998, 37–39) states ontologies fail to distinguish between folk theories or "stories" of daily social life by individual and collective actors, and accounts of causal events. He notes that "methodological individualism" suffers from the same problem because of "insisting on human individuals as the basic or unique social reality... [yet in] more economistic versions... the person in question contains a utility schedule and a set of assets, which interact to generate choice within well-defined constraints" (39). Yet this view includes "a market-like allocated structure that is external to the choice-making individual . . . [and] rarely [do] methodological individualists examine by what means those allocated structures actually do their work" (40).

Tilly alludes to observable activities and settings but leaves it to the reader to imagine the kinds of studies and evidence that would clarify the work of social interaction and conversation in face-to-face or electronic encounters, and the way documents are written and interpreted.

While he does not elaborate the connection to the comparative observational methods I describe, "holism" is an important doctrine Tilly has addressed with considerable skill. For Tilly, holism is defined as

> the doctrine that social structures have their own self-sustaining logics. In its extreme form—once quite common in history but now unfashionable—a whole civilization, society, or culture undergoes a life of its own. Less extreme versions attribute self-producing powers to major institutions, treat certain segments of society as subordinating the rest to their interests, represent dominant mentalities, traditions, values, or cultural forms as regulators of social life, or assign inherent self-reproducing logics to industrialism, capitalism, feudalism, and other distinguishable varieties of social organization. (1998, 40)

Holism must examine "to what extent, how, and why small-scale social life, including individual experience, articulates with these overarching patterns"

(1998, 40). Tilly underscores his view of the concept of "social structures" as being reified by the theoretical notion of "holism."

"Relational realism," the fourth, and Tilly's favored, alternative doctrine, refers to

> transactions, interactions, social ties, and conversations constitute the central stuff of social life, once predominated in social science, if not history, concentrates on connections that concatenate, aggregate and disaggregate readily, from organizational structures at the same time as they shape individual behavior. Relational analysts follow flows of communication, patron-client chains, employment networks, conversational connections, and power relations from the small scale to the large and back. (1998, 41)

The redescriptive details attributed to the relational realist "portray both individuals and collectivities as continuously changing products of interaction" (Tilly 1998, 43), and they "incessantly invoke indirect effects, cumulative effects, unintended effects, and effects mediated by the non-human environment."

The notion of a realist, therefore, metaphorically "covers the waterfront" but lacks a wide spectrum of unspecified "effects." "Standard stories refers" to "stories in which connected, self-propelled actors, individual or collective, cause events, outcomes, and each other's actions" (Tilly 1998, 42–43).

A key point (Tilly 1998, 46) is that when "standard stories" are the products of research, they make explanations of daily social life difficult and restrict our ability to link micro and macro processes. Social processes said to contradict standard stories are conditions of "inequality, organizational change, contentious politics, network-mediated communication, state transformation, revolutionary struggle, labor market operation, nationalism, and migration" (46). To summarize, the everywhere dense, essential details of daily life presupposed by the concept of standard stories become insurmountable obstacles by ignoring inherent, detailed, communicative processes of ethnography.

Macro theory and research thus conveniently ignore essential details of daily life; instead of leveraging details to provide a more valid and nuanced link between micro and macro, macro theory often reproduces standard stories that are empirically misleading.

Achieving Demographic Comparability

Demographic theory and research exemplify Euclidian multidimensional modeling while ignoring real-time, observable behavioral data and ecological validity. Keyfitz (1975), a distinguished demographer, embraced the modeling, but challenged the absence of behavioral data.

The problems identified here are often seen clearly in demographic work. Demographic theory and research exemplify Euclidean multidimensional modeling while ignoring real-time, real-life, observable behavioral data and ecological validity. Keyfitz (1975) embraced the modeling, but also challenged the absence of behavioral data.

Federal, statewide, county, and city bureaucratic agencies routinely elicit, classify, and make available a number of useful aggregated human demographic characteristics. The reader, however, is required to imagine the likely behavioral activities possible.

Lenoir (1995) addressed elements of thinking that might have led to the development of demographic big-picture categories useful for summarizing and assessing a large range of social, economic, environmental, and political conditions within a society. Lenoir refers to a correspondence between "demographic thinking" and "state thinking" that enabled demography to grow and consolidate its legitimacy.

The categories used by nineteenth-century French governmental registry offices emulated those employed by demographers. The diffusion of demographic categories helped to create an aura of bureaucratic neutrality and contributed to their legitimacy when used by the state, and subsequently by academic and commercial research groups.

The creation and existence of currently even larger datasets has hugely extended speculative social science and historical interpretation of macro data. The data have become especially popular with macro social scientists dedicated to modeling policy issues and influencing political change. Even proponents of "big data" acknowledge the danger of using ever-larger data sets to produce findings that are "precisely incorrect" (McFarland and McFarland 2015) and whose ecological invalidity is weak (Cicourel 1982).

Keyfitz begins his classic theoretical paper endorsing mathematical modeling as enabling the avoidance of "the irregularity of empirical [demographic] data as they appear in charts and tables" (1975, 267). Mathematical modeling, states Keyfitz, avoids flawed secondary data derived from sample surveys, and organizational practices such as those at census bureaus and local, national, and world health organizations.

Cultural factors, notes Keyfitz, compromise the use of quality empirical data. He begins with a familiar demographic finding:

> Demographers know that a population that is increasing slowly has a higher proportion of old people than one that is increasing rapidly; and that differences in birth rates have a larger influence on the age distribution than do differences in death rates. They also often claim that a poor country whose population is growing rapidly will increase its income per head faster if it lowers its birth rate than if it maintains a high birth rate. (Keyfitz 1975, 267)

Keyfitz's reference to received demographic theory and data underscores macro research on fertility, population growth, and decline, and then challenges this received knowledge.

> How do demographers know these things? Many readers will be surprised to learn that in a science thought of as empirical, often criticized for its lack of theory, the most important relations cannot be established by direct observation, which tends to provide enigmatic and inconsistent reports. (1975, 267)

Keyfitz underscores a basic challenge to macro theory an inability to show that "the most important relations cannot be established by direct observation . . . [and the danger of creating] enigmatic and inconsistent reports" (267). Thus, direct observation remains a conundrum in demography. Keyfitz adds:

> Yet this argument is in the end unconvincing . . . To know the net drop in overall fertility as a result of the restriction requires behavioral data. That alone can discriminate between the competing models and predict the quantitative effects of an induced change in age of marriage. (1975, 277)

Keyfitz's remarks on the essential role of behavioral data and direct observation are exceptionally cogent, despite not having been pursued empirically. We are left with insightful possibilities, despite the lack of empirical details on the theories and measures necessary to satisfy the demands of ecological validity.

Economic Micro and Macro Levels of Analysis

A "micro–macro" perspective by the economist Brian Arthur refers to an interdependence between of levels of analysis and notes: "Complexity portrays the economy not as deterministic, predictable, and mechanistic, but as process dependent, organic, and always evolving" (1999, 107–109). Arthur continues:

> Common to all studies on complexity are systems with multiple elements adapting or reacting to the pattern these elements create. . . . Elements and the patterns they respond to vary from one context to another. But the elements adapt to the world—the aggregate pattern—they co-create. Time enters naturally here via the processes of adjustment and change: As the elements react, the aggregate changes; as the aggregate changes, elements react anew. Barring the reaching of some asymptotic state or equilibrium, complex systems are systems in process that constantly evolve and unfold over time. . . . But unlike ions in a spin glass, which always react in a simple way to their local magnetic field, economic elements (human agents) react with strategy and foresight by considering outcomes that might result as a consequence of behavior they might undertake. This adds a layer of complication to economics that is not experienced in the natural sciences. (107–108)

Arthur underscores an unavoidable, invariant interpenetrative dynamic: the contextual nature of complexity inherent in the social sciences "not experienced in the natural sciences." The inherent contextual complexity of the behavioral and social sciences noted here requires the study of moment-to-moment nonverbal, observational theory, methods, and authentic speech events, yet are pursued in a minimal way by only a few research scholars. Arthur notes the way agents "react with strategy and foresight by considering outcomes that might result [due to] behavior they might undertake."

Thus agents constantly rely on self-conscious, subconscious, reflexive, evolving cognitive mechanisms enabling the cocreation of evolving, process-dependent systems "with multiple elements adapting or reacting to the pattern these elements create."

Arthur continues:

> Conventional economic theory chooses not to study the unfolding of the patterns its agents create but rather to simplify its questions in order to seek

> analytical solutions. Thus it asks what behavioral elements (actions, strategies, and expectations) are consistent with the aggregate patterns these behavioral elements co-create . . . ? Conventional economics thus studies consistent patterns: patterns in behavioral equilibrium that would induce no further reaction. (1999, 107–108)

A salient point noted by Arthur is how economists (all macro social scientists) focus on net-aggregated levels of analysis while ignoring "the unfolding of the [behavioral] patterns its agents create."

The complication that human agents add to economic (and other cognitive, affective, cultural, and social) choices includes recognizing that emergent behavior is contingent on summarizations of perceived interpersonal and organizational constraints and consequences. Essential conditions of Arthur's reference to the "how" of "the unfolding . . . patterns its agents create" are contingent on social action motivated by the individual and collectively perceived constraints.

Even when they acknowledge insights about the connections between context and in situ behavior, economists and most sociologists and political scientists do not directly study real-time, real-life processes or adjustment and change by observing how agents in real-time, real-life organizations interact moment-to-moment during daily life, nor do they address the effects of variation in the way individuals experience limited capacity processing constraints in making decisions. Hence, the continued importance of leveraging theoretical and empirical linkages offered by comparative sociological ethnography.

Implications for Theory and Practice of Social Science; Two Forms of Reasoning in Micro and Macro Research

Earlier in the chapter, following Rumelhart and Abramson (1973), a distinction was made between two forms of analogical thinking; the first is viewed as measurable using Euclidian multidimensional space based on subjects' problem-solving ability to readily pursue *structural* cognitive problems relying on conscious, episodic remembrance memory based on similarity judgments using tasks with a scale from zero to ten, where zero indicated two objects were identical, and a value of ten signified that two objects were highly different.

Rumelhart and Abramson, however, in their final closing page, state that their model could be viewed as a special case of multidimensional, analogical problem-solving when patterned experimental tasks were employed, but noted the algorithms employed were not sustainable if they required unraveling complex (noncompositional) semantic meaning of relationships among words.

In a subsequent paper, which I will paraphrase here, Rumelhart (1989) directly acknowledged that qualitative analogical reasoning was required to resolve novel, daily life problems typical of real-time, real-life, individual and collective multiparty problem-solving. Rumelhart's summary of cognitive elements essential for daily life reasoning is captured in the following remarks. Reasoning in novel settings requires three common processes to understand how subjects become familiar with problem-solving tasks.

Rumelhart's 1989 paper will be viewed as applicable to elements of attempted collaborative problem-solving between clinicians and patients within the healthcare clinic activities described earlier. For example:

1. Reasoning by similarity or the ability to invoke a solution to a known, previous, problem-solving task requires deciding if it is similar to a current situation typical of real-time, real-life settings.
2. Reasoning by mental simulation, namely, imagining some action, and the consequences that follow when solving a problem, requires redescription to achieve task solutions.
3. The latter process activates implicit knowledge associated with episodic and procedural memory of a problem.

Practicing physicians' emergent tacit knowledge from unconscious procedural memory, and identifying explicit episodic conscious memory, create patient accounts of past clinical experiences to guide the way clinicians look for similar and different symptoms, thus enabling formal, abstract, redescriptive aspects of symptoms in medical histories.

For example, in the case of a patient with a possible infectious disease, the physician begins with eliciting redescriptive episodic memory information from the patient about a possible recent visit to a restaurant, farm, geographical locations such as an outing in uninhabited countryside, or a camping trip. If no leads emerge with this line of questioning, the physician may ask the patient about home living conditions (e.g., pets in the house, foods consumed). An infectious disease specialist, for example, may think a patient's symptoms are similar to those of someone who has been exposed to an infected farm domestic animal or a food source such as shellfish.

Formal reasoning relies on emerging, redescriptive heuristics, and remembering previous problem-solving procedures—for example, carefully titrating medication for a patient, including explicit, redescriptive instructions about when and how to take medication appropriately.

The clinical process I outlined here paraphrases formal theoretical reasoning examples of Rumelhart's (1989) paper and suggests how elements of my empirically oriented medical examples can capture "essential abilities" associated with reaching logical conclusions without having to be logical.

The following essential abilities noted by Rumelhart (1989) are assumed to be helpful in clarifying reasoning processes.

1. *Pattern matching.* This ability enables a person to attend to sensory and mental input while quickly "settling" into interpretation and pattern matching. Physicians, for example, rely on implicit, qualitative reasoning while employing implicit cognitive mechanisms to generate redescriptive interpretations, and obtain redescriptive input from a patient to create an analytic summary.
2. *Modeling the world.* Humans acquire the ability to anticipate new states of affairs as a consequence of direct actions or while observing events.

   Rumelhart also notes that survival would not be possible unless it was feasible for human animals to build up expectations by (redescriptively) representing their experiences internally. Nor could mental simulations be performed unless humans could model taken-for-granted environments. Physicians, for example, immediately begin to imagine possible diagnostic categories and treatments after only a few elicitation procedures and descriptive responses from the patient to perform redescriptive mental simulations even when the patient's responses are vague or abstract, especially if the physician is, for example, an infectious disease specialist.
3. Manipulating the environment. The ability to manipulate elements of the environment is an essential aspect of human tool invention and use.

Direct study of real-time, real-life behavior, and the ability to manipulate physical, biological, and sociocultural systems, enabled humans to redescriptively represent innovative thoughts, relationships, and events engendering sociocultural change during the achievement of unique, routine, practical, intellectual activities.

Concluding Thoughts of the Study of Humans in Situ

David Premack (2004) described cognitive differences between human and nonhuman animals, particularly other primates. While acknowledging the necessity of language use and recursion in human development, he also underscored flexible properties inherent in evolution: human intelligence and problem-solving. For example, humans possess

> the only flexible processes on Earth capable of producing endless solutions to the problems confronted by living creatures . . . although evolution can do "engineering," changing actual structures and producing new devices, it cannot do science, changing imaginary structures and producing new theories or explanations of the world. (Premack 2004, 320)

In *Primate Cognition* (1997, 399–400), Tomasello and Call refer to primate cognitive skills as the ability to discriminate, categorize, and quantify objects in different environmental contexts. Likewise, they note that essential third-party relations probably evolved in social domains in which competitive group social action was necessary to resolve the distribution of limited resources. Such sociocultural notions as "domination" and "alliances," or "agonistic and affiliated relations," are presumed to be outgrowths of nonhuman and human primate competition for limited resources.

Dramatic changes in the adaptive nature of human cognitive development, state Tomasello and Call (1997, 401–402), changed cognition "from a basically individual enterprise to a basically social-collective enterprise."

The evolutionary description of "a basically individual enterprise to a basically social-collective enterprise" refers to comparative psychological and social ways of defining the concept of ecology and social structure, and firmly underscores the essential human ability to ethnographically benefit from in situ study of themselves. Clinical and evidence-based medicine exemplify micro and macro views of the concept of social structure.

This chapter has outlined a few suggestions by which behavioral and social scientists can characterize the concept of social structure by examining concepts and research methods from other disciplines to explain the big-picture or macro-level explanations, and moment-to-moment or micro-level characterizations of evolving human communal life. Unless theoretical concepts and research methods can be developed to integrate the two levels of analysis theoretically and empirically, the concept of social structure will remain ambiguous.

Academic and funding institutions fail to insist that micro-level and macro-level behavioral and social scientists must directly challenge each other conceptually, methodologically, and empirically when employing the concepts of social ecology or social structure.

References

Arthur, W. Brian. 1999. "Complexity and the Economy." *Science* 284 (April 2):107–109.

Becker, Howard S. 1963. *Outsiders, Studies in the Sociology of Deviance*. New York: Free Press.

Brunswik, Egon. 1957. "Scope and Aspects of the Cognitive Problem." In *Contemporary Approaches to Cognition: A Symposium Held at the University of Colorado*, edited by Jerome S. Bruner, 5–31. Cambridge, MA: Harvard University Press.

Cicourel, Aaron V. 1964. *Method and Measurement in Sociology*. New York: Free Press.

Cicourel, Aaron V. 1977. "The Cognitive and Linguistic Aspect of Social Structure." In *Communication & Cognition*, edited by M. de Mey, R. Pinxten, M. Poriau, and F. Vandamme, 25–31. Ghent, Belgium.

Cicourel, A. V. (1982). "Interviews, Surveys, and Ecological Validity." *The American Sociologist* 17, 11–20.

Cicourel, Aaron V. 2002. "La gestion des rendez-vous dans un service médical spécialisé." *Actes de la recherche en sciences sociales* 143: 3–17.

Cicourel, Aaron V. 2011. "Contrasting Reasoning Strategies and Evidence in Micro-Level Clinical Practice and Macro-Level Research and Policies." In *Handbook of Communication and Professions*, edited by S. Sarangi and C. Candlis, 4–61. Berlin: De Gruyter-Mouton.

Cressey, Donald. 1971. *Other People's Money: Study in the Social Psychology of Embezzlement*. Montclair, NJ: Patterson Smith.

Dalton, Melville. 1959. *Men Who Manage*. New York: Wiley.

Davies, N. B., J. R. Krebs, and S. A. West. 2012. *An Introduction to Behavioral Ecology*. Cambridge: Cambridge University Press.

Fauconnier, Gilles, and Mark Turner. 2002. *The Way We Think: Conceptual Blending and the Mind's Hidden Complexities*. New York: Basic Books.

Fillmore, Charles. 1982. "Frame Semantics." In *Linguistics in the Morning Calm*, edited by Linguistic Society of Korea, 111–137. Seoul: Hanshin Publishing Co.

Glaser, B. G., and A. L. Strauss. 1968. *Time for Dying*. Chicago: Aldine

Goffman, Erving. 1953. *Communication Conduct in an Island Community*. PhD diss., Department of Sociology, University of Chicago.

Goffman, Erving. 1956. *The Presentation of Self in Everyday Life*. Edinburgh: University of Edinburgh, Social Sciences Research Centre.

Holyoak, K. J. 2012. "Analogy and Relational Reasoning." In *Oxford Library of Psychology. The Oxford Handbook of Thinking and Reasoning*, edited by K. J. Holyoak and R. G. Morrison, 234–259. New York, NY: Oxford University Press.

Karmiloff-Smith, Annette. 1992. *Beyond Modularity: A Developmental Perspective on Cognitive Science*. Cambridge, MA: MIT Press.

Keyfitz, Nathan. 1975. "How Do We Know the Facts of Demography? *Population and Development Review* 1, no. 2: 267–288.

Lakoff, George, and Mark Johnson. 1980. *Metaphors We Live By*. Chicago: University of Chicago Press.

Langacker, Ronald. 1986. *Foundations of Cognitive Grammar*. Stanford, CA: Stanford University Press.

Lenoir, Remi. 1995. "L'invention de la demographie et la formation de l'etat." *Actes de la recherché en sciences sociales* 108: 36–61.

Lindesmith, Alfred. 1964. *The Addict and the Law*. Bloomington, Indiana: Indiana University Press.

Lombrozo, T. 2012. "Explanation and Abductive Inference." In *Oxford Handbook of Thinking and Reasoning*, edited by K. J. Holyoak and R. G. Morrison, 260–276. Oxford, UK: Oxford University Press.

McFarland, Daniel A., and H. Richard McFarland. 2015. "Big Data and the Danger of Being Precisely Inaccurate." *Big Data & Society* (July–December): 1–4.

MacIver, R. M. 1942. *Social Causation*. Boston: Ginn.

Mahamid, Julia Stefan Pfeffer, Miroslava Schaffer, Elizabeth Villa, Radostin Danev, Luis Kuhn Cuellar, Friedrich Förster, Anthony A. Hyman, Jürgen M. Plitzko, Wolfgang Baumeister. 2016. "Visualizing the Molecular Sociology at the HeLa Cell Nuclear Periphery." *Science* 251, no. 6276 (February 26): 969–97.2

Mead, G. H. 1934. *Mind, Self, and Society*. Chicago: University of Chicago Press.

Premack, David. 2004. "Is Language the Key to Human Intelligence?" *Science* 303, no. 5656: 318–320.

Rumelhart, David. 1989. "Toward a Microstructural Account of Human Reasoning." In *Similarity and Analogical Reasoning*, edited by S. Vosniadou and A. Ortony, 298–312. New York: Cambridge University Press.

Rumelhart, D. E., and A. A. Abramson. 1973. "A Model for Analogical Reasoning." *Cognitive Psychology* 5, no. 1: 1–28.

Squire, L., and E. Kandel. 1999. *Memory: From Mind to Molecules*. New York: Scientific American Library.

Sutherland, Edwin. 1949. *White-Collar Crime*. New York: Dryden.

Tilly, Charles. 1998. "Micro, Macro, or Megrim?" In *Mikrogeschichte—Makrogeschichte: komplementaer oder inkommensurablel?*, edited by Juergen Schlumbohm, 33–51. Goettingen: Wallstein Verlag.

Tomosello, Michael. 1999. *The Cultural Origins of Human Cognition*. Cambridge, MA: Harvard University Press.

Tomasello, Michael, and Joseph Call. 1997. *Primate Cognition*. New York: Oxford University Press.

Whyte, W. F. 1943. *Street Corner Society: The Social Structure of an Italian Slum*. Chicago: University of Chicago Press.

SECTION II

NEW AND EXISTING CRITICAL APPROACHES TO COMPARISON

5

An Ethnography of Comparative Ethnography

Pathways to Three Logics of Comparison

Ching Kwan Lee

If "thinking without comparison is unthinkable" (Ragin 1981), then ethnography without comparison is undecipherable storytelling. How then does comparative ethnography come about? Like any object of sociological inquiry, the cases in comparative ethnography have to be *constituted* by the researcher, who has to make choices about the units of empirical and explanatory analysis, as well as the theoretical agenda that informs both. Translating these general methodological principles into practice is the bread and butter of graduate seminars on the ethnographic method. Yet missing from such standard, if also sanitized, curriculum is something more messy and idiosyncratic but no less central to the production of knowledge. It is the tangled dialogs and compromises between theoretical inspirations and methodological precepts the ethnographer brings with her on the one hand, and her personal encounters in the field on the other. This bridging work in doing ethnography, comparative or not, is perhaps not codifiable, more art than craft. In this chapter, using my three comparative ethnographic book projects as illustrations, I reflect on this hidden crucible of ethnographic practice. As a critical account of a personal journey of discovery and engagement with the method, it is, in essence, an ethnography of ethnography. Much like the other ethnographies I have written, this one has to be contextualized within the larger forces of political economic change, academic and intellectual currents, and personal fortunes and endeavors.

China's rise in the global economy has been the most critical factor motivating my three ethnographic book projects. My fascination with China has partial roots in my personal background. I was born and raised in Hong Kong when it was still a British colony. For the first twenty some years of my

Ching Kwan Lee, *An Ethnography of Comparative Ethnography* In: *Beyond the Case*. Edited by: Corey M. Abramson and Neil Gong, Oxford University Press (2020). © Oxford University Press.
DOI: 10.1093/oso/9780190608484.003.0006

life, Communist China felt like at once an alienated next-door neighbor and a mysterious foreign country. While I was pursuing my PhD in sociology at UC Berkeley in the late 1980s, China began its fascinating, tumultuous, and consequential transformation. All my research projects to date have sought to understand the "labor question" in various critical moments and regions of China's development, linking the politics, livelihoods, and subjectivities of the working class to the evolution of state power, labor markets, and international and domestic capital flows. Beginning with a study of the labor regimes that make possible China's spectacular rise as the world's workshop, I then moved on to chronicle the regional patterns of labor protests that intensified in tandem with the country's turn from socialism to capitalism. Recently, as Chinese capital expands abroad, most energetically in the Global South, my research agenda has also taken a global turn. My most recent project explores China's engagement with African labor and government in Zambia, Africa's top copper producer. All these projects share some underlying theoretical interest, but they illustrate different strategies of comparison.

Variable Comparison: Factory Women in Two Regimes of Production

When I was a graduate student, I first aspired to become a comparative historical sociologist. To fulfill the method requirements of the program, I took Kim Voss's comparative historical method seminars, reading classics by Bendix, Dore, Skocpol, Tilly, Thompson, Moore, and others. When the 1989 Tiananmen movement erupted, I even toyed with the idea of writing a dissertation comparing the Chinese student movement with the Polish Solidarity movement as cases of popular dissent under Communism. Personal circumstances intervened and I had to take a two-year leave of absence from graduate school. Let loose in the wilderness, my reading became unhinged from systematically organized syllabi and subfields. Somehow I stumbled upon Paul Willis's *Learning to Labor* (1977), the first book-length ethnography I had ever read. It was an instant revelation! The vividness of human agency, social interactions, and power relations in working-class lads' everyday life were all analyzed in relation to the British class structure and its reproduction through the cultural logic of patriarchy. Right there, I found the method to realize C. Wright Mills's sociological imagination, which was what drew me to sociology as an undergraduate in the first place. Compared to comparative historical sociology, ethnographic sociology gives me greater access to agency (or biography) without ignoring structure and history. This serendipitous discovery of ethnography led me to read the work of Michael Burawoy and Aihwa Ong, who would soon become my mentors. If my own scholarship had any Marxist, feminist, and Foucauldian insights, it was largely due to their inspirations. Also, at that time both of them studied industrial workers by theorizing their politics and identities in the contexts of various national political economies—machinists in Chicago, steel workers in Russia and Hungary, and female workers in electronics in Malaysia. Their celebrated monographs, *Manufacturing Consent* (1979) and *Spirits of Resistance and Capitalist Discipline* (1986), became the models for a formative and aspiring sociologist in search of a dissertation project.

It was around 1991, when I resumed my graduate studies at Berkeley, that China embarked on an uncertain trajectory of economic integration with global capitalism in a bid to overcome the twin crisis of legitimacy and accumulation after the Tiananmen crackdown. The Chinese government was "crossing the river by feeling stones," as Deng Xiaoping put it most vividly, when it first experimented with setting up special economic zones along the southeastern seaboards. Chinese diasporic capital, mainly from Hong Kong initially, and Taiwan and Southeast Asia later, met the massive migrant workforce hailed from the vast countryside and partially set free by economic reform. The border town Shenzhen, linked to Hong Kong by a bridge, was quickly transformed from a geographically and economically peripheral outpost from Beijing's perspective to become the world's newest mega-manufacturing hub. In less than a decade, the entire South China region would become the powerhouse of China's export-led economic miracle.

Seizing this historic moment and taking stock of the labor process theories and feminist interventions I had read, I began formulating a theoretical question: How can class-first Marxist theorization of factory regimes be "engendered" in light of the prevalence of women workers at the point of production in China and many Third World industrializing countries? Comparison was emphatically *not* on my mind at this stage as I conjured up a dissertation prospectus in Berkeley, based on disparate journalistic accounts about exploitations of women workers in Shenzhen's global factories. I was more worried about gaining access to what Marx famously called "the hidden abode of production on whose threshold there hangs the notice 'No admittance except on business' " (Marx 1990, 279–280). Luckily, I happened to have a good friend who was a manager in the commercial loan department of a major Chinese bank in Hong Kong. He solicited the consent of one of his clients who owned Liton Electronics Limited (a fictitious name), an electronics factory in Hong Kong that had just opened a new plant in Shenzhen. Neither my friend nor I could ever gauge the extent to which Liton's consent was due to the bank's creditor status and the subtle coercion it wielded. When I met the boss for the first time, he was relaxed and welcoming, telling me how my Berkeley affiliation triggered his fond memory of UCLA, where he had obtained his MBA. Before he left me for the golf course, he put me in the ward of his executive manager, who would have the ultimate say on what I could do in his factories. After touring the two production lines in the Hong Kong and Shenzhen plants with the manager, I knew my ethnography should be comparative.

"'The Field' itself is . . . a powerful disciplinary force: assertive, demanding, even coercive" (1996, 119), wrote Clifford Geertz in his memoir *After the Fact* (1996). It rang particularly true when the two factories I visited cried out for comparison. Even on my first visit, I could see the interesting similarities and differences. Owned by the same enterprise, managed by the same team of border-crossing managers who shuttled between the two factories every week, producing the same home audio entertainment products for exports, and using the same technological labor process (the exact alignment of work positions along the production lines), I noticed distinctive shop-floor cultures which I later would call regimes of work. The veteran married women workers in Hong Kong, most in their forties, were playful and domineering, teasing and talking back to their male supervisors, while the younger migrant women workers in their late teens and early twenties in Shenzhen were disciplined, controlled, and subservient to male supervisors and managers. Brief discussions with the managers confirmed that they too felt they had to manage the workforce differently. This initial trip led to an empirical puzzle: Why the difference, given the striking similarities? To answer my initial theoretical question about gender in the labor process, I could have conducted a single case ethnography using the extended case method. But comparative ethnography not only suggested itself in this particular case; it also turned out to be a more robust tool to engage and reformulate theory.

In June 1992 I started working as a full-time production worker assembling home audio (hi-fi) entertainment sets in the Hong Kong plant for two months. I then went to the Shenzhen plant working as a line production assistant for another two months, and ended with an additional two-month period in 1993. As a novice ethnographer, fieldwork was an intensely exhausting experience, physically and mentally. Simple things like controlling the electric rivet gun hung from the railing several feet above my seat while keeping pace with the assembly line was not as simple as I thought. I remember thinking about the classic scene from Charlie Chaplin's *Modern Times* whenever things started accumulating in front of me. In the China plant, the heat, humidity, long hours (12 on average) and unappetizing canteen food took a little longer to get used to. Paying attention to the jokes, arguments, stories, personalities, and relationships that swirled around me amidst mountains of electronic motherboards, disaggregated CD players, and amplifiers constantly moving along the many conveyor belts was the least of the challenges. What kept me up at night were questions of conceptualization and theorization—what do my fieldnotes mean sociologically? How do I construct concepts, develop arguments, and engage theories with the empirical data I collect among workers and managers?

Thinking comparatively on two fronts, empirical and theoretical, kept me oriented during the fieldwork process. First, in deciding what to compare across the two factories, I relied on Burawoy's theorization of factory regimes, which offers an analytical structure for organizing the differences and commonalities I observed in the two factories. Basically, a factory regime refers to the overall political form of production, including the political effects of the "labor process" (i.e., the technical and social organization of tasks in production) and the "political apparatus of production" (i.e., how state institutions regulate and shape workplace politics). There are two generic types of factory regime: the despotic and the hegemonic. A despotic regime of production is founded on workers' dependence on wage employment for their livelihoods, and wages are tied to performance in the workplace. State interventions such as providing welfare and regulating industrial relations remove the basis for coercion and give rise to a hegemonic regime in which consent prevails over coercion. Building on these sets of concepts, but drawing from my ethnographic data, I formulated two factory regimes that I called "localistic despotism" and "familial hegemony." In Shenzhen, localistic despotism describes management control over a migrant workforce through a coercive disciplinary regime that exploits workers' localistic networks and constructs women as docile maiden workers. This contrasts with the regime of familial hegemony in Hong Kong, where management establishes control through shop-floor discourses of familialism, factory policies facilitating women's family responsibilities, and the construction of women as veteran matron workers.

The second moment of comparison was identifying anomalies vis-à-vis theory. After months of dialogs between data and theory, I formulated three empirical anomalies from Burawoy's theory, giving me the opportunity to reformulate it into a "gendered theory of factory regime." The first anomaly is about the role of the state. Even though Hong Kong workers lack a base of livelihood independent of wage work and have almost no recourse to any state insurance or welfare—conditions that would theoretically foster a despotic regime—a hegemonic regime emerges in the Hong Kong plant. In the Shenzhen plant, even though migrant workers can return to their home villages to pursue an agrarian livelihood independent of wage work, a despotic regime is found, contrary to Burawoy's theory. My fieldwork reveals that management does not always have an interest in coercive means of control even when it has the capacity to impose despotism, something that has been assumed in Marxist theories. Also, as managers are relatively free from state intervention in both places, the state is not the theoretical linchpin in determining types of control at work, as Burawoy's theory has proposed.

Second, in lieu of the state my cases suggest that the organization of the labor market is a critical determinant of workers' dependence. How the labor market is socially organized shapes the choice of managerial strategy of control. In Shenzhen, networks originating in a common rural village or county channel migrant women workers from farmlands to factories. Workers depend on these localistic ties for survival, while management exploits these ties to control labor through job and dormitory assignments. In Hong Kong, women's labor force participation is conditioned by their fulfillment of family and kin obligations, compelling management to consciously introduce flexibility to facilitate their combination of work and familial responsibilities.

Finally, whereas my shop-floor experience in both factories is saturated with gender, Burawoy's theory fails to elaborate how gender contributes to class power and resistance. The diverse constructions of women's gender is the medium through which shop-floor power is conceived, legitimated, and contested. "Maiden workers" and "matron workers" were the summary labels I created to describe notions and practices of womanhood arising within production and under the specific but diverse political economic conditions, especially labor market conditions, in South China in the early 1990s.

With hindsight, I realize I was deploying the logic of variable analysis. Controlling for some theoretically relevant and significant variables, namely technology, product, management, ownership type, and the state in the two cases, I looked for other variables such as labor market organization and gender construction which account for the different outcomes, that is, gendered regimes of work. I basically disaggregated the two worlds of factory women into analytical elements, comparing one labor market with another labor market, one state with another state, following an "additive" notion of causality. It was crisp and compelling to scholars familiar with the reasoning of statistical control but mechanical and reductive for those seeking more complex and conjunctural approaches to comparison. For instance, rather than eliminating or controlling for the state as a competing explanation (based on state nonintervention in both cases), I could have theorized how the colonial state in Hong Kong and the socialist state in Shenzhen shaped the organization of the labor market in different ways, the former through minimal welfare pushing women into the workforce, and the latter through reforming the stringent policy on rural–urban migration. Had I pursued that route, I might have developed two rather than one gendered theory of production politics, one for each type of political regime.

Another auto-critique on my use of variable comparison is that I missed the contextual connections between the two cases that I treated as independent from each other. In those days, running parallel workshops across the borders was a common strategy for Hong Kong industrialists who were eager to exploit the fresh supply of cheap labor and land but not yet certain how committed the Communist regime would be to market reform. But such hedging did not last long. Joining a more general trend of relocation, Liton closed the Hong Kong factory several months after I exited the field and moved all its production lines to Shenzhen. With hindsight, I realized I was witnessing a larger and gradual process of economic integration between Hong Kong and Mainland China, developing in tandem with the latter's strategy of political, economic, and social absorption of a former colony under Chinese Communist rule. The difference I observed could have been due to capital's expectation of relocation, and the respective business significance of the two factories in their overall profit structure.

Later, as I became more experienced and confident as an ethnographer, more independent-minded as a sociologist and less encumbered by disciplinary standards and rewards, my practice of comparative ethnography also changed. Thinking comparatively in variables is a valid process that helps clarify and simplify realities so that we can analyze them. But as I turned to tackle more amorphous and less institutionalized subject matters, I realized variable comparison can be triangulated with, even transcended by, other modes of comparison that bring complexity and contingency into ethnography.

Encompassing Comparison: Labor Protests in China's Rustbelt and Sunbelt

By the time I finished writing my first book, *Gender and the South China Miracle: the Two Worlds of Factory Women* (1998), China's market reform had advanced from a few enclaves in the southeast to the rest of the country, accompanied by a rising tide of labor unrest. Two interlinked political economic dynamics were happening simultaneously. On the one hand, the rapid decline of the state industrial sector was marked by a drastic reduction of the state industrial workforce from 43 million in 1996 to 13 million in 2003. On the other hand, the capitalist boom fueled by foreign and private investment in the export and construction sectors brought about a 100 million–strong migrant workforce. Mass unemployment, rampant pension default, nonpayment of wages, exploitation, industrial injuries, and violation of labor rights sparked numerous incidents of collective action among both state and migrant workers. This development prompted me to formulate my next project focusing on working-class resistance, rather than regimes of managerial control. Why were workers under an authoritarian regime able to sustain so much activism? Why did worker unrest not bring about political challenge to the regime? Whereas I began with theoretical ideas and puzzles in the previous study, this time I began with an intriguing empirical phenomenon, and searched for theory and field sites along the way.

Inspired by E. P. Thompson's monumental *The Making of the English Working Class* (1963), I framed the study as the making and unmaking of the Chinese working class. The comparative ethnography that would later become the book *Against the Law: Labor Protests in China's Rustbelt and Sunbelt* (2007) chronicles the fate of the two main segments of the working class in two provinces. It compares the "rustbelt" (old industrial bases with a high concentration of state-owned enterprises, veteran and unemployed workers) in Liaoning and the "sunbelt" (new industrial regions with a heavy presence of foreign invested factories employing young migrant workers) in Guangdong in terms of the local government's strategies of development, workers' mobilization of the law and moral economy, and the limits to their activism, all shaped by the central government's project of economic liberalization and claims to lawful governance. The goal was to explain the divergent and convergent features of labor protests and survival strategies of two generations of workers by contextualizing them in the regional and national political economies.

No amount of theoretical inspiration could materialize into an ethnography had I failed to gain access into a politically sensitive phenomenon. In a country where workers have no legal right to strike, where would I find subjects willing to talk about their collective mobilization? Also, unlike the bounded, institutional life worlds of the factories in my first book, protests and strikes do not have time tables or fixed locations. The thought of finding subjects and field sites seemed like an elusive pipe dream of an overzealous sociologist. But to my pleasant surprise, I discovered that behind the facade of a formidable authoritarian state machine lie dense layers of social connections that nurture hidden spaces of autonomy and agency for fieldworkers and workers alike.

Among the researchers I came to know while conducting a side project on factory politics in state-owned enterprises going through market reform in Guangdong was a party researcher from a small industrial town in the northeast province of Liaoning. Swept up in the sea change unleashed by marketization and enticed by higher salaries in the south, he took a "long holiday" from his official job as a Communist Party historian in his hometown and came to Guangzhou as a contract researcher in an institute where some of my friends worked. At first he moonlighted for me, helping me compile newspaper reports on unemployment and state-owned enterprise reforms. That was invaluable, labor-intensive work in the days before the Internet and Google. Then as he fed me ever more stories from home about protests by pensioners, unemployed, and furloughed workers, many of whom were his relatives, friends, former classmates, and neighbors, I asked him to host me in his home and introduced me to his acquaintances. He and his wife welcome my stay and gladly accepted my offer of a room and board fee. Using my friend's working-class neighborhood in an old industrial town as a base, I made forays to other towns known for their Soviet-style manufacturing facilities, visited workers in their homes, collected the handbills and petitions they wrote, went with them to their crumbling but imposing enterprises to recover unpaid compensations and pensions, and observed several rallies in front of government buildings and road blockages while traveling around town. Altogether, between 1997 and 2003 I interviewed more than 150 workers, unionists, and managers caught up in the momentous and wrenching collapse of permanent employment, long hailed as the hallmark of socialism's superiority over capitalism, in a region that was considered the dragon head of the China's national planned economy.

Locating the subjects is one thing; getting them to open up and participate in coproducing knowledge is another, especially in a purportedly repressive authoritarian one-party state. Surprisingly, aggrieved workers were much less fearful than one would assume, because labor protests were so numerous in those days that they became normalized everyday occurrences. Taxi drivers developed local knowledge about when and where to avoid road sit-ins, the method of choice for many elderly pensioners who found them physically less demanding than rallies. Besides finding strength in numbers, another important factor motivating workers to participate in my research was their sense of righteousness in what they were doing. Thanks to assurance of confidentiality and anonymity by a mutual acquaintance, many workers talked vividly about socialist factory lives, political campaigns during Mao's time, and their present predicament when bankruptcy swept through the region, and how they went about organizing road blockages, demonstrations, and petitions. Having contributed their life-long low wage labor to the cause of socialist industrialization and national development, the state arbitrarily abandoned them en masse. Some men broke down in tears; others were so upset by my interviews that they quit before I finished. These workers were the most articulate and impassioned subjects I had ever met, thanks to years of official propaganda and political campaigns that sharpened their awareness of exploitation, surplus value, cadre corruption, and working-class power. They now used their experience and memories of the Mao era to criticize market reform, cadre corruption, and payment defaults in moral economic terms—the regime's betrayal of the socialist social contract that instituted an implicit exchange between the paternalistic state and a politically acquiescent populace.

State repression was a constant threat, but also a selective practice. The political space that allowed workers to stage tens of thousands of protests every year also gave me the opportunity to carry out ethnographic research. That space existed not only because the local police were part of the local community with families and friends affected by the wave of massive layoffs, and therefore refrained from the use of force. I also found that the government differentiated single-factory, socioeconomic protests from cross-factory, politically motivated ones. The former were deemed legitimate, even lawful, discontents. Just as workers learned through occasional arrests by public security the boundary of permissible protests, I had my own brush with the police state that informed me of the red line for data collection. It happened one morning when I was sitting in a cab parked in a small alley, waiting to see if workers would come out in protest against the arrest of four worker representatives who had led the spate of citywide protests the week before. Six plainclothes police descended and surrounded the cab and brought me to the Public Security Bureau for an hour of menacing interrogation, at the end of which they made me sign a confession acknowledging my violation of Chinese law by not seeking official permission for research. They confiscated my notebook and my camera, and laughed out loud when I requested a lawyer before answering their questions. The moment they realized that I was not a reporter who would write to the Chinese public, but an unknown academic writing in English, their voice softened. That was the red line they drew. I was taken to the highway exit at the outskirt of town, and told never to come back without permission.

After focusing on the rustbelt for a couple of years, I turned to an equally assertive working class in the bustling export sector. Migrant workers combined various modes of resistance—strikes, rallies, arbitration, and lawsuits—in response to wage nonpayment, abusive management, and horrendous working conditions. Back to my old stomping ground, with the assistance of a local reporter, I obtained access to aggrieved migrant workers who approached his newspaper in the hope of gaining public and government attention. On many occasions, I visited factories and workers' dormitories with my reporter friend and I was introduced as his assistant. Later, he quit his job and committed himself full-time to running an independent research and labor advocacy organization, funded by various international foundations. Using his office as base, I interviewed workers who came to report and seek advice on disputes and lawsuits. In many cases, I was even able to follow the development of these conflicts and observed how they bargained with their employers or engaged government officials in labor bureaus, arbitration tribunals, courtrooms, construction sites, and on the street.

Fieldwork is always messy because it entails data collection in constant dialog with emergent analysis, conceptualization, and theorization. Getting inside worker activism while staying out of trouble was just the visible aspect of fieldwork. Less visible but no less challenging was an ongoing struggle to formulate a framework to both understand and guide my emergent analysis. The work of Charles Tilly in sociology and Elizabeth Perry in China studies have long alerted me to the interactive relationship between state power and social protests, leading me to think about the state's strategy of using the law as a channeling and containment device. From the political economy literature, I took the idea of decentralization as an accumulation strategy, but noticed how this by itself could not explain how workers reacted to market reforms. It has to be considered together with the rich traditions of working-class politics, memories, and aspirations that gave rise to diverse patterns and logics of protest. This is where E. P. Thompson's cultural Marxism became helpful.

Theorizing with data, I began to see how the socialist social contract in the rustbelt and the market-embedded legal contract in the sunbelt oriented the two generations of workers to different discursive claims (moral economic rights and legal rights, respectively). This affects their distinct repertoire of action, with rustbelt workers more inclined to take to the streets and sunbelt workers more prone to use the courtrooms, marches to labor bureaus, and strikes. The common features in worker activism across the two regions—that is, cellular single-factory action making socioeconomic demands framed in policy and legalistic terms—sprung from the central government's emphasis on legalistic authoritarian rule.

Data sometimes talked back and compelled the ethnographer to expand the original framework. This happened when after several years of getting inside worker activism and working-class lives, I began to realize the impact of what Marxist sociologists term the "social reproduction of labor" on labor unrest. It refers to how the capacity to work is reproduced on a daily and generational basis. Wage is important to workers' survival but it is usually supplemented by nonwage entitlements, community services, and family subsistence. Hanging out in working-class neighborhoods and spending a lot of time visiting workers in their homes in the rustbelt, it dawned on me that they had become homeowners after the government sold them work-unit housing at subsidized prices. That is, they were unemployed or owed wages and pensions, but they benefited from state policy that turned them into property owners. Similarly, observing how frequently migrant workers dissipate into the vast countryside during a prolonged labor dispute or plant closure, I decided to travel with some of them back to their villages during periods of their unemployment. These trips made me realize that their entitlement to land in the countryside protected them against the vagaries in the labor market. Some have thriving rural sideline businesses; others have hired help with farming; most could fall back on household self-provisioning of food. Therefore, in both cases, there are nonmarket mechanisms embedded in the urban work-unit system and the rural economy that mitigate exploitation at the point of production and limit their militancy against the existing order in which they have a stake.

Unlike my treatment of the two cases in the factory regimes study, the comparison in this project can be described as "case oriented" rather than "variable oriented" in that the cases are constituted by the conjunctural configuration of a set of factors and not broken down into distinct variables for control and contrast (Ragin 1987). Moreover, rather than treating the two cases as analytically separate, I underscore their relational dynamic in which the rustbelt was being displaced by the sunbelt, socialist social contract by legal contract, and state workers by migrant workers, all shaped by an evolving national strategy of political economic development—decentralized legal authoritarianism. The relation between the cases actually tells an important national-level story. This comparative strategy is akin to what world-system sociologists called "encompassing" or "incorporating" comparison" (Silver 2003, 29–30). Subunits of a totality are seen as structured by their locations within it while their interactions (re)produce the system overtime. The substantive argument emerging from applying this encompassing comparative perspective is this: despite the large numbers of cellular and localized labor protests, the two cases together indicate that the two generations of workers pursued independent struggles. The absence of a powerful nationwide labor movement in a country with the world's largest workforce was the cornerstone of China's labor-intensive export driven economy.

To recapitulate, as China's capitalist boom intensified and expanded across the country, so did class conflicts. Veering away from the mode of variable comparison I adopted in my factory ethnography, this study theorized the conjunctural effects among variables—state legitimation strategies, working-class history, and the social reproduction of labor—in two ideal typical regional political economies (i.e., the rustbelt and the sunbelt), and the relational dynamic between the two cases—connecting their similarities to a national strategy of development and their differences to explain the absence of a working-class movement in China. As the subject matter became more political, it was only natural that my fieldwork became more difficult. What I had learned was that authoritarian state power is real and repressive (never forget plainclothes police!), but there are always more hidden spaces for popular resistance and for ethnography than we imagined possible. This lesson would serve me well for my next project as I followed the footsteps of China's capitalist development to Africa.

Eventful Comparison: Varieties of Capital in Zambia

Around the time *Against the Law* was released, China's socioeconomic development seems to have reached another critical juncture. In response to the domestic pressures of business competition, falling rates of profit, overcapacity, increased demands for raw materials, and contracted demands for its products in the advanced industrialized world, the Chinese government orchestrated a new initiative—"going out." This state-sponsored policy of encouraging the outward flows of capital and labor complimented the spontaneous strategy of private companies and individuals to seek their fortunes outside China. Africa became the frontier of this global expansion of Chinese capital, generating both enthusiasm and criticism from different quarters. The most salient and urgent question being asked in the global media was, and still is: Is China launching a neocolonial scramble for Africa, or is it pioneering an alternative model of South–South development? To me, a "China in Africa" study beckoned as a logic extension of my previous projects. It would allow me to take the labor question of Chinese capitalism one step further, beyond its own borders into the contested terrains of transcontinental capital and labor migration, the complex interplay of class and race conflicts, and the struggle for development in the Global South.

Among the fifty-four countries on the African continent, where should I go to conduct ethnographic research? Although no single country is representative of Africa, where diversity in political economic conditions and natural endowments defy continent wide generalizations, I decided to focus on Zambia early on because it is a critical case for methodological and theoretical reasons. First, Zambia has long been Africa's top copper producer and its Chambishi mine was the first overseas mine ever acquired by a Chinese state-owned company. Second, Zambia is also the inaugural site for a number of Chinese state-owned special economic zones in Africa. As the first of its kind, the footprint of Chinese state capital is deeper there than elsewhere, allowing for an analysis of the process and dynamic of transformation. Third, the logic of comparative extended case method also points me to Zambia. I thought I could use Michael Burawoy's classic work *Color of Class on the Copper Mines* (1972), which was based on his ethnographic research in Zambia in the late 1960s, as a benchmark for historical comparison and theoretical engagement. Whereas Burawoy studied the immediate postindependence years when colonial capital remained dominant over Zambian state and labor, I would be analyzing state capital from China in a neoliberalized Zambia forty years later. Has the relation between state, foreign capital, and labor changed?

Besides historical comparison, I realized early on the need for comparing Chinese with non-Chinese capital, if I were to specify what is specifically "Chinese" as opposed to generic "capitalist" behavior. On my first trip to the copperbelt, I was astonished to see China was only one among a host of foreign investors from India, South Africa, Brazil, Canada, and Switzerland, making the copperbelt a natural site for comparative ethnography. Only after more fieldwork did I realize that the popular and official practice of designating investors by nationality (e.g., Chinese, Indian, or South African mines) was spurious. Chinese *private* capital is not that different from Indian private capital. What is uniquely Chinese in Zambia is Chinese *state* capital that pursues state-defined political economic objectives, distinct from global private capital's interest to maximize shareholder value. During the latter half of my seven-year research, I arrived at a two-way comparison: between state capital and global capital, and between copper (a place-bound, strategic, capital intensive industry employing organized labor) and construction (a footloose, nonstrategic, labor-intensive industry employing informal labor).

But what to compare among these four cases? In formulating an analytical framework I began with the "varieties of capitalism" literature, which proposes that capitalist economies have distinctive national characteristics depending on the configurations of institutions for macroeconomic policymaking, firm-level corporate governance, interfirm relation and industrial relations, and so on. From the influential distinction between liberal and coordinated market economies in the member countries of the Organisation for Economic Cooperation and Development, the "varieties of capitalism" rubric has spread to studies of East Asia, Latin America, and East and Central Europe. But my fieldwork made me realize that capital is too globally mobile and politically contested to be contained within national frameworks of institutional complementarity. From the perspective of African states and citizens there are no varieties of capitalism, but rather "varieties of capital" competing under the same global neoliberalized market economy. To analyze the two varieties of capital I found in Zambia, I drew on classical sociology and Karl Polanyi to formulate a comparison along three dimensions of capital: logic of accumulation, regimes of labor, and ethos of management. The questions I wanted to address were: What are the peculiarities of Chinese state capital compared to global private capital in all these dimensions? Do they bring with them different impacts on Zambian development? I still vividly remember the day, time, and location when the comparative design, the dimensions, and constitution of empirical and theoretical cases came together for the first time in my mind. By then, it had been four years since I first set foot in the copperbelt.

Access is an ongoing process of negotiation and improvisation, with unexpected twists and turns that open and end abruptly. Compared to the two previous ethnographic projects that took place in China where I had acquaintances and contacts, I parachuted into Zambia without any local connection. Perhaps my tenure had given me the freedom and audacity to take risks, and my naiveté and curiosity had gotten the better of me. Ignorant about African realities, I was soon shocked to find obstacles to fieldwork that did not exist in China. There were no more plainclothes police, but the lack of infrastructure and roads, poor communication, the scarcity of statistics and local scholarship, many of which were the adverse legacies of colonialism, took time and patience to get used to. But the biggest challenge this time was access to copper mines and construction sites owned by powerful state-owned companies from China and global London Exchange-listed multinationals and other private investors. The difficulty of studying up from the humble position of an academic is the reason why sociology knows so much more about the powerless than the powerful.

The first breakthrough came in 2009, when by chance I spent a few days at the Ndola International Trade Fair, a national exhibition event dating back to preindependence days (1956), and attended a presentation by the director of the National Council for Construction, the government body that oversees the registration and regulation of all construction companies operating in Zambia. Away from his office in Lusaka, and having just finished his official duty, the director was relaxed and in the mood to sit down with a curious sociology professor from the United States. After an hour-long amiable and animated conversation, in which he shared with me his observations and concerns about the dominance and practices of Chinese contractors flooding the Zambian market, I proposed that his agency and I conduct a collaborative study, comparing Chinese with non-Chinese contractors. Having written a dissertation for his doctorate in architecture in Newcastle, England, the director understood instantly how this study could furnish him with objective facts rather than rumors about how foreign contractors actually operate. We signed a memorandum, stating our respective responsibility and co-ownership of the data collected.

Mining proved to be a much harder nut to crack. Foreign-invested copper mines, state-owned or publicly listed, are powerful players in the universe of corporations. Like gated kingdoms, they bore a menacing physical presence, greeting visitors with layers of security checks and of course proprietary claims on company information. Even though I had a sense of what went on inside the mines through interviews with the major miners' unions, their shop stewards, and rank-and-file miners, as an ethnographer, I knew interviews could never substitute for participant observation. My first opportunity came when a Chinese friend who worked in the personnel department of the newly built Chinese state-owned smelter introduced me to her boss and proposed that I work in the smelter to teach English to his Chinese staff. But my job interview with the general manager, who was also the Chinese Communist Party secretary there, ended disastrously. The party boss did what a twenty-first-century manager would do—he Googled me, and was horrified to see my publications on labor protests in China and Zambia. After lecturing me about how the global discourse on "China's scramble for Africa" was just the latest instance of the West's humiliation of China, he sent me packing. I had no choice but to defect to the other side. With another stroke of significant luck, I befriended a Zambian opposition politician who took an interest in a paper I wrote on China in Zambia. We hung out in Lusaka over after-hour drinks, trading frustrating stories about our respective line of work: Zambian politics and researching China in Zambia. Consoling me after my failed job interview at the smelter, he said, "Wait until we are in power." I did, and his party, the Patriotic Front, won the 2011 election. On becoming the vice president of the Republic, my friend made good his promise, called up the CEOs of the major mines, and ushered me in as a Zambian government consultant.

From 2012 to 2014, I spent a total of six months in five copper mines owned by multinationals. Keeping the production process constant, I eventually decided to compare only the three mines with underground operations in the copperbelt, leaving the two newer open-pit mines in Northwestern Province out of this study. The ethnographic fieldwork in these mines entailed shadowing managers as they went about their work underground and in the processing plant, observing production meetings and collective bargaining negotiations, living among expatriate managers in company housing, and interviewing them in their offices. On weekends, I continued my visits to mining townships and talked to miners in their homes. In addition,

I worked with, observed, and interviewed Zambian government technocrats and politicians on how they handled China–Zambia relations. As the vice president's informal advisor on Chinese affairs whenever I was in town, I was invited to sit in meetings where he met with Chinese officials and businessmen. He also asked me to tag along during his first trip to China, right after the Patriotic Front took power. Toward the end of the research in 2014, the vice president called a meeting where I presented my findings to the ministers and their permanent secretaries in the Ministries of Finance, Labor, Mines, Commerce, and Industry. In short, the process of obtaining fieldwork access to Chinese state capital via the Zambian political elite resonates with a major argument of the book: Chinese state capital is less powerful abroad than at home because of it had to accommodate local politics, from giving access to a researcher to negotiating with workers on strike.

A salient ethical and power issue I contended with during fieldwork was informed consent. This issue came to sharp relief when at one point, toward the end of my stint at one of the mines, the company lawyer who was not previously informed by the CEO or anyone else of my presence and my fieldwork wanted me to sign a legal document renouncing my right to publish my finding. I refused, maintaining that he should talk to the government or the vice president who sent me as their consultant. The lawyer did not give me consent to study the company, but the CEO and other senior managers did, albeit reluctantly, because they did not want to alienate the vice president and his government. Did I violate the ethical principle of informed consent? This study of the power elite was possible only because I was given the opportunity to leverage the power dynamic between the powerful (i.e., state and capital). Informed consent is a liberal notion of human subjects' equal and legal rights to be informed of the purpose of our study and to participate voluntarily. But anyone who has done fieldwork would know that in practice, treating all human subjects equally perpetuates the inherent power inequality; some human subjects need more protection than others. Are these global London-listed multinationals and Chinese state-owned companies "human subjects" in the same sense as miners and construction workers? Do these companies warrant or need the same kind of protection as miners? And what kind of protection can I, a mere ethnographer, offer them? I asked myself these questions many times in the course of this research and I have come back time and again to the same conclusion that Troy Duster, David Matza, and David Wellman arrived at more than three decades ago: "An uncritical across the board application (of informed consent) unwittingly favors certain human subjects," especially in ethnographic studies of racism, fraud, or discrimination by businesses or public institutions (1979, 136–142). Like them, I am not suggesting that we should throw informed consent out of the window, but we should allow researchers discretion to determine how best to practice it, when and if they can.

In a nutshell, is Chinese state capital different from global private capital? My research found that yes, it can be *made* different. Chinese state capital came to Zambia with a set of encompassing imperatives—securing a supply of copper ore at the source (for national resource security), expanding political influence in Africa (for strategic and diplomatic interest), and profit-making (for economic sustainability of state firms, market expansion, and creation for its huge foreign reserves). This encompassing set of imperatives—for which China is assailed as colonialist—contrast with the one-dimensional driver of profit maximization or shareholder value maximization found in global private firms. The former runs a production-driven, low-wage regime of labor whereas finance-driven global private mines tend to use retrenchment and extensive labor subcontracting to control labor. Finally, Chinese state capital had at its disposal a more disciplined and controlled management that displays an ethos of "collective asceticism," distinct from the "individualistic careerism" found among expatriates working in global firms. In other words, counterintuitively, I found that Chinese state capital's encompassing imperatives, which cannot be reduced to financial gains alone, in reality compel it to be different and more negotiable, more open to political and economic concession than private capital in responding to African developmental impulses and labor demands. This has happened in Zambia during my fieldwork, which coincided with a strong political current of resource nationalism in both Zambian state and society and the election of a populist president, buoyed by a period of high global commodity prices. But this configuration of forces and dynamic exists unevenly across industrial sectors (in copper but not in construction), depending on variations in labor's organizational capacity and in elite political vision and will. In the informalized and nonstrategic construction sector, there is less pressure from the general public and labor to discipline political elites; Chinese concession loans as a form of state capital pose the threat of recreating Zambia's indebtedness and political dependence.

Compared to the two previous projects, I was ever more conscious to historicize my ethnography in this study. Burawoy's fieldwork four decades ago was a constant reminder that the political economic conditions I was observing cannot be taken for granted. Compared to the late 1960s, the global neoliberal economy in the twenty-first century brought a more diversified range of capital to Zambia. For all its fiscal and capacity deficit and dependence on copper, the Zambian state was compelled in the wake of political liberalization to respond to the amplified pressure of political competition and popular resource nationalism with more assertive policies toward foreign investors. Even as Zambia's structural economic subordination in the global economy persists, global capitalism has unleashed a variety of capital that offers different bargains to Zambia, and triggered political backlash that open up unforeseen possibilities.

But an important event during my fieldwork also alerted me to contingencies and crisis that should be analyzed in tandem with structural tendencies and imperatives of capital or capitalism. During my second trip to Zambia in the fall of 2008, the global financial crisis sent copper prices plummeting and created widespread panic. How the two types of capital reacted differently to critical moments like this was revelatory of their distinctive imperatives and politics—while private global investors announced massive layoffs, the Chinese state mining company expanded its portfolio and refrained from retrenching labor; it accommodated to the Zambian state's "value addition" development strategy by building two special economic zones, while global investors deemed it economically unviable and refused to assist.

Perhaps we could call this "eventful comparison" in that events are opportunities for knowledge that can be leveraged by the comparative ethnographer. If encompassing comparison emphasizes relatively stable and patterned institutional configuration and articulation (such as the relation between regional economies, state strategies of governance, and working-class history in my second project), eventful comparison makes use of crisis moments, or the disruption of structure and institution to highlight differences among the cases under study. These two modes of comparison are not mutually exclusive or incompatible. As a matter of fact, the resulting book *The Specter of Global China* (Lee 2017) relies on both.

Interestingly, William Sewell's idea of "event" (i.e., a subclass of happenings that *may* transform structure instead of being determined by structure) is also a theoretical claim that includes both structure and crisis. In his conception of "eventful capitalism," the temporalities of capitalism are on the one hand abstract and repetitive, but on the other also restless and hyper-eventful.

> One can confidently predict that capitalism will expand, but it is impossible to predict the actual direction of future expansion—which seems to

> be governed by highly contingent and eventful logics. (Who, forty years ago, would have predicted a runaway capitalist boom in China, Internet shopping, back offices in India, an international derivatives market worth trillions of dollars?) The expansiveness of capitalism is an existing force capable of being instantiated at any given time in a number of alternative ways, just as the repetitive rhythm of capitalist business cycles can manifest itself in whatever medium of production, trade, finance, and investment is available in any historical present. (Sewell 2008, 523–524)

"China in Africa" can exactly be framed as an event and like other historical events of capitalism—for example, the Great Depression, the collapse of Communism, the opening up of China, and the 2008 financial crisis. It is dialectically bound to capitalism's powerful self-reinforcing logics and its abstract temporality (as in boom-and-bust cycles, endless accumulation, and inexorable expansion). But events can also change and channel these logics and their effects in contingent ways. What this means is that whether or not Chinese state investment, with its peculiar logic of accumulation depicted in my study, will enable African countries to break the colonial legacy of underdevelopment dependent on commodity production and to jumpstart their belated industrialization will depend on many factors beyond the volition of the Chinese state or African governments. One possible scenario is that the current crisis of overaccumulation, deindustrialization, and underdemand for labor at the global level will structurally deprive African industrialization of any market. On the other hand, aggregate growth of African economies may become a new frontier for global capital, just as China was decades ago, and allow the world economy to surmount the current crisis and launch another boom.

Conclusion

By now, the reader should know that the messy production process of comparative ethnography belies the seamless appearance of the final product—a neatly bound book, a crisp table of contents, chapters flowing in cascading order from theory to method to cases and back. Like an old and reliable compass, the method of comparative ethnography provides me with reassuring orientation whenever I feel adrift in the field, from factories in South China, to the streets and courts of the rustbelt and sunbelt, or copper mines and construction sites in Zambia. While the extended case method calls for grounding fieldwork in theories and forces that shape the daily encounters with our subjects, it is only through comparison that I was able to understand and analyze both the macro and the micro. As I turned from the more bounded institutionalized factory regimes to more contested, national-level, and then global phenomena, I had to deploy more nuanced comparison—from the more mechanical control and contrast logic of variable comparison between two gendered factory regimes in Hong Kong and Shenzhen, to the encompassing comparison of two patterns of working-class formations in the rustbelt and sunbelt of China, and then adding eventful comparison of Chinese state capital and global private capital in Zambia. These three modes are ideal types that can be combined in any comparative ethnography. I was still using the logic of variable comparison in the last project, but allowing for more contingency and interaction among the variables (the three moments of capital). Beginning with either theoretical inspirations or fieldwork imperatives, the pathways leading to these respective types of comparison in different studies was always a dialog and compromise between both. Comparison can be deliberately designed at the beginning of a study or it can emerge during the course of fieldwork in response to circumstances and opportunities. Either way, everything being equal, comparison makes ethnography better, more theoretically robust and empirically interesting. Finally, in retracing the research processes and field challenges that shaped my practices of comparison, I also discovered the secret ingredient that I had all along relied on—persistence.

References

Burawoy, Michael. 1972. *The Colour Class on the Copper Mines: From African Advancement to Zambianization*. Lusaka, Zambia: Institute for African Studies, University of Zambia.

Burawoy, Michael. 1979. *Manufacturing Consent*. Chicago: University of Chicago Press.

Duster, Troy, David Matza, and David Wellman. 1979. "Fieldwork and the Protection of Human Subjects." *The American Sociologist* 14, no. 3: 136–142.

Geertz, Clifford. 1996. *After the Fact: Two Countries, Four Decades, One Anthropologist*. Cambridge, MA: Harvard University Press.

Lee, Ching Kwan. 1998. *Gender and the South China Miracle: Two Worlds of Factory Women*. Berkeley and Los Angeles: University of California Press.

Lee, Ching Kwan. 2007. *Against the Law: Labor Protests in China's Rustbelt and Sunbelt*. Berkeley and Los Angeles: University of California Press.

Lee, Ching Kwan. 2017. *The Specter of Global China: Politics, Labor and Foreign Investment in Africa*. Chicago: University of Chicago Press.

Marx, Karl. 1990. *Capital, vol. 1*. London: Penguine.

Ong, Aihwa. 1986. *Spirits of Resistance and Capitalist Discipline*. Albany: SUNY Press.

Ragin, Charles. 1981. "Comparative Sociology and the Comparative Method." *International Journal of Comparative Sociology* 22, nos. 1–2: 102–120.

Ragin, Charles. 1987. *The Comparative Method*. Berkeley: University of California Press.

Sewell, William H. 2008. "The Temporalities of Capitalism." *Socio-Economic Review* 6: 523–524.

Silver, Beverly 2003. *Forces of Labor: Workers' Movement and Globalization since 1870*. Cambridge: Cambridge University Press.

Thompson, Edward Palmer. 1963. *The Making of the English Working Class*. New York: Pantheon.

Willis, Paul. 1977. *Learning to Labour: How Working Class Kids Get Working Class Jobs*. New York: Columbia University Press.

6

Critical Realism and Contrastive Ethnography

The Curious Case of Autism in Somali Refugee Communities

Claire Laurier Decoteau

As part of the broader postmodern turn that accompanied globalization, George Marcus first introduced multisited ethnography in the 1980s, suggesting that anthropological techniques of ethnographic analysis needed to adapt to the dynamics of a shifting world order (Marcus 1986, 1988, 1995). Multisited ethnography "moves out from the single sites and local situations of conventional ethnographic research designs to examine the circulation of cultural meanings, objects and identities in diffuse time-space" by exploring multiple interdependent locales that cross national boundaries (Marcus 1995, 96). Instead of seeing globalization as an external force imposing itself upon situated locales, multisited ethnography attempts to get inside globalization itself (Burawoy 2009, 201). Marcus proposed that there were multiple means by which this could be accomplished: by following the people (as in migrant studies), following the object (as in commodity-chain studies), following the metaphor (for example, Emily Martin's work on immunity [Martin 1994]), and following an individual biography or a particular conflict (Marcus 1995). However, it is the ethnographer's own logic of association that ties these sites together, which, as Gille and Ó Riain (2002, 287) point out, is arbitrary and problematic. Burawoy further notes that the "site" can become just as reified or naturalized as the village or tribe (2009). Rather, Burawoy notes, objects of analysis should be theoretically constructed, and he advocates for multi*case* rather than multi*site* ethnography. "Constituting distinct sites as cases of something leads us to thematize their difference rather than their connection, which, then, poses questions of how that difference is produced and reproduced" (Burawoy 2009, 202).

Claire Laurier Decoteau, *Critical Realism and Contrastive Ethnography* In: *Beyond the Case*. Edited by: Corey M. Abramson and Neil Gong, Oxford University Press (2020). © Oxford University Press.
DOI: 10.1093/oso/9780190608484.003.0007

For Burawoy, the case is "doubly constituted" by the broader "context within which it is embedded" as well as the "social processes it expresses" (2009, 203), which consist of the variations and dynamics of historical change within macrostructural regimes. For Burawoy, then, context and process are realist, exogenous dynamics of case. But how these cases are perceived also depends on the researcher's positionality and theoretical framework, which are the constructivist, endogenous dynamics (2009). Burawoy's approach to ethnography is inspired by and adopted from the Manchester School of Social Anthropology's extended case method, or ECM (Burawoy 1998; Burawoy et al. 2000). In ECM, one begins with the extension of the observer into the world of the participant (which is typical in any ethnographic approach), and then moves to observations over time and space (often by conducting ethnohistories of sites or peoples under investigation). It extends from micro-processes to macro-forces, and then extends the existing theory to accommodate new anomalies (Burawoy et al. 2000, 27). "For us, the macro-micro link refers not to such an 'expressive' totality, but to a 'structured' one in which the part is shaped by its relation to the whole, the whole being represented by 'external forces.' That determination is often made accessible by explaining the divergence of two similar 'cases'" (27).

Burawoy admits that many of his own ECM studies have remained limited by comparing across the scale of the nation-state and that global ethnography can problematize the third step in ECM (the extension from micro-processes to global forces) in order to counter the objectification of these forces and their causal impact (Burawoy et al. 2000, 29). This can be done by considering how global forces are *received* by populations (not just via imposition, but by negotiation and even resistance), by recognizing that global forces are contingent on social processes and result out of networks or flows of people and ideas, and finally by understanding that what we mean by "global" might be imagined differently by different actors (29). While I recognize that these caveats to nation-based comparative studies are important in a globalized world, I also think that a focus on the fluidity and fragmentation of globalization obscures the ongoing significance of national difference and the "nation-state's continuing influence on global forces and connections" (Burawoy et al. 2000, 34).

There are many similarities between an ECM and critical realist approach to empirical evidence—they both heed the mutual constitution of subjects and structures and situate the empirical case within a broader set of structural conditions. Putting the two in conversation brings advantages to each approach. Critical realism is helpful in complicating Burawoy's ECM in two distinct ways: 1) by showing that one can compare across both events and causal mechanisms; and 2) by considering *conjunctural* causal features due to the fact that "complex events are codetermined by constellations of causal mechanisms" (Steinmetz 1998, 177). Critical realism, when it has been applied to empirical investigation, has not often been applied to *ethnographic* research.[1] Critical realism's emphasis on causality is complicated by ethnographic research, which sheds light on the mutual causal relationship between structures and agents.

Critical Realism, Contrastive Demi-Regularities, and Conjunctural Causality

Because the "social" is an open and not a closed stem, experimentation in the social sciences can be difficult. Positivism's insistence on the "constant conjunction of events" presumes a controlled experimental environment. Conversely, critical realism assumes that underlying causal mechanisms (the causal powers of structures,[2] which operate even when unobservable) are ontologically distinct from the events to which they give rise, otherwise, it would be impossible to take results determined in the lab and apply them to the world (Steinmetz 1998, 176). In other words, scientists presume that the causal mechanisms under analysis in artificially controlled lab experiments also operate outside the laboratory. The scientist is only responsible for triggering a mechanism already in existence and controlling for interference from other mechanisms. The scientist does not create the mechanism being tested (176). Critical realists then argue that mechanisms are independent from the events they generate.

Even as critical realists recognize the open and dynamic nature of the social world, "certain mechanisms may, over restricted regions of time-space, be reproduced continuously" and come to form partial or demi-regularities (Lawson 1998, 149). Lawson gives the example of women being concentrated in secondary sectors of the labor market. These demi-regularities are not universal, but they do show the actualization of a mechanism in a semiconsistent fashion over a specific time-space. Lawson suggests that it is because of these demi-regularities that contrastive cases become an important means of analysis in the social sciences. Instead of artificially controlling for all but one variable in an experimental design, critical realist social scientists attempt to find comparable populations or events with similar histories, where we would expect to find similar outcomes. When critical realists find instead a puzzling difference in outcome, we hypothesize a heretofore-unknown causal mechanism and then we empirically test for this missing mechanism (Lawson 1999, 37).

> In short, any patterning, any "standing-out," of phenomena which turns upon differences or unanticipated or surprising or implausible relationships of some kind, whether primarily social, historical, or geographical, can serve to alert us to the existence or way of acting of some item previously unknown, unrecognized or perhaps known only implicitly, in some taken for granted way. (Lawson 1998, 153)

In fact, Lawson suggests that scientific explanation is inherently contrastive (153).

George Steinmetz complicates Lawson's general contrastive method, which relies on isolating *singular* causal mechanisms in a comparative research project. Because, as explained, critical realism insists on the ontological distinction between events and causal mechanisms, one can compare, Steinmetz urges us, across either generative causal mechanisms *or* across empirical-level events (2004, 373). The founder of critical realism, Roy Bhaskar, explains this distinction as such:

> The world consists of mechanisms not events. Such mechanisms combine to generate the flux of phenomena that constitute the actual states and happenings of the world. They may be said to be real, though it is rarely [*sic*] that they are actually manifest and rarer still that they are empirically identified by men [*sic*]. They are the intransitive objects of scientific theory . . . They are not unknowable . . . they can become manifest to men in experience . . . This is the arduous task of science. (Bhaskar 2008, 47)

Ontological stratification between levels of the empirical (the level of events) and the real (the level of causal mechanisms) are combined with a kind of horizontal stratification where causal structures are always understood to be multiple and diverse, combining in wholly contingent and unpredictable ways (Steinmetz 2004, 377).

> Now, it is characteristic of open systems that two or more mechanisms, perhaps of radically different kinds, combine to produce effects; so that because we do not know ex ante which mechanisms will actually be at work (and perhaps have no knowledge of their mode of articulation) events are not deductively predictable. Most events in open systems must thus be regarded as "conjunctures." (Bhaskar 2008, 119)

This means that no one event is caused by any one, isolated causal mechanism. Rather, events are always overdetermined by "constellations of causal mechanisms" (Steinmetz 1998, 177). Causal constellations are nonrepeatable and unpredictable. Further, any comparable event may not be caused by the same constellation of causal factors, no matter the event's similarities. To make matters more complicated, mechanisms may be exercised without being realized or they may be realized but unperceivable (176). Explanation, then, demands that we contend with all of this causal complexity. Steinmetz suggests that case comparisons of the small-N type can be most explicative in terms of unpacking the complexity of both events and their conjunctural causal features.

> The elements that constitute causal constellations may vary from case to case. And even if we do find recurrent empirical patterns, these can never be assumed to be universal or to be determined by the same set of mechanisms in each case. Comparison thus can focus on the differing empirical effects of a single mechanism, or on the differing conjunctures leading to similar outcomes. (Steinmetz 2004, 383)

Dave Elder-Vass suggests that explanation in the social sciences requires the concept of emergence, where the entity or structure created comes to have properties distinct from its component parts (2010). Within the natural sciences, water is the prototypical example of emergence because it comes to have its own ontological existence as a substance, distinct from hydrogen and oxygen. "The powers and properties of an object or entity can be ascribed to the organization of its parts into a particular kind of complex whole" (Elder-Vass 2010, 45). Elder-Vass suggests that some explanations may require a "laminated" view of the entity being explained, where the whole is stratified into an ensemble of parts at various ontological levels, each of which may exert causal force (49). For example, in explaining a particular effect of capitalism, one might need to view capitalism as its own global force, acting on a population or event, or one may extract a composite part of capitalism, like the property relation, to explain an event.

> Causation is never truly "independent" of what is happening at other levels in the individual instance; it is only analytically independent when generalized. Cause as we generally understand and apply it is therefore an attempt to simplify and extract from the impossible complexity of actual causation. (Elder-Vass 2010, 53)

One further complication I would like to add to this critical realist account comes from William Sewell, who is not an avowed critical realist, but who holds similar views on causality, namely that structures and events can be studied as separate phases of analysis, that events are contingent and therefore unpredictable, and that causality is always conjunctural (Sewell 2005). Sewell augments critical realism by suggesting that structures exist at different depths, vary widely in the kinds of powers they can mobilize, and may be long and enduring or consist of sudden ruptures. He adds an analysis of structural depth, strength, and endurance to the critical realist toolkit. Further, Sewell always insists on the duality of structures, or that they only exist in and through the people who make them up and have the power to change them (2005). This is a point that is also consistently made by Margaret Archer in her work on morphogenesis (Archer 1995). Archer explains that society has no predetermined shape or set of powers, and that structures take shape and are formed by agents, even if we separate these two different modes of action (structural and agential) in our analysis. Ethnography can highlight this point about the mutual causality of agents and structures. This is what ethnographic analysis offers critical realism: an explication of the reverse nature of causality; that agents positioned differentially act back upon structural mechanisms in sometimes unexpected ways, further complicating a critical realist account of causality. In the next section, I explain how I combine components of ECM and critical realism to compare the experiences and beliefs of Somali refugee communities in Minneapolis and Toronto, who are contending with high rates of autism spectrum disorder (ASD) and have forged epistemic communities united around an etiology, ontology, and treatment protocol that challenges mainstream science.

The Epistemic Communities of Minneapolis and Toronto

Idman Roble[3] migrated from Somalia to Toronto, Canada, in 1991. Seven years later, she had her first child, a son she named Mohamed. He was a healthy baby—big and tall. He walked at seven months, and according to Idman he was a "normal, good-lookin' kid," and everything was perfect. As she sat in the pediatrician's office for his eighteen-month well-baby check-up, she read a large sign indicating developmental milestones and the age at which children should reach them. She realized that by his age, her son should know ten words and she knew he did not. She told her pediatrician she was worried about his speech delay, and the pediatrician tried to call Mohamed over to him, from where he was sitting playing with toys. Mohamed did not respond. The pediatrician assessed Mohamed and made a referral to a developmental pediatrician and told Idman that he suspected Mohamed was likely autistic. He said, "Idman, I wish I could give him some pills that could make what he has go away, but your son has something called autism." Idman recalls these words exactly. "I came home that day, and I was just so sad and so confused. I didn't know what was going on . . . Finding out was tough for me . . . because we were very ignorant about what autism was because we never saw someone who was autistic back home."

Mohamed was given a battery of tests, as well as a diagnostic assessment for autism. "They kept telling me it was a life-long disability and his whole life, he would be autistic—my son. That was very devastating for me and my family . . . I wish I knew what I know today, but I didn't have any idea, and I didn't know anybody to turn to and ask for information about how to help my son. Nobody. Nobody I knew in my community, or anyone in Toronto. None, none, none." At that time, there was no process in place for referring parents to local governmental services for children with developmental disabilities. Two years later, Idman noticed advertisements about children with special needs and called the community agency on a billboard, which led to an interagency assessment and eventually one-on-one behavioral therapy through a local autism agency. Her son was getting services, and his language and skill set immediately started improving, but she still felt isolated. In 2002, when her son was attending a summer camp for children with developmental disabilities, she met Adar Hassan who has two sons with autism. This was the first Somali that Idman had met who was dealing with the same issues. They became fast friends and collaborators, and soon came to learn that many other Somali parents in Toronto had children with autism and were also struggling to cope in isolation.

Idman tells me that one of the most frustrating things she has dealt with is that doctors keep telling her that autism is just behavioral. But after years of research, Idman has come to believe that her son's behavioral difficulties are caused by underlying physiological disorders. She thinks that the behavioral symptoms of autism (challenges in language, social skills, and social repertoire) are caused by biological disorders in her child's gastrointestinal tract, immune system, and metabolic and cellular function.

> Look if I go to a doctor, they believe that autism is a behavior . . . But I don't believe that. Our kids have so many health issues. They have gut issues . . . Some of them they don't sleep well. Sleep disturbances. Some of them, they have an eating disorder. Their diet is very limited. Some of them, they have eczema. Some of them, they have asthma. I mean, our kids have so many complex issues . . . They're all related . . . So you cannot say that, oh they have autism behavior. What is the cause of autism behavior? Because their body is not functioning the proper way. There's so many things, the minerals, vitamins, they're missing something. Or they have a stomach issue. They cannot digest the food . . . Some of them don't go regularly to the washroom . . . Imagine how you'd feel if you didn't go for a couple days. How does your brain function? Tell me. So all those things, they ignore it . . . [Autism is] a health issue. Those health issues cause behavior.

This belief that autism is really a biological and not a behavioral or even psychological issue is related to the fact that, for Idman, and many other Somalis who have children with autism, autism is caused by a whole host of environmental insults to the vulnerable bodies of their children—children whose bodies were made vulnerable because of forced migration. Idman believes that forced migration from Somalia to Canada altered her gut microbiota and other features of her immune and metabolic systems, which made her children vulnerable to autism. For Idman, Mohammed's autism is the result of numerous environmental insults, including a caesarian section that damaged her son's microbiome, vaccinations while breastfeeding, and exposure to "superbugs" in the hospital after birth. These theories about the etiology and ontology of autism inform her approach to treatment and support for her son. Idman has tried a host of biological remedies, including nutritional supplements, probiotics, enzymes, chelation, and glutathione therapy.

"Autism is a big puzzle, so you have to get all the pieces to connect together. It won't help you if you do just one thing . . . If something works for one child, it won't necessarily work for another child with autism. Every child's autism is unique." She tries various therapies, expecting she will eventually hit on the right combination to help Mohamed's behavior improve.

Idman did not come to these theories of autism causation alone, nor is she isolated in her continuous quest for therapies. In fact, she and Adar have formed a support group for Somali parents of children with autism in Toronto, which has transformed over time into a tight-knit epistemic community united around a common etiology, ontology, and treatment regimen for autism.

In 2012, I came across a newspaper article explaining that the Centers for Disease Control (CDC) had launched a surveillance study on autism prevalence among the Somali population in Minneapolis, based on parental and educational reports that Somalis were experiencing high rates of autism. As I began to look into the issue, I discovered that the public health and education communities in Minnesota had gotten involved in this issue because of fears about drops in MMR (measles, mumps and rubella) coverage, as well as Somali parent mobilization. In fact, the surveillance study results confirmed that Somalis constitute an autism "cluster."[4] One in 32 children of Somali descent, aged seven to nine in 2010, were identified with autism (University of Minnesota 2013). This prevalence rate is roughly equivalent to white children in Minneapolis (1 in 36), but much higher than the national average, which is 1 in 59 (Baio et al. 2018). One hundred percent of the Somali children with autism had an accompanying intellectual disability. Soon thereafter, I came across a video discussing the same issue in the Somali community in Toronto (ABC Four Corners 2009). I was intrigued and decided to embark on a comparative ethnography of autism among Somali refugees in Minneapolis and Toronto.

Similar to the ECM approach, my decision to embark on a *comparative* ethnographic project was driven by theoretical interests. I was intrigued by the ways that Somalis' experiences of racial, religious and national marginalization influenced how they made sense of their children's autism diagnoses and pursued therapies. Ethnography was the only methodological technique that would allow me to excavate their meaning-making processes and experiences of marginalization. A comparative approach was necessary because both the Minneapolis and Toronto Somali communities had forged coherent epistemic communities, though they differed in scope and content.

The existing literature focusing on health social movements (Petryna 2002; Rose and Novas 2004; Epstein 2007; Nguyen 2010) fails to take into account how people suffering from the same illness may forge divergent social movements. In other words, it assumes that bonds form between people who share a common biosocial identity (like being HIV-positive, or a parent of someone with autism), which leads to "politicized collective illness identities" (Brown et al. 2004) and eventually social movements. But why do people who share a biosocial identity form conflicting groups? I was interested in what makes the same population (Somali immigrants and refugees), exposed to the same phenomena (high rates of autism) forge divided and often contentious explanations, target different authority figures for blame, and join divergent, "embodied health movements" (Brown et al. 2004; Brown 2007). In addition, the literature on health social movements and biosocial groupings has thus far failed to consider experiences of populations marginalized on the basis of race, religion, and nationality.

There are certain features of the Somali autism experience which hold constant across the two national contexts, but many of the structural features informing group formation vary between the two sites, including racial formations, refugee policies, autism health policies (and the broader difference between private and public health provision), responses to vaccine hesitancy, and the involvement of local public health, education, and medical communities. These different structural contexts have influenced the content, composition and coherence of the Somali autism communities over time. I needed a methodological approach that would allow me to compare both the event in question: the formation of epistemic communities around autism causation and therapy in minoritized populations, and the structural context and conjunctural causal mechanisms.

As such, this study compares across the levels of structural mechanism and event (the real and the actual). At the level of the event, there are several features that hold constant in both national settings. The majority of the Somali parents of children with autism I met and spoke with in both locations insisted that autism does not exist in Somalia, and therefore, genetic explanations for the disorder make little sense.

ADAR: I remember I literally called my mom. At that time she was alive. I called her. I called my uncle, I called my aunt, asking them, you know, anybody, please tell me if you've seen anything like this behavior before because they're telling me this is caused by genetics.

IDMAN: Why is it so epidemic if it's genetic? That's the real question.

Another commonality across the Somali communities was the general tendency to see autism as an environmentally acquired illness. Even Somalis who think it is possible that their children have an underlying genetic disorder or mutation also insist that autism is triggered by something environmental. For example, Safia Gassem explained: "I think it's genetic, but very sensitive to this environment . . . because, in Somalia, we don't have all this environmental toxic . . . Maybe we are more susceptible to this environment. Maybe our genes don't accept this environment" (interview June 10, 2015). Somali parents in both Minneapolis and Toronto point to a whole host of environmental insults including: lack of Vitamin D, shifts in gut heterogeneity due to changing diets, environmental toxins, stress, the overuse of antibiotics in health and food production, the overuse of caesarian sections in birthing practices, and vaccines. Of the 54 parents I officially interviewed across the two locations, only five parents did not think that vaccines were a primary causal factor for the development of autism. Because of these common beliefs about the cause of autism, there was some overlap in how parents sought therapies for their children. Many of the parents tried various forms of alternative or biomedical therapies, meaning therapies other than applied behavioral analysis—the only agreed-upon mainstream approach to treating autism. But this is not unique to the Somali community. Estimates of the usage of alternative therapies within the autism community vary widely, but most suggest that it is very common for parents of children with autism to try multiple alternative therapies (Hanson et al. 2007; Silverman 2012; Hart 2014).

In both Toronto and Minneapolis, Somali parents of children with autism also point out that their children have more severe forms of autism. The CDC study in Minneapolis found that Somali children with autism had higher rates of intellectual disability than most children with autism and provided evidence to support these beliefs. Somali parents of children with autism in both Toronto and Minneapolis have formed support groups and political organizations, which are largely headed by charismatic, well-educated, and strong-willed women. Parents in both Toronto and Minneapolis have also teamed up with researchers to forge lay-expert collaborations, though the resulting types of research have varied dramatically.

There are several underlying causes of these consistencies across national sites. Because most Somali refugees and immigrants fled to the United States and Canada due to the Somali civil war, their movement to the Western Hemisphere happened around the same time period. The largest migrations began in the early 1990s and have remained relatively steady, although the numbers entering Canada and the United States on an annual basis have declined since the 1990s. Somalis in both Toronto and Minneapolis were settled into high-density urban settings, and the majority remain reliant on public welfare. Due to their racial and religious identity, Somalis have faced discrimination and remain segregated from other ethnic communities. In addition, due to the strong sense of Somali identity and desire to sustain Somali culture in North America, first-generation Somalis remain very close-knit and insulated. Somalis remain in close contact throughout the diaspora, and often move back and forth between Minneapolis and Toronto (the two largest sites of Somali settlement in North America.) There are various social media and telephonic forums that keep Somali immigrants connected to one another and in constant conversation about politics in the West and in Somalia. Autism is often a topic of this transnational conversation and debate. These demi-regularities (Lawson 1998) make it unsurprising that similar epistemic communities might form in two different national sites. The comparison of these communities is an actualist comparison, at the level of event. And yet the structural and cultural settings in Canada and the United States also lead to tremendous differences in how these epistemic communities have emerged and matured, their ability to form social movements and their impact on local politics, policies, and research. The structural mechanisms combine in unique constellations to impact these two communities differentially. To address these unique constellations, I now turn to a comparison across mechanisms, a "depth-realist comparison" (Steinmetz 2004, 394).

This level of analysis required me to "extend out" from the micro-processes (Burawoy 1998, 2009) of the Somali community to explore the national and global forces influencing the formation, coherence, and maintenance of these epistemic communities. This entailed a different set of methodological techniques, including interviews with 150 professionals who work in the field of autism provision, education, policy, and research, as well as Somali professionals, activists, and community organizers. I engaged in extended archival research, including newspaper sources, social movement documents, policy documents, funding reports, immigration policies and statistics, and academic research on autism causation and therapy.

A variety of divergent structural features impact the Somali epistemic communities in Toronto and Minneapolis. I will outline several of the key factors, but then highlight one feature to provide a detailed demonstration of this depth-realist comparative technique. The United States and Canada have very different racial formations (Omi and Winant 1994). Canada has adopted a racial ideology of multiculturalism against the United States' assimilationist ideology. Moreover, the racialized state violence that Somali populations face in Toronto and Minneapolis have varied in form and extremity: Somalis in Canada face criminalization on the basis of drug use and gang involvement, whereas Somalis in the United States have been the target of FBI surveillance over terrorist threats. Refugee policies in the United States and Canada also varied dramatically. Canadian refugees were assigned a liminal citizenship status for extended periods of time. As a result, Somalis faced barriers to employment and education for many years during the time that the bulk of Somalis immigrated to Canada. In the United States, refugees are required to seek employment and their benefits rely upon proof of employment. This creates its own challenges for Somali communities, but refugees are immediately thrown into educational and employment settings in the United States. In addition, one might expect that Canada's nationalized healthcare system would afford better access to autism services for marginalized populations than the privatized US healthcare system. But autism is not considered a medical condition in Canada; therefore, therapies are not provided by the Canadian national healthcare system. Applied behavioral analysis (in a variety of forms) is available to Canadian citizens free of charge, but the waiting lists are long, not every child with autism is guaranteed a spot, and transportation and timing issues make attending sessions difficult for families with two working parents and multiple children. Most of the Somali-Canadian parents I interviewed are extremely unsatisfied with the autism services they have received (or not received) and believe the system is biased against them. Due to lengthy battles by parents and advocates in the United States (and a strong history of disability rights mobilization), the privatized health system in the United States affords most children with autism slightly better access to services than in Canada. But many Somali parents still complain that the best services are only available to those who can afford to pay for private therapies out of pocket. In addition, heightened concerns over vaccine hesitancy and resistance in the United States (and declining rates of MMR coverage) have generated extensive surveillance of Somali health practices in Minneapolis that does not exist in Canada. This is just a small sample of the structural features that combine to shape Somalis' experiences in the two national contexts and inform the emergence of epistemic communities antagonistic to mainstream autism policy and research. Each community, in each national site, faces isolation and discrimination, more severe forms of autism due to lack of access to resources, and heightened surveillance of their health choices. These dynamics converge in causal constellations of mechanisms at particular historical moments in the development of these communities, which directly affects their impact on local (and even national) policy and research. At any one moment, a particular structural mechanism may be more or less prominent, more or less effective due to the broader political and scientific landscape. Therefore, the depth, strength, and endurance of the mechanism can differentially affect the epistemic community and its mobilization at any particular time. To demonstrate this argument, I will focus on one example of how structural dynamics differentially impact the epistemic communities in Toronto and Minneapolis.

In Minneapolis, Somali parents began bonding together in the early 2000s, when they noticed that Somalis were overrepresented in early childhood special education programs. Along with a motivated special education teacher, they contacted Minnesota Department of Health officials, who held a community forum with parents and agreed to engage in administrative prevalence research focused on the Somali population (Minnesota Department of Health 2009). In 2009, the Minnesota Department of Health published a study revealing that Somali children in Minneapolis were two to seven- times more likely to receive ASD special education services than non-Somali children (Minnesota Department of Health 2009). The parents began organizing among themselves and started an organization called Parents United Against Autism. According to several researchers who eventually became involved in the CDC study, these early mobilizations effectively used accusations of racial disparities and racial discrimination to draw attention to the issue. The parents were extremely active—conducting interviews with media, writing blogs, and meeting with government officials, educators, health providers, public health officials, and researchers. This eventually led to a collaboration between the CDC, the National Institutes of Health (NIH), Autism Speaks, the Minnesota Department of Health (MDH), and University of Minnesota (UM), that carried out an Autism and Developmental Disabilities Monitoring (ADDM) surveillance study from 2011–2012 in Minneapolis.[5] This study confirmed a high prevalence rate of ASD in the Somali population (University of Minnesota 2013). Many Somali parents and Somali professionals were actively involved as researchers in the study, and others become involved as cultural liaisons with the MDH and UM.

Collaborations between the Somali community and the local public health and research communities did not end with the 2011–2012 CDC study. Somali parents remained active in advocating for a new Autism Benefit, which was rolled out in Minnesota in 2016; Somali professionals and parents meet monthly at a Somali Public Health Advisors group, which directly advises the Minnesota Department of Health on issues in the community, and other research collaborations and publications have resulted from relationships that began with the CDC study. In fact, the CDC declared Hennepin and Ramsey counties (in Minnesota) an official federal ADDM site starting in January 2015. These counties were part of the CDC 2014 and 2016 cycles.

The story is quite different in Toronto. Despite their best efforts and trying many of the same tactics as the parents in Minneapolis, Somali parents of children with autism in Toronto have had little success in garnering any attention or resources from local service providers or government officials.

> As soon as the news came out in Minnesota, when they found out that a lot of Somalis have autistic kids . . . Everybody, they came to the rescue. They paid attention and it resulted in better access to education, speech [therapy] and ABA [applied behavioral analysis] . . . Where is ours? Where is ours? We did a documentary with David Suzuki. Before that, we published an article in the *Globe and Mail*. Of all of that, not one Canadian stood up to try to help these poor, poor people who don't know . . . what's happening to their kids; who don't know how to help them. (Adar Hassan, interview June 12, 2014)

As Adar explains in this quote, Somalis in Toronto made a film with David Suzuki called *Autism Enigma* (ABC Four Corners), which aired on major media outlets throughout Canada. Adar was also featured in a *Globe and Mail* newspaper article (Jiménez 2009). Members of the support group have met with numerous officials from the Ministries of Health, Children and Youth, and Education to raise the issue of Somalis' vulnerability to autism, as well as their struggles to access services for their children. Their efforts have largely fallen on deaf ears.

There are a number of reasons that the Somali community in Minneapolis has been more successful in garnering public and professional recognition of their plight than Somalis in Toronto. One of the most important reasons is the threat they posed to vaccine compliance. This is a complicated issue that I do not have the space to address here, but MMR coverage rates among Somalis in Hennepin county fell from 90% in 2004 to just under 55% in 2010 (Bahta and Ashkir 2015).[6]

But another reason Somalis in Minneapolis have been more successful than their counterparts in Toronto is due to differences in the racial dynamics of the two countries. Key leaders in autism advocacy, research, and policy in the United States are keenly aware that the racial dynamics of autism are sorely underexplored and unknown. In fact, according to one anonymous source, the Somali parents were responsible for the federal governments' attention to this issue because they "called people racist and shamed the CDC into the study." Public health and education professionals in Minneapolis have worked hard to respond to demands from the Somali community. They have been receptive to arguments that racial disparities impact access to healthcare and have worked diligently to not only address these issues, but to involve Somalis in figuring out how to address them. According to parents in Toronto, however, the multicultural racial politics of Canada make race a less salient political category for social movement mobilization than accusations of racial discrimination and racial disparities in the United States. Idman told me that when people are accused of being racist in Canada, they back away instead of step up. People try so hard, she said, to avoid conversations about race, that they make racism worse. Idman explained that when she and Adar discuss the high rates of autism in the Somali community with government officials, they are told, "We cannot look into this without any proof of what you are saying," but Idman asks, "How are we to get proof if no one is willing to help us?"

This is not simply a matter of a structural causal mechanism (racial formation) operating differently in Toronto and Minneapolis. The Minneapolis Somali community activated this structural mechanism and, through the strategic manipulation of US racial politics, managed to transform existing structural dynamics in Minneapolis. This was less successful in Toronto because of the different content, depth, and power of the Canadian racial system. It was the parents in Minneapolis who made the racial structure so crucial in determining the outcome of these events. According to Sewell (2005), conceiving of structures as multiple and overlapping matters for two reasons. First, subjects are formed by multiple different structures and sit at the intersection of a conjuncture of interpellating systems (2005, 212). And second, this means that agency and creativity are easier to understand: "It follows that they should have some intellectual distance on the structural categories themselves, that they should be able to view one set of cultural categories from the point of view of others that are differently organized, to compare and criticize . . . categorical logics, to work out ways of . . . harmonizing . . . the seemingly contradictory demands of different cultural [and structural] schemes" (2005, 213). Recognizing the conjunctural nature of causality helps the researcher analyze how agents come to exercise agency and creativity in navigating the system that informs and shapes their actions. Somalis in Minneapolis were able to use the vulnerabilities of the US racial system to advocate for better health resources for their children. Critical realists highlight two crucial aspects of causality: that causal mechanisms can be compared independently of the events they inspire and must be understood as contingent and conjunctural. But, critical realists often fail to highlight the mutual constitution of agents and structures. Ethnographic methods can overcome this limitation. In this example, agents strategically utilized the "conjuncture of structures" (Sewell 2005, 221) to not only navigate their social world, but intervene in it, thereby shifting the content and force of those structures moving forward.

In addition to highlighting subjects' agency, understanding the conjunctural nature of causality can help the researcher unpack the combination of structures that informed the eventful outcome of Somalis in Minneapolis being able to impact local autism advocacy and systems of care. Race did not operate in isolation, as the key variable in question. Rather, its salience arose in part from its relationship to other structures, including the medical, education, and public health systems. Similarly, the outcome reverberated beyond simply changing the racial system. Other features of the conjuncture of structures included the unique history of vaccine hesitancy, autism causation, and the response by US public health officials to concerns about a relationship between the two, privatized healthcare and racial health disparities that lead to late diagnosis and higher severity of autism in marginalized populations, and the history of refugee policy in Minnesota—a state known as a haven for refugee resettlement. Minneapolis government officials were invested in sustaining their reputation as a haven through partnerships with the Somali community, one of the city's largest, newest, and most visible immigrant communities. "The specific nature of the structure of the conjuncture will differ. . . but we do know what to look for: a conjuncture of structures that sets off a synergistic interaction between actors attempting to make structural sense of a highly volatile situation" (Sewell 2005, 223).

How is it possible to use ethnography to identify all of the structures acting within a particular conjunctural constellation? I have addressed this issue in another article (Decoteau 2017), but it is important to begin by understanding the complexity of the ethnographic situation by first asking respondents to identify the causes they see impacting their actions, beliefs, and experiences. Then, one extends out to macro forces and draws on other sources of data (in my case interviews with service providers, policy specialists, immigration specialists, and educators, as well as archival and historical data) to identify and describe the causal powers (and their interaction effects) in operation. From this, the researcher builds a conjunctural causal model, which, if accurate, elucidates the effects seen in the ethnographic locale. The model is both theoretical and explanatory, but it is also fallible and contingent, requiring ongoing testing. The best causal models have strong evidentiary basis, the greatest explanatory power, and the widest theoretical scope (Gorski 2004, 21).

Heeding Burawoy's insistence that the positionality of the researcher always matters in ethnographic research (2009), I want to conclude this section by showing how my own positionality as a sociologist mattered in Toronto and Minneapolis *because* of the different histories of local investment (or lack thereof) in addressing autism in Somali communities. By the time I arrived in Minneapolis in 2013, the city had a long history of researcher involvement in the topic. Some people were unimpressed with my interests and failed to see the relevance of yet another research project, especially an ethnographic one. In addition, because I was not from Minneapolis, some people questioned whether I would show up regularly or be invested in their communities. Therefore, it took a long time and a lot of hard work to convince people in Minneapolis that I was serious about this project and could contribute something to the existing knowledge. In the end, I was able to conduct ethnographic research with Somali parents of children with autism in Minneapolis and to develop an understanding of the contemporary contours of existing epistemic communities between 2013 and 2016. Very few of the early Somali parent pioneers were still involved or interested in being part of my research project, therefore, my analysis of the history and transformation of the parents' movement had to come from people who worked with the Somali community and not from interviews with the founders of the movement.[7]

In Toronto, the opposite was true. After initial vetting in 2013, the Somali community in Toronto welcomed me with open arms. They invited me to observe meetings of their support group, carry out extensive ethnographic research and interviews with support group members, gave me references for service providers and activists, and basically did everything in their power to open access for me. I was intimately involved in the community, and as a result, my ethnographic data from Toronto is much more extensive than my data from Minneapolis. I suspect that one of the reasons for this differential treatment stemmed from the fact that the Toronto community was desperately trying to attract attention to their plight; something the leaders of the Minneapolis community felt they no longer needed. Still, many Somali parents in Minneapolis were more than happy to share their stories and welcome me into their homes. Some of these parents told me that their stories were not being heard by the leadership of the local Somali parents' movement. As a result, I was able to gather more backstage data in Minneapolis and more of the official story of the Somali movement in Toronto.

Conclusion

As in Burawoy's analysis (2009), context, process, positionality, and theory inform my analysis. I analyzed the structural features (context) that affected the epistemic communities in Toronto and Minneapolis—in terms of their etiology, ontology, and approach to treating autism and in terms of the impact of the epistemic communities on local policies and service provision. I also showed that these epistemic communities are not static in nature; they change over time in relationship to structural dynamics, which are also changing both in response to parent activism and on their own (process). I analyzed how my positionality mattered in gathering data in these two communities. I also showed that theory was integral to casing the phenomena under analysis. Theory will also be integral to my analysis of why these epistemic communities matter in the broader context of autism science and policy, though that part of my analysis is beyond the scope of this chapter.

I have shown that critical realism offers ethnographers helpful tools with regard to causal inference and comparison. Critical realism reveals that there are multiple levels at which phenomena can be compared—at the level of the event itself and at the level of the real, where causal mechanisms operate. These mechanisms never act alone but always in concert with other mechanisms, making any event overdetermined by a constellation of forces that are difficult to isolate in the open system of the social. Critical realism and the work of William Sewell (2005) offer us methodological tools for parsing out the complexity of causal mechanisms that generate contingent conjunctions. And yet critical realism can also benefit from further engagement with ethnography—particularly by recognizing the mutual causal relationship between the actual and the real. As agents navigate, use, and strategically deploy the schemas and resources made available to them by their structural positionalities, they actively transform those same structures. Agents do not passively accept the unchanging powers and forces of static systems that inform them, but rather have the power to transform existing structures precisely because of the contingent and conjunctural nature of causality.

Notes

1. Exceptions include Decoteau (2017), Rees and Gatenby (2014), and Porter (2002).
2. "A mechanism is basically a way of acting or working of a structured thing. Bicycles and rockets work in certain ways. Of course they cannot work or act in the ways they do without possessing the power to do so. Mechanisms then exist as causal powers of things. Powers of structured things are usually exercised only as a result of some input: the striking of a match, the lifting and wielding of the hammer, the switching on of a computer or interacting with it, the flexing of vocal chords, the arrival of teachers and children at school or employees at the workplace. And mechanisms when triggered (where relevant) have effects. Structured things, then, possess causal powers which, when triggered or released, act as generative mechanisms to determine the actual phenomena of the world" (Lawson 1997, 21).
3. Those subjects whose names are used in this study have consented to the use of their names. All other participants' identities remain confidential.
4. Autism "clustering" in the US occurs in white, wealthy populations because of social networks, the widespread availability of pediatric healthcare, diagnostic expansion, and better detection and reporting (King and Bearman, 2011; Liu et al. 2010; Mazumdar et al. 2013; Bakian et al. 2015). To my knowledge, the Somali autism cluster in Minneapolis is the first cluster discovered in a racially marginalized and economically disadvantaged population.
5. This project was carried out by a series of researchers from the University of Minnesota and the Minnesota Department of Health. Experts screened, abstracted, and reviewed school and medical records, which included not only children with official ASD diagnoses, but those who were reported to have behaviors consistent with ASD. Findings from the survey can be found here: http://rtc.umn.edu/autism/.
6. There was a measles outbreak in March of 2011, which prompted a county epidemiological report on MMR uptake, and it was discovered that the rate had dropped from 2007 (when it was 90%), to 55% in 2011 and then to 30% in 2013 (fieldnotes June 13,

2013). There was recently a severe measles outbreak within the Somali community in Minneapolis (in May of 2017), which has brought added scrutiny to this issue.

7. I did end up interviewing several people who had been involved in the early years, but I was missing interviews with some of the key players.

References

ABC Four Corners. 2009. *Autism Enigma*. Aired August 27, 2012. Produced by C. Sumpton, R. Benger, and M. Gruner.

Archer, M. 1995. *Realist Social Theory: The Morphogenetic Approach*. Cambridge: Cambridge University Press.

Baio, J., L. Wiggins, D. L. Christensen, M. J. Maenner, J. Daniels, Z. Warren, M. Kurzius-Spencer, W. Zahorodny, C. Robinson, T. White, M. S. Durkin, P. Imm, L. Nikolaou, M. Yeargin-Allsopp, L-C. Lee, R. Harrington, M. Lopez, R. T. Fitzgerald, A. Hewitt, S. Pettygrove, J. N. Constantino, A. Vehorn, J. Shenouda, J. Hall-Lande, K. Braun, and N. F. Dowling. 2018. "Prevalence of Autism Spectrum Disorder Among Children Aged 8 Years—Autism and Developmental Disabilities Monitoring Network, 11 Sites, United States, 2014." *Centers for Disease Control Morbidity and Mortality Weekly Report, Surveillance Studies* 67, no. 6: 1–23.

Bakian, A., D. Bilder, H. Coon, and W. McMahon. 2015. "Spatial Relative Risk Patterns of Autism Spectrum Disorders in Utah." *Journal of Autism & Developmental Disorders* 45, no. 4: 988–1000.

Bhaskar, R. 2008. *A Realist Theory of Science*. New York: Verso.

Bahta, L., and A. Ashkir. 2015. "Addressing MMR Vaccine Resistance in Minnesota's Somali Community." *Minnesota Medicine* (October): 33–36.

Brown, P. 2007. *Toxic Exposures: Contested Illnesses and the Environmental Health Movement*. New York: Columbia University Press.

Brown, P., S. Zavetoski, S. McCormick, B. Mayer, R. Morello-Frosch, and R. G. Altman. 2004. "Embodied Health Movements: New Approaches to Social Movements in Health." *Sociology of Health & Illness* 26, no. 1: 50–80.

Burawoy, M. 1998. "The Extended Case Method." *Sociological Theory* 16, no. 1: 4–33.

Burawoy, M. 2009. *The Extended Case Method: Four Countries, Four Decades, Four Great Transformations*. Berkeley: University of California Press.

Burawoy, M., J. Blum, S. George, Z. Gille, T. Gowan, L. Haney, M. Klawiter, S. Lopez, S. O. Riain, and M. Thayer. 2000. *Global Ethnography: Forces, Connections and Imaginations in a Postmodern World*. Berkeley: University of California Press.

Decoteau, C. L. 2017. "The AART of Ethnography: A Critical Realist Explanatory Research Model." *Journal for the Theory of Social Behaviour* 47, no. 1: 58–82.

Elder-Vass, D. 2010. *The Causal Power of Social Structures: Emergence, Structure and Agency*. Cambridge: Cambridge University Press.

Epstein, S. 2007. *Inclusion: The Politics of Difference in Medical Research*. Chicago: University of Chicago Press.

Gille, Z., and Ó Riain, S. 2002. "Global Ethnography." *Annual Review of Sociology* 28: 271–295.

Gorski, P. 2004. "The Poverty of Deductivism: A Constructive Realist Model of Sociological Explanation." *Sociological Methodology* 34, no. 1: 1–33.

Hanson, E., L. A. Kalish, E. Bunce, C. Curtis, S. McDaniel, J. Ware, and J. Petry. 2007. "Use of Complementary and Alternative Medicine among Children Diagnosed with Autism Spectrum Disorder." *Journal of Autism & Developmental Disorders* 37, no. 4: 628–636.

Hart, B. 2014. "Autism Parents & Neurodiversity: Radical Translation, Joint Embodiment and the Prosthetic Environment." *BioSocieties* 9, no. 3: 284–303.

Jiménez, M. 2009. "The Somali Autism Puzzle." *Globe and Mail*, April 7. http://www.theglobeandmail.com/life/health-and-fitness/health/conditions/the-somali-autism-puzzle/article572688/.

King, M., and Bearman, P. 2011. "Socioeconomic Status and the Increased Prevalence of Autism in California." *American Sociological Review* 76, no. 2: 320–346.

Lawson, T. 1997. *Economics and Society*. Cambridge: Cambridge University Press.

Lawson, T. 1998. "Economic Science without Experimentation." In *Critical Realism, Essential Readings*, edited by Margaret Archer, Roy Bhaskar, Andrew Collier, Tony Lawson, and Alan Norrie, 144–169. New York: Routledge.

Lawson, T. 1999. "Feminism, Realism, and Universalism." *Feminist Economics* 5, no. 2: 25–59.

Liu, K-Y., M. King, and P. Bearman. 2010. "Social Influence and the Autism Epidemic." *American Journal of Sociology* 115, no. 5: 1387–1434.

Marcus, G. E. 1986. "Contemporary Problems of Ethnography in the Modern World System." In *Writing Culture: The Poetics and Politics of Ethnography*, edited by J. Clifford and G. E. Marcus, 165–193. Berkeley: University of California Press.

Marcus, G. E. 1995. "Ethnography in/of the World System: The Emergence of Multi-Sited Ethnography." *Annual Review of Anthropology* 24: 95–117.

Marcus, G. E. 1998. *Ethnography Through Thick and Thin*. Princeton, NJ: Princeton University Press.

Martin, E. 1994. *Flexible Bodies: The Role of Immunity in American Culture from the Days of Polio to the Age of AIDS*. Boston: Beacon Press.

Mazumdar, S., A. Winter, K-Y. Liu, and P. Bearman. 2013. "Spatial Clusters of Autism Births and Diagnoses Point to Contextual Drivers of Increased Prevalence." *Social Science and Medicine* 95 (October): 87–96.

Minnesota Department of Health. 2009. "Autism and the Somali Community—Report of Study." https://www.health.state.mn.us/diseases/autism/somalireport.html.

Nguyen, V-K. 2010. *The Republic of Therapy: Triage and Sovereignty in West Africa's Time of AIDS*. Durham, NC: Duke University Press.

Omi, M., and H. Winant. 1994. *Racial Formation in the United States: From the 1960s to the 1990s*. New York: Routledge.

Petryna, A. 2002. *Life Exposed: Biological Citizens after Chernobyl*. Princeton, NJ: Princeton University Press.

Porter, S. 2002. "Critical Realist Ethnography." In *Qualitative Research in Action*, edited by T. May, 53–72. London: SAGE Publications.

Rees, C. and M. Gatenby. 2014. "Critical Realism and Ethnography." In *Studying Organizations Using Critical Realism: A Practical Guide*, edited by P. K. Edwards, J. O'Mahoney, and S. Vincent, 132–147. Oxford: Oxford University Press.

Rose, N., and C. Novas. 2004. "Biological Citizenship." In *Global Assemblages: Technology, Politics, and Ethics as Anthropological Problems*, edited by Aihwa Ong and S. J. Collier, 439–463. Oxford: Blackwell.

Sewell, W. 2005. *Logics of History: Social Theory and Social Transformation*. Chicago: University of Chicago Press.

Silverman, C. 2012. *Understanding Autism: Parents, Doctors and the History of a Disorder*. Princeton, NJ: Princeton University Press.

Steinmetz, G. 1998. "Critical Realism and Historical Sociology: A Review Article." *Comparative Studies in Society and History* 40, no. 1: 170–186.

Steinmetz, G. 2004 "Odious Comparisons: Incommensurability, the Case Study, and 'Small N's' in Sociology." *Sociological Theory* 22, no. 3: 371–400.

University of Minnesota. 2013. *Minneapolis Somali Autism Spectrum Disorder Prevalence Project*. http://rtc.umn.edu/autism/#project_docs.

7

Sequential Comparisons and the Comparative Imagination

Iddo Tavory and Stefan Timmermans

Despite some protestations to the contrary, ethnographers necessarily work comparatively. Even a single site study entails important comparative dimensions and decisions, as observations and situations are compared for analytical leverage, and as the ethnographer thinks about it in relation to other texts. But what, exactly, is a comparison? What kinds of comparisons can we engage with in our work? This chapter outlines some of the ways in which ethnographers work comparatively as a way to enrich our comparative imagination, and makes a partisan case for one comparative research strategy, that of *sequential comparison*.

As ideal types, we begin by suggesting that there are at least three broad ways in which ethnography can be comparative. First, given that research takes its meaning in relation to a community of inquiry, *shadow comparisons* constantly lurk behind our work. On this basic level, any ethnography worth its salt is comparative. An ethnography of marginalized black urban men necessarily evokes comparisons to Liebow's (1967) *Tally's Corner* and Anderson's (1976) *A Place on the Corner*; an ethnography of working-class teenagers necessarily takes Paul Willis's (1977) "lads" as a point of reference. Working within a community of inquiry, our work resides in a larger historical matrix of those who came before us and who work alongside us, and the meaning of what we do is importantly defined by its location in a structure of similarities and differences to other research within this world. As with all signs, the meanings of ethnography emerge through difference and reference.

But this, perhaps, seems too general. If shadow comparisons are everywhere, is it even useful to highlight their importance as comparisons? As we proceed to show, explicit attention to such a comparative dimension is crucial, but insufficient to capitalize on the comparative potential of

Iddo Tavory and Stefan Timmermans, *Sequential Comparisons and the Comparative Imagination* In: *Beyond the Case*. Edited by: Corey M. Abramson and Neil Gong, Oxford University Press (2020). © Oxford University Press.
DOI: 10.1093/oso/9780190608484.003.0008

ethnography. Beyond shadow comparisons are more overt comparisons. But even here, what "comparison" means remains unclear. We suspect that for most people the words "comparative ethnography" evokes images of an ethnographer spending a year in one place, then a year in another; perhaps going to one group on Tuesday and Thursdays, another on Mondays and Wednesdays. Then we imagine her building her ethnographic narrative and claims around the similarities and differences that she finds between different—albeit carefully chosen—ethnographic sites. This second kind of comparison can be thought of as an *external comparison*, loosely organized around a set of expected similarities and differences.

Third, these kinds of comparisons can be productively juxtaposed to other kinds of comparisons—those that we constantly attend to as we conduct any "single site" ethnography. These *internal comparisons* are of a somewhat different order. Rather than thinking among sites or research projects, it focuses on the internal variation between what happens in one situation and the next; between how we see people act in one part of their social world, and another; between the lives of our interlocutors when we began our study, to their lives years later when we leave the field.[1]

Bringing these various forms of comparison into sharper focus, this chapter advances two arguments. First, and most basically, it aims to widen the scope of our comparative imagination. The relationship between shadow comparisons, internal comparisons, and external comparisons provides us with new ways to think about our work. There are multiple ways to compare, and each project needs to develop its own kind of comparison based on both the questions that motivate the research, and those that emerge in the research act. Widening the scope of our comparative imagination would thus help us avoid straightjacketing our own research into preset ways of conceptualizing, and moving among, cases.

Second, we make a partisan case. We argue that a neglected consideration—and resource—in thinking about comparative ethnography is requires us to re-evaluate how research is situated in time. Ethnographers think about time carefully when they trace objects as they move between situations, or when they trace people's careers. But they often neglect to think about the time of analysis. Those of us who ply the trade of external comparison often try to get their fieldwork in two places done as soon as possible, sometimes visiting two or more sites during the same period (especially when the sites are close by). The timeline of a PhD program, or the promises made on a grant application, exacerbate this tendency. We think, however, that this approach doesn't play to the strengths of ethnographic comparison—the theoretically productive recursive relation between analysis and observation.

Instead, we argue that people would be better off practicing sequential comparisons in their fieldwork. That is, working through one field site carefully, attending to the internal comparisons that emerge there, and abductively figuring out the theoretical and empirical story we want to tell, and only then moving to another field, that (we have reason to hope) provides an interesting counterpoint to the analytic and empirical story we have constructed. We argue that although this sequential comparative strategy is time consuming, it will allow for more productive comparisons, and less straightjacketing of theoretical claims, a problem that haunts many external comparisons.

Deepening Shadows: Revisits, Reminiscence, and Comparing Notes

Ethnography takes place in a matrix of methodological conventions, tricks of the trade, and ongoing discussions about strengths, limitations, and variations. These writings, in turn, are embedded in iconic ethnographic exemplars. These ethnographies constitute the field's community of inquiry and its definition as something like a "field." Whether or not we agree with each other, we refer to the same discussions, take positions in regards to shared texts we assume we all read. In other words, this community forms a comparative shadow reference point for ongoing work. Especially in urban ethnography but also in the fields of healthcare, medicine, education, and immigration, researchers enter well-established traditions and new projects have to engage their predecessors: to build on their work, fill in gaps, extend their reach, update in light of new structural configurations, or take issue with the past.

Moreover, for each specific study, there are iconic works that the ethnographer needs to tackle, orienting points the ethnographer needs to orient herself in relation to. No study of dying is complete without careful thought about Glaser and Strauss's (1965) *Awareness of Dying*; no study of Orthodox Jews can sidestep Samuel Heilman's (1976) *Synagogue Life*.

While this is true for all ethnographic work—much as it is true for academic work more generally—some shadows are thus deeper than those we usually evoke. Ethnographers often treat their shadow comparisons opportunistically, as these emerge, and as they help them think in interesting ways about their field. The deeper shadows, on the other hand, become more like what Michel Callon (1986) called "obligatory passage points"—points that actors *have to* move through in order to make their claims. And while many of these obligatory passage points are perfunctory, a performance of the relation rather than a true attempt to grapple with such shadows, others are more deliberate.

One such instance is the strategy of "revisiting." This approach to ethnographic work, made famous by Michael Burawoy's (2003) serendipitous discovery that the machine shop he was conducting his ethnography in was the same that Donald Roy studied years before (see also Duneier 2004), uses comparison as its motivating force. Previous work, conducted by a different ethnographer at a different time is the foil that the ethnographer uses. The tenor of such revisits is variable. Usually, revisits are ways to rethink and retheorize a substantive field along a linear temporal dimension. And yet a revisit is perhaps most powerful in allowing us to think about how history shapes our field—something that ethnographers yearn for, but that their methods cannot neatly capture.

Revisits thus use other people's work and theory as a comparative vantage point. However, unlike more shallow shadow comparisons, a revisit has the unique advantage of holding the place (and sometimes even some of the people) constant, thus allowing for a more focused leverage. As in all shadow comparisons, the cases leveraged are largely "silent"—they provide the background against which we work, and although we may question the conclusions of the earlier ethnographer, the original ethnography is where we take off from, not where we aim to get to at the end of our journey.

Another distinct way of deepening shadows consists of comparing notes. Thus, although ethnographers are (speaking in terms of doing the actual research) solitary creatures, they talk and think together. One outcome of such exchange is that ethnographers may come to realize that aspects of their work are productively seen in relation to each other—either because a shared framework or process can illuminate their observations in both fields, or precisely because the observations are so different that putting them side by side is theoretically and empirically productive.

This is the case with articles such as Nina Eliasoph's and Paul Lichterman's "Culture in Interaction" (2003) as well as other joint publications (e.g., Tavory and Winchester 2012). To take Eliasoph and Lichterman's work, as they compared notes from their ongoing ethnographies of civil society in churches

(Lichterman) and small groups that mostly avoided politics (Eliasoph) they came to see that in both cases the groups they observed crystallized general cultural tropes in ways that had a distinctive group style. This, then, became the basis of an important theoretical intervention about the way in which culture and interaction are intertwined. Although they could, perhaps, have developed this theoretical model using only one ethnographic project, the ongoing comparison of their projects allowed them to make more ambitious claims.

Lastly, some ethnographers use their own past work as their "significant other." This is rarer than one would expect. Most ethnographers do not produce more than one or two serious ethnographies in their lifetime (after which they usually begin writing endless methodological and theoretical tracts such as the one you are currently reading). But some ethnographers—such as Gary Alan Fine and Diane Vaughan—have used their own trajectory as a way to continue working on the same set of problems, deepening and expanding on a core set of concerns. Thus, Gary Fine has produced more than ten separate ethnographies—ranging from groups playing Dungeons and Dragons (Fine 1983), to kitchen workers (Fine 1996), meteorologists (Fine 2010), and mushroom collectors (Fine 1998). And, although the fields are quite different, Fine continuously works on the same set of concerns—the construction and inner working of little group culture, or "idiocultures" (Fine 1979). Similarly, in Diane Vaughan's work (Vaughan 1986, 1992, 1996, 2004), whether in NASA, in marriages or with flight controllers, the ethnographies build on each, constructing an increasingly sophisticated theory of organizational breakdown.

In short, then, revisits, reminiscence and comparing notes are modes of comparison that punch the logic of "shadow comparisons" to its extreme, deepening the shadows so that they almost become an external comparison.

Internal Comparisons in Grounded Theory and Beyond

A second analytic strategy, that of *internal comparison*, was most explicitly developed in the grounded theory literature. Grounded theory has a rather convoluted attitude toward comparison. The approach puts comparison front and central as a data analytical strategy, even as it largely downplays its potential as a research design tactic. Perhaps most tellingly, grounded theory also travels under the heading of the "constant comparative method," a term that Barney Glaser, one of the two architects of grounded theory, introduced in 1965 in an article published in *Social Problems* (Glaser 1965). In the paper, Glaser proposed a three-stage set of comparisons.

Researchers, according to Glaser, should code every instance in their data in as many categories as possible. The added value of this strategy was that the researcher should compare the newly observed instance with the already present instances of the category. Comparisons done in this way should alert the researcher to salient theoretical properties, which, Glaser recommended, should be spun off as analytical memos. Next, the researcher should integrate different analytical categories and their properties, again by comparing the instances between and across categories. In the third stage, the researcher is concerned with parsimony and scope of the emerging theorization and works on pruning down the data categorization to maximize generalizability. The deciding criterion is what Glaser and Strauss famously called "saturation": if no new information is found in subsequent observations, the analytical construct can be considered saturated. Only then, after this threefold process of comparison, should the researcher write-up their emergent theory.

The comparative aspect of grounded theory thus consists of continuously comparing categories that emerge in the coding process with each other in order to delineate their theoretical properties. This was different from, for example, analytical induction where researchers develop theoretical properties from a deliberate search for negative cases as way to recursively construct the theoretical categories and scope conditions of the emergent theorization (Becker 1993; Katz 2001; see also Lakatos 1978).

Glaser and Strauss revolutionized qualitative data analysis with their emphasis on conceptualizing observations in ways that were not pregiven, but they did the field of qualitative research a dubious service by presenting grounded theory as an inductive research method. Glaser, in particular, remains adamant that existing theories and research would contaminate the researcher's engagement with her field. As a data analysis strategy, the constant comparisons of grounded theory were thus hobbled by the strong admonition to not engage existing literatures and research until the project's wrap-up.

In the language developed here, the problem with grounded theory is that it rejected the shadow comparisons that must be a part of parcel of both the process of research design and the ongoing context of research. The difference between grounded theory and abductive analysis, which we have developed elsewhere (Tavory and Timmermans 2014b; Timmermans and Tavory

2012), is precisely there. In abductive analysis, shadow comparisons are evoked throughout the research context. A site is chosen because we have an inkling that it would be theoretically interesting, but we continue to compare our findings to various literatures throughout the research project, leveraging these shadow comparisons to identify analytic and empirical surprises.

Interestingly, although grounded theory was conceived as a form of internal comparison, the relation to *external* comparison haunted is from its very inception. As with most data analytical innovations, grounded theory originated from a specific research project and carries some of the specificity of this project along with it. The formative project was a study of hospital dying in the Bay Area (Glaser and Strauss 1965). This study had tremendous comparative potential: Glaser and Strauss observed dying in six different hospitals and on different hospital wards, differentiating, for example places where dying was expected from unexpected dying, dying of the young from dying from old age, dying in secrecy and dying in the open. Yet to contemporary readers, *Awareness of Dying* does not read as a comparative study because Glaser and Strauss downplay the specificity of dying in the different San Francisco hospitals. They spell this out:

> We might have organized our analysis in this book to highlight differences and similarities among the various medical services. Instead, we chose to offer our readers a more abstract—and so more powerful—explanatory theoretical scheme. This scheme arose from scrutiny of the data and should illuminate the data far more than a comparative analysis of the medical services. (Glaser and Strauss 1965, ix)

Indeed, even though the hospitals include such diverse institutions as a mental health hospital, a VA hospital, an academic center, and a general public hospital, none of the institutional specificities made it into the analysis. Instead, Glaser and Strauss develop the notion of awareness contexts to capture a general process of social isolation during dying in hospitals. They pay attention to institutional factors, but none of these factors is situated within any of the hospital settings. In fact, the hospitals themselves are not described in their book. The commitment to treat all observations in terms of an overarching internal comparison thus sacrifices specificity, history, and context for conceptual abstraction, consolidating what could have been considered different sites into one meta-site within which comparisons are made "internally."

Still, despite the problems and elisions of grounded theory, it has made a number of crucial contributions to theorizations of comparison in ethnography. First, alongside analytic induction, grounded theorists stressed that internal comparisons are the sine qua non of the research process. But second, the grounded theory notion of "theoretical sampling" as a basis for comparison is promising. Theoretical sampling takes advantage of findings in one site to determine the most appropriate second site or community to set-up a comparison. The key take-home message of theoretical sampling is less its role in opening up theory-construction following grounded theory's open-ended coding approach but as a means to think through the most plausible grounds for comparison. In other words, we need to find a way to link sites to compare, and this linking can only be done through the work conducted within a site.

External Comparisons

Within this landscape of shadow and internal comparisons, we can now think about the place that external comparisons play. In the typology developed here, what distinguishes external comparisons is that (a) the researcher actively engages two or more sites; so that (b) the comparison become an obligatory passage point for claims-making; and where (c) this engagement is recursive, either in the moment of data collection, or as the ethnographer tries to make sense of their materials. Even here, however, there is more than one way to think about external comparison. Generally speaking, we may think about two warrants for external comparison—*causal analysis* and *theoretical provocations.*

First, and despite some protestations to the contrary, many external comparisons are loosely based on Mill's methods of similarity and difference (Mill 2002 [1843]). Even as they know that no perfect controls exist in the social world, the specter of such neat causal inference haunts such comparisons. Very few ethnographies pull this off in a consistent way, in part because reducing rich historicity for a number of key characteristics, and turning the overdetermination of lives into specific variables that we control is usually anathema to the ethnographer's work ethic. Still, in specific cases, this Millian logic leads to incisive work.

One such research project is Katherine Kellogg's study of educational reform in three hospitals (Kellogg 2011). Concerned about sleep-deprived medical residents harming patients, the federal government set a maximum number of hours residents could work in a shift. A lack of compliance could result in a loss of accreditation of the residency programs. Starting her project prior to the implementation of the reform, Kellogg conducted fifteen months of ethnographic observations in two hospitals and added a third hospital one year later. The three hospitals were not only similar in organizational characteristics and surgery programs but also subject to the same external regulatory pressures to reform their residency programs. All three hospitals initiated similar reform processes supported by the hospitals' medical directors. Yet in the first hospital, reformers succeeded in changing working hours, in the second hospital reform never took off, and in the third hospital reform initially was implemented but later defeated. Why these different outcomes?

As Kellogg shows, surgery is an extraordinarily hierarchical and masculinized specialty in which everyone is expected to remain responsible for "their" patients and "scutwork" is delegated to the lowest on the hierarchy. Surgeons demand total dedication for the seven years of residency. Limiting residency hours required interns to hand-off patients to senior residents working the night shift and these seniors refused to do to be what they considered demeaning tasks. The resulting "dropped balls" in patient-care came back to haunt the interns rather than the night shift residents: interns would rather capitulate than endanger their reputations. In the hospital that succeeded to reform resident hours, reformers were able to build alliances; work out scripts to redefine the derogatory, feminine language associated with reform efforts; and isolate defenders of the old policies. The leaders of reform were mostly transient residents, doing a one-year surgery residency as part of a different specialty. These transient residents' reputation was less vulnerable to defender attacks.

Kellogg's key theoretical contribution is that struggles for macro-political reform require equivalent processes of micro face-to-face "collective combat" at the institutional level for reforms to be implemented as intended. Kellogg's study then comes the closest to a traditional experimental comparative ethnography where the researchers controls for certain factors in case selection (made easier in her case by the standardization of hospitals and residency programs), looks at a similar external force (the educational reform), and uses ethnographic data grounded in various theories to tease out the key explanatory interactional processes.

And yet the decision to turn to quasi-experimental logic comes at a high price. While an insightful study, and perhaps one that comes quite close to a true Millian method, Kellogg's ethnography is focused on answering a narrow question: Why did reform work in one site but not in another? Her ethnographic appropriation of the experimental approach produces an added value: she discovers a social mechanism of joining forces collectively that we would not have obtained in its specificities from any other methodology but the trade-off is that she leaves much on the cutting floor. For a book of surgery residents, we learn almost nothing about how surgery is performed (Bosk 1979) and, importantly, the impetus for the reform (that sleep deprived residents endanger patient lives) remains also unexplored. In other words, the price of the Millian method is purifying ethnography from what people may see as its unique strengths—the abilities to capture different social worlds in their fullness.

While the pursuit of the Millian method is one possibility opened by external comparison, it is not the only one. Another possibility is that of *theoretical provocation* (see also Krause 2016). Here, rather than finding a specific difference, researchers proceed by showing how a shared theoretical framework helps bring the finding culled in the (usually) two or more sites to life. The origin of this approach to comparison can be found in the heuristics developed by Everett Hughes (1971 [1945]). Hughes encouraged students to draw far-out comparisons in order to nail the specificity of a case. For instance, he noted that scholars learn much about physicians from studying plumbers and from psychiatrists from studying prostitutes. The first pair practices esoteric techniques to help people in distress while the second pair cannot become too personally involved in intimate matters of their clients. They, then, share similar occupational challenges. Hughes proposed that theories can be strengthened by incorporating a wide range of seemingly dissimilar comparative cases into analytical view.

Two examples of this kind of ethnography are those of Ofer Sharone (2013), and of Jeff Guhin (forthcoming). First, Sharone (2013) shows how different understandings of the relationship between selfhood and employment structure the labor markets in Israel and the United States. In Israel, workers see the job openings through what Sharone calls a "specs" game. That is, they understand their hiring (or lack thereof) in terms of job descriptions, as well as through the network ties they have (or don't have, as the case may be). In the United States, in contrast, workers understand their ability to get a job through what Sharone calls a "chemistry game," that is, they internalize their successes and failure, and make them about the fit between the person him or herself and the job. As Sharone shows, playing these different games in the two national contexts have profound effect for how white-collar workers understand both hiring and unemployment, thus giving rise to different experiences of work.

Taking a very different object of analysis, Guhin (forthcoming) compares four religious schools in New York—two Muslim Sunni Schools and two Christian Evangelical ones—in order to parse out when and how do specific practices and ideas become morally salient. The importance of evolution in the Evangelical schools or of gendered religious practices in the Sunni ones cannot be derived from abstracted beliefs, but they emerge in the intersection of core practices and histories with aspects of religious doctrine. Thus, as Evangelicalism practically focuses on the literal reading of the bible, and in relation to the history of the church (e.g., the Scopes "monkey trial"), evolution becomes a rallying cry and salient boundary; as Sunni Muslim families are dealing with their status as immigrants and their American kids, and in relation to the "veil debates" gendered practices emerge as salient boundaries.

These examples, like others (e.g., Lee 1998; Snyder 2016), may sometimes play loosely with the Millian method, but the power of the analysis is not derived from such comparative logic. Rather, the sites recursively work to focus the researcher's attention of a shared theoretical architecture as well as to defamiliarize aspects of each case that we may take for granted. So, in Sharone's case, the American and Israeli cases are not really comparable, but they show how different national games can refract the precarity of employment in late capitalism; in Guhin's case, the institutional context of the school, and the specific differences between the two Evangelical and the two Sunni schools take second fiddle to the larger theoretical point he develops about the salience of specific boundary practices.

In short, external comparisons are often motivated by a Millian hope to identify particular differences or similarities, or by a mode of thinking that uses the different ethnographic cases more to shed light on each other than to strictly compare them. Indeed, the best ethnographies that leverage external comparison manage to artfully blend these two warrants, so that at one moment they imply a *differentia specifica* between the field sites, and at the next they relax the comparison to gain a wider appreciation of the way worlds are structured.

Toward a Sequential Comparative Ethnography

Elsewhere we argued that delineating social mechanisms plays to the particular strengths of ethnography (Tavory and Timmermans 2014a). Social mechanisms refer to processes the ethnographer traces to link an explanandum to an explanans. We proposed that the relevant building blocks of such an attempt to trace processes are the meaning-making sequences that people engage in in the unfolding moments of action. Second, we proposed that the explanatory value of these building blocks can be assessed by examining variation across cases. Lastly, we argued that a necessary step in the research process was to engage the proposed mechanism within the various plausible alternatives offered by a broader intellectual community. In other words, we spent most our effort on thinking through the relationship between shadow comparisons and internal comparisons.

Here, we want to push our argument further by looking for comparative history for inspiration. In making the case for comparative historical research, Haydu (1998) notes that comparative research either sacrifices thick understanding of historical particularities for causal generality, or offers distinctive in-depth understanding of a limited number of cases. Generalizing following an experimental model runs in the problem of independence and equivalence of cases. As Sewell (1996) noted, the more independent cases are, the less they tend to be similar. Comparative historians therefore often move to study societies or communities that are closely related. However, that raises the opposite problem. The more equivalent, the more likely they are connected through explicit links. In Skocpol's comparative study of revolutions, the Chinese Revolutionaries did not only directly model their revolution on the Bolsheviks revolution in Russia but received direct support from them—something of a problem given that Skocpol's causal model analyzed the revolutions as independent events.

To partly solve that problem, Haydu suggests that historical comparative analysis would get analytical mileage out of connecting events over time as repeated attempts to solve similar problems. The advantage of putting human problem-solving front and central is that it focuses the comparative historian on how to carry forward the explanatory weight of the past to shape later turning points and critical choices. Dependence, rather than independence, is the operating assumption to debunk before one can speak of different cases or different periods. Solutions in one period create problems in subsequent periods that require new solutions, looking for both contrast and continuity. Previous actions not only close off future courses of action (as in path dependency), but open up new historical pathways due to contradictory or unintended consequences. Periods are distinguished based on contrasting solutions for recurring problems and the goal of the analysis is to explain why people pursued different solutions to enduring problems. Problems qualify as organizing principles of historical analysis on empirical observable or theoretical grounds, but, as Haydu requires, they cannot be imposed by social scientists. There needs to be some correspondence to how actors themselves experience the world.

Translating an iterative problem-solving approach from comparative history to contemporary ethnography is obviously not going to be a panacea for all forms of comparative ethnography. And yet it has some advantages. The key insight, following Haydu, is that sites are linked by a common issue—by a similar problem that requires a solution. The comparison consists in examining both the interdependency and the solutions to similar problems.

There are two ways that such an iterative problem-solving approach can inspire ethnographic work. One, well established, is the idea of a multisited ethnography which—in its pure form—is by definition *not* comparative but rather follows an object from one site to the next. Here, interdependence becomes the central linchpin of the analytical project. The other, which we refer to as "sequential" comparative ethnography, starts from an abductive identification of a phenomenon in one site, before the ethnographer begins tacking back and forth with other sites where a similar structure of meaning making is apparent. Here, while the problem-solving instances may or may not be interdependent in terms of their genesis in the field, they are interdependent in the biography of their analytical development by the ethnographer. We review each in turn.

Multisited Ethnography

Millian comparison presumes that dissimilarities and similarities are analytically explored while holding other things constant. In ethnography, this approach inevitably implies that we can access a common structure of human experience, something that has become contested in certain corners of anthropology. At the end of the twentieth century, anthropologists increasingly questioned representation and the ethnographer's scientific authority as part of a humanist, postmodern critique and postcolonial awareness. The idea of going to a far-away tribe and describing it in light of the reader's own society was deeply problematized as the relationship between anthropology and colonialism was interrogated. Consequently, the notion of *comparison* itself became problematized in a globalizing world, where the assumption that places and peoples can be treated in isolation became increasingly indefensible. The late modern world seemed to call for multisited, rather than comparative, ethnography.

Multisited ethnography, as advanced by George Marcus (1995), follows an issue across different sites focusing on movement and geographical transformation. The method arose out of the realization that people are globally interconnected through goods, political systems, conflicts, and ideas. Ingredients for a commodity may be gathered in one place, processed in a different part of the world, packaged in another place, and then sold in yet a different global market. Some topics, such as migration, organ trafficking, or commodity chains, immediately suggest movement, and a nimble ethnographic method not stuck to one site allows to capture this movement. The focus of the analysis is on connections and associations, mapping both sites of resistance and accommodation, as well as action-at-a-distance in turn. In an exemplary study, Anna Tsing (2004) examines globalization in an Indonesian rain forest industry not as a homogenizing force but as a set of actions that only receive universality through resistance with local specificity. Such resistance is messy but still influential because it greatly transforms the lives of the people at the bottom rungs of society. Methodologically, Tsing's analysis involves a changing cadre of actors building contingent global alliances based on cultural fantasies about frontiers.

Similarly, within sociology, Dan Menchik (2017) made the case for studying tethered venues, persistent cross-venue linkages that link different sites together across distances and institutions. This approach takes issue with ethnographies that analytically privilege one place and resulting set of similar situations and instead aims to analytically capture the distributed nature of activities. Thus, if one wants to study a teacher's understanding of the curriculum a more traditional ethnography may focus on the classroom work but a multisited ethnography may instead examine the teacher's contacts with their local union, school board meetings, feedback from principal, fellow teachers, and parents, and attendance at professional development meetings. Menchik's point is that we need to study these venues in their own right for the resources they provide and the geographical constraints they put on getting work done.

More generally, any time an ethnographer attends carefully to the complex ways in which actors move among situations, they necessarily construct an intersituational ethnography (Trouille and Tavory 2019). However, these connections are not explicitly comparative. Instead, they break the ethnographic mold of single site ethnography for following phenomena across different geographic spaces. Instead of studying people on a street corner only, we follow them into their jobs, relationships, leisure, and travels. Instead of a unified self, we study the multiple roles of a distributed self.

Sequential Comparative Ethnography

Whereas intersituational and multisited ethnography focuses on the ways in which different moments are interconnected, there are other ways in which ethnographers can keep their comparative impulse alive. To do so, however, would require us to change some of the ways in which we practically organize external comparisons. With sequential comparative ethnography, we refer to a deliberate form of comparative ethnography where ethnographers explore emerging themes and theoretical puzzles in one site, and only then explore a second site for analytical payoff—only to then tack back and forth between the fields again.

This approach differs from the external comparison modeled (explicitly or implicitly) after experiments in important ways. For many external comparisons, it is critical that the sites are as similar as possible except for one explanatory variable and that the sites are considered independent of each other. The aim of sequential comparison, in contrast, is to strengthen a set of analytical claims by exploring a different site. Sequential comparisons hinge on an abductively emergent theoretical insight as the ground for comparison.

The key practical difference between sequential comparison and most comparative ethnographies is that the decision to expand to a second site is not made in the research design stage but is a decision made halfway through the research project based on accumulated analytical and theoretical insights. The standard for initiating a comparison should be high: the study should lose critical analytical scope if the comparison is not pursued. And, while the difference between such an approach and the more experimental external comparisons seems small—a matter of when we decide to proceed—both the epistemology grounding it, and the potential analytic payoff is large.

This prerequisite takes care of the recurring problem in comparative ethnography—that comparisons do not pan out. Many, probably most, studies start off in the design stage as comparative ethnographies where the explicit goal is to compare two sites. This is often done because of the conviction that a comparison constitutes some kind of research insurance, in the sense that if one site is good, two sites should be even better, and in the sense that a comparison will guarantee stronger lines of analysis. However, because the comparison has been decided based on what the researcher's hopes and literature review, but prior to the observations, the ethnographer may discover that the sites are either very similar (which renders the comparison moot) or too different to facilitate a meaningful comparison. In other words, these comparisons often falter because the preconceived notions or theoretical expectations remain unfulfilled, either forcing the ethnographer to shave the most interesting aspects of each case to achieve meaningful comparison, or to position the cases side by side with an embarrassed admission that the connection between them is unclear. Instead of a comparative study, the project is often repackaged as a study that took place over two sites without any pretense of comparison. Or alternatively, the researcher stubbornly plays the circus contortionist, pursuing the initial comparison even while the differences in both explanans and explanandum makes such an exercise increasingly tenuous. In the latter case, the researcher is subjected to much criticism related to unwarranted causal statements that probably would not have occurred if they had opted for more modest causal claims limited to one site.

The reason why comparisons often fail in ethnography is no mystery. One of the exciting analytical tasks of conducting ethnographies is figuring out what the site is good for. Most research methodologies presume that the researcher first asks a question and then looks for an answer. Doing ethnography is more akin to solving a Jeopardy puzzle: the accumulated observations come in the form of an answer and the trick is to figure out what the question is. Of course, researchers enter the site with potential scientific and theoretical rationales of what they hope or could find based on their reading of the literature. But these rationales are often only loosely coupled to the actual analytical payoff of the site. Much of qualitative method data analysis tries to answer the reverse engineering question of "What is this set of observations in this site a case of?" Surprising findings, surprising in light of prior expectations and literature or prevailing theories, constitute the portal for abductively puzzling out what is happening from a sociological perspective (Tavory and Timmermans 2014b).

Yet exactly because there is some readjustment of what the study is about from the initial design and theoretical expectations may a comparison be a game changer in broadening the study's analytical scope. Sequential comparative ethnography requires the researcher to first figure out precisely what case they have in their original site (and this does not need to be one geographical singular site but can be multisited or tethered as we discussed here) and then decide whether it would help to add a second comparative site for analytical purposes, and which kind of site it should be. Adding sites for comparison is not done because it is expected or as a form of analytical insurance in the design stage of the project, but because without adding the second site, the explanation would fall short and the findings stand isolated.

An example: Neil Gong started with a study of mental health provision in Los Angeles' Skid Row (Gong 2019). The problem he saw was that at a time that institutions for the mentally ill had closed down, public resources were scarce, and patients were empowered to refuse treatment, a growing urban mentally ill homeless population posed challenges for city living. Police or mental health authorities could not force the mentally ill into therapy or lock them up just for being on the street and talking to themselves, unless they were a danger to themselves or others. Many found shelters or board-and-care homes undesirable or unworkable, and thus lived on the streets. But the presence of mentally ill homeless people still remained disruptive for businesses and city dwellers. How did city officials address this problem?

With a strong commitment to comparative ethnography at the design stage, Gong initially planned to contrast the United States and Scandinavia, but was unsure whether the axis of variation was different welfare systems, patient rights laws, culture, or something else. He decided to start on Skid Row and hold off until he knew his first case better. Once he delved deeper into his research, Gong observed a highly tolerant approach to engaging mad people who resisted standard treatment placements but could not be legally coerced. Here workers utilized the "housing first" logic—subsidized apartments without disciplinary demands for medication compliance, sobriety, or therapeutic engagement. Given the limited capacity to treat and monitor people, the providers also accepted deviant behavior as largely inevitable. Thus, in stark contrast to theoretical expectations of controlling or paternalistic state services for the poor, these impoverished mad people received considerable autonomy.

Here the combination of civil liberties and the public sector's limited resources for treatment led to a "patient choice" that could be seen as either respectful or neglectful. This then raised an interesting comparative vantage point. What would treatment and choice look like for Los Angeles' wealthy? They also faced a changed institutional landscape of restricted legal means to compel treatment outside of dangerousness, but were far better resourced. Gong added elite private clinics as a comparison site and found a completely different approach to managing mental health. Here the clinics worked with families to dangle financial support as carrot and stick for treatment compliance, and mobilized intensive therapeutic regimes to try and actually transform privileged patients. This greater capacity for care and surveillance, as well as classed expectations for behavior, also meant a different vision of "choice." Far from tolerating idleness, nonadherence, or substance use, these clinics disciplined clients in the name of health. In isolation, treatment of the poor mentally ill seemed an aberration, but in contrast to how the same problem was dealt with among the wealthy, the significance of these counterintuitive approaches became clearer: the choice for the poor was in part a lack of care capacity, and the constraint of the wealthy was precisely seen as care. The key point was that the grounds for an SES comparison emerged as a result of the initial research.

With Haydu, we may assume that an ethnographic site is good for solving a particular problem but what the exact problems, its contours, resources, consequences, and limits on future aspirations are, is the outcome of the ethnographic inquiry. These results may take the shape of a social mechanism by which various elements change over time. Thus, in a study of the return of newborn screening results, the problem requiring solving was that babies born without any visible symptoms may still be suffering from potential fatal diseases, but the result of the test may also be false (Timmermans and Buchbinder 2010, 2013). Adjudicating the results took time and in the meantime, parents and clinicians wondered whether the infant was sick or should be treated as healthy unless problems manifest. Ethnographically following the journey of parents over various testing regimens showed how the possibility of a diagnosis anchored itself in the lives of the families. Lying out the social mechanism of dealing with fundamental uncertainty in the life course opens up various comparative possibilities. Some of these are shadow comparisons as when connections are drawn with other literatures such as the plight of people facing contested illnesses (Timmermans and Buchbinder 2010) or internal when we compare asymptomatic infants with infants admitted to intensive care units with multiple health issues (Timmermans and Buchbinder 2013).

But the study also opened up more explicit grounds for comparison in our sequential comparative mode, such as with the return of genomic testing results to patients. Here, the ground of comparison is the inherent indeterminacy of genomic information. Technologically, it is relatively easy to sequence thousands of genes at once, but interpreting the clinical relevance of variants of which little is often known in the biomedical literature becomes an overwhelming, resource-intensive problem that both commercial and academic labs will need to solve if they want to commercialize genomic testing. The comparative hinge linking both projects then is the problem of interpreting an explosion of genetic test results that may have far-reaching consequences for patients. Newborn screening forms a small-scale but high-stakes manifestation of a much larger issue.

This kind of comparison relaxes independency of the external comparison in an additional important way. Sequential comparisons inevitably take place one after the other, and therefore events observed in the second site will take place after the events in the second site. This adds a possible alternative explanation for observed differences; maybe it is not the different sites but the different time points that explain the observed differences. Rather than seeing this confounding as a drawback, it actually opens up analytical opportunities to explore the iterative nature of problem-solving. Gong, for instance, can revisit the Skid Row homeless outreach people to see whether anything in their approach has changed. And in the case of genomic testing, the learning curve of dealing with ambiguous test results across different applications can itself become a topic of inquiry. We can then examine how solutions to similar problems may accrue different meanings, like boundary objects (Star and Griesemer 1989), across sites, undergoing transformations, local adaptations, attempts at standardization, and so forth. Comparing such processes over time and across sites will reveal the power of various stakeholders to impact situations in recursive ways.

Conclusion

Like alpacas ogling grass to graze on, ethnographic observations look always more alluringly green in a next site or in more far away fields, because this promises more food to chew on. However, once we prance to that comparative site, we may find that what looked from a distance to be a thick verdant tapestry of greenery actually is a completely different flora. It is, to push the metaphor to its unsavory limits, much more complicated and less digestible than anticipated. Adding an external comparative component does not create an analytical shortcut. While it opens up opportunities for strengthening an explanation, it more often results in impoverishing the work we have done in an attempt to create false Millian equivalence.

And yet there is no real question about making comparisons in ethnography. We all make comparisons. The question is, instead, what the relationship between shadow, internal and external comparisons is. Different projects call for different modes of comparisons, and different moments within which external, internal, and shadow comparisons are evoked. The generative question is thus never "Should I compare?" but rather "What kinds of comparisons should I focus on?" As we argued here, to the degree that ethnographer want to throw themselves into external comparisons, a fruitful way to do so is sequentially, after the analytical and theoretical contours of the first site have abductively emerged and a second site promises an incontrovertible payoff.

Note

1. As ideal types, these three kinds of comparisons are simplifications. Especially between external and internal comparisons lies a vast grey zone. Thus, for example, Niewöhner and Scheffer (2010) make the case for comparison as a process of analytical thickening, in which a straightforward comparison between sites is inadvisable because it requires some basic discursive and hermeneutic commonalities that are often lacking but where the comparative ethnographer aims to examine how and when layers of comparison shift, overlap, and respond. This works best at an intermediate level of abstraction. Here, the theoretical construct forms the comparative hinge that connects multiple sites. Because legal terms are often highly context specific, Niewöhner and Scheffer, for example, focus on the indexical meanings of legal discourse across European jurisdictions, following similar problem situations over time in different legal settings. When devoid of local specificity, it is unclear how such theoretical constructs are useful for understanding any of the legal systems.

References

Anderson, Elijah. 1976. *A Place on the Corner*. Chicago: University of Chicago Press.

Becker, Howard S. 1993. "Theory: The Necessary Evil." In *Theory and Concepts in Qualitative Research: Perspectives from the Field*, edited by D. J. Flinders and G. E. Mills, 218–229. New York: Teachers College Press.

Bosk, Charles L. 1979. *Forgive and Remember: Managing Medical Failure*. Chicago: University of Chicago Press.

Burawoy, Michael. 2003. "Revisits: An Outline of a Theory of Reflexive Ethnography." *American Sociological Review* 68: 645–679.

Callon, Michel. 1986. "Some Elements of a Sociology of Translation: Domestication of the Scallops and the Fishermen of St Brieuc Bay." In *Power, Action, and Belief: A New Sociology of Knowledge?*, edited by J. Law, 196–229. London: Routledge.

Duneier, Mitchell. 2004. "Scrutinizing the Heat: On Ethnic Myths and the Importance of Shoe Leather." *Contemporary Sociology* 33, no. 2:139–150.

Eliasoph, Nina, and Paul Lichterman. 2003. "Culture in Interaction." *American Journal of Sociology* 108, no. 4:735–794. https://doi.org/10.1086/367920.

Fine, Gary Alan. 1979. "Small Groups and Culture Creation: The Idioculture of Little League Baseball Teams." *American Sociological Review* 44, no. 5: 733–745.

Fine, Gary Alan. 1983. *Shared Fantasy: Role-Playing Games as Social Worlds*. Chicago: University of Chicago Press.

Fine, Gary Alan. 1996. *Kitchens: The Culture of Restaurant Work*. Berkeley: California University Press.

Fine, Gary Alan. 1998. *Morel Tales: The Culture of Mushrooming*. Boston: Harvard University Press.

Fine, Gary Alan. 2010. *Authors of the Storm: Meteorology and the Culture of Prediction*. Chicago: University of Chicago Press.

Glaser, Barney G. 1965. "The Constant Comparative Method of Qualitative-Analysis." *Social Problems* 12, no. 4: 436–445. https://doi.org/10.1525/sp.1965.12.4.03a00070.

Glaser, Barney, and Anselm Strauss. 1965. *Awareness of Dying*. Chicago: Aldine.

Gong, Neil. 2019. "Between Tolerant Containment and Concerted Constraint: Managing Madness for the City and the Privileged Family." *American Sociological Review* 84, no. 4. 664–689.

Guhin, Jeffrey. Forthcoming. *Make Belief: A Study of Muslim and Christian Schools*. Oxford: Oxford University Press.

Haydu, Jeffrey. 1998. "Making Use of the Past: Time Periods as Cases to Compare and as Sequences of Problem Solving." *American Journal of Sociology* 104, no. 2: 339–371. https://doi.org/10.1086/210041.

Heilman, Samuel. 1976. *Synagogue Life: A Study in Symbolic Interaction*. Chicago: University of Chicago Press.

Hughes, Everett. 1971 [1945]. *The Sociological Eye: Selected Papers*. Chicago: Aldine-Atherton.

Katz, Jack. 2001. "Analytical Induction." In *International Encyclopedia of the Social and Behavioral Sciences*, Vol. 1, edited by N. J. Smelser and P. B. Baltes, 480–484. Oxford: Elsevier.

Kellogg, Katherine C. 2011. *Challenging Operations: Medical Reform and Resistance in Surgery*. Chicago: University of Chicago Press.

Krause, Monika. 2016. "Comparative Research: Beyond Linear-Causal Explanation." In *Practising Comparison. Logics. Relations, Collaborations*, edited J. Deville, M. Guggenheim, and Z. Hrldckova, 480–484. Manchester: Mattering Press.

Lakatos, Imre. 1978. *The Methodology of Scientific Research Programmes*. Cambridge: Cambridge University Press.

Lee, Ching Kwan. 1998. *Gender and the South China Miracle: Two Worlds of Factory Women*. Berkeley: University of California Press.

Liebow, Elliot. 1967. *Tally's Corner: A Study of Negro Streetcorner Men*. Lanham, MD: Rowman & Littlefield.

Marcus, George E. 1995. "Ethnography In/Of the World-System: The Emergence of Multi-Sited Ethnography." *Annual Review of Anthropology* 24: 95–117. https://doi.org/10.1146/annurev.an.24.100195.000523.

Menchik, Daniel A. 2017. "Tethered Venues: Discerning Distant Influences on a Field Site." *Sociological Methods and Research* 48, no. 4: 850–876. https://doi.org/10.1177/0049124117729695.

Mill, John S. 2002 [1843]. *A System of Logic: Ratiocinative and Inductive*. Honolulu: University Press of the Pacific.

Niewöhner, Jörg, and Thomas Scheffer. 2010. *Thick Comparison: Reviving the Ethnographic Aspiration*. Leiden: Brill.

Sewell, William Jr. 1996. "Historical Events as Transformations of Structures: Inventing Revolution at the Bastille." *Theory and Society* 25, no. 6: 841–881.

Sharone, Ofer. 2013. *Flawed System/Flawed Self: Job Searching and Unemployment Experience*. Chicago: University of Chicago Press.

Snyder, Benjamin. 2016. *The Disrupted Workplace: Time and the Moral Order of Flexible Capitalism*. Oxford: Oxford University Press.

Star, Susan Leigh and James R. Griesemer. 1989. "Institutional Ecology, 'Translations' and Boundary Objects: Amateurs and Professionals in Berkeley's Museum of Vertebrate Zoology, 1907–1939." *Social Studies of Science* 19, no 3: 387–420.

Tavory, Iddo, and Stefan Timmermans. 2014a. "A Pragmatic Approach to Causality in Ethnography." *American Journal of Sociology* 119, no. 3: 682–714.

Tavory, Iddo, and Stefan Timmermans. 2014b. *Abductive Analysis: Theorizing Qualitative Research*. Chicago: University of Chicago Press.

Tavory, Iddo, and Daniel Winchester. 2012. "Experiential Careers: The Routinization and De-Routinization of Religious Life." *Theory and Society* 41, no. 2: 351–373.

Timmermans, Stefan, and Mara Buchbinder. 2010. "Patients-in-Waiting: Living Between Sickness and Health in the Genomics Era." *Journal of Health and Social Behavior* 51, no. 4: 408–423.

Timmermans, Stefan, and Mara Buchbinder. 2013. *Saving Babies? The Consequences of Newborn Genetic Screening* Chicago: University of Chicago Press.

Timmermans, Stefan, and Iddo Tavory. 2012. "Theory Construction in Qualitative Research: From Grounded Theory to Abductive Analysis." *Sociological Theory* 30, no. 3: 167–186.

Trouille, David, and Iddo Tavory. 2019. "Shadowing: Warrants for Intersituational Variation in Ethnography." *Sociological Methods and Research* 48, no. 3: 534–560.

Tsing, Anna Lowenhaupt. 2004. *Friction: An Ethnography of Global Connection*. Princeton, NJ: Princeton University Press.

Vaughan, Diane. 1986. *Uncoupling: Turning Points in Intimate Relationships*. New York: Vintage.

Vaughan, Diane. 1992. "Theory Elaboration: The Heuristics of Case Analysis." In *What Is a Case? Exploring the Foundations of Social Inquiry*, edited by C. C. Ragin and H. S. Becker, 173–203. Cambridge: Cambridge University Press.

Vaughan, Diane. 1996. *The Challenger Launch Decision: Risky Technology, Culture and Deviance at NASA*. Chicago: University of Chicago Press.

Vaughan, Diane. 2004. "Theorizing Disaster: Analogy, Historical Ethnography, and the Challenger Accident." *Ethnography* 5, no. 3: 315–347.

Willis, Paul. 1977. *Learning to Labor: How Working Class Kids Get Working Class Jobs*. New York: Columbia University Press.

SECTION III

CONTEXTUALIZING COMPARISON

8

Using Computational Tools to Enhance Comparative Ethnography

Lessons from Scaling Ethnography for Biomedicine

Alissa Bernstein and Daniel Dohan

Introduction

Ethnographers have long been drawn to thinking about how to compare and the logics of comparison: what makes cases, places, ideas, or concepts comparable or incommensurable, who compares and how, and how can comparisons be best represented (Lock 2002; Marcus 1995; Maurer 2005; Kleinman 1978; Ong and Collier 2005; Ragin and Becker 1992; Small 2009). In this chapter we consider approaches to enrich ethnographic methods through transdisciplinary influences that foster a dynamic engagement with comparison. These approaches reflect our grounding in ethnography as well as our daily encounters with biomedicine, an arena where ethnography has a rich history of impactful engagement with both scientists and practitioners. Our techniques incorporate computational tools that complement ethnography, but we emphasize their utility as methodological innovations within our particular research setting rather than as technical solutions. Our standpoint is that of ethnographers employed and embedded in an academic medical center, and our arguments in this chapter reflect our experience as ethnographers (from anthropology and sociology) in and of the medical field. As have past generations of ethnographers, we have found biomedicine to be a fruitful site for engaging in comparative ethnographic analysis. The innovations we describe here have fostered interdisciplinary engagement across the social sciences and biomedicine, and thus a central goal of this chapter is to share our experiences and reflections about how these computational tools have engendered this meaningful engagement. We consider the insights these innovations have provided on the variance of culturally

Alissa Bernstein and Daniel Dohan, *Using Computational Tools to Enhance Comparative Ethnography* In: *Beyond the Case*. Edited by: Corey M. Abramson and Neil Gong, Oxford University Press (2020). © Oxford University Press.
DOI: 10.1093/oso/9780190608484.003.0009

embedded practices across practice settings, patient populations, clinical conditions, and treatment modalities. We also consider the limitations of these methodologies and the ways in which they not only complement but potentially also threaten the ethnographic project.

The computational techniques we describe originated in biomedicine, public health, and geography, and we have shaped and extended them to inform comparative ethnography. Broadening the scope of ethnographic case analysis and data presentation enables researchers to more directly examine and interrogate the data, representation, and conclusions of an ethnographic study. We also suggest ways social scientists can benefit from engaging with models of science that extend beyond their disciplinary orthodoxies. Thus, while our empirical examples in this chapter are drawn from the fields of health and medicine, we see these techniques as potentially useful for ethnographers of other domains as well.

Medicine, Ethnographic Engagements, and Comparison

The practice of medicine depends on eliciting patients' narratives, and observational research has been a valuable tool in our attempts to understand and improve practice (Glaser and Strauss 1967; Bosk 1979; Timmermans and Shen 1999). Ethnography, which involves collecting narratives and conducting participant observation, is thus a potentially powerful tool for advancing research and, ultimately, improving practice. However, when it comes to shaping research and practice, researchers and policymakers typically turn to quantitative analysis. Qualitative methods are often seen as insufficient to advance scientific research and improve practice. Social scientific studies of biomedicine thus confront a quandary that resembles that which engulfed the social sciences broadly in the late twentieth century. In the 1980s to the 2000s, "quantitative" versus "qualitative" social science investigators wrestled over the legitimacy of these research approaches. In the social sciences, scholars became more comfortable with a pragmatic epistemology that focused on using either approach as long as it advanced understanding of significant theoretical and empirical questions. Quantitative methods remain dominant for a variety of reasons—they monopolize other fields of science, they are more efficient for making generalizability claims, and advances in computer technology has broadened the scope and power of numeric data and analysis. Researchers often turn to qualitative methods when their goals are developmental or exploratory, such as refining close-ended survey items or mining focus group data to identify new concepts. In medicine, analysts appropriately note that such studies contribute to the field—and should be evaluated—in ways that are distinct from the hypothesis-testing or causally driven studies that typically use quantitative methods (Reeves, Kuper, and Hodges 2008; Devers 2011; Devers 1999; Kuper et al. 2008). This "exceptional" treatment afforded qualitative data brings ethnographers to the biomedical research table, but it brings them there as guests rather than as full scientific contributors. Medical anthropologists and sociologists who use qualitative data must still navigate epistemological tensions when they engage biomedicine.

One potential pathway to navigate this tension and legitimize qualitative methods in medicine is for qualitative researchers to develop new ways of plying their craft that speak to the culture of biomedicine while maintaining the integrity of their approach. In our work, we have found that our concept of what ethnography is, how it can be done, as well as the question of how to represent our work is fundamentally changing through our encounter with biomedicine in our role as researchers in a biomedical setting. This occurs both in the encounters we have in our research with the culture of biomedicine as well as our adaptation and incorporation of aspects of biomedicine's methodological approaches, concepts, and technologies. In reflecting on her own work, anthropologist Marilyn Strathern (1988) critiques social scientists' attempts to describe, understand, and analyze others through their own taken-for-granted disciplinary language and frameworks. These modes of thinking, she suggests, enter into researchers' analyses, and become unquestioned assumptions (Strathern 1988, 9). Strathern suggests that a more fruitful starting point for analysis may be found in the expansion and extension of concepts that happens in the encounter between the researcher and the field. In our work, this encounter is represented through our interactions, as social scientists, with the fields of biomedicine that we study through ethnography. Biomedicine's practices, concepts, and methodologies have fundamentally shaped the concepts and methodologies. As such, our way of doing ethnography reflects the culture of biomedicine and we in turn aim to intervene in and shape the culture of medicine. We have developed methodological extensions based on these encounters and the requirements of ethnography in a biomedical setting. Biomedicine has thus productively "elicited" methodological innovations from us in the realm of comparative ethnography as we try to communicate, translate, and scale ethnography for biomedicine (Strathern 1990, 201). Furthermore, our approach to ethnography must constantly change, adapt, and extend—both our methodologies and the concepts we use—through these encounters. In the examples we describe in this chapter we show how the methodologies we use have been infused with and reshaped by the language and tools of biomedicine and health.

The Ethnoarray: Increasing Ethnographic Accessibility and Transparency

Ethnographers who work with or within the medical research community recognize the need to bridge the scholarly divide between conventional ethnography and the norms of scientific scholarship. Qualitative social scientists educate their biomedical science colleagues about the insights that ethnography brings to their work, the distinct types of rigor which ethnographers bring to analysis, and how the epistemological foundations of ethnography stand in distinction to that of the natural sciences (Reeves, Kuper, and Hodges 2008a; O'Brien et al. 2014). This educational approach creates a bridge which some clinical and health policy researchers traverse to embrace ethnography.

Nothing prevents ethnographers from crossing the bridge in the other direction—toward the conventional science of biomedicine—and a number of notable efforts have been made to do so in recent decades. Ethnographers, familiar with the scientific critique of the method, do not lack for understanding of normal science. But their attempts at bridge-crossing have struggled to find theoretical and epistemological solutions that can link the ethnographic enterprise with conventional science at a more foundational level (Lamont and White 2008; Ragin et al. 2004). Meanwhile, the medical community has pursued technical and methodological fixes. When applied practitioners in medicine (and other fields) use ethnography, they do so with an eye toward procedural orthodoxy—an orientation that disciplinary ethnographers who learned the ethnographic craft at mentor's knee may find anathema (Becker 2009). Ironically, grounded theory has provided the most common source of procedural orthodoxy in medicine. Biomedicine embraced the approach because it spoke to core substantive questions rather than for its ability to groundbreak new theory through application of humanistic phenomenology (Charmaz 1995; Strauss and Corbin 1990; Strauss

1987; Creswell 2007). An additional irony is that applied ethnography has moved into biomedicine along with computer-assisted qualitative analysis (Miles and Huberman 1994). Like grounded theory procedures, computer assisted qualitative data analysis (CAQDA) enhanced the apparent rigor of ethnographic analysis. But as implemented, CAQDA actualized in software what ethnographers had done on paper for a century. This embrace of skeuomorphism meant ethnography missed out on a potential pathway by which technology could help cross the bridge to conventional science. If there is a common desire for a genuine link between ethnography and biomedicine, the results of bridge-crossing to date have not arrived there. For ethnographers, the status quo may feel frustrating. Biomedicine is using qualitative approaches to address the questions they care about, but despite repeated attempts, ethnographers have had limited success at reshaping the fundamental questions that are asked nor in redefining the rules for what counts as valuable evidence (Greenhalgh et al. 2016).

From this inauspicious starting point, we describe here a sense that elements are in place to create a more genuine connection between the ethnographic and conventional-biomedical scholarly enterprise. New approaches for sharing and displaying data have shown their capacity to advance the ethnographic project of sharing experience and illustrating culture. The alt-right and Arab Spring illustrated that the Internet has cut the Gordian knot of empowering previously muffled voices in ways unimagined by postmodern theory two decades ago. Academic ethnographers have found ways to visualize data in ways that bring readers closer to social dynamics that had previously been described through narrative and prose (Desmond n.d.). We argue here that ethnography can embrace methodological tools and paradigms that will allow it to share more of its narrative more transparently. Mostly what is needed is a CAQDA approach that breaks from previous skeuomorphism by using a different data analytic and presentation approach.

Origins of the Ethnoarray

As is common in science, the innovations to address these questions did not arise from an abstract desire to advance theory or method but rather from a practical problem. In 2010, we began a project to examine how cancer patients with late stage disease began enrolled in early-phase clinical trials for new cancer therapies (Garrett et al. 2017; Dunn et al. 2016; Koenig et al.

2015). In early phase trials, new treatments of unknown benefit are examined in humans. The patients who participate in these trials typically have terminal disease and may have suffered from cancer for many years and have tried many other treatments. They may be physically or emotionally frail. Early phase trials are small—enrolling as few as a one to two dozen patients nationwide—with stakes that are potentially considerable for pharmaceutical industry profits and cancer researcher careers. Early phase trials had already proven a rich ground of ethnographic exploration (Fisher and Kalbaugh 2011; Fisher, Cottingham, and Kalbaugh 2015; Petryna 2009).

Our applied setting and goals made a sociological approach to trials less than fulfilling. Our study promised to advance practical understanding of the early phase trials experience with an eye toward addressing the persistent challenge of recruiting patients to participate in these studies. This promise helped secure funding from the National Cancer Institute (NCI), which in turn helped establish our legitimacy at the clinics in which we embedded ourselves. A solo ethnographer might have been able to gain access to some of the field sites, but our focus on the medical community's problem of trials enrollment allowed us to place a team of ethnographers at multiple sites and thus collect data at a larger scale. The warrant for our study thus draws on Katz's insights about ethnography that provides a naturalistic approach on historically emergent or policy-relevant phenomena (Katz 1997). But our warrant was not to produce a study of interest to sociologists. It was to provide insights that the policy and biomedical community would find convincing and actionable, for example, what strategies do patients follow as they manage late stage disease and how can clinicians help patients make good treatment decisions given the patient's strategic approach to their illness experience (Garrett et al. 2018). It was that practical goal that led our research team to attempt a technological jump toward the biomedical research community by developing a different approach to ethnographic data management, analysis, and visualization.

Other disciplines have embraced new technological approaches for sharing and illustrating data with great vigor and less ambivalence. Biomedical research includes computer-aided representations of the microscopic world, and sharing data is the norm in the field—even if biomedicine is considered a relative laggard in developing the intellectual infrastructure to share data broadly as compared to fields such as physics and aeronautics (Stokols et al. 2008; Stokols 2006). In biomedicine, the sequencing of the human genome played a role in advancing transdisciplinary team science, and coincidentally, a genetic analysis technology inspired our efforts to experiment with how a stronger embrace of technology might allow ethnography to move closer to biomedicine. The data management and visualization techniques used in genetics seemed able to address some of the challenges of qualitative research in biomedicine, including analytical and data transparency due to the large volume of data collected during qualitative research, the context of the clinical setting, and the need to preserve informants' identities. The approach, the ethnoarray, presents ethnographic data visually. It was modeled after the genetic microarray, a visual approach to data presentation and analysis developed by biologists. The logic of the ethnoarray itself, how it compares to other types of computational methods, and its empirical application, have been published elsewhere (Abramson and Dohan 2015; Abramson et al. 2018). Here we summarize its key features as a strategy for scaling ethnography for biomedicine.

In developing the ethnoarray through our encounter with biomedicine, we adopted the biomedical community's conventional definition of science—without impugning the legitimacy of the epistemological stance that grants conventional ethnography its scholarly, intellectual, and humanistic value. The ethnoarray accepts the need for data reduction and quantification, which provide a plausible pathway for making ethnographic data and analysis consonant with biomedical science norms. The ethnoarray uses thematic data coding of ethnographic texts for the purpose of data reduction. This is a standard procedure for many ethnographers, including those working in the tradition of inductive discovery such as grounded theory and phenomenology. The ethnoarray is a tool for comparative data analysis, so data coding may begin with induction and exploration, but it typically is not complete until analysts arrive at a more deductive coding strategy that can applied across multiple cases. To this point, the ethnoarray is consistent with conventional ethnography, but it then departs. Analysts constructing an ethnoarray must deductively define what constitutes an analytical case and establish data categories and elements to apply to each case. Once analysts define consistent cases and data elements, statistical software can discover patterns in the coded ethnographic data using nonparametric techniques such as principal component analysis. The resultant patterns of cross-case similarity and difference can then be displayed graphically, as shown in Figure 8.1.

Figure 8.1 shows an ethnoarray based on ethnographic case studies of thirteen patients with advanced cancer. These patients were enrolled in a study that examined the reasons and pathways that cancer patients enrolled in clinical research studies, a focus that is reflected in the categories (e.g., role in treatment conversations, medical knowledge) and codes (high involvement, multiple consults, etc.) shown on the right side of the array. To simplify this array, its cells reflect merely the presence (black) or absence (white) for a particular patient (each represented by a single column and identified at the bottom of the array). To aid in the interpretation of the array, we used hierarchical clustering to order the patients based on the similarity of the thematic patterns in their case. Based on the results of the quantitative analysis, the patients were then sorted into two groups, Reliant Insiders (group A) and Active Outsiders (group B).

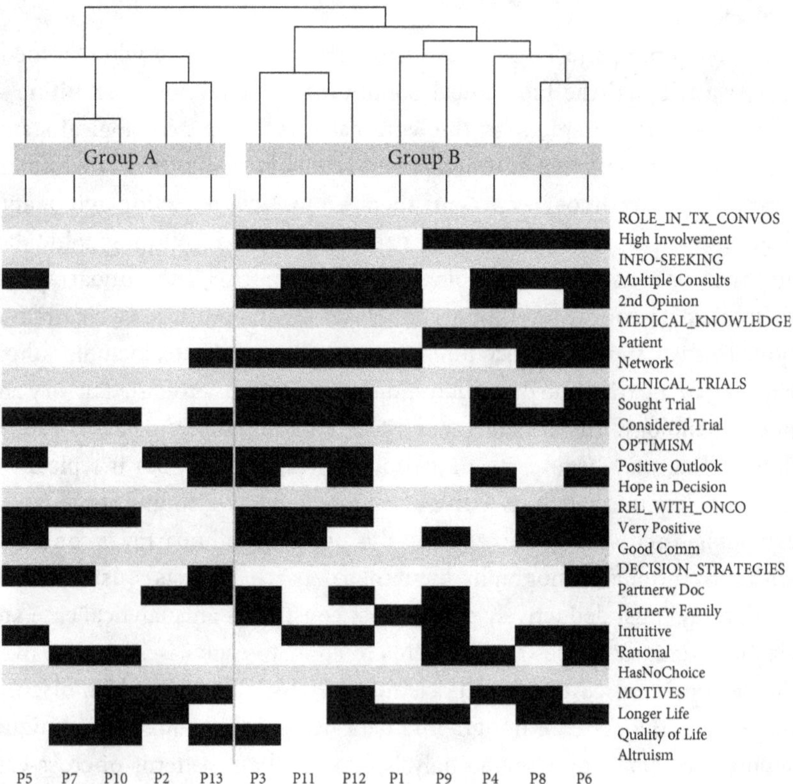

Figure 8.1 Example of an Ethnoarray

Columns represent individual patients. Rows represent the presence or absence of themes in patient data. Group A and Group B labels and a vertical grey line have been added for clarity.

A conventional thematic analysis of these data might highlight the importance of patients' involvement in treatment conversations and their information-seeking behaviors. Such an analysis might even note that these differences appeared to distinguish different types of patients, such as that most patients seemed to be highly involved in treatment conversations while a few patients were less so. But when all the cases can be examined and considered simultaneously, more systematic patterns become apparent. The two groups of patients are similar in many respects; few systematic differences separate the groups when it comes to their larger motives for seeking care, their decision-making strategies, and their relationship with their oncologists. Some patients in both groups approached their situation with optimism. The ethnoarray uses visual analysis to reveal patterns and systematicity in a broader range of ethnographic data than could be included in a conventional narrative analysis.

By displaying comprehensive data from an ethnographic study, the array can capture the entirety of an ethnographic project—findings that typically consume hundreds or thousands of pages of field notes and transcripts—in a summary fashion within a single image. This provides a window of transparency on ethnographic studies and encourages readers to dive more deeply into the data. In addition, however, the ethnoarray is consistent with two strategies for preserving ethnography's unique narrative richness.

One strategy is to provide readers with a broad overview of the entirety of the ethnographic dataset. Quantitative data analysts point out that thoughtfully constructed visual data displays are important not merely because they put an attractive face on one's data, but also because they provide opportunities for critical examination. Tukey, for example, highlights the potential for disastrous consequences when inelegant visual displays of data obscure important, actionable findings. The ethnoarray seeks to reveal variety and nuance in ethnographic data by encouraging readers to examine the narratives of each individual case within a dataset. Reading down the column of an ethnoarray captures the narrative dynamics of a single case. Conventional ethnography provides the opportunity for authors to richly describe the narrative histories of a limited number of cases. Typically these cases come from key informants. Some informants provide access to the field site and thus are the source of significant amounts of observational data while others may become key informants when they provide particularly rich interview data by drawing on their own powers of self-reflection and observation to articulate and interpret the social dynamics of the own social setting. The narratives in conventional ethnography are, therefore, selected by the author as particularly rich examples of evidence or themes that the author values.

A vertical read of an ethnoarray provides a different type of narrative experience. Readers can examine any case they wish and examine how the evidence or themes they consider relevant are reflected in that case. They can select cases that may contrast with or even contradict the argument made by the author. They may discover counterfactual examples that shed new light on the author's claims, or they may gain new understanding of a subject's experience by reading down the ethnoarray column that captures the entirety of their case. Table 8.1 shows vertical narratives of two patients depicted in the ethnoarray. Comparing their narrative histories with the depiction of their case within the ethnoarray—as well as how their case compares to others both within and outside their group—provide the kind of narrative reassurance and immediacy that is a hallmark of ethnography.

A second strategy for capturing narrative richness is to provide readers with the ability to develop an emic appreciation of a subject's worldview, experiences, and locale. As envisioned (but not yet implemented), this richness could be provided to readers by linking coded raw data to each of the ethnoarray's visual cells. These data would provide a rich narrative sense of the data, and if combined with a vertical read of the ethnoarray could potentially provide unprecedented data transparency that allows readers to appreciate the experiences of many individuals or other cases in an ethnographic project—not just those of selected key informants.

The ethnoarray is thus an analytic approach to expand the breadth of ethnographic analysis and reportage while retaining the ability to explore narrative and empower readers to undertake interpretation. For the biomedical research community, this type of scaled ethnography presents itself as a familiar visual. It also challenges biomedical scientists—as well as social scientists—to acknowledge the tension that patterns of social life emerge from data reduction without erasing the narrative specificity and interpretive ambiguity that constitute all meaningful lives. Ethnography of greater breadth and scale has the potential to communicate this quality of social experience. In biomedicine, it can do so for an audience that already has the ability to code-switch between scientific rigor and clinical narrative. A tool that elegantly bridges rigor and narrative may ensure ethnographers a full seat at the table of biomedicine.

Table 8.1 Vertical Narratives

Reliant Outsider	Active Insider
Dennis (P7) is a white carpenter in his 50s who was referred to the cancer center after a lengthy diagnosis process. After learning he had melanoma, "there was only one option. It was go to SF and start treatment with [the oncologist]." He tells the interviewer that he does not know much about the different treatments available to him: "It's all mumbo jumbo to me . . . I'm not big into reading up on stuff like that." His caregiver wife, a cashier, keeps track of this information. In the course of this experience Dennis did not look for second opinions. He described his decision-making process as "always our decision, but I would always ask [the oncologist], you know, which way does he want to go. 'Cause I don't see how you ask a patient which direction you want to go, you know, when a doctor's been doing this for however many years. It makes no sense. So we pretty much just kind of let him—I mean, we agreed to everything that he wanted to do so we let, you know, pretty much followed his lead." He could not remember any point when he and his wife second-guessed a decision made that way. After a year of care at the cancer center he was told there were no remaining anti-cancer options for him unless he was willing to travel outside of California for trials, something he was not willing to do.	Gary (P12) is a white semiretired engineer in his 60s. When he was diagnosed he and his wife did not know anyone with melanoma, so they relied on research they did, their MD son's insights, and information and referrals they secured from doctors at three different institutions. Gary and his wife were proactive and effective in pushing for the care they wanted with the providers they wanted. Gary described his approach to decision-making as relatively "cautious": "We make sure we got the whole picture before we make a decision." He described weighing the pros and cons of different courses of action. Gary, his caregiver wife, and MD son used information they found via research and medical networking to make decisions together as a team. Throughout his care, Gary scrutinized oncologists' descriptions of the risks of different treatments, as his MD son had told him that oncologists tended to minimize the severity of treatment side effects. From early on Gary saw PD1 trials as the only potentially efficacious option available to him: "They've given me the distinct impression that this is a much better, although still experimental drug, both for minimizing side effects and chances of success . . . I want to get into [it] very badly and . . . as soon as possible . . . We have never wavered from that approach."

Integrating Mapping Technology with Ethnography to Expand the Scope of Data Collection

As ethnographers in the medical research and health sciences settings, we are particularly concerned with how to design research questions and collect, integrate, and represent different types and scales of data in ways that are relevant to the health sciences and clinical audiences. These concerns about research design and implementation are matched by our desire to maintain the integrity and rigor of the ethnographic method, which has traditionally focused on in-depth fieldwork and rapport-building that enables a deep and nuanced understanding of social contexts and processes, as well as attention to how meaning is made (Messac et al. 2013). As such, from project development to implementation, our encounter with the medical research environment necessitates—and in fact, offers—new ways of thinking about how to ask and frame questions, how to integrate different methods to provide new insights into important problems where there have previously been roadblocks to progress, and, importantly, how to frame the work we do so that our research findings may lead to actionable interventions with implications for improving clinical practice or health policy.

Historically, anthropologists, whose primary method is ethnography, used many modes of data collection to try to gain a "holistic" view of a particular culture or aspect of society, including studying language, kinship structures, rituals, governance structures, and other aspects of everyday life (Evans-Pritchard 1976; Lévi-Strauss 1969; Benedict 2005; Mead 2001). This approach to fieldwork has been replaced with experiments with many different units of study, which constitutes a shift away from studying cultures as bounded entities. For example, anthropologists now explore assemblages of information through cases that are globally connected at many different scales (Ong and Collier 2005). Anthropologist Joao Biehl (2013) used an innovative approach by investigating one woman's life story as a way to understand the politics of mental illness and social abandonment in Brazil. Jerry Zee (2017) follows pathways of dust storms across multiple sites from Inner Mongolia to Beijing to South Korea via communities of scientists, bureaucrats, and local citizens in order to understand relationships between historical, political, and environmental factors in anti-desertification effort in China. These are just a few examples among countless ethnographers who have worked with different scales and practices in order to change the scope and modes of data collection. This multiplicity of approaches is enabled by the inherent flexibility of the ethnographic approach to adapt to different research settings and morph to fit different types of encounters and research questions. There is a clear precedent for fostering connections with biomedical and health sciences to develop ethnographic approaches which themselves emerged from the research questions being asked and the particular context of the research being conducted (Cohen 2007 on bioavailability; Landecker 2007 and Solomon 2016 on metabolism; Haraway 1999 on immunity, and Mol 2002; Mol and Law 2004 on multiplicity and enactment). If what characterizes ethnography is a deep sensitivity and interest in encounters, as both the setting for ethnographic work and all social life, then the questions that the health sciences push ethnographers to pose and the contexts of the studies we do in these settings enable new connections to emerge (Faier and Rofel 2014). Ethnography in this form has expanded from its earlier emphasis on a bounded research object—an ethnos—toward an experimental approach that reflects on itself and the object or problem on which it centers.

Much as Strathern (1988) argued for an expansion of the concepts we use through the encounter between the researcher and the field, in our work we are constantly drawn to the question of what ethnography looks like and how it changes in its encounter with biomedicine and the health sciences. This approach allows for new relations between ethnographers and scientists or medical personnel to emerge which have both collaborative and mutually productive potential. As part of this project, we also ask how we can be better enabled to translate our findings and approaches across disciplinary boundaries. In the case we discuss here, we examine how ethnography conducted within the biomedical setting led to new research questions. Furthermore, with the goal of identifying potential interventions, we were led to an approach that would allow us to collect and analyze data to help healthcare providers, community resource providers, and policymakers reach a better understanding of the social, emotional, and spatial dimensions of loneliness, social isolation, and burden among caregivers of people with Alzheimer's disease. We specifically attend to ways of expanding the modes of data collection and the scope of information or data that can be collected during a certain period of time. The scope of data, understood in this way, relates to the type and amount of data that can be collected, stored, and analyzed, as well as approaches to representation and visualization. Through these analytical approaches, new types of analyses and data representation are made possible.

Origins of Ethnographic Engagement with Mapping: Addressing Caregiver Burden in Alzheimer's Disease

The imperative to incorporate multiple scales and modes of inquiry within an ethnographic study emerged in this case from an identified problem in our research among caregivers of people with Alzheimer's disease and related dementias. As a medical anthropologist in a clinical setting, I (AB) am embedded within a team of researchers in a memory clinic within a Department of Neurology implementing a clinical trial, the Care Ecosystem, focused on implementing care navigation for people with dementia and their caregivers. The Care Ecosystem is a telephone- and web-based supportive care intervention for people with dementia and their caregivers based at the University of California, San Francisco and the University of Nebraska Medical Center. One major focus of the study was to support caregivers and improve caregiver quality of life. I was tasked with gaining a qualitative understanding of the experiences of caregivers, both in their everyday life and through their interaction with the care navigators, in order to complement the quantitative and survey measures being collected and analyzed as part of the study.

More than 15 million family members or friends provide care for individuals with Alzheimer's disease or other dementias in the United States, which involves immense emotional, physical, and practical support. Social isolation impacts as many as 17% of all older adults in the United States (65+), and loneliness is experienced by as many as 40% of these older (Theeke 2010; Hawkley and Cacioppo 2010). Due to additional burdens of caregiving, caregivers of people with Alzheimer's disease are at an even higher risk for these negative health outcomes. Social isolation and loneliness contribute to caregiver burden, depression, and disease, conveying a higher risk for dementia, cardiovascular disease, inability to continue caregiving, and early death (Luo et al. 2012; Jennings et al. 2015; Valtorta et al. 2016). To date, efforts to support caregivers have focused heavily on skills acquisition, education, counseling, and respite (National Academies of Sciences 2016). Yet studies show only a quarter of caregivers access these services. Despite these numbers, the same types of services continue to be implemented, even though many caregivers are not making use of them.

With this context in mind, I began my ethnographic research for the project. In Nebraska I conducted interviews and participant observation with fifteen family caregivers of people with dementia, as well as care team navigators and clinical team members. I sought to understand experiences of everyday life as a caregiver through my interview questions, and by meeting people in their homes and participating in their daily activities. I asked participants to describe what life is like as a caregiver, what happens on good days and what happens on difficult days, as well as to share the emotions involved in these experiences and to tell me about their social networks and the community resources they use. Simultaneously, the Care Ecosystem study collects quantitative data about these caregivers at six-month intervals. Measures include caregiver burden, quality of life scores, depression scores, and other quantitative data. The richness and depth I was able to see into the lives of the caregivers was strengthened by spending time in their homes where, with some caregivers, I was able to use a traditional participant observation approach to engage in their day-to-day activities with them. Through my visits in vastly different settings in both urban and rural Nebraska, I felt the need to get both a deeper and broader understanding of caregivers' day-to-day social and emotional experiences, how they spend their time, their use of resources, and how their surroundings, both in the home and in the community, shaped their experiences.

In particular, a common refrain I heard was, "My world keeps getting smaller." From my interviews, I knew this description depicted the social, spatial, and temporal experiences of being a caregiver: not being able to leave the home as often, less time to engage in activities, less social connections as people dropped away. Following are examples from my fieldnotes and an interview with two a caregiver that represent a more traditional approach to ethnographic fieldwork.

> I visited Mr. and Mrs. J. in their one-bedroom apartment in a low-income housing development in urban Omaha. The apartment is dark, cramped, and messy with medications scattered all over the table in a jumble. Mr. J (who has advanced Alzheimer's disease) sits in a giant easy chair in the back room, his coloring book sprawled on a table and his intricate drawings on the wall. Mrs. J, his wife and caregiver, discovered that while he has limited ability to communicate or remember anymore, he finds great joy in coloring. Year-round Halloween decorations adorn the walls because they make him happy, it's his favorite holiday. Mrs. J sequesters him to the back room because sometimes, she said, he gets violent. She sleeps in the front room on the couch with her cat. They communicate through the language of "coffee." When he needs something, anything, she told me, he says "coffee." She spends most of her time with the cat while he is sleeping or agitated. She feels very isolated. She told me she only gets out of the house twice a week to take a taxi to Walmart to grocery shop. She explains that Walmart is where she socializes. She otherwise sees herself as extremely independent, but still cries when discussing her loneliness, telling me, "*The hardest thing dealing with this is the solitude.*"

Following is an excerpt from our interview:

INTERVIEWER: So you were saying you do some walking now, so you've been able to extend your walks?

CAREGIVER: Yes.

INTERVIEWER: That's great.

CAREGIVER: And when I go to Walmart, I talk to everybody, so they're all kind of, oh there's the crazy lady! (Laughs). And when I have the cart I'm more mobile, i can walk better, so it's almost like having a walker. It usually takes me about a half hour or forty-five minutes at Walmart.

INTERVIEWER: How do you get there?

CAREGIVER: Cab.

INTERVIEWER: How often do you usually do that?

CAREGIVER: Usually about twice a week.

INTERVIEWER: That's nice, so it's a little outing.

CAREGIVER: Yes, it is, I feel like I escape.

INTERVIEWER: Have you ever thought about doing a support group or a meeting or anything like that?

CAREGIVER: No, because it's hard for me to get out. There are times when I can tell him I'm leaving, but see how his hand is twitching, he will get so his whole body is doing that, and I get nervous, so I don't like to leave him alone, so I can't just pick up and go when I want. There are windows when I can get away.

INTERVIEWER: What's your fear?

CAREGIVER: That he would try to get out or something would happen, he would get up and he would fall, or he would be hurt while I was gone. And, the guilt would not be happy. Caretaker, babysitter, a pain in the ass. I'm sure he has several different names for me.

The preceding description fits a more traditional ethnographic approach to both fieldwork and the representation of data: a description of participant observation with a narrative that illustrates a single person's experiences. Through this early fieldwork it became clear that we do not fully understand how to intervene in caregivers' social and physical experiences in the home and community environments to reduce the social isolation and loneliness so commonly experienced. One of the limitations of ethnographic research in a medical setting is the ability to spend the same kind of time we might spend during more traditional fieldwork. Another is that there are many elements of the person's environment, physical, social, and structural, that might have implications for the problem I was looking at, including what services people access, when, and how that were out of the purview of the time I spent with the family. While I was able to spend a brief amount of time with people in their day-to-day lives, I wanted to expand the scope of the data I was using to address this common problem. What were their neighborhood or community characteristics? How much time did they spend in different rooms in their homes or accessing different services in the community? Who did they interact with? Where did these interactions happen? How did they get there? What happened when I was not around?

Furthermore, while the case description and thematic analysis approach is useful for representing some of the richness ethnographers experience during fieldwork, it did not always seem a satisfying approach to represent the issues I encountered in a way that could be useful to clinical or policy audiences. I wanted to be able to illustrate core dynamics involved, both for individual caregiver-patient dyads as well as for making comparisons across caregivers, locations, or other points of interest. I thus questioned what strategies could be used to make the data speak to clinicians, policymakers, and scientists, while still being legible to other social scientists. As such, I sought an approach that would allow me greater insight into people's activity, movement, social networks, and emotional experiences that were connected to the ways they moved about in space and where they spent their time, and could be represented computationally. Furthermore, I hoped that such an approach would allow for case comparisons using different types of data and units of comparison.

As I moved into thinking about new iterations to my approach, I became captivated by both the emotional experiences of social isolation and loneliness, as well as the spatial and temporal and geographical dimensions and implications, with the goal of eventually developing interventions that would actually be located at sites where caregivers spend the most time. Both anthropologists and geographers examined how people understand, use, and make social and political meaning through space and in time (Gupta and Ferguson 1997; Caldeira 2000; Marcus 1995; Caquard 2013; Buliung and Kanaroglou 2006; Kwan 2008; Malkki 1992). Similarly, I wanted to understand aspects of space and time in regards to where people went during the day—both in their homes and in their communities, how long they spent in different places and why, who they talked to, what feelings or experiences they had in different locations and spaces, how neighborhoods, transportation, and resource environment impacted their experiences, and ways to think about comparing across caregivers that did not make assumptions about the salience of pregiven categories such as "rural" and "urban," or take for granted what counts as a social connection. These questions, I felt, would help me to answer the more applied question: How could we find new ways to identify caregivers at risk for social isolation and loneliness, and intervene in ways that people would actually find meaningful and adaptable to their current experiences and environments?

As a member of the Care Ecosystem research team, I was engaged with the questions that were most concerning to clinicians. I was also inspired by another colleague's work. As a geriatrician and an engineer, he had developed a functional monitoring component for the Care Ecosystem study. The idea was to provide smart watches and smart sensors to the person with dementia in order to track his or her physical activity and movement. Implications from this work include the possibility of creating falls-prediction modeling based on patient movement in the months leading up to a major fall or health emergency (Zylstra et al. 2018). To expand the scope of data collection and the possibility for this type of modeling that could be relevant to applied audiences, I wanted to collect a lot more data in a short period of time through a number of different instruments and computational techniques (specifically, monitoring, observations, interviews, and public data sets). I felt that engaging in multiple modes of data collection could increase both the depth and breadth of data in order to create new assemblages of information that could lead to more possibilities for insightful comparative analysis. My encounter as part of a clinical research team led to another cross-disciplinary interaction, as I formed a collaboration with a geographer in order to gain insights into how ethnographic data in the traditional sense might be incorporated into technological and visual systems both as a mechanism to study experiences, but also for representational purposes

An ethnographic approach that uses geographic information systems (GIS) technology, interviews, and observations can be used to map and describe caregivers' experiences of social connection and isolation in relationship to their activity within the home and community at multiple different scales (Kwan and Ding 2008; Fielding 2009; Shaw, Yu, and Bombom 2008; Jung and Elwood 2010; Buliung and Kanaroglou 2006). This approach allows for mixed-method data collection that incorporates GPS tracking, activity data, a social dimensions surveys, and publicly available data with ethnographic interviews and participant observation (Table 8.2). Data about

Table 8.2 Types of Data for Use in Mapping

Caregiver Tracking	**Measurement**
Location and time	GPS data: geographic location and duration
Social dimension survey	Survey of social contacts
Activity data	Qualitative findings
Community Environment	**Measurement**
Home/residence	Point on maps, layout of home
Location of medical centers, hospitals, public clinics	Points on maps, counts of sites in neighborhoods
Location of caregiver support sites	Points on maps, counts of sites in neighborhoods
Location of AD-related services and organizations	Points on maps, counts of sites in neighborhoods
Community social events, classes, supports	Points on maps, counts of sites in neighborhoods
Location of transportation routes	Lines on maps, counts of routes in neighborhoods
Location of pharmacies	Points on maps, counts of sites in neighborhoods
Location of grocery stores	Points on maps, counts of sites in neighborhoods
Location and type of housing	Points on maps, counts of sites in neighborhoods
Location of "other" as defined by caregivers in interviews	Points on maps, counts of sites in neighborhoods
Socioecological Characteristics	**Measurement**
Median household income	Median income of all household members in 2009
Concentrated poverty	% of households under the poverty line
Racial heterogeneity	% of African Americans, % Whites, % Asians, % non-White Hispanics
Racial isolation	% of one racial group/all others
Walkability score (Moudon and Lee n.d.)	The number of typical consumer destinations within walking distance of a house, with scores ranging from 0 (car dependent) to 100 (walkable)
Social and Emotional Characteristics	**Measurement**
Social and emotional experiences	Qualitative findings
Survey results	Survey findings

locations, time spent, and experiences is analyzed both through qualitative software (e.g., ATLAS.Ti), and through ArcGIS, a software used to map and analyze geospatial activity. In this approach, caregivers wear GPS trackers to continuously monitor geolocation. The output reveals activity space, locations, and duration, which give an accurate and objective read of people's movement in space and the time they spend at different places. Caregivers also complete a social dimensions survey, which provides insights into their social interactions. In this survey they describe the social relationship with each contact, including 1) frequency of typical contact; 2) emotional support from contact; and 3) service provided. During ethnographic interviews, caregivers reflect on social and emotional experiences at different locations that are identified through the GPS data collected prior to interviews. Interview responses can be integrated with the mapping data, which also includes publicly available data related to census, transportation, walkability, health services, and AD resources.

All of this data is brought together in a mixed-methods geo-database that can be linked to coding and qualitative analysis in ATLAS.ti, with community environment and socioecological characteristics stored as layers, and integrated with ethnographic findings, which provide more depth and nuance. Maps produced based on these layers can help researchers to visualize and analyze caregivers' physical activity space in their home and community environments, the time spent at different locations, and how physical activity space and time intersects with qualitative social and emotional experience. Some aspects of caregiver experience that can be analyzed using this approach include: movement, activities, time, duration, social contacts, and social emotional experience. For example, we can evaluate the quality of the home and community environment for the social needs of a caregiver (e.g., resources available, proximity of activities and contacts, time spent), and assess their role in a caregiver's activity space. We can visually represent and analyze the intersection of caregivers' physical and social experiences by analyzing the maps and ethnographic data together, and integrating the ethnographic data into the maps. The computational program, ArcGIS can be used to create map layers to integrate social and emotional characteristics from interviews, observations, and surveys with the physical activity space maps to examine the interactions of social experience and space and time dimensions. Based on inputs we will create maps and analyze relationships between movement, resources, time spent in particular salient places, and caregiver experiences.

One example of a mapping method used in GIS is called space-time paths. Space-time paths allow for the mapping and identification of contextual influences and how they vary across space and time, using GIS and detailed GPS data (Kwan 2012; Lee and Kwan 2011). This approach allows for the representation of a trajectory in 3D space in ArcGIS as a way to visualize the caregiver's movement in space and time in combination with social and emotional experiences (Figure 8.2). The vertical axis shows temporal progression, and the horizontal axis shows geographical movement of the caregiver's activity space (Richardson et al. 2013). Space-time paths enable assessment of how aspects of the social or built environment integrate with spatial and temporal movement. Maps show caregivers' activities, including use of resources, social interactions, and emotional experiences, and how these unfold across space and over time. These maps can help in assessments of social and emotional dimensions related to individual and aggregated caregivers' movement through their physical activity space. Ethnographic data provides insights into thoughts, decisions, social networks, context, emotions, and experiences. We aim to use these maps to enable complex comparisons of results across caregivers based on different parameters or characteristics such as where they live, caregiver burden score, or other factors.

Overall, this approach allows for new ways of expanding the scope of data collected and the kinds of comparisons that are possible while also maintaining the depth and nuance of traditional ethnography through in-depth interviews and participant observation with caregivers. We are able to

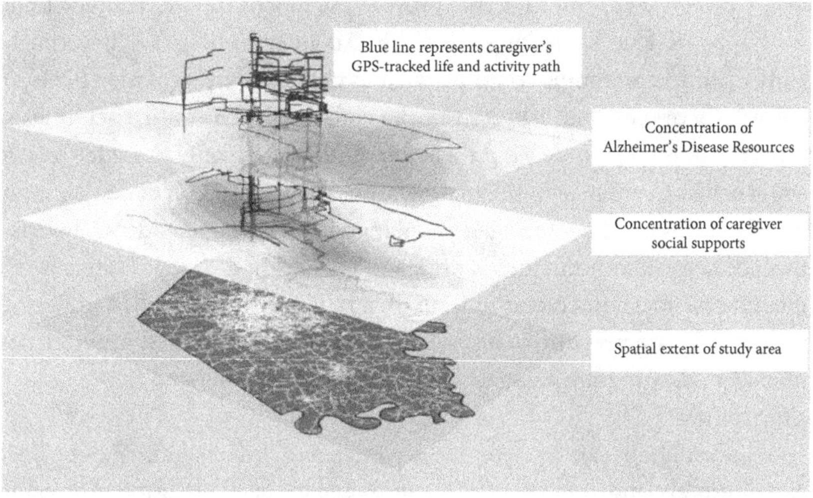

Figure 8.2 Example of Caregiver Space-Time Path Map Using ArcGIS Software

Life paths of caregivers provide assessments of their social and environmental contexts and contacts and how they are related to movement. Caregiver life paths are shown as trajectories that unfold along the vertical axis, which represent time; the bottom horizontal plane represents the spatial extent of the study area. Above this are two horizontal planes that illustrate the spatial distribution of social and resource factors shaping caregiver experience. Dark line represents caregiver's GPS-tracked life and activity path. Adapted from Richardson et al. (2013).

think about new ways to understand dynamics that clearly have intersecting spatial, temporal, and social elements at play, and are connected to resource environments, activity space, and social and emotional experience. This computer-assisted approach to fieldwork offers an expanded scope of data, where more data is collected and the amount of useful information at a given period of time is higher, allowing for more depth and nuance of understanding of a caregiver's experiences.

Applied Implications and Future Directions

While this approach is still in development, there are many potential implications for the method that can be used to help develop applied interventions in both community and clinical settings. In what follows, I discuss three potential areas of forward movement.

Integrating interviews, observations, and GIS data can provide insights into where to locate and how to adapt caregiver interventions that have been shown to be efficacious in addressing caregiver burden so that they are more accessible to caregivers. For example, once we identify the locations where caregivers spend time that provide the most supportive interactions, we might be able to adapt evidence-based interventions so they can be embedded in community settings, such as chain stores, local merchants, or places of worship, and delivered in the course of such routine activities as grocery shopping. To develop this intervention, we would consider how to adapt existing evidence-based interventions to be successful in new community locations and how to engage local merchants as stakeholders. There is a precedent for relocating interventions to novel care delivery settings where meaningful social interactions occur. In a randomized controlled trial study to reduce blood pressure in black men, a pharmacist-assisted hypertension management program was most successful when integrated into a barbershop setting.

GIS information can provide local clinicians with insights about which caregivers are most at risk for loneliness and social isolation. For many providers, it is often difficult to identify when more support is needed and for whom. My previous research on strategies to integrate dementia care into primary care highlights the need for designing an intervention that will be accessible to clinical teams and compatible with their busy clinic schedules.

Thus, intervention development will focus on how to effectively integrate GIS data with the electronic health record (e.g., using a smartphone or other activity tracker data) to inform a primary prevention intervention. Sharing GIS data with providers, including physicians, social workers, and nurses, can help them identify whether someone is especially isolated compared to individual, neighborhood, and community-level normative characteristics. Ethnographic and GIS analysis can help identify areas where caregivers encounter government and policy programs that are outside of the healthcare system, and where investment in novel support programs might be most effective. A long-term goal is to engage community resource providers and city policymakers in developing resources to help caregivers better connect to support. For example, in the United Kingdom, postal carriers were identified as a nontraditional means for intervening to provide support for older adults who were isolated at home. These postal workers helped connect older adults with community resources. By knowing where caregivers spend their time (GIS) and with whom they interact (ethnography) we will identify targets for novel caregiver support interventions that reduce artificial boundaries between sectors and may inform policy.

Overall, expanding the scope and type of data collected can help to identify assets and resilience in caregivers who remain connected with social networks, mechanisms involved in those who are especially burdened, and identify interventions into loneliness and social isolation that exist at the intersection of space, place, time, and sociality. Integrating social and spatial information into studies of caregiving, can offer health and community resource providers a better understanding of the mechanisms of social isolation, loneliness, and connection that contribute to caregiver burden or well-being. Expanding the scope of ethnographic research through the integration of geographic-based computational techniques offers the potential to enhance health and resource providers' interactions with caregivers in places and at times that are most relevant, as well as to tailor services provided outside of healthcare settings. Furthermore, GIS allows for anticipatory modeling, for example, by using inputs from multiple sites and cases to eventually create a model that can simulate behavior or simulate the impact of interventions. While GIS is one example of how this can be done, integrating other types of passive monitoring with ethnographic analysis can help ethnographers understand links between structural features of the environment and people's actual practices.

Discussion

In this chapter we highlight the value of ethnography for studies in medicine and suggest ways that social scientists can advance ethnographic inquiry by engaging with models of science beyond their disciplinary orthodoxies. Ethnography is a diverse and contested field of practice, and the computational innovations we describe build on traditions that have been used in the social sciences for decades. These innovations have diffused poorly to ethnography, however, and some view them as antithetical to the ethnographic tradition. We conceive of ethnography broadly and suggest that these innovations are commensurate with the ethnographic project both methodologically and theoretically. Methodologically, we focus on providing robust interpretative analysis of the meaningful behaviors and cultural practices of groups, movements, organizations, or institutions. Theoretically, our ethnographic work is epistemologically consistent with sociological research on the causes and consequences of social action—even as we recognize that ethnography's mandate extends more readily to elucidating potential mechanisms of action than to drawing conclusions about cause and effect.

Our techniques and the origin stories behind them differ, but both respond to needs we experienced in our work in the applied biomedical research environment. The techniques and innovations we describe typically require specific types of data collection and analysis practices. Both approaches build on the textual data recorded in field notes derived from participant observation of research subjects in naturalistic settings. Other types of ethnographic data, including in-depth interviews with research subjects or key informants, text data, or visual data, can also be incorporated in this approach. Analytically, ethnography includes a range of approaches along the deductive/inductive spectrum. These innovations assume the ethnographer enters the field with some a priori analytical foci or priorities; purely exploratory, inductive studies, such as studies that truly start with the grounded theory question of "what is going on here" are unlikely to benefit from the types of innovations we describe. Consistent with the deductive approach, analysts who seek to use these innovations will typically be comfortable conducting thematic analysis of ethnographic data. Both innovations require computer-assisted qualitative data analysis.

This chapter examines the potential for ethnographers and ethnographic studies to be shaped in encounters with other disciplines, and specifically to inform the practice of biomedicine. The rich ethnographic literature on medicine has often adopted a critical perspective on medical practice or used medicine as a case study for studies of more general social principles or dynamics. Our focus is more practical and applied: How can ethnography inform and improve healing practices across a range of settings from the clinic to the community to policy? Medicine's longstanding appreciation for narrative and culture make it a potentially fertile ground for ethnographic contribution. The profession's focus on quantification leads us to consider how larger-scale comparative ethnographic projects—including projects that use novel approaches for representing and interpreting ethnographic findings—may advance the practice of medicine and the health of populations. In comparative studies in particular, ethnographers seek to examine how phenomenon or behavioral practice varies across and among distinct contexts including practice settings, patient populations, clinical conditions, or treatment modalities.

References

Abramson, Corey M., and Daniel Dohan. 2015. "Beyond Text: Using Arrays to Represent and Analyze Ethnographic Data." *Sociological Methodology* 45, no. 1 (August): 272–319.

Abramson, Corey M., Jacqueline Joslyn, Katherine A. Rendle, Sarah B. Garrett, and Daniel Dohan. 2018. "The Promises of Computational Ethnography: Improving Transparency, Replicability, and Validity for Realist Approaches to Ethnographic Analysis." *Ethnography* 19, no. 2: 254–284.

Becker, Howard S. 2009. "How to Find Out How to Do Qualitative Research." *International Journal of Communication* 3: 9.

Benedict, Ruth. 2005. *Patterns of Culture*. Boston: Houghton Mifflin.

Benedict, Ruth, and Ian Buruma. 2006. *The Chrysanthemum and the Sword: Patterns of Japanese Culture*. New York: Mariner Books.

Biehl, João. 2013. *Vita: Life in a Zone of Social Abandonment*. Berkeley: University of California Press.

Bosk, Charles. 1979. *Forgive and Remember: Managing Medical Failure*. Chicago: University of Chicago Press.

Buliung, Ronald N., and Pavlos S. Kanaroglou. 2006. "A GIS Toolkit for Exploring Geographies of Household Activity/Travel Behavior." *Journal of Transport Geography* 14, no. 1: 35–51.

Caldeira, Teresa Pires do Rio. 2000. *City of Walls: Crime, Segregation, and Citizenship in São Paulo*. Berkeley: University of California Press.

Caquard, Sébastien. 2013. "Cartography I: Mapping Narrative Cartography." *Progress in Human Geography* 37, no. 1: 135–144.

Charmaz, Kathy. 1995. "Grounded Theory." In *Rethinking Methods in Psychology*, edited by Jonathan A. Smith, Rom Harré, and Luk Van Langenhove, 27–49. London: SAGE Publications.

Cohen, Lawrence. 2007. "Operability, Bioavailability, and Exception." In *Global Assemblages: Technology, Politics, and Ethics as Anthropological Problems*, edited by A. Ong and S. Collier, 79–90. Oxford: Blackwell.

Creswell, John W. 2007. *Qualitative Inquiry and Research Design: Choosing Among Five Approaches*, 2nd ed. Thousand Oaks, CA: SAGE Publications.

Desmond, Matthew. 2019. "Eviction Lab." https://evictionlab.org.

Devers, K. J. 1999. "How Will We Know 'Good' Qualitative Research When We See It? Beginning the Dialogue in Health Services Research." *Health Services Research* 34, no. 5, Pt. 2 (December): 1153–1188.

Devers, Kelly J. 2011. "Qualitative Methods in Health Services and Management Research: Pockets of Excellence and Progress, but Still a Long Way to Go." *Medical Care Research and Review* 68, no. 1 (February 20): 41–48.

Dunn, Laura B., Jim Wiley, Sarah Garrett, Fay Hlubocky, Christopher Daugherty, Laura Trupin, Pamela Munster, and Daniel Dohan. 2016. "Interest in Initiating an Early Phase Clinical Trial: Results of a Longitudinal Study of Advanced Cancer Patients." *Psycho-Oncology* 26, no. 10: 1604–1610.

Evans-Pritchard, E. E. 1976. *Witchcraft, Oracles, and Magic among the Azande*. Oxford: Clarendon Press.

Faier, Lieba, and Lisa Rofel. 2014. "Ethnographies of Encounter." *Annual Review of Anthropology* 43, no. 1 (October 21): 363–377.

Fielding, Nigel, and César A. 2009. "CAQDAS-GIS Convergence: Toward a New Integrated Mixed Method Research Practice?" *Journal of Mixed Methods Research* 3, no. 4 (October): 349–370.

Fisher, Jill A., Marci D. Cottingham, and Corey A. Kalbaugh. 2015. "Peering Into the Pharmaceutical 'Pipeline': Investigational Drugs, Clinical Trials, and Industry Priorities." *Social Science & Medicine* 131 (April): 322–330.

Fisher, Jill A., and Corey A. Kalbaugh. 2011. "Challenging Assumptions about Minority Participation in US Clinical Research." *American Journal of Public Health* 101, no. 12 (December): 2217–2222.

Garrett, Sarah B., Corey M. Abramson, Katharine A. Rendle, and Daniel Dohan. 2018. "Approaches to Decision-Making among Late-Stage Melanoma Patients: A Multifactorial Investigation." *Supportive Care in Cancer* 27, no. 3 (August): 1059–1070.

Garrett, Sarah B., Christopher J. Koenig, Laura Trupin, Fay J. Hlubocky, Christopher K. Daugherty, Anne Reinert, Pamela Munster, and Daniel Dohan. 2017. "What Advanced Cancer Patients with Limited Treatment Options Know about Clinical Research: A Qualitative Study." *Supportive Care in Cancer* 25, 10 (October): 3235–3242.

Glaser, Barney G., and Anselm L. Strauss. 1967. *The Discovery of Grounded Theory: Strategies for Qualitative Research*. New York: Aldine Publishing Company.

Greenhalgh, Trisha, Ellen Annandale, Richard Ashcroft, James Barlow, Nick Black, Alan Bleakley, et al. 2016. "An Open Letter to The BMJ Editors on Qualitative Research." *BMJ* (February): i563.

Gupta, Akhil, and James Ferguson. 1997. *Culture, Power, Place: Explorations in Critical Anthropology*. Durham, NC: Duke University Press.

Haraway, Donna. 1999. "The Biopolitics of Postmodern Bodies: Determinations of Self in Immune System Discourse." In *Feminist Theory and the Body: A Reader*, edited by J. Price and M. Shildrick, vol. 1, no. 1, 203. New York: Routledge.

Hawkley, Louise C., and John T. Cacioppo. 2010. "Loneliness Matters: A Theoretical and Empirical Review of Consequences and Mechanisms." *Annals of Behavioral Medicine* 40, no. 2 (October 22): 218–227.

Jennings, Lee A., David B. Reuben, Leslie Chang Evertson, Katherine S. Serrano, Linda Ercoli, Joshua Grill, Joshua Chodosh, Zaldy Tan, and Neil S. Wenger. 2015. "Unmet Needs of Caregivers of Individuals Referred to a Dementia Care Program." *Journal of the American Geriatrics Society* 63, no. 2 (February 1): 282–289.

Jung, Jin Kyu, and Sarah Elwood. 2010. "Extending the Qualitative Capabilities of GIS: Computer-Aided Qualitative GIS." *Transactions in GIS* 14, no. 1: 63–87.

Katz, Jack. 1997. "Ethnography's Warrants." *Sociological Methods & Research* 25, no. 4: 391–423.

Kleinman, Arthur. 1978. "Concepts and a Model for the Comparison of Medical Systems as Cultural Systems." *Social Science & Medicine* 12: 85–93.

Koenig, Christopher J., Evelyn Y. Ho, Laura Trupin, and Daniel Dohan. 2015. "An Exploratory Typology of Provider Responses That Encourage and Discourage Conversation about Complementary and Integrative Medicine during Routine Oncology Visits." *Patient Education and Counseling* 98, no. 7 (July): 857–863.

Kuper, A., S. Reeves, W. Levinson. 2008. "An Introduction to Reading and Appraising Qualitative Research." Bmj.Com, May, 2019. https://www.bmj.com/content/337/bmj.a288.full.pdf+html.

Kwan, Mei Po. 2008. "From Oral Histories to Visual Narratives: Re-Presenting the Post-September 11 Experiences of the Muslim Women in the USA." *Social and Cultural Geography* 9, no. 6: 653–669.

Kwan, Mei-Po. 2012. "How GIS Can Help Address the Uncertain Geographic Context Problem in Social Science Research." *Annals of GIS* 18, no. 4: 245–255.

Kwan, Mei-Po, and Guoxiang Ding. 2008. "Geo-Narrative: Extending Geographic Information Systems for Narrative Analysis in Qualitative and Mixed-Method Research." *The Professional Geographer* 60, no. 4 (September 16): 443–465.

Lamont, Michèle, and Patricia White. 2008. Workshop on Interdisciplinary Standards for Systematic Qualitative Research. National Science Foundation. Washington, DC: National Science Foundation.

Landecker, Hannah. 2007. *Culturing Life: How Cells Became Technologies.* Cambridge, MA: Harvard University Press.

Lee, Jae Yong, and Mei-Po Kwan. 2011. "Visualisation of Socio-Spatial isolation Based on Human Activity Patterns and Social networks in Space-Time." *Tijdschrift Voor Economische En Sociale Geografie* 102, no. 4: 468–485.

Lévi-Strauss, Claude, John Richard Von Sturmer, James Harle Bell, and Rodney Needham. 1969. *The Elementary Structures of Kinship.* Boston: Beacon Press.

Lock, Margaret M. 2002. *Twice Dead: Organ Transplants and the Reinvention of Death.* Berkeley: University of California Press.

Luo, Ye, Louise C. Hawkley, Linda J. Waite, and John T. Cacioppo. 2012. "Loneliness, Health, and Mortality in Old Age: A National Longitudinal Study." *Social Science & Medicine* 74, no. 6: 907–914.

Malkki, Liisa. 1992. "National Geographic: The Rooting of Peoples and the Territorialization of National Identity Among Scholars and Refugees." *Cultural Anthropology* 7, no. 1 (February): 24–44.

Marcus, George E. 1995. "Ethnography in/of the World System: The Emergence of Multi-Sited Ethnography." *Annual Review of Anthropology* 24, no. 1 (October): 95–117.

Maurer, Bill. 2005. *Mutual Life, Limited: Islamic Banking, Alternative Currencies, Lateral Reason.* Princeton, NJ: Princeton University Press.

Mead, Margaret. 2001. *Coming of Age in Samoa: A Psychological Study of Primitive Youth for Western Civilisation.* 1928. Reprint, New York: Perennial Classics.

Messac, Luke, Dan Ciccarone, Jeffrey Draine, and Philippe Bourgois. 2013. "The Good-Enough Science-and-Politics of Anthropological Collaboration with Evidence-Based Clinical Research: Four Ethnographic Case Studies." *Social Science and Medicine* 99: 176–186.

Miles, Matthew B., and A. Michael Huberman. 1994. *Qualitative Data Analysis: An Expanded Sourcebook.* Thousand Oaks, CA: SAGE Publications.

Mol, Annemarie. 2002. *The Body Multiple: Ontology in Medical Practice.* Durham, NC: Duke University Press.

Mol, Annemarie, and John Law. 2004. "Embodied Action, Enacted Bodies: The Example of Hypoglycaemia." *Body & Society* 10, no. 2–3 (June): 43–62.

Moudon, Anne Vernez, and Chanam Lee. 2018. "Walking and Bicycling: An Evaluation of Environmental Audit Instruments." *American Journal of Health Promotion* 18, no. 1: 21–37.

National Academies of Sciences, Engineering, and Medicine. 2016. *Families Caring for an Aging America.* Edited by R. Schulz and J. Eden. Washington, DC: National Academies Press.

O'Brien, Bridget C., Ilene B. Harris, Thomas J. Beckman, Darcy A. Reed, and David A. Cook. 2014. "Standards for Reporting Qualitative Research: A Synthesis of Recommendations." *Academic Medicine: Journal of the Association of American Medical Colleges* 89, no. 9 (September): 1245–1251.

Ong, Aihwa., Stephen J. Collier, and Wiley InterScience. 2005. *Global Assemblages: Technology, Politics, and Ethics as Anthropological Problems.* Oxford: Blackwell.

Petryna, Adriana. 2009. *When Experiments Travel: Clinical Trials and the Global Search for Human Subjects.* Princeton, NJ: Princeton University Press.

Ragin, C. C., and H. S. Becker. 1992. *What Is a Case?: Exploring the Foundations of Social Inquiry.* Cambridge: Cambridge University Press.

Ragin, Charles C., Joane Nagel, Patricia White, and National Science Foundation Sociology Program. 2004. Workshop on Scientific Foundations of Qualitative Research. National Science Foundation, Washington, DC: National Science Foundation.

Reeves, Scott, Ayelet Kuper, and Brian David Hodges. 2008. "Qualitative Research Methodologies: Ethnography." *BMJ (Clinical Research Ed)* 337 (August): a1020–a1020.

Richardson, D. B., N. D. Volkow, M.-P. Kwan, R. M. Kaplan, M. F. Goodchild, and R. T. Croyle. 2013. "Spatial Turn in Health Research." *Science* 339, no. 6126 (March): 1390–1392.

Shaw, Shih Lung, Hongbo Yu, and Leonard S. Bombom. 2008. "A Space-Time GIS Approach to Exploring Large Individual-Based Spatiotemporal Datasets." *Transactions in GIS* 12, no. 4: 425–441.

Small, M. L. 2009. "'How Many Cases Do I Need?': On Science and the Logic of Case Selection in Field-Based Research." *Ethnography* 10, no. 1 (March): 5–38.

Solomon, Harris. 2016. *Metabolic Living: Food, Fat and the Absorption of Illness in India.* Durham, NC: Duke University Press.

Stokols, Daniel. 2006. "Toward a Science of Transdisciplinary Action Research." *American Journal of Community Psychology* 38, no. 1–2 (September): 79–93.

Stokols, Daniel, Shalini Misra, Richard P. Moser, Kara L. Hall, and Brandie K. Taylor. 2008. "The Ecology of Team Science: Understanding Contextual Influences on Transdisciplinary Collaboration." *American Journal of Preventive Medicine* 35, no. 2 (August): S96–115.

Strathern, Marilyn. 1988. *The Gender of the Gift: Problems with Women and Problems with Society in Melanesia*. Berkeley: University of California Press.

Strathern, Marilyn. 1990. *Negative Strategies in Melanesia*. Edinburgh: Scottish Academic Press.

Strauss, A. L. 1987. *Qualitative Analysis for Social Scientists*. Cambridge: Cambridge University Press.

Strauss, Anselm L., and Juliet M. Corbin. 1990. *Basics of Qualitative Research: Grounded Theory Procedures and Techniques*. Thousand Oaks, CA: SAGE Publications.

Theeke, Laurie A. 2010. "Sociodemographic and Health-Related Risks for Loneliness and Outcome Differences by Loneliness Status in a Sample of U.S. Older Adults." *Research in Gerontological Nursing* 3, no. 2 (April): 113–125.

Timmermans, Stefan. 1999. *Sudden Death and the Myth of CPR*. Philadelphia: Temple University Press.

Valtorta, Nicole K., Mona Kanaan, Simon Gilbody, Sara Ronzi, and Barbara Hanratty. 2016. "Loneliness and Social Isolation as Risk Factors for Coronary Heart Disease and Stroke: Systematic Review and Meta-Analysis of Longitudinal Observational Studies." *Heart* 102, no. 13: 1009–1016.

Zee, Jerry. 2017. "Holding Patterns: Sand and Political Time at China's Desert Shores." *Cultural Anthropology* 32, no. 2 (May): 215–241.

Zylstra, Bradley, George Netscher, Julien Jacquemot, Michael Schaffer, Galen Shen, Angela D. Bowhay, et al. 2018. "Extended, Continuous Measures of Functional Status in Community Dwelling Persons with Alzheimer's and Related Dementia: Infrastructure, Performance, Tradeoffs, Preliminary Data, and Promise." *Journal of Neuroscience Methods* 300 (April): 59–67.

9

Elite Ethnography

Studying Up or Down in US and French Sociology

Lynn S. Chancer

For many years, I have been struck by the apparent tendency of ethnographers in the United States to study "down" more than "up." By this, I mean that the magnifying lens of this immersed, richly detailed and time-honored qualitative practice tends to be brought disproportionately to bear on the problems and practices of poor and marginalized groups relatively more than on those of the rich and powerful. By extension, since racism has historically affected class disadvantages, this has resulted in ethnographers disproportionately concentrating their research on communities of color more than groups of whites. By contrast, studying elites—and disproportionately white elites—has been a relatively less trodden path. It is an observation verified at least anecdotally by the books that spring to mind when conjuring names of well-known contemporary ethnographies: it may be, for instance, Philippe Bourgois's award-winning *Searching for Respect* that is quickly remembered or other works that include, among many deservedly well-known monographs, Loic Wacquant's *Body and Soul*; Elijah Anderson's *Code of the Street*; Mitchell Duneier's *Sidewalks*; Martín Sánchez-Jankowski's *Cracks in the Pavement*; and Terry Williams's *The Cocaine Kids*. Easily memorable, too, are younger ethnographers who have likewise studied down including, for instance, Matthew Desmond's now Pulitzer Prize–winning study *Evicted*; Alice Goffman's widely discussed *On the Run*; Randol Contreras's *Stick Up Kids*; and Victor Rios's *Punished: Policing the Life of Black and Latino Boys*.

Yet—and here is the rub—if a graduate or undergraduate student were to ask to be directed to comparably influential ethnographies of major upper-class occupations including (say) hedge fund managers, successful real estate developers, or multimillion dollar–earning law firm partners, many sociology professors would likely hesitate before names of books would be so

Lynn S. Chancer, *Elite Ethnography* In: *Beyond the Case.* Edited by: Corey M. Abramson and Neil Gong, Oxford University Press (2020).
DOI: 10.1093/oso/9780190608484.003.00010

quickly and analogously cited. To be sure, as soon summarized, the situation is changing: many sociologists are (re)turning to the study of elites, in both the United States and France, a shifting inclination that correlates with worsening world-wise class inequalities and with the frighteningly sharp economic recession that occurred around the world (and strongly hit America) in 2007–2008. For example, there is now Shamus Khan's itself award-winning book on an American boarding school that some children of elites attend—bluntly titled *Privilege*—that deserves mention. Other instances, from the work of Rachel Sherman and Annette Lareau in the United States through that of Bruno Cousin and Sebastian Chauvin (among others) in France, also offer noteworthy instances of studying up in the last ten to fifteen years.

However, my point is that a trend, a disparity, has existed, and persisted, calling out for theoretical and empirical exploration rather than overlooking or dismissal. For why has there been a disparity all told, and how has it arisen? It is to investigating this "sociology of sociology" query that these reflections are devoted while exploring why, in any case, such skewing matters. Ensuing pages also place this query in comparative perspective to inquire whether elites have been studied relatively more often outside the United States even though such studies may not be as known, or frequently cited, in the American context. Specifically, I consider the case of French ethnography while recognizing, of course, that other comparisons can, have, and ought be made as well (see, for example, Aguilar and Schneider's interesting cross-cultural edited volume titled *Researching Amongst Elites*).

Why, though, compare primarily the United States and France? A major justification is that US sociology has been greatly and obviously influenced by French thought, distinctively among its precursors: classical sociological theory in the United States is virtually unimaginable without looking back on Comte and Durkheim (and, if, less well-known, on Mauss); in contemporary thought, the work of Bourdieu has had analogously outsized significance in America. Nor has Bourdieu's influence been only theoretical but methodological: Bourdieu would have likely admired the careful case made by Robert Alford in *The Craft of Sociological Inquiry* against artificial and still conventionally upheld distinctions in the field between studying theory and methods. For both these reasons, contrasting US and French ethnographic approaches may be enlightening about whether elites should be studied but also whether insuperable obstacles of method (read: access) have prevented more research from occurring. In other words, a comparative orientation can be helpful to discern whether a similarly disproportionate sociological "gaze"—that is, a proclivity toward studying down rather than up—connects, or perhaps differentiates, French and US ethnography.

I commence with the observation just adduced only casually: Is there indeed evidence, other than of an impressionistic kind, for claiming that American ethnographers have studied the poor and marginal relatively more than the elite and privileged—at least until recently? Second, if indeed this looks to be the case, does the pattern hold when viewed through a comparative lens? Third, whether in the United States or France, has the primary reason for disparities in studying down or up been that access to elites has been difficult to obtain, thereby limiting the shape of ethnographic research in the sociological field? Alternatively, I explore a "dispositional" hypothesis—namely, whether reasons stemming from emotional inclination and not just rationally calculated methodological factors have also influenced the direction of ethnographic research. Finally, I return to why anyone in or outside the walls of the sociological discipline should care whether ethnographers study up with the same assiduous attention and craft-like prowess that has been brought to bear on research habitually gazing downward.

A Brief Review—and More Than Anecdotal Evidence

Other scholars have lately emphasized not so much a lack as a resurgence of research into elites when viewed on a longer timeline of American sociological scholarship. In a review article published in the *American Review of Sociology* (2012), Shamus Khan describes postwar research into elites that included major studies conducted by C. Wright Mills and later G. William Domhoff on interlocking political and economic elites. According to Kahn, this research was followed by a "relative lull" before three factors resulted in the more recent rise of elite studies. These factors were, first, sharply worsening income inequality nationally and globally going back to the 1970s, as lately depicted in Thomas Piketty's encyclopedic work on twenty-first-century neoliberal capitalism and its discontents. A second factor, Kahn argues, has been the furthering development of network analysis as a "technical" resource that allows interconnections among elites to be traced in more sophisticated detail than before the information revolution (Khan 2012). He cites, thirdly, a "cultural turn" in sociology and the theoretical sway in the United States of Pierre Bourdieu, whose work influenced a generation of scholars immersed in the French as well as American academic fields such as Michele Lamont and Loic Wacquant.

An unpublished paper by Princeton graduate student Jeremy Cohen classifies past research relatedly but also somewhat differently from Khan's categorization. Cohen suggests that elite scholarship has fallen into three broad areas he dubs institutional/organizational, cultural, and mobilization/movement, related respectively (Cohen 2016). He includes both the Mills/Domhoff tradition in the institutional category as well as organizational studies such as one done by Lauren Rivera (2012) on hiring practices in elite firms and professions. Cohen and Kahn overlap in their identification of cultural research, with the former suggesting a long historical line from the late nineteenth-century work of Thorsten Veblen about elite consumption through Bourdieu's late twentieth-century study of cultural distinctions. But Cohen also highlights mobilization studies that fit into social movement scholarship insofar as the latter has focused on both elite networks and elite grass-roots campaigns.

A benefit of such classifications is that they attest to ethnography as one (but not the only) way to study elites, past and present; simultaneously, they confirm ongoing and expanding interest in studying up. Revitalized interest can also be adduced in "sociology of knowledge" terms as scholars provide growing mutual support for each others' ethnographic research on elites. For example, a "sociology of elites" mini-conference held at the 2016 Eastern Sociological Society (ESS) conference in February 2016 was organized by Patrick Inglis and Hugo Ceron Anaya, both of whom study elites, and featured an array of speakers including Khan, Rachel Sherman, and Ashley Mears, among others. And new plans are underway to reorganize at least one special issue, another mini-conference for the ESS in 2017, and a graduate center conference in 2018. New studies published, special issues organized, conferences and mini-conferences held and planned: taken together, all of this confirms renewed interest in studying elites at the same time attesting to the dynamic character of sociology itself.

Yet the fact remains that when ethnographic research on elites is concentrated upon, the resulting picture demonstrates not just what Khan calls a "lull" but an ongoing disparity. For when it comes to ethnography, it still seems that far more scholarly attention is still accorded marginalized groups than those who are elite. To ascertain this, Omar Montana and I looked at the entire period during which the journals *Ethnography* (2000 to 2017),

Qualitative Sociology (1978 to 2017), and the *Journal of Contemporary Ethnography* (1972 to 2017) were published. We selected these three journals because they are well-recognized and obviously devoted to publishing ethnographic work. For *Ethnography*, published beginning in 2000, a total of 66 issues and 388 articles appeared: of these, 73 out of 388 articles focused on topics related to people who are poor or working-class. In other words, 18% of all articles published in the journal focused on studying down whereas only 1% (or 4 out of 388) articles concerned elites; this means that *Ethnography* was 18 times more likely to feature articles centered on the poor and marginalized than on the wealthy and more powerful.

A similar conclusion resulted from looking through *Qualitative Sociology*: of 1,165 articles published from 1978 to the present, 470 concerned the working-class and poor while only 8 focused on studies of upper-class elites. In other words, 40% of the articles in *Qualitative Sociology* have concentrated on studying the poor and working class compared to only less than 1% articles about elite research subjects. Finally, looking at the *Journal of Contemporary Ethnography* from 1972 to the present yielded a broadly similar result. This time, of 1,045 articles published, 402 concentrated on the working-class and poor as opposed to 15 articles studying upper-class elites; this amounts to 38% of articles about the former as opposed to 1% about the latter (in other words, the poor were written about 38 times more often than the upper class).

Let us come back to the original query, then, as this empirically manifested disparity seems both intriguing and important. For one thing, ethnography is clearly a practice through which sociologists convey and shape impressions and affect stereotypes within the outside world as well as inside university walls. Published ethnographies are often read—and sometimes by larger numbers than would peruse drier academic writings—with the kind of avid engagement people bring to novels. Thus, for instance, the work of Sudhir Venkatesh (i.e., his ethnographic account in *Gang Leader for a Day*) was featured in airport bookstores as obviously popular reading; Alice Goffman appeared on *Ted Talks* after *On the Run* was published; and Matthew Desmond's *Evicted* is an easy candidate for monthly book club reading groups (my own included). This does not mean that ethnographers themselves are not also sometimes marginalized; however, at least in some cases, their studies have obvious resonance in terms of reaching the larger world as a form of public sociology.

But probing the disparity is also merited because of a theoretical question relatively less explored in other elite studies despite their obvious strengths: again, for what reasons should the directionality of research be shifted? What and where are the potential gains (or not) from studying elites? Moreover, reflecting on *why* anyone should care can itself contribute to shifting sociological attention by clarifying whether researchers *ought* change the overall and still disparate trend.

To Continue, Then: Why the Disparity? Access, Disposition, or Both?

To frame discussion, I pursue two lines of argumentation. First, I start with the assumption—let's say the thesis—of access being the primary reason for the patterned skewing of ethnographic research in the United States manifested by (among other possible indicators) the disparity in major ethnographic journals' published articles. Second, I turn to an alternative possibility—let's say to an antithesis—that dispositional inclinations, to some extent, have also influenced the disparity. In conclusion, I offer suggestions aimed at synthesizing prior points.

A Thesis: Access Qua Explanation

Of course it is commonsensically apparent that access is a major reason for disparities between studying up and studying down. It is certainly the easiest and most self-evident explanation. For why wouldn't people who are poor and marginalized seek (rather than seek to avoid) contact with researchers who have the potential to understand and sympathetically portray the serious and overlooked problems they have experienced? As a thesis, therefore, access is necessarily a two-sided coin. On the one hand, the explanation encompasses difficulties of gaining entry into the realms habituated by elites; and, on the other, it posits the apparent relative *ease* of developing relationships with those who have been socially excluded. Discussing these in reverse order, and as Terry Williams understood in *The Cocaine Kids* (1989), many ethnographers have sought to de-stigmatize those who have been demonized, whose problems are left to be tackled as though merely of individualistic origin in American (as opposed to European) culture. Within this context, and taking Philippe Bourgois's *In Search of Respect* (1995) as an excellent example, ethnographers have reason to believe their writings can call attention to structural causes of problems people experience such as attempting to find jobs that may not exist, at which their expectations are mismatched, or where they encounter disrespect and discrimination. Then, too, scholars including Wacquant, Sánchez-Jankowski, Contreras, and Rios, among many others, show conditions of urban violence often correlated with poverty and desperation with which people have to cope—and to which people often respond creatively and sometimes heroically, albeit sometimes also (self)-destructively given extraordinarily challenging circumstances within which they find themselves living and surviving.

Consequently writing about socially abandoned groups of people matters: it calls attention to who and what has been forgotten given the ongoing pervasiveness of American individualism that leaves people to their own devices rather than offering social support and safety nets. In turn, this has ramifications for questions of access. Good can and does clearly come from studying the poor since the potential exists for changing biased attitudes and collective sentiments frequently used to justify vastly unequal distributions of social resources. For quite intelligible and intelligent reasons, then, people may be quite willing—once trust has been established—to let ethnographers into their lives. There may be enjoyment, sociability, connections available—and it can feel affirming if a representative of "outside" society puts herself or himself in your shoes (as George Herbert Mead long recommended "taking the role of the other") so as to learn, to understand, to see one's own all-too-easily overlooked world as important. The social tables may even feel reversed as now this relatively more powerful outside party (the ethnographer) clearly needs those he or she is researching. Relative powerlessness may become its opposite vis-à-vis this studying down ethnographic situation in which the scholar nevertheless depends upon, and requires, people who have been socially marginalized for access.

But now contrast this with the perspective that emerges if we consider the situation in just the opposite way, that is, from the vantage point of elites at the opposite end of the class spectrum. What is in it for them—for the investment banker, the hedge fund manager, the powerful corporate lawyer and his or (sometimes, infrequently) her partners? It is likely these groups' trust that will be harder to earn. Sociologists are, and are known to be, for the most part progressively oriented, and thus perhaps relatively suspect as a group from the get-go. It would not be surprising if people who live at the upper echelons of society imagined researchers to harbor disdain toward them, the very elite groups whom liberals/progressives/Marxists are likely to blame for creating, maintaining, producing, and reproducing chronic inequalities that poor and marginalized people experience and endure.

Thus to allow ethnographers to come into one's (now) elite world—and to thereafter study/see/gaze on this world's day-to-day operations of power and privilege—may be to invite problems vis-à-vis lack of understanding (rather than its reverse), and perhaps cultural and even legal problems to boot. Why would you/I/they want this? Nor might the elite, the powerful, and the extremely well-to-do have much interest in having people live with researchers at their homes, in their neighborhoods—to come along to fancy dinners, vacations, social gatherings, and social clubs as they go about their literal and figurative business in multiple dimensions of their lives. Finally, whereas the marginalized may gain relative power (in relation to actually experienced powerlessness) given the ethnographer's need for access to them, elites could feel just the opposite. The ethnographer's presence may estrange their habitual sense of power, and modify it into relatively more powerless and uncontrollable feelings of uncertainty about what the gazing other is thinking, and possibly judging, once allowed into elite people's lives with little assurance about the conclusions he or she will reach and convey.

But here is where the opposite argument, as an antithesis, arises: Is it conceivable that the "access thesis" is too simple, too rapidly (even eagerly?) presumed because so apparently self-evident? For example, in talking about this chapter to an American colleague who has done ethnography, he quickly declared that the reason scholars in sociology and criminology do not study down is obvious: scholars cannot "get into" Wall Street, he observed, citing one of his student's experiences. But for both empirical and theoretical reasons, perhaps the access hypothesis needs to be—as is a term worth coining in this and other situations—complexified, that is, explored in a more nuanced way.

An Antithesis: Plumbing the Psychosocial in the Researcher and the Researched

To start, it is misleading to presume only elites have grounds for suspiciousness; people who have experienced marginalization and discrimination obviously have good reason, too, for cautiousness toward researchers. Thus, when studying down, access is hardly automatic nor easy; rather, skill and commitment were, and are, analogously required to reassure people that an ethnographer is not an unfriendly outsider. Still, it can and should be granted that something must be different when studying groups who have accumulated great amounts of social power, wealth, and privilege compared with those struggling to attain equalities at great and sometimes impossible seeming odds.

Let us grant then, for argument's sake and also because commonsensically apparent, elites have more to protect insofar as they own/have/possess just this—more—and may well fear that this very inequality, when viewed through an ethnographic lens, could result in sociological criticism rather than being viewed with sympathy (or empathy). But if self-protectiveness on the part of elites (which, in turn, affects access) is truly the main reason for disparities in research attention to studying up or down, how is that detailed ethnographic studies of elites have still been done and published—past and present? It is here that comparing French and US ethnography appears instructive. For background for this theoretical chapter, I talked with approximately ten sociologists and ethnographers who work in France. Many referred to the foundational work of Monique Pinçon-Charlot and her husband Michel Pinçon-Charlot, sociologists who studied with Bourdieu, married, and then devoted nearly the entirety of their academic careers working together at a French research institute to studying up and publishing ethnographies of French elites. Collecting detailed research about the culture and interactional patterns of the bourgeoisie and haute bourgeoisie, "les Pinçon Charlot" (as they have been called) published well over a dozen books that are clearly elite studies. These titles included, among many others, *Dans Les Beaux Quartiers* (1989), *Grandes Fortunes: Dynasties Familiales et Formes de Richesse en France* (1996), *Voyage en Grande Bourgeoisie* (1997), *La Violence Des Riches* (2013), and *Les Ghettos du Gotha: Comment La Bourgeoisie Defend Ses Espaces* (2010).

Interestingly, though, the work of Michel and Monique Pinçon-Charlot seems relatively unknown in the United States—in part, no doubt, because many of the couple's Bourdieu-inspired studies have not been translated from French into English nor distributed by academic or commercial publishers in the United States. But the language barrier also raises the question of why more interest has not been shown in translating the work of Monique and Michel Pinçon-Charlot, especially since (again) they are extremely well-known sociologists in France and given that—as previously discussed—a resurgence appears to be taking place in the United States with regard to studying up. Moreover, in France, the books of "les Pinçon Charlot" regularly sell large numbers of copies—analogous, say, to the sales of Goffman's *On the Run* or Desmond's *Evicted*—while a mass-distributed French documentary has been made about their lives and research. Indeed, when I visited France in July 2016, I was struck at seeing the latest book written by Michel et Monique Pinçon-Charlot prominently displayed in FNAC, one of Paris' major bookstores that is broadly comparable to Barnes and Nobles in New York City.

How then, and for example, did "les Pinçon-Charlot" gain access and overcome suspiciousness the access thesis predicts? One reason may be that Monique and Michel Pinçon-Charlot worked together as a pair, and may have found that their work was helped by their being a married couple. Perhaps this signaled something in common between the researched and the researchers, that is, a cultural matching of sorts insofar as their fitting a common family form (the romantic heterosexual pair) was familiar and not culturally threatening to the people les Pinçon-Charlot were meeting. Perhaps this created a point in common that assisted with access.

But it is hard not to wonder if more than this also occurred that facilitated associations of the kind les Pinçon-Charlot obtained and other ethnographers studying elites have also established as a sine qua non of their research. Other studies done by people in France have likewise penetrated deeply into the cultural, quotidian lives of the haute bourgeoisie. Again, in French research, Bruno Cousin and Sebastian Chauvin have likewise studied upper-middle-class, elite culture through ethnographic observation of people in St. Barts. In the United States—and as is fascinating given my colleague's confidence that the access problem was insurmountable—a study of Wall Street bankers by Karen Ho, titled *Liquidated: An Ethnography of Wall Street*, was indeed published in the field of anthropology in 2009 by Duke University Press. The edited volume *Research Amongst Elites* (2012), contains a host of other studies of elites that have been conducted not only in France and the United States, but also around the world in the last several decades.

Thus it is empirically evident, not only from the research of Les Pinçon Charlot but many other scholars, that ethnographic access to the daily lives of elites can be managed outside and inside the United States. Perhaps this offers an entrée to tackling our antithesis theoretically not just on the basis of empirical studies of elites and the upper middle-class already done.

Obviously access has occurred, but for what reasons did it (and is it) possible? To theorize post facto what has not only been potential but actuality, I turn to a psychosocial mode of analysis defined here as follows. Psychosocial analysis, increasingly developing in British sociology (see, for US and British psychosocial writings in the edited collection *The Unhappy Divorce of Sociology and Psychoanalysis*), pays close attention to social and cultural contexts as well as psychological meanings—to both—in order to probe individual and collective behaviors that, without an explicitly multidimensional approach, will be understood far more superficially. This is because both levels—the psychological and the social, the emotional and the rational as well as the conscious and unconscious—regularly combine in quotidian motivations and practices. What is more, and crucially for this argument, multidimensional motivations and practices that involve regular intercourse between the social and psychic occur routinely and daily for both the researched and the researcher: they have this, humanly, in common whatever else are their likewise highly salient social differences.

Thus in the case at hand, psychosocial analysis can be used to explore why the access thesis has started to seem too simple: for example, it is really or necessarily the case that only, or primarily, people who experience social marginalization and economic pressures are likely to enjoy having their lives looked at? Let us start, then, with the psychological part of a psychosocially oriented approach. The successfully undertaken and completed work of les Pinçon-Charlot and others who have studied elites (such as, again Karen Ho, in anthropology) raises the possibility that narcissistic pleasures experienced to some extent by everyone—as the psychoanalytic tradition concludes—simultaneously takes variant forms depending on class status and other distinctly social factors. In other words, not only people who are poor but those who are quite well-to-do may well find it enjoyable—similarly but also differently, once relationships of sufficient trust have been established—to have one's life and life's work granted importance through the gaze of apparently nonjudgmental observers. Consequently narcissistic pleasures vary and overlap—existentially speaking—up, down, and across the class hierarchies of capitalism.

For elites, enjoyment clearly will not involve compensation for social insensitivity at one's (structurally caused) problems having been overlooked, but may emanate from a sense of pride at feeling one's material power, advantages, and achievements mirrored in the observer/researcher's eyes. In this scenario, elites may imagine the ethnographer as admiring of, if not awestruck by, an elite person's wealth and power—a quite different projection, of course, than envisioning the ethnographer as relatively uncontrollable due to judgments he or she will eventually publish and convey. I find myself thinking here of Donald Trump taken here as representative of one Weberian-style type: in fact, Trump's personality has frequently been written about as classifiable along a narcissistic continuum. However powerful Trump was (and is) as an example of an economic and now political elite, it is hard to believe that he does not still experience admiration from outsiders as, quite simply, pleasurable. Why else continue to go to rallies even after his election if not for phenomenological (as well as political) enjoyment, at this "psycho" level of "psychosocial" analysis, of precisely such immediate, visceral, gazing admiration and recognition?

But other psychological interpretations of the psychosocial may likewise illuminate why, in other cases involving elites, people may appreciate—and not necessarily shirk or shy away from—contact with ethnographers. In contrast with people whose marginalization understandably generates angers that can be expressed to a researcher, some members of elite groups may feel exactly the opposite emotion in some cases—guilt—whether or not this feeling is explicitly expressed or consciously recognized. In other words, like everyone else, people who are elite evidently vary among themselves even as also evincing sociological similarities. For instance, and as an important instance of such intraelite variability, Rachel Sherman has spoken about guilty feelings noticeable after she conducted interviews with upper-class urban women who live in the New York City metropolitan area. Her interviewees know well that they have far more economic power than others (including, likely, ethnographers) amidst the deeply stratified structures of a politically progressive city. Perhaps, as a result, defensive mechanisms are observable that could arguably be interpreted as seeking to neutralize guilt as elite women recounted their regular habit of teaching their families, their children, to cloak and minimize conspicuous displays of their privilege. This may be an elite version of what, in the very different social context of lower class crime, David Matza superbly called "techniques of neutralization" (of, in both cases, guilt). And, indeed, the very first sociologist to theorize the psychosocial cultural traits, the social psychology, of elites was arguably Max Weber himself, famously plumbing the guilty anxieties of early Calvinist Protestants who did not want to conspicuously and sensuously enjoy their pleasures. Rather, they used religion to neutralize guilt via the belief system of accumulating wealth in the service of a deity rather than only and crassly in the service of themselves; this is how, indirectly, they would (hopefully) gain entrance to heaven.

And thus the guilty elite person may feel quite differently toward the liberal social scientist than the narcissistically suspicious one—and he or she may wish to impress an ethnographer not so much with his wealth as with her or his progressivism. But the point is that whether interspersed with myriad forms of narcissism, or with larger-or-smaller tinges of guilt, people who are elite—not just those who are working-class or poor—may be quite willing, at least sometimes and in some situations, to have other people listen to, watch, and inquire about them across one or more dimensions of their lives. And, at both ends of the class spectrum, such ethnographic interest may be experienced as potentially justifying of the validity of one's life—a concern for *meaning* that it seems foolish to attribute, as a human want or need, to only some people in some class situations. A caveat, though: a thorny problem, at once theoretically and methodologically, is that narcissistic enjoyment found in ethnographers reporting on or about elite lives may result in just the opposite strong reaction, that is, the shutting down of access, when or if strongly critical ethnographic narratives eventually appear in print. This may be what happened when, following their official retirement from academia, the publications of Michel and Monique Pinçon-Charlot became more critical of the people they had studied in their previously published monographs (take, for example, the postretirement book les Pinçon-Charlot wrote about French elites titled *La Violence Des Riches*).

But, for now, let us concentrate on these psyche-related theoretical observations suggesting that disparities in sociologists studying down versus up cannot be reduced to only problems of access. The question has indeed begun to appear more complicated, as is further confirmed when turning now to a social piece of this particular psychosocial puzzle. Are there additional reasons, more traditionally sociological, that may have assisted in the successful gaining of access and published work on elites by Les Pinçon-Charlot, Bruno Cousin, and Sebastian Chauvin in France as well as (among others) Shamus Khan, Ashley Mears, Rachel Sherman, and others in the United States? For similarities of class, gender, race, and ethnicity could have, at least in some cases and if only to some extent, facilitated research by rendering the researcher familiar; this may facilitate what could be called, again, cultural matching or (as Bourdieu might put it) a kindred sense of interrelated habitus/i. Moreover, and adding to this, academic status (whether or not strictly aligned with class status) may pertain between researcher and the sought out elite researched-to-be: say, in the United States, does the sociologist bear/wear an (elite) contagious effect of the famed University of Chicago, from Harvard or Berkeley? In France, does the researcher come from the highly esteemed Sciences Po in Paris? If so, this too may be a pedigree in status-conscious contexts that can bestow degrees of legitimization and facilitate entrée in some, if not all, cases. For it is certainly possible, and again if only in some instances, that such commonalities help to dilute a scholar's potentially suspect character in wanting so badly and determinedly to study up?

Take class and cultural capital. Karen Ho writes that her ability to conduct ethnographic study among Wall Street bankers was helped by strategically drawing on her own educationally elite background of having gone to Harvard and Princeton so as, one presumes, to forge a common connection that may mitigate against suspiciousness. As she writes about her background, "I then became a graduate student at Princeton University, a recruiting hotbed for investment banks . . . My path to Wall Street was made possible by the institutional, elite 'familial' connections between particular universities and Wall Street investment banks . . ." (Ho 2009, 13). In the case of Shamus Khan, as recounted in *Privilege*, Khan himself went to St. Paul's School, a social fact that seems to have assisted with access via common and previously established cultural academic capital. And Bruno Cousin, when asked about why ethnographic studies of elite are being undertaken lately, cited among other important reasons (such as worsening inequalities) that more upper-middle-class scholars are drawing on their class backgrounds to facilitate research.

A similar analysis might also be applicable to gender: for instance, would Philippe Bourgois's study *In Search of Respect* have been possible if conducted by a scholar who was a woman, that is, were it not for masculinity-based commonalities and homosocial bonding, without which the young men he came to know may not have been comfortable recounting stories of their sexist and sometimes violent practices toward young women? Of course class, racial, and gender commonalities also combine (why would they not?) when researching class hierarchies at other points in class spectrums: as Randol Contreras has observed, his ability to research *The Stick Up Kids* was facilitated by his stepping out of his back door where he grew up in the Bronx.

It is important to note that these observations are in no way normative. By no means am I suggesting that an ethnographer ought or cannot study outside his or her own social background; such a suggestion would be highly problematic, let alone essentialistic. Rather, in counterarguing with the access thesis, I am positing that whether one likes this or not, in a pragmatic sociological sense at this historical moment, problems of access may be diminished by strategically tapping connections one already has. It may sometimes be strategically useful to tap conventional ties that can conceivably be established—ranging from the cultural familiarity of "in love" couples through class, racial, ethnic, and gendered similarities.

But even more significantly, and theorizing further, the social part of psychosocial analysis suggests that such strategic drawing on similarities between researcher and researched is especially germane when studying elites for a structural reason that is distinctly sociological. Again: elites groups and individuals may feel they have more to lose (rather than gain) from granting ethnographers access. And, consequently, researchers may be compelled to maximize the degrees of reassuring familiarity on offer to parties responding most self-protectively (for structural reasons) to the idea of an ethnographer studying about their lives. On the other hand, when studying down, people who have been marginalized can (for structural reasons) be anticipated as relatively more likely to welcome—again after trust, in both cases, has been established—researchers who may or may not be from similar backgrounds as their own. As previously argued, given economic and social invisibility marginalized groups experience in ways elites do not analogously encounter, social recognition may be—for this structurally based reason—particularly appreciated for its relative paucity.

Thus, by implication, sociological researchers who are themselves middle- or upper-class (and, in this sense, possibly also elite and in degrees privileged) may not need to draw on their backgrounds as much to make connections when studying down rather than up. The reverse may also be the case. But can there be exceptions to this structural prediction such that people in a relatively powerless group manage perfectly well to access elites who are relatively more powerful along one or more sociological axes? Of course, and significantly so: in some cases, those from working or lower class backgrounds can and do study up just as women can and do study groups of (predominantly) men, and people of color study can and do study groups of (predominantly) whites. Les Pinçon-Charlot, for example, were from working-class backgrounds but may have had other cultural familiarities to draw upon; in some contexts, diverse backgrounds may be perceived as advantageous rather the reverse. What I am positing, though, is the existence, the persistence, of a structurally based tendency that simultaneously leaves room for phenomenological outcomes which regularly render psychosocial life complex, contingent, and full of surprises.

Yet the positing of a tendency matters. For if this argument holds in theory regarding access to elites becoming potentially easier if and when tapping social similarities between researcher and researched, has this been occurring in practice? Although I have not studied the question systematically, it is conceivable that many ethnographers—both in the United States and France—who have tended to study down, in the past, have elected to do so even though their own middle, upper-middle, or upper-class backgrounds might have assisted with access had they chosen to study up (or laterally across). This is an empirical question I leave to others: namely is it possible that despite the structurally based prediction theorized here, a greater percentage of sociological ethnographers of middle- and upper-class origins have elected in practice to study down more often than up (both in France and the United States, but certainly in the United States)? Of course, this is not to say that people do not also study across: for example, some middle-class scholars study the middle class (though, as is another empirical point worthy of further research, lateral ethnographies of the middle class by middle-class scholars appear on the surface to be relatively less frequent). Moreover, scholars from marginalized groups may tend to study people with whom they have sociological commonalities in greater proportions based on ramifications of the same structurally based proclivity.

Another caveat: by no means does this argument impugn the social value and sociological craft of outstanding ethnographies of marginalized groups written by middle or upper-middle-class scholars studying down. Such a surmise would miss the point here, namely, that something intellectually noteworthy may be afoot that touches on the "access thesis" as though a Mertonian self-fulfilling prophesy. And, if so, our noted disparity in sociology between studying up and studying down in turn suggests a corollary disparity between researchers who *might* tap their own middle- or upper-class connections to study up and those who actually do not—electing, instead, to study down. With this, then, I move to counterarguing with the access thesis from the standpoint of what I call dispositional leanings.

Dispositional Leanings that Complexify the Access Thesis

In turning to connections perhaps not fully tapped until more recently, I offer several dispositional reasons why sociological ethnographers from middle, upper-middle, and upper-class backgrounds have until recently turned more often—in a skewed way that could even be sociologically unconscious—to studying down rather than up. For if disposition is also entailed in the skewed character of studying down, why might this be? I propose three interrelated, and purposely speculative, explanations beginning with what Erving Goffman astutely diagnosed as contagion effects.

For, perhaps quite understandably, one would rather be associated with groups that have been downtrodden, marginalized, and discriminated against than with those who have been the seeming cause of tremendous human misery. Being or becoming putatively connected with the apparent arrogance of elite groups may evoke embarrassment at best, disdain or contempt at worst. It may, literally and figuratively, feel as though one has become stuck on and associated with the wrong side of history—with the victimizer rather than the victim, the oppressor rather than the oppressed, the "bad guys" as opposed to the "good." And, once more, this explanation will tend to operate as a two-sided coin: by contrast, association with groups who have been wronged (and who therefore seem "good") can seem to produce a contagion effect such that the researcher is positively affected too. Moreover, to opt (rather than one's position forcing one) to associate with the group who has been deprived equal social recognition may even be to experience a "cool" contagion effect, kindred to what anthropologists have long referred to as "going native": I could have been hanging out with the rich, but I chose not to; now others in the wider world will see me not as "one of them" but as having come closer to jettisoning my ethically/morally dubious class of origins. Moreover, people one befriends in marginalized groups may seem—and, sometimes be—nicer, more "authentic" and warmer once their own reasons for social protectiveness have been overcome (and trust earned).

In other words, for the reasons articulated here that relate to the motivations of the researcher and not merely the contents of the research, a sociologist ethnographer from a middle- or upper-class background may prefer and feel psychosocially more drawn and comfortable—dispositionally—toward studying and hanging out with people who have been socioeconomically marginalized, as opposed to immersing oneself amidst persons closer to one's own class background (assuming access could become possible). This confirms what from a psychosocial perspective is obvious, namely, both the subject and object of ethnography, that is, researcher and researched alike, share motivations that are at once rational and emotional, explicit and unwitting—dare I say unconscious as well as conscious.

But, with this, a second explanation emerges insofar as to study elites may be to elicit feelings of guilt related to precisely such contagion effects. If studying down can make one feel less culpable, quite the contrary experience can be anticipated to result when studying up. Now, by contrast, one enters the so-called belly of the beast; hardly surprising if, therefore, scholars tend to "vote with their feet" asymmetrically. Then too, if feelings of guilt could (in an ethnographer's projective imagination) ensue from studying elites, this would again recall analogous guilty reactions observed both within the classical tradition of Max Weber and the contemporary context of Rachel Sherman's work.

For if elites sometimes neutralize guilt by minimizing and trying hard not to display their privilege, why wouldn't a psychosocial version of this impulse also sometimes apply to a social researcher? The latter, too, may aim to and experience neutralization of guilt pangs when studying down rather than up—especially in an academic discipline, namely sociology, that concerns itself with and has excellent reason to decry gaping, worsening local and global capitalist class inequalities.

More, too, stems by implication from this analysis. Once again, a benefit of studying down is allowing groups who have been stigmatized by the dominant society, and thereafter rendered virtually invisible, to be depicted fairly and nonstereotypically. Whether on the basis of Weber's advocacy of Verstehen, or Mead's symbolic interactionistic admonition that sociologists put themselves in the mind of another, or the advice of the naturalistic school of ethnography: qualitative sociologists are interested in seeing the world through someone else's inner lens. This is an enterprise, a craft, inclined to diminish distance between self and other, subject and object.

But what if the other within whose life one becomes immersed strikes the ethnographer as distasteful? In response, the observer may feel capable of describing elite practices—but humanizing them? This may be a far more difficult challenge than studying down. It may make the ethnographic study of elites seem more akin to undertaking an expose, a muckraking journalistic investigation—a raison d'etre hard to square with naturalistic advice to put oneself in the minds, the shoes, of the other. Even more: to humanize elites may be to reactivate those Goffman-like contagion effects, not only in the larger world but among progressive fellow scholars likely to bristle if elites are portrayed in ways that seem, in these depictions' apparent neutrality, to equate with political wishy-washiness or even flattery. Where does that leave one afterward, then—still a good guy or potentially appearing to have crossed over to the other side?

Last but hardly least, dispositional proclivities away from studying up rather than down may emanate from not being sure why studying elites even matters. For after all these reasons are said and done, what—other than exposé—is to be gained? Some sociologists may even decide that given actually existing social problems and inequities, the inner world of elites is well known enough a priori that research is not even called for.

When All Is Said and Done Then: Why Study Elites Anyway?

It is with this last query that I started and to which I now return: why, in the end, go through all the painstaking work and trouble of gaining access in any case? In concluding, I enumerate minimally four ways sociology can benefit from ethnographic study of elites in proportion to—rather than noticeably out of line with—the amount of scholarly time that has been devoted to studying down. I refer to these benefits, respectively, as cultural/ideological (involving the relationality of class); political/theoretical (involving distinctions between elites that have real-world ramifications); philosophical/humanistic (involving commonalities as well as differences between people); and sociological/reflexive (involving greater self and disciplinary awareness). Of course reasons have already been stated amidst resurgent interest occurring with renewed energy and conviction, and given the growing number of studies being conducted and published about French, American, and other globalizing elites around the world (see, for instance, Inglis's and Naudet's studies of inequalities and elites in India). Thus, I apologize in advance if the reasons cited here are at all repetitive; at the same time, I trust that the ensuing formulations are useful to present in my own way.

First, studying elites ethnographically matters for a cultural and ideological reason: namely, understanding class relations is virtually inconceivable except within the context of a relational, and hierarchically structured, continuum. Drawing on the work of Bourdieu, including but not limited to his extraordinarily thorough study of cultural distinctions, how is it possible to grasp hegemony of the Gramscian kind—wherein dominant classes exert steady influence over subordinated ones—without reference to relationality, that is, to what some people "have" in direct contrast with what others "have not"? Thus it makes little sense to overstudy the lower end of the class-stratified hierarchy of capitalism that by necessity exists in relation to the upper. This was precisely what may have motivated Monique and Michel Pinçon-Charlot's earlier trailblazing works, convinced as they were of this point by their own Bourdieu-influenced background. Moreover, flowing from the benefits of investigating cultural relationality is that values, constructions, and ideological formulations that become accepted—doxic, as per Bourdieu's lexicon—are disproportionately influenced, though not wholly controlled, by conceptions generated at the highest and most elite echelons of society. For this reason, too, to study one end without the other—including the class and cultural experiences of many people who are, or consider themselves, in the middle—is to overlook how social/sociological common sense becomes generated, circulated, and accepted rather than challenged. It should be noted, though, that ethnographies that end up criticizing elites—in the course of viewing them on a continuum that is, by definition, comparative—risk, in so doing, cutting off precisely the access which had been assiduously and carefully gained. This is a methodological as well as theoretical conclusion that studying elites has to view in almost intellectually strategic terms, as to the point at which critical analyses are rendered.

But a second reason to study elites, though, is equally significant and can be labeled political/theoretical; it is a reason that, like the others to come, suggests that studying elites does not in any simplistic or one-dimensional way result solely in the kind of critique that might cut off access. For without detailed study of the kind of intra- and interpersonal variation that exists within any social group, significantly patterned differences between elites may be missed or left incomprehensible and unpredictable. Another way of stating this is that ethnographic studies have the potential to illuminate why some elites end up contributing to progressive causes (for instance, becoming like Bill Gates or George Soros or Harry Guggenheim, thereafter starting progressive foundations and Open Societies) while, alternatively, others end up funding right-leaning or ultra-conservative parties, candidates, and causes (for instance, becoming like Sheldon Adelson). This has evidently major political and policy implications since, practically speaking, whether elites donate money in redistributive or regressive directions makes huge differences in the immediacy of people's day-to-day lives. It could be young and talented individuals to whom this makes a difference, affecting their ability to get good educations and develop their own critical consciousness. Or the question may turn on whether support is forthcoming (or not) to a host of nonprofit organizations centrally focused on a gamut of needs from healthcare and housing provision through many other distributive programs that seek to avoid negative human effects (like mass incarceration, with its disproportionately harmful repercussions for poor and minority communities). Worth remembering, too, is that contemporary US history verifies that social movements are more apt to thrive when progressive rather than conservative elites hold power and influence.

But in calling this rationale "political/theoretic," I also mean to say that probing intraelite divisions—that is, why some elites lean leftward and others relatively more rightward—demands psychosocial modes of investigation. One can view elite studies, in fact, as a case study in the previously elaborated need to illuminate (through a wide range of case studies) patterned psychosocial dynamics. For whether members of elite classes lean leftward or rightward is likely to entail not only neighborhood, community, and business associations but also childhood factors—for example, what was one's father like? One's mother and siblings? What emotional and psychic dispositions did these influences bequeath?—affecting a given individual and his or her psychosocial habitus. In other words, a sophisticated awareness of multidimensionality will be key to comprehending, and making pattern-based predictions about why particular individuals within elite groups become relatively more progressively rather than conservatively oriented. Likewise, and analogously, psychosocial studies are needed outside elite contexts to multidimensionally illuminate why a young person raised in a poor neighborhood ends up in college or drops out of school and becomes locally involved with illegal activities.

A third reason studying elites is worthwhile can be deemed philosophic/humanistic. This re-evokes the volume *Sadomasochism in Everyday Life*, wherein I described how people situated in relatively powerless positions find themselves compelled by "sadomasochistic dynamics" to the point where personal or political revolutions occur—thereafter catapulting one/them from a subordinate to a dominant position. This can happen at a personal level: before I was the powerless child but, look, now I have become a powerful adult in charge of a child myself. Or a political one: I was a member of a downtrodden and oppressed group but, look, now we have finally taken power ourselves and have to decide how much punishment to mete out (or not) to our former oppressors. But the "social facts" of either and both kinds of revolutions have at least one dimension, and pose one dilemma, in common: a key decision must be faced, namely, will I or will I not reinvent the wheel? Will the left person who may have had (well hidden?) authoritarian leanings turn into the right-wing one once power is achieved—transforming with terrible and historico-tragic irony into his or her mirror image (at once similarly and differently). Of course, this is precisely what happened with Stalinism in and over historical time, as this miscarriage eventually bred its own counterrebellious reactions back toward neoliberal capitalisms of the twenty-first century.

Put slightly differently, change regularly and unavoidably happens such that individuals and groups once marginalized sometimes find themselves about to, or actually becoming, their opposites. How, then, can (sometimes) individuals and (sometimes) groups manage not to repeat cycles—how will they avoid becoming precisely what they vowed and wanted never to be themselves? While perhaps seemingly beside the point, rather, this discussion is quite germane to ethnographic study of elites insofar as recommending an attitude of critical humility: people can become other than what they meant to by intention or desire, but why and how? For ethnography can (and does) illuminate what it is like to have and hold power, and whether this can potentially happen over the course of time as dynamic social processes occur, recur, and evolve.

Moreover, "Could this happen to me?" is a (self)-reflexive question that returns social theorists to both Karl Marx (among classical thinkers) and Erich Fromm (among recent Frankfurt School ones) in terms of both structuralism and humanism. Karl Marx comes to mind insofar as his analyses focuses on structures rather than individuals (even as the omission of the latter obviously created its own huge problems). A benefit of Marxist approaches, though, is to make clear that anyone occupying particular positions—up, down, or middle—might and could behave in particular ways influenced by structural requisites and mandates. Moreover, in his book *The Radical Humanism of Erich Fromm*, Kieran Durkin goes back to Fromm's Frankfurt School understandings that psychoanalytic factors (at the individual level) combine with structural factors (at the social level) to compel what I have here called psychosocial analyses.

Thus elite ethnographies are distinctively capable of illuminating what people do, can or cannot do when in possession of multifaceted and complicated permutations-and-combinations of power. Do people in elite positions come to behave admirably (or not), why (or why not), and how could they possibly behave otherwise (and how might I, if I were or ever became them)? Here, I would also interweave Einsteinian relativity into the theoretical mix to make an interconnected point. Studying up, like studying down, is a project within which "subjects" and "objects," the researched-and-the-researcher, are highly likely to affect one another. This goes beyond outdated positivistic distinctions between the supposedly separable realms of objectivity and subjectivity, and seems fairly apparent when studying down—namely, a researcher is likely not the same after getting to know the people she or he studies, just as he or she is likely to influence communities and neighborhoods of people in turn. Similarly, why wouldn't studying elites possibly affect the very question—relativity-wise—of whether someone well-to-do and powerful leans left, right, or center? In this sense, studying up can also produce social good in ways different to but also possibly kindred with what can, and has, happened as a result of studying down.

This brings me to the last reason I cite here for redirecting scholarly interest from studying down to studying up, and hopefully in the middle too, in reasonably equitable proportions. Ethnographic study of elites also underscores the significance of sociological and individual self-reflexivity on both levels. Again, whether studying up or down, researcher-and-researched share motivations that are social, psychological, and both in intricate patterns of interactive complexity. Studying elites thereby becomes an occasion to call not only for humility (since I have the capacity to become the other, or the other me) but to insist that researchers explore both themselves and others in the social worlds they study. For isn't it the stuff of sociology, as well as social psychology and the psychosocial, to reflect on why one chooses to study up, down, or both? Why did I choose what I am about to research—and why isn't including, and exploring, my reasons for so doing part-and-parcel of understandings to result? By now, though, I hope it has become clearer that studying up has the capacity to expand and fill in our sociological imaginations. By further illuminating the intersections of personal biography, politics, culture and society, elite ethnographies in the United States, France, and globally are in keeping with future intellectual challenges laid down for sociologists in the past from Marx through Weber, deBeauvoir through Fromm, and Mills through Bourdieu.

References

Aguiar, L. L. M., and C. J. Schneider. 2012. *Researching Amongst Elites: Challenges and Opportunities in Studying Up*. Burlington, VT: Ashgate Publishing.

Alford, Robert. 1998. *The Craft of Inquiry: Theory, Methods, Evidence*. New York: Oxford University Press.

Anderson, Elijah. 1999. *Code of the Street: Decency, Violence and the Moral Life of the Inner City*. New York: Norton.

Bourgois, Philippe. 1996. *In Search of Respect: Selling Crack in El Barrio*. Cambridge: Cambridge University Press.

Chancer, Lynn. 1992. *Sadomasochism in Everyday Life*. New Brunswick, NJ: Rutgers University Press.

Chancer, Lynn, and John Andrews, eds. 2014. *The Unhappy Divorce of Sociology and Psychoanalysis*. London: Palgrave Macmillan.

Contreras, Randol. 2013. *The Stick Up Kids: Race, Drugs, Violence and the American Dream*. Berkeley: University of California Press.

Cousin, Bruno, Shamus Khan, and Ashley Mears. 2018. "Theoretical and Methodological Pathways for Research on Elites." *Socio-Economic Review* 16 (April 2): 225–249.

Desmond, Matthew. 2016. *Evicted: Poverty and Profit in the American City*. New York: Crown.

Duneier, Mitchell. *Sidewalk*. 2000. New York: FSG.

Durkin, Kieran. 2014. *Radical Humanism of Erich Fromm*. New York: Palgrave Macmillan.

Goffman, Alice. 2015. *On the Run: Fugitive Life in an American City*. New York: Picador.

Ho, Karen. Zouwen. 2009. *Liquidated: An Ethnography of Wall Street*. Durham, NC: Duke University Press.

Inglis, Patrick. 2019. *Narrow Fairways: Getting By and Falling Behind in the New India*. New York: Oxford University Press.

Khan, Shamus Rahman. 2011. *Privilege: The Making of an Adolescent Elite at St. Paul's School*. Princeton, NJ: Princeton University Press.

Khan, Shamus Rahman. 2012. "The Sociology of Elites." *Annual Review of Sociology* 38: 361–377.

Naudet, Jules. 2018. *Stepping into the Elite: Trajectories of Social Achievement in India, France and the United States*. New York: Oxford University Press.

Piketty, Thomas. 2013. *Capital in the Twenty-First Century*. Cambridge, MA: Harvard University Press.

Pinçon, M., and Pinçon-Charlot, M. 1989. *Dans les beaux quartiers*. Paris: Seuil.

Pinçon, M., and Pinçon-Charlot, M. 1996. *Grandes fortunes: dynasties familiales et formes de richesse en France*. Paris: Editions Payot & Rivages.

Pinçon, M., and Pinçon-Charlot, M. 1997. *Voyage en grande bourgeoisie: journal d'enquéte*. Paris: Presses Univ. de France.

Pinçon, M., and Pinçon-Charlot, M. 2007. *Les Ghettos du Gotha: comment la bourgeoisie défend ses espaces*. Paris: Editions Du Seuil.

Pinçon, M., and Pinçon-Charlot, M. 2013. *La violence des riches: chronique d'une immense casse sociale*. Paris: Zones.

Rios, Victor. 2011. *Punished: Policing the Lives of Black and Latino Boys*. New York: New York University Press.

Rivera, Lauren. 2012. "Hiring as Cultural Matching: The Case of Elite Professional Service Firms." *American Sociological Review* 77, no. 6: 999–1022.

Sánchez-Jankowski, Martín. 2008. *Cracks in the Pavement: Social Change and Resilience in Poor Neighborhoods*. Berkeley: University of California Press.

Sherman, Rachel. 2017. *Uneasy Street: The Anxieties of Affluence*. Princeton, NJ: Princeton University Press.

Venkatesh, S. A. 2008. *Gang Leader for a Day: A Rogue Sociologist Takes to the Streets.* New York: Penguin.

Wacquant, Loic. 2004. *Body and Soul: Notes of an Apprentice Boxer*. New York: Oxford University Press.

Williams, Terry. 1990. *The Cocaine Kids: The Inside Story of a Teenage Drug Ring.* Cambridge, MA: Da Capo Press.

10

A Dialog with Aaron Cicourel on Comparative Ethnography

Aaron V. Cicourel and Corey M. Abramson

In this chapter, eminent ethnographer and cognitive sociologist Aaron Cicourel shares insights gleaned from using ethnographic methods for the past six decades. In conversation with Corey Abramson, Cicourel addresses a number of important issues about both the practice of comparative ethnography and the academic contexts in which it takes place. The dialog is primarily based on a tape-recorded conversation between Cicourel and Abramson in late 2017. The final form presented here was updated to integrate ideas from subsequent conversations as well as email correspondence.

Approaches to Comparison

ABRAMSON: One of the motivations for this volume is that important ethnographic approaches and traditions, including yours, are frequently misrepresented or ignored. I think that a lot of potential insight is lost in the process, particularly for younger generations of scholars who are less familiar with ethnography's variability.

CICOUREL: You know more about it than I do.

ABRAMSON: Perhaps. But I'd like to get your take on it.

CICOUREL: The problem of measuring qualitative theoretical concepts begins with complex unexamined, daily life, everyday language usage among "native" speakers who invariably take for granted their use of metaphoric, metonymic speech, nonverbal expressions, among countless other speech acts they rely on for essential, taken-for-granted communicative activity. For example, social science research personnel translate standardized theoretical concepts using standardized syntactic and semantic statements presumed to convey the "same" meaning to the recipient of

Aaron V. Cicourel and Corey M. Abramson, *A Dialog with Aaron Cicourel on Comparative Ethnography* In: *Beyond the Case*. Edited by: Corey M. Abramson and Neil Gong, Oxford University Press (2020). © Oxford University Press. DOI: 10.1093/oso/9780190608484.003.0011 sample survey questions, and limited fixed choices presented to a randomly selected sample of respondents. Respondents are assumed to attribute comparative meanings to the theoretical concepts operationalized by fixed-choice questions and responses inherent in sample surveys.

I suggest both quantitative and qualitative measurement groups in sociology are heavily influenced by what Erving Goffman called, addressing a totally different problem, " 'being 'taken in' by one's own speech acts,"[1] thinking they have the 'upper hand' in their pursuit of research methods. Neither qualitative nor quantitative research adherents realize that they rely on misleading cognitive/linguistic roots; spend little time considering how daily life discussions of their beliefs compare with theoretic concepts and measures represented by open-ended interviews and sample survey language use.

Consider the demographer Nathan Keyfitz's view of demographic data.

Keyfitz's (1975) well known paper espoused an unusual solution to complaints about the accuracy of demographic data; one should not trust "official," existing, quantitative data-sets.[2] Users of official data have relied on the reliability of sample surveys since, I believe, the second half of the nineteenth century, and did not pursue ethnography nor emergent forms of laboratory research on memory. It is an example of a strong belief in the validity of sample survey data; faith in individual respondents' memory, informed by routine exchanges with others, informal learning at home, and formal learning in school. The invention of survey questions is an example of being taken in by one's methodological act of creating a clever early form of "big data."

Keyfitz underscored a basic challenge to macro theory; its inability to show essential behavioral data, and the focus on using official quantitative data such as the census, world bank and other organizational summaries.

Keyfitz adds (1975, 277):

> Yet . . . [an earlier] argument is in the end unconvincing . . . To know the net drop in overall fertility as a result of the restriction requires behavioral data. That alone can discriminate between the competing models and predict the quantitative effects of an induced change in age of marriage.

[1] Goffman (1956).
[2] Keyfitz (1975).

Keyfitz remarks can be interpreted as underscoring the essential role of behavioral data, but he does not discuss what counts as behavioral data.

ABRAMSON: Mm-hmm [affirmative].

CICOUREL: Quantitative social scientists, using "official" [administrative] and sample survey data, often ignore the essential role played by direct behavioral observation and direct field sampling of communal, local, daily life, face-to-face, vocal and nonverbal exchanges. The problem becomes even more complicated with comparative, interdisciplinary data and translation in general. Ethnographical data are necessary to claim that macro data has not obscured the role of local cultural practices for assembling "big data."

ABRAMSON: Right. And a lot of the approaches miss the role of cognitive reasoning and *challenges of translation*. And it becomes an issue of what gets lost or gained in a given approach. It seems like there are two positions that have become popular, perhaps because they are so extreme. One is, the notion that everything is so messy and situationally contingent that social scientists cannot make ethnographic comparisons, must avoid generalization, and cannot speak broadly beyond specific cases. The other fetishizes parsimonious models that control out variation in the pursuit of covering laws, and in the process produces abstractions that are so hopelessly clean they are divorced from the realities of social life. My take on this, which mirrors aspects of yours, is that the most fruitful approaches to comparison must lie somewhere in between and look at both variance and invariance, including what you have aptly described as "structural invariance with accountable exceptions" that makes complex social forms possible. And in your approach, this often is tied to the cognitive and linguistic underpinnings of both micro and macro structure, and the evidence we use to evaluate them, as discussed in your chapter in this volume.

CICOUREL: The problem for macro social scientists is their reliance on a compositional approach to language, a kind "dictionary approach." The evolution of communal life has made libraries essential and the creation of bureaucratically organized values, norms, and official rules. Everyday communal and emotionally charged interpersonal relationships, emotional experiences, informal and bureaucratic thinking and reasoning cannot exist nor survive without situated, foundational, memory, and colloquial language use. You and I will go to a dictionary for information, and what we learn is essential to resolve elements of everyday life emotional experiences, thinking, reasoning, and semantic, nonverbal communicative problem-solving. Structural, macro-level research does not openly accept nor rely on the invariant role of situated social interaction enabling ecological daily living.

ABRAMSON: Right. And as we have discussed, conversation analysis has a parallel problem. They focus on micro speech acts, but often ignore broader ethnographic and ecological issues that frame language use and comprehension. Fortunately, your chapter in this volume talks about the issue and some alternatives.[3]

Levels of Analysis, Comparative Ethnography, and Ecological Validity

ABRAMSON: Switching gears, I'd like to ask you a few things more specifically about comparative ethnography. First, for the younger generation that may not know your work as well, how would you describe your general approach to ethnography and ethnographic comparison?

CICOUREL: The notions of "comparative ethnography" and "levels of analysis" are similar to how increased population size influenced human development of increasingly complex forms of local, face-to-face communal life; the use of innovative metaphoric and metonymic forms of language use to represent specific and more complex communicative settings, technology, and their differential adoption in other communities. Communal representation included the invention of forms of normative living and governing devices, forms of transportation, and other ways of simulating human life called "servo-mechanisms," "robotic" life forms, and comparative forms of human life across the planet Earth.

For novice ethnographers, a helpful start would be self-conscious tape-recording of initial interactions with a doctoral student recently returned from the field. When a novice ethnographer first enters the field, asking for details from a local translator about initial exchanges with "natives," especially when one was about to conduct an interview in a foreign language is useful. For example, noting any sense of discomfort vis-à-vis one's self-awareness of speaking with a new "native" friend about your

[3] See Cicourel (this volume).

thinking about elements of your first days "in the wild." For example, record the way you described your project to early and later respondents. Keep a record of unusual lexical items, metaphors, and metonyms used by the respondents, and difficulties you encountered.

A Curious Example of Comparative Language Use

Our family spent a research year (1963–1964) in Argentina [wife, six-year-old son, four-year-old daughter, and fourteen-month-old son]. The research attempted to replicate a study of Jamaican fertility done by Judith Blake while Blake was Kingsley Davis's graduate student at Columbia University. Judith and Kingsley gave me permission to replicate her dissertation[4] in Buenos Aires. I was familiar with fifteenth-century Spanish but only a modest facility with what in Spain is called "Castellano" and "Spanish" in Latin America. Having met Gino Germani while working in Kingsley Davis's research center in Berkeley in the summer of 1962 and additional visits during the 1962–1963 academic year, I was fortunate to be allowed to discuss my attempt to replicate Judith's dissertation with Germani, who along with Davis, were very instrumental in my acquiring research funds for a year in Argentina.

When in Buenos Aires a few months later, I also asked to be a visiting professor at the University of Buenos Aires and teach two graduate classes during the 1963–1964 academic year. A curious language problem emerged, primarily in my teaching. I was born in the United States, but my mother only spoke to me in a form of fifteenth-century "Castellano" (called "Ladino" by Sephardic Jews) and called "Spanish" in Argentina and Latin America. I began to learn American English when I was three years old.

I began to learn "modern Spanish" hurriedly in Argentina because of my teaching and research. My first class became a problem because after about three weeks, one of the students informed me the class was planning a strike against me because of my "Spanish." Namely, that they had not been informed that fifteenth-century "Spanish" was a required prerequisite. It took me about four to five months before I could sound "authentic." I also had to cope with learning Argentine "Spanish."

[4] Blake (1961).

Engaging respondents in Spanish was difficult initially, but fortunately, Germani enabled me to hire several doctoral students to help me interview respondents. I managed, fairly quickly, to engage in additional interviews and the number gradually increased. I receive other help from two Germani's outstanding doctoral students, Miguel Murmis and Dario Canton, who helped me translate Judith Blake's questionnaire into Spanish.

In Buenos Aires, I was initially engaged in some preliminary work at the Buenos Aires Children's Hospital. I met a woman who had brought one of her two children to see a pediatrician. She was willing to speak with me about fertility issues, and we arranged to meet in her home. At her home, the woman said she did not like speaking with her husband about fertility issues because he believed they should have as many children as she was capable of having. Her viewpoint was summarized by saying, "I don't want another child. I don't want it, and I do everything I can to not have more. I get 'sick,' I get headaches. I have two, and couldn't stand having more children."

I was very fortunate to have met this woman. She was willing to become part of study, and I used her story when interviewing other women.

ABRAMSON: It's an ecological validity problem; the details of everyday life are absent in the laboratory setting and in sample-survey questionnaires, often missing key insights like this and producing erroneous models.

CICOUREL: After learning about ecological validity and meeting two of Brunswik's former students, I began reading his work and participated for five years in a biology seminar at UCSD learning about "behavioral ecology." I realized how crucial studying animals in the wild was for understanding human animals. The animals were captured and brought into laboratory settings for experimental research. The importance of ecological validity was obvious. For example, Caribbean female fish capable of recognizing and pursued males by the beautiful colors in their tails made "mistakes" because of the brackish water of the Caribbean hindered their genetic-based judgments. In laboratory tanks, the females did not make "mistakes."

Brunswik (1956),[5] one of the first persons in the behavioral sciences who directly addressed the ecological validity problem, was a quantitative, hard line, highly respected experimentalist, yet clearly recognized

[5] Brunswik (1956).

the importance of transforming ethnology in the wild into a necessary laboratory problem-solving, practical way of achieving ecological validity. For example, Brunswik would take a subject outside of the laboratory to an actual building to estimate its height by asking them to estimate their own height, the height of nearby humans, estimate the height of other objects (trees smaller buildings) nearby, and then asked to estimate the size of the building.

ABRAMSON: Yes. The notion is that you look at patterns to discern invariance and then infer what accounts for the exceptions.

CICOUREL: I think it's possible to pursue systematic ethnological field research, and then pursue quasi-experimental research patterns under controlled conditions by studying daily life activities "in the cultural wild," say "small groups" under controlled conditions. Ecological validity conditions would be essential; first seeking invariant verbal and nonverbal behavioral patterns in the "*cultural wild*." Data on thinking and reasoning are presupposed but seldom addressed by social scientists, nor is situated daily use of language, gestures embedded in identified normatively framed and complex during social interactional.

CICOUREL: Another way is to outline interesting empirical field research issues. For example, at the beginning of my Argentine research I began thinking I needed a sense of what everyday life settings looked like by observing many parts of Buenos Aires and Gran Buenos Aires, including isolated areas near established communities. A graduate student offered to help. He suggested we hire an experienced, independent taxi driver to take us around large incorporated areas and various smaller areas. The idea was to have the driver describe neighborhoods within the randomized, aerial samples of Buenos Aires that Germani and Davis allowed me to use. In each area we stopped at the driver's choice of a bar, a place that served small dishes, coffee, tea, and alcoholic drinks. At every stop, after visiting the bar and speaking with a few of the bar attendants, we would walk around two or three blocks as I took notes of my impression of its socioeconomic level; the kinds of stores, bars, restaurants, how people were dressed, and my descriptions of the housing. I took a few pictures. I wanted a personalized sense of each area.

As a graduate student at UCLA, I did a Master's student paper on a small factory. I engaged in voluntary work on an assembly line and interviewed each worker. The workers appeared to be doubtful of how I obtained permission from the owner of the facility. They also appeared to be suspicious about my relationship with the owner, a friend of my in-laws. After thinking I was able to get to know the workers fairly well, I inferred the workers were not happy with the owner, and as one worker noted, he and others did not trust the owner. I was unable to convince the two workers I thought I understood their views of the owner. I inferred some of the workers believed a small questionnaire I asked the workers to fill out was an attempt to obtain questionable information for the owner. My study satisfied my faculty supervisors, but I became suspicious of the owner's remarks about his relations with his workers. I came to believe the workers and viewed my study as a failure.

I encountered a different reaction when seeking permission to study cognitive changes in aging senior citizens at a community center organized by the wife of a Cornell faculty professor. I also learned that a few members of the center were former doctoral students at Cornell. One of organizers was the mother of a well-known Ithaca pediatrician. Her close friend was the mother of a professor on my doctoral committee. These two met each Friday afternoon over cocktails to discuss activities pursued by the Center. I was asked to join these meetings. The two women had also attended a one-year program at a Cornell University estate previously donated to the university by a former president of Cornell. The estate was used by [the] university for special affairs. My new friends were former attendees at the estate where they had spent a sabbatical year on improving the health of aging persons sponsored by the School of Medicine. I was invited by my friends for a week to a special meeting at the estate to discuss how to improve their health sabbatical. Friday nights were devoted to special speakers; for example, the head of the United Nations, a well-known Princeton professor. The meetings were often devoted to learning about innovative research on the health of aged. The attendees I met appeared to be primarily persons with considerable means. Needless to say, the weekend enabled me to acquire considerable information about the wealthy and their concerns with improving their health, and underscored how different the weekend event was from my research contacts with low-income subjects in Ithaca.

I attended all weekly luncheons at the Center for nine months. After approximately four months, subjects began inviting me to their homes, asked to meet my wife, and subsequently were very anxious to meet our first child. I organized a men's group that met every Saturday for lunch and outings. I was able to obtain films from the *New York Times*, organized picnics and luncheons on Saturday once each month. When I finished a draft of my dissertation and about to leave Ithaca, I organized a party for the men. The men gave me a very emotional bottle of coins for our baby.

Cicourel on Ethnographic Comparison

ABRAMSON: One of the characteristics of your approach, as I understand it, is its attempt to connect individual and group activities at meso-level and macro-level structures, and especially to underscore that social scientists needed different cognitive data obtainable primarily by ethnographic research methods.

CICOUREL: My research is contingent on the concept of "social cognition": socially organized and interpreted conscious and unconscious thinking and reasoning during daily life communal social interaction. For example, the use of metaphorical and metonymical expressions during formal and informal daily life events as studied by linguistic anthropologists in cross-cultural daily life settings. Laboratory research of human subjects is notable for its very suggestive conceptions of analogical thinking and reasoning while simultaneously avoiding the study of nonverbal, colloquial language use. Field and laboratory studies differ markedly from survey questionnaires and a primary use of demographic data. The two groups each believe their research is more objective.

The study of comparative ethnography can be defined as the study of ongoing, cognitively organized, culturally motivated, moment-to-moment experiences of conscious and unconscious memory and verbal and nonverbal communication. The study of colloquial and standardized language use relies on difficult to study real-time, real-life, ethnographic facial expressions, bodily movements, and subtle verbal prosody. The latter conditions are presupposed but seldom addressed in laboratory research on thinking and reasoning.

This discussion requires asking how many levels of analysis should be identified? It is a difficult issue, and hinges on what we can agree must be theoretically and methodologically operationalized. An example taken from my chapter in the present volume refers to Anselm Strauss's work with Glaser on death and dying.[6] Their reporting appears to have captured

[6] Glaser and Strauss (1965, 1968).

daily life hospital conditions of death and dying. His narratives consist of metaphorically speaking, "jam-packed" valuable macro summaries of observed, selected field settings. The moment-to-moment details are missing; how we should unpack his informative macro remarks remains a conundrum.

Tacit and self-conscious contractual and noncontractual conditions, constitutive of all communication, enabled humans to cope progressively with rapidly increasing populations requiring organization, bureaucratization of daily life activities and contingent on personal, collective, and emotional memories. These organizational activities enabled complex social forms—

dense forms of daily life, sociolegal systems, and macro socioeconomic differences.

ABRAMSON: Right, this parallels discussions about the limits of "sticking to the letter of the law." The fact is there are many that simply overlook that law presupposes language, shared understanding around personhood and property, and a form of social organization and enforcement that make the formal rules (i.e. the letter of the law") and contracts intelligible. I mean, that was one of Durkheim's classic points from his dissertation (even if he looked at this through the rose-colored glasses of an unequivocally positive notion of social solidarity rather than domination).[7] Explanations that don't acknowledge these underpinnings can lead to errors in not only holistic explanation but identifying explaining causal mechanisms.

The Connection to Ethnomethodology

ABRAMSON: So, what would be the difference between your approach and ethno-methodology, a tradition that also examines some of these issues and with which you are often associated? Is it that ethno-methodology doesn't look adequately at the formalization via behavior at the meso-level?

CICOUREL: In [Harold] Garfinkel's[8] dissertation, he recognized important flaws in Parson's theoretical work, and the usefulness of the methodology

[7] Durkheim (1933).

[8] Garfinkel was one of the foundational, and most widely known, figures in the ethnomethodological approach.

employed by social psychologists[9] Parsons brought into his newly formed Department of Social Relations at Harvard. The social psychologists influenced Garfinkel's dissertation methodologically. As a student, Garfinkel alerted Parsons to work by Alfred Schütz.[10]

Okay, so this is critical. Harold and I were writing a book together. We started in the spring of 1958, and we had already independently written a couple of chapters. I was focusing on methodological issues, including the way Garfinkel has deceived his student subjects about a key issue: the fake "interview" subjects told an interview the heard was between an administrator posing as a dean. The students believed the official interview had actually taken place. I objected to Harold's use of deception with student subjects in his dissertation and subsequently.

I was disturbed that the narrative of the fake administrator because the students applied to medical school and believed the interview between Harold's graduate student friend posing as a university official created a very difficult emotional strain for the students until they were finally told the interview never took place.

I was also very upset when the same strategy was replicated by Garfinkel at UCLA by one of his graduate students, who pretended he was a therapist. Again, he was not bothered [by] once again lying to the subjects. I said Harold, you obtained evidence that's tainted. He was quite angry with me.

ABRAMSON: Mm-hmm [affirmative].

CICOUREL: He would not acknowledge that this was a problem. So, we finally broke our collaboration.

ABRAMSON: So, some of it is they overstate the universalism, some of it is that they miss the situated translational interactional components of it in order to look at the sort of the cognitive macro-structures (i.e. ecological aspects), and some of it is that they lacked methodological rigor in the construction of empirical research.

CICOUREL: So, this was a delicate issue, but it should be clarified as a reason why we did not work together. It is worth clarifying. Garfinkel would not recognize the basic methodological problem—how do you enlist people in your study and what does one tell the subjects [and how does that affect the data]? I had to do it with old people in my dissertation. I wanted them

[9] Garfinkel (1952).
[10] Subsequently published as Schutz and Natanson (1962).

to let me live for many months with them, visit their homes frequently, go to their meetings with others at luncheons, and go with them to movies and stuff.

ABRAMSON: Right, one of the things that distinguishes your work is that there is a concern for the procedural issues and reflexivity about how the research process and theoretical priors affect data and interpretation.

CICOUREL So, on the one hand, I see Garfinkel as being one of the first sociologists to really apply social psychology and its experimental methodology to challenge the classical notion of social structure.

ABRAMSON: So, it seems like on the one hand, you have a contrast between survey research and ethnomethodology. Surveys sort of ignore processual aspects of moment-to-moment interaction, and then on the other hand, you there is the emergence of new types of ethnography that are so focused on brief but intensive examination of micro-details that they miss essential connections to connect micro and macro. What you seem to be saying we need to take both seriously and observe the links at all levels, including the meso-level.

CICOUREL: You have to pursue both of them seriously; the differences between the two levels of methodology, both the quantitative and qualitative. Early on, it got me in trouble with people from two sides of sociology, and at times, the social sciences. Because I said the different groups are not systematic enough. They are not paying attention to the language used in surveys and lack of a concern for moment-to-moment verbal and nonverbal communicative practices. They don't want to be bothered with the messiness of real-world behavior. I was fortunate to have studied with two kinds of statisticians; one at UCLA (Bill Robinson in anthropology and sociology), and Cornell (Jack Kiefer, mathematics department). They both encouraged studying details [as well as patterns].

Feasibility, Logistics, and Team Science in the Context of Contemporary Academia

ABRAMSON: One barrier to the way in which you approach comparative ethnography is that what you propose is very difficult both intellectually and logistically. You have to be there collecting the data for long periods of time, you have to be reflexive about the process, you have to know statistical approaches, you have to systematically record speech and behavior, and you have to triangulate everything with other data types. So, in terms of workflow, it's complex and demanding.

CICOUREL: Yes. You put your finger on a very crucial point, Corey, which is how much more work it takes and the barriers that must be overcome to achieve what we are calling comparative ethnography. We have a big nemesis. People who decide how money will be dedicated for research largely support sample-surveys that view tests of significance as a necessary form of validity, rather than pursue the goal of ecological validity, or what biologists call behavioral ecology; systematic observation of nonhuman animals in the wild using audio and video recordings to establish key empirical findings enabling laboratory research to uncover basic theoretical concepts under controlled conditions. The study of animals in the wild has produced highly cogent, essential findings of ecological validity by first engaging in long-term, moment-to moment, behavioral research on animals in the wild and then under controlled experimental, animal habitats.[11]

ABRAMSON: Right, and it's a complicated contingent thing that involves a lot of work that is often ignored or devalued in the profession. Some people have argued that perhaps the way that we could do this, have a fruitful integration of different levels of analysis, is to have something like an "organic" division of labor in the Durkheimian sense. That perhaps you have quantitative people that have recognized these issues charting the aggregate patterns, ethnographers observing in the field, and the micro-level cognitive linguists that are examining the speech patterns all working together on a project, each acknowledging their contributions and limits. Hence, the trick would not be finding a single person who could do all of those. I'm sure you'll acknowledge that not a lot of people could do all of those; but being able to connect them together to execute the broader vision might be possible But, as you've said in the past, that presupposes a degree of co-operation and methodological humility about the limits of any given method that makes it difficult to execute in practice.

Clarifying the Analogical and Digital in Sociology

CICOUREL: You've been after me on these things and with good reason.

ABRAMSON: For more than a few years, yeah.

[11] Davies, Krebs, and West (2012); cf. Cicourel (2006).

CICOUREL: I want to acknowledge that and am glad you're persistent because it's hard for me to say this on my own. With your pushing and knowing what you know.

ABRAMSON: That's a high compliment. Thank you.

CICOUREL: We have this thing that is a very clever compromising approach combining quantitative data, computers and ethnography.[12] People have to respect it because it has consistency to it. The process is clear and it's open. In your dissertation, you did it in a way that's very convincing.[13] People who do surveys, quantitative research, are convincing because of their correlations, but they don't know how to examine those correlations and turn them inside-out and say, what kinds of observable behavior should be pursued? Now, sample-survey research is good on pointing out macro-level summaries based on their correlations and general summaries of the knowledge they obtain about other research on the same or similar topics. But it's a curious kind of thing that they do. They do not engage in participant observation such as what you did with the aged and real time with real people, in daily life conditions. They do not agree that we need both micro and macro—

actual, communal social interaction with subjects with whom you have spent considerable time.

ABRAMSON: You have often talked about this as the fetish for the imposition of digital [deductive] logics over analogical reasoning.

CICOUREL: I have tried to show that analogical reasoning involves invariant, universal elements. All human animals must use analogs, and similar forms of thinking, and reasoning. Otherwise, they could not have gradually engaged in more and more complex forms of communication; verbal and nonverbal behavior activities and practices. Now [what] we do in the so-called social sciences is call attention to what humans have created, but we must all recognize the fact that we must involve ourselves in direct relationships with others to understand the way this has been accomplished; difficult tasks that are presupposed when research on concepts like analogs, thinking, reasoning and face-to-face and indirect behavior are discussed and examined empirically.

[12] Cf. Abramson, Joslyn, Rendle, Garrett, and Dohan (2018); Abramson and Dohan (2015).
[13] Abramson (2015).

On Theory and Method: Against Atheoretical Description

ABRAMSON: I wonder too, about the dangers of the other side of methodology—that is, extreme anti-reductionism and atheoretical description.

As you have said, one solution to addressing the complexity of human culture advanced by social scientists is a tendency toward making the world overly simplistic through reduction. In your terms, often involves imposing a digital or experimental logic, a deductive ruling out approach that can produce misleading or at best incomplete answers. But the other extreme is problematic as well. You see this in postmodernism and even some interpretivist anthropology,[14] and you see it making a resurgence in sociology as well. The idea being that we should abandon strong theory and explanation and focus on description, an approach that might be understood as a spin on Geertz's call for "thick description."[15] For instance, there was a recent piece by Besbris and Kahn that some of my graduate students liked called "Less Theory, More Description." It makes the argument that ethnographers should focus on describing what we see rather than trying to extend concepts, generate or test theory, or produce higher-level generalizations.

In a similar vein, I had a critic of my comparative ethnography on inequality in later life[16] note that evocative literary description was "what ethnographers do" and my work privileged a conceptual model over "thick" narrative description. I responded that trying to force my work, which is explicitly situated as a form of analytical sociology concerned with creating generalizable models using observational data, into the model of "thick description" was intellectually and practically problematic.[17] It reveals either a lack of understanding of the diversity of ethnographic approaches (which this volume captures) or is an attempt to reify ethnography in spite of this diversity. Yet this framing of "what ethnography does"—i.e. it provides descriptive accounts judged by their literary merits and ability to give outsiders a vivid account of social life—is pervasive in undergraduate methods classes, some graduate programs, and

[14] Cf. Clifford and Marcus (1986).
[15] Geertz (1973).
[16] Abramson (2015).
[17] See Abramson and Gong (this volume).

beyond. And, it is often invoked without so much as a footnote acknowledging there are multiple ethnographic traditions.

I'd add that it seems to me that this move risks pushing various forms of ethnography perilously close to journalism, or at minimum, the qualitative analog to the "abstracted empiricism" warned against by C. Wright Mills.[18] Many traditions represented in this volume (including my own) see such a move as undesirable, especially as a general approach to ethnography.

How would you respond to this line about eschewing or at least deemphasizing theory?

CICOUREL: The paper by Besbris and Khan[19] is informative and addresses the weakness of the concept "cultural capital" and the way sociologists have used it despite its "theoretical inconsistency." The authors note a large number of sociologists (and many other disciplines) have joined the bandwagon. The authors note, "As the concept (of cultural capital) spreads, scholars become incapable of precisely stating what it is and it ends up depicting many things that are unrelated to or in consistent with on another" (Besbris and Khan 2017, 148). Thus, decreasing the concept's usefulness. Further, "concepts thereby become bloated—in other words rich and nuanced—and lack the possibility of being refuted" (148).

I believe the key issue can be found first in the following quote from Bourdieu paraphrased by Besbris and Kahn, but not pursued by them empirically: "The original formulation—from Bourdieu—defined cultural capital as 'goods' transmitted to individual children through family practices that were more or less valued depending on how closely they matched the cultural practices deemed important by institutions like schools." (see Bourdieu and Passeron 1977, 30)[20]

Let me say quickly: it is important to look not just at the acquisition of family practices, but how did the family members acquire this knowledge and where can we find empirical evidence for such remarks? Neither Bourdieu, Passeron, nor Besbris and Kahnaddress this [multi-level problem] empirically. The literature by developmental psycholinguists and some linguistic anthropologist on children's socialization and

[18] Since conducting this interview, Michael Burawoy has produced a piece making a parallel argument is response to recent critiques of ethnography. Burawoy criticizes the logical and practical problems of an atheoretical approach to ethnography. See Burawoy (2019). See also Mills (1959).
[19] Besbris and Khan (2017).
[20] Besbris and Kahn 2017, 149.

acquisition of "goods," much less the acquisition of cognitive and emotional skills observable in the home, and wherever children are taken, presupposes moment-to-moment study of the acquisition of language and nonverbal communicative practices in the home *and* outside from birth on has seldom been addressed by sociologists. I have addressed aspects of the latter issues, but this is not the place to discuss my work nor the huge number of publications by others.

Strong empirical research, including qualitative studies, require strong theory. If you can't show the micro behavioral details are presupposed by descriptive macro concepts, thick description does not clarify but actually distorts a given theory, and calls into question what happens in a given ecology empirically. They don't understand social theory because it's never really studied empirically with the micro behavioral observations noted earlier. Thick description has created a kind of self-evident reality using unexamined common-sense concepts not addressed empirically and using others "thick descriptions" as data. [This supersedes] recording real-time, real-life events and risks ignoring the problem of ecological validity and behavioral ecology as pursued by behavioral biologists and others.

ABRAMSON: Many of your criticisms, although unfortunately not always attributed to your now classic works like *Method and Measurement*, have made their way into sociology and shape the way many think about the limits of quantitative research and their ability to test theories and uncover laws.[21] But what we're talking about is this other, perhaps related, trend on the qualitative side. It takes part of the critique, but misses a key part of the corrective which involves recognizing the limits on all approaches and the irreducible role of theory for both methodology and explanation. You've always made the argument in our discussions that one needs to have a strong theory of action *and* a strong theory of method. Without both, social scientists impose latent theories of behavior and how to understand it. Under such circumstances, common-sense notions about nature, society, and "evidence" remain unexcavated but come to prominence (in large part because they have a certain face-validity or resonance with an audience who shares similar beliefs). Their purported "a-theoretical" nature makes them seem to be more objective and less problematic, even though they ultimately only replace "social

[21] See Cicourel 1964 and Cicourel 1982.

theory" with latent "common-sense" and their own culture. As Bourdieu correctly noted (under other circumstances), "There's no way out of the game of culture." Even when we study culture, we're producing culture, and ultimately trapped by it. Ignoring the connection rather than explicating and engaging with it does not remove the underlying problem.

CICOUREL: We [qualitative researchers] make the same mistake when we assume survey research, demography, experimentation, historical methods, ethnography, ethnomethodology, [and] conversational analysis justify "standing on their own," and that each notion of research methods is the primary way to "do" sociology. We should be asking what concepts are essential for particular theories and methods? For example, particular concepts may be viewed as invariant in aspects of social behavioral science but not viewed as empirical variables; memory, moment-to-moment aspects of speaking and nonverbal skills are at the heart of all human research. How, therefore, does each of these concepts enter theory and research?

ABRAMSON: Right. There's no simple solution, which creates challenges, in part because the current model of academic production seems to privilege quick (tweetable) answers rather than the sort of deep engagement with the longstanding challenges of method and measurement that have been one of your central contributions to social science. It seems the best we can hope for is that scholars will treat these challenges with the seriousness and intellectual rigor that you have, and translate their responses (whatever those may be), to principled research design, execution, and writing (something to which I hope this volume will contribute).

Advice to Future Ethnographers

ABRAMSON: So, the last thing I wanted to ask is for the future generation, younger ethnographers, is there any advice you'd like to share?

CICOUREL: Several years ago (Fall 1999 and 2004), I was invited to be a Fellow at the Hanse Institute for Advanced Studies, Delmenhorst, Germany, and visiting professor, University of Bremen, Germany. In 2004, I was again invited to be a Fellow at the Hanse Institute for Advanced Studies, Delmenhorst, Germany. While giving lectures at Bremen, I was fortunate to meet two innovative professors who had almost completed an important study of women whose working careers were interrupted on different occasions by the decision to have a family. The study was a collaboration between colleagues who had conducted a survey of the subjects from which random cases were selected for intensive ethnographic research. My memory of actual details may be imperfect, but somewhere in my files, I have a copy of the actual work. I underscore this study because it is one in which not only the conclusions of the survey did not capture essential issues the women actually faced, but the research colleagues who had done the survey did not pursue the different findings the ethnographers could show. Note, I am underscoring the research methods pursed by the scholars and the fact that they had a very important subsample from a careful survey and addressed the same substantive issues but relied on different methods and produced different conclusions.

The advice is that they have enough of a get together and agree that it's damn hard to agree on anything, and that they always have to challenge [findings that do not represent on the ground realities] as much as they can when they know they are right. And even if something gets published we have to ask: is it valid? Have we made any progress? Have we shown something that can be replicated?

ABRAMSON: This has been really illuminating and useful. Thank you again for the opportunity to have this discussion.

References

Abramson, Corey M. 2015. *The End Game: How Inequality Shapes Our Final Years*. Cambridge, MA: Harvard University Press.

Abramson, Corey M., and Daniel Dohan. 2015. "Beyond Text: Using Arrays to Represent and Analyze Ethnographic Data." *Sociological Methodology* 45, no. 1: 272–319. https://doi.org/10.1177/0081175015578740.

Abramson, Corey M., Jacqueline Joslyn, Katharine A. Rendle, Sarah B. Garrett, and Daniel Dohan. 2018. "The Promises of Computational Ethnography: Improving Transparency, Replicability, and Validity for Realist Approaches to Ethnographic Analysis." *Ethnography* 19, no. 2: 254–284.Besbris, Max, and Shamus Khan. 2017. "Less Theory. More Description." *Sociological Theory* 35, no. 2: 147–53. https://doi.org/10.1177/0735275117709776.

Blake, Judith. 1961. *Family Structure in Jamaica: The Social Context of Reproduction*. PhD diss., Columbia University, New York.

Bourdieu, Pierre, and Jean Claude Passeron. 1977. *Reproduction in Education, Society and Culture*. London: SAGE Publications.

Brunswik, E. 1956. *Perception and the Representative Design of Psychological Experiments*, 2nd ed. Berkeley: University of California Press.

Burawoy, Michael. 2019. "Empiricism and Its Fallacies." *Contexts* 18, no. 1: 47–53.

Cicourel, Aaron V. 2006. "Cognitive/Affective Processes, Social Interaction, and Social Structure as Representational ReDescriptions: Their Contrastive Bandwidths and Spatio-Temporal Foci." *Mind and Society* 5, no. 1: 39–70.

Cicourel, Aaron V. 1964. *Method and Measurement in Sociology*. Glencoe, Ill.: Free Press of Glencoe.

Cicourel, Aaron V. 1982. "Interviews, Surveys, and the Problem of Ecological Validity." *The American Sociologist* 17, no. 1: 11–20.

Clifford, James, and George E. Marcus. 1986. *Writing Culture: The Poetics and Politics of Ethnography*. Berkeley: University of California Press.

Davies, N. B., J. R. Krebs, and S. A. West. 2012. *An Introduction to Behavioral Ecology*. Cambridge: Cambridge University Press.

Durkheim, Émile. 1933. *Émile Durkheim on The Division of Labor in Society*. Translated by George Simpson. New York: Macmillan.

Garfinkel, Harold. 1952. *The Perception of the Other: A Study in Social Order*. Cambridge, MA: Harvard University Press.

Geertz, Clifford. 2000 [1973]. "Thick Description: Towards an Interpretive Theory of Culture." In *The Interpretation of Cultures: Selected Essays*, 3–30. New York: Basic Books.

Glaser, B. G., and A. L. Strauss. 1965. *Awareness of Dying*. New Brunswick, NJ: Aldine Transaction.

Glaser, B. G., and A. L. Strauss. 1968. *Time for Dying*. Chicago: Aldine Publishing Co.

Goffman, Erving. 1956. *The Presentation of Everyday Life*. Edinburgh: University of Edinburgh Social Science Research Centre.

Katz, Jack. 2002. "Social Ontology and Research Strategy." *Theoretical Criminology* 6, no. 3: 255–278. https://doi.org/10.1177/136248060200600302.

Katz, Jack. 2004. "On the Rhetoric and Politics of Ethnographic Methodology." *Annals of the American Academy of Political and Social Science* 595: 280–308.

Keyfitz, N. 1975. "How Do We Know the Facts of Demography?" *Population and Development Review* 1, no. 2:267–288. https://doi.org/10.2307/1972224.

Mills, C. Wright. 1959. *The Sociological Imagination*. New York: Grove Press.

Schutz, Alfred, and Maurice Alexander Natanson. 1962. *Collected Papers Volume 1*. The Hague: Nijhoff.

Conclusion

A Comparative Analysis of Comparative Ethnographies

Neil Gong and Corey M. Abramson

This volume is guided by the goal of productive pluralism—the simple notion that even though ethnographic approaches may be partially incompatible with one another, the field as a whole benefits from diverse contributions to understanding social life. Beyond a mutual tolerance that leaves ethnographers in their silos, such a pluralism supports sustained scholarly dialog to clarify points of disagreement, as well as illuminate opportunities for collaborative problem-solving. To this end, we have included the works from prominent scholars representing contemporary iterations of traditions such as positivism, symbolic interactionism, the extended case method, interpretivism, and grounded theory to articulate what, why, and how they engage in ethnographic comparison. The resulting works show that examining ethnographic comparison is timely given the resurgence of comparison in the field and offer a useful window for understanding ethnography's diverse traditions. We leave it to readers to decide which frameworks are most useful for their goals and the audiences they aim to reach. Our hope remains that by engaging with alternative positions on comparison, scholars will be able to improve their own practice while understanding why others take a different path.

The contributors to this volume come from diverse methodological traditions, with contrasting philosophies of science, empirical and theoretical interests, and practical research suggestions. There are clear disagreements in how to best approach comparative field research. Both our introductory chapter and the work of our contributors speak to the significant differences and apparent incompatibilities between approaches. Yet they are united in the belief that comparative ethnography makes crucial contributions alongside typical single case studies. As C. K. Lee provocatively puts it, "If 'thinking

Neil Gong and Corey M. Abramson, *Conclusion* In: *Beyond the Case*. Edited by: Corey M. Abramson and Neil Gong, Oxford University Press (2020).
DOI: 10.1093/oso/9780190608484.003.0012

without comparison is unthinkable,' then ethnography without comparison is undecipherable storytelling" (Lee, this volume). Although it differs in the form of explanation, this parallels Sánchez-Jankowski and Abramson's argument for the necessity of comparison in generating generalizable explanation that goes beyond bounded cases. In each, comparison offers a route past narrative and the idiographic to a specifically causal analysis of divergent outcomes. DeGloma and Papadantonakis, on the other hand, focus on interpretation rather than causal explanation and show how a comparative approach to storytelling itself may reveal unforeseen structural regularities.

Not all of the authors would agree on what comparison should do, or the specific mode of analysis, but each contribution speaks to what comparison offers. As Tavory and Timmermans note, there are necessarily moments of comparative thinking even in a bounded case study. Often these are "shadow comparisons" that serve as a contextualizing backdrop. This echoes Cicourel's longstanding concern with how microstructures (cognition, analogical reasoning, language) shape both human action and research. Even when ethnographic work is not directly comparative, human reasoning (both that of the researcher and subjects) involves analogs, contrasts, and latent comparisons. But the contributors in this volume are expanding the discussion. Each speaks to the importance of addressing two or more cases to accomplish analytical goals: charting variance and invariance, mapping causal mechanisms, identifying general meaning or interactional structures, understanding the local impact of macro-historical phenomena like capitalism, or more deeply theorizing an initial case by adding another.

In this concluding chapter we contextualize the contributions of our authors, pointing to both divergences and (perhaps) surprising synergies in the way they approach ethnography. We begin by considering the basic questions of how and why our contributors perform comparison. Having summarized the approaches, we move to specific comparisons of research processes, research products, and the criteria used for evaluating both. We conclude by suggesting how their synergies open the possibility for a chance to address further concerns in comparative methodology.

Approaches to Comparison

In this section we summarize each contribution and its take on the "how" and "why" of comparison.

Comparative Participant Observation in the Behavioralist Tradition

In chapter 1, Sánchez-Jankowski and Abramson argue that comparative participant observation is crucial for the advancement of variable-based social science. By providing longitudinal data about human behavior in real-world settings, a behavioralist approach to participant observation illuminates the operation of causal mechanisms that can only be imputed using tools such as surveys, interviews, or experiments. The imperative to compare in this behavioralist approach is derived in part from the goal of using observable variation (i.e., difference in patterns of behavior across space and time) as well as invariance (i.e., commonalities across space and time) to chart *when* and *how* mechanisms combine to produce outcomes of theoretical and practical significance. They argue the payoff is substantial—when done well, they argue, this form of ethnography provides unparalleled resources for observing causal mechanisms in situ and produces robust models that link micro-, meso-, and macro-level social processes, and reduces inferential error.

In chapter 2, Abramson and Sánchez-Jankowski describe their behavioralist process in detail and compare it to other methodological approaches to the collection, analysis, comparison, and extension of ethnographic data. They describe the mode of research design, sampling, data collection, analysis, and explanation associated with this approach, giving examples from their prior empirical works. The chapter then addresses longstanding concerns about ethnographic reliability and replication. The chapter concludes by explaining the contributions that can be made by repositioning participant observation within the spectrum of realist approaches to understand causal processes in the social sciences.

In both opening chapters, Sánchez-Jankowski and Abramson articulate a form of comparison that produces durable explanations of when and how macro-structural context, meso-level social forces, and individual action combine to produce observable patterns in aggregate behavior. They pursue this task through an embrace of realism, use of a probabilistic variable-centered logic, and the construction of multilevel samples that include control groups that account for the coconstituency of individuals, groups, and institutions. As an example of invariance, they describe Sánchez-Jankowski's finding of a shared "defiant individualist" psychological profile among gang members from across different types of gangs. Such a finding required observation of numerous cases to demonstrate that this profile is not an artifact of a particular location, ethnic culture, or gang organizational structure. Regarding variation in aggregate patterns, they point to Abramson's (2015) work exploring the ways mechanisms of social stratification shape the lives of Americans aging in unequal circumstances. By observing older Americans in different communities, Abramson identified numerous means by which personal history, class background, racial difference, or neighborhood ecology translated to health outcomes. The analysis parses differences between neighborhood disadvantages and individual resources, prior inequality and present behavior, in a comparative analysis that charts the causes and forms of variation in a way that would not be possible in a case study of a single neighborhood or population.

Interactionist and Simmelian Formalism: The Thematic Lens

Chapter 3 turns to an alternative vision of the search for invariance and generalization, drawn from symbolic interactionism, cultural sociology, analytical sociology, and Simmelian formalism. Authors DeGloma and Papadantonakis use comparison to chart what underlies the empirical manifestation of general meaning structures or interactional patterns. Unlike Sánchez-Jankowski's and Abramson's use of mechanisms to explain empirical outcomes of interest, the authors argue for the value of examining transsituational forms that connect substantively different empirical cases. Getting at these formal components requires comparing the structures that underlie and produce empirical manifestations in diverse settings. They argue that to identify what is general, ethnographers must compare seemingly disparate objects in way that broadens, rather than narrows, comparison. Their comparisons are not selected in advance to resolve a scientific question (as in positivism) or extend a given existing theory (as in the extended case method), but develop a series of linked cases that reveal general cultural structures. These insights become crystalized as a thematic lens, which ethnographers can apply to other cases to better understand commonalities and differences.

A key example from the text is subversive anonymity, a way that actors use masking of faces to elicit particular responses from those they seek to incorporate or oppose. The authors note, for instance, that the Ku Klux Klan and the Zapatistas might be far apart politically, but their organizational tactics and mythology have considerable overlap in this anonymous presentation.

Elsewhere, DeGloma has shown how a narrative structure of awakening to new identities is shared across empirical instances, helping to hone a general theory of awakenings that has transsituational validity and may predict features of other linked processes. Only with comparative cases can scholars separate out what is a feature of subversive anonymity or awakenings and what is a particular contingency of the object. These structures of meaning or interaction, they contend, reveal formulaic patterns of action that can further explain behavior in unfamiliar or seemingly unlinked cases.

Cognitive Sociology and Ethnomethodology: Connecting Micro and Macro Structure

Chapter 4 turns to Cicourel's comparative approach to understanding invariance and the human cognitive bases of social structure. Cicourel begins by explaining the essential importance of looking at micro-structures—forms of social cognition, tacit knowledge, memory systems, analogical reasoning, and knowledge processes. Communal life, and the macro-structures that sociologist often study, are only possible through these micro-structures which enable complex historically situated macro-structures. Participant observation plays a unique role in charting these, as it allows the observation of people, behaviors, and communicative events in real time in a way no other method can. He argues that other modes of research, in their attempt to get at macro-structure without acknowledging its micro-foundations (e.g., demographic and survey research), frequently make errors by taking these processes for granted and missing important connections. The result is that these macro-structural approaches transpose the deductive forms of digital reasoning implicit in those methods onto all which they study and risk employing measures that do not map onto the real-life situations they study (i.e., they lack ecological validity). Ethnographers who only focus on the situation or conversation make a similar error and fail to connect to the macro-contexts that constrain the operations of micro-structure.

Cicourel's approach requires a form of comparison that involves temporal, vertical, and horizontal dimensions. Participant observation for Cicourel, by its nature, always examines real-world situations temporally. By examining these over time, and leveraging inherent temporal variation, it is possible to see which aspects of a phenomenon are invariant with accountable exceptions. Likewise, horizontal comparisons across institutions and contexts serve a parallel role for uncovering both micro and macro-structure. The approach also involves vertical comparisons across levels of analysis, data types, and repositories of information, which Cicourel sees as redescriptions of the realities underlying social structure. The notion of combining data types to connect phenomena is likely most familiar to most readers as a form of triangulation—with ethnography adding both ecological validity and the direct observation of behavior. For Cicourel, however, the comparison is bigger, and requires examining the underlying systems of memory, representation, and communication embedded in different data types (i.e., the scientific version of collective memory). The point for him is not simply to combine these data, but to compare differences in what they produce and make this process of production a central methodological and empirical object leveraged for connecting micro- and macro-structure. Rather than relying on the books produced earlier in his distinguished career, Cicourel provides here an example with original data examining how a flood of information and cognitive overload are managed in medical clinics. The example points to the importance of connecting language, behavior, and context to explain individual and institutional responses to a shared challenge.

The Extended Case Method: Leveraging Variance to Theorize Micro–Macro Connections

In chapter 5, Lee explores her own evolving approach to comparison, grounded in the overarching tradition of the extended case method (ECM). The reasons ECM practitioners compare is intimately tied to the chief goals of the ECM itself: the search for micro-macro connections and the elaboration of existing social theory. Comparison at the macroscopic level offers a route to better *seeing* invisible social structure as it impacts the visible, observed world. Given that the theories to be extended are often macro in scope, ECM helps ethnographers stay attuned to both micro-level and political economic questions. This approach typically compares meso-level forms (factories, casinos) in different macro-level settings (nation-states, economic systems) to observe and explain variation in micro-level interactional outcomes (e.g., style of management). Finding micro-variation while engaged with often macro-theories of, say, shifts in global capitalism offers puzzles for reformulating these theories.

A key instance of comparison in ECM is found in Lee's study of factories located on either side of the China/Hong Kong border, with the same owners but different management styles. In dialog with Burawoy's theory of states' influence on different management styles, Lee shows how gendered labor markets in each setting shape management. There she employed what she called a variable approach to comparison, but found the logic of controlling for factors overly reductive, and sought in her second book to show interconnections between her compared cases. In her most recent book she does not compare the same company across countries, but mining companies of different national origin within a single country, and leverages historical moments in an eventful comparison. When the global price of copper takes a hit, Lee is able to compare how Chinese, Indian, and other forms of capital react to answer her question: is there something unique about Chinese capital in Africa? She finds that the private Chinese companies react similarly to other private organizations, but Chinese State capital is unique. From here she is able to elaborate a theory of varieties of capital, versus varieties of capitalism. Without comparison at a macro-level, her projects could not make these specific claims about national or state influence. In her candid elaboration of the research process, she also shows how the ECM can be deployed in more flexible ways than critics have assumed.

Critical Realism: Actualist and Realist Comparison

In chapter 6, Decoteau shows how a Critical Realist (CR) philosophy of science can enhance existing approaches to ethnographic comparison. Decoteau's contribution takes the extended case method (ECM) as a starting point, but then draws on the vocabulary of CR to help think through multiple levels of analysis. Like other ECM practitioners, Decoteau is interested in micro-macro connections and extending theory. As a critical realist she makes certain distinctions that somewhat reorient the logic of comparison. With the principle of ontological stratification, critical realists separate out the empirical phenomena (manifestations of the "actual") from what they call "the real" (the mechanisms that underlie them). Thus, for Decoteau, ECM practitioners need not be so actualist with their case selection (e.g., factories and factories, casinos and casinos), and can instead focus on mechanisms that underline empirical manifestations. This is akin to Steinmetz's (2004) point that he studied German colonization of Africa, China, and Samoa not simply because all are colonies, but because they were likely to provide comparative leverage on shared mechanisms and generative structures. For Decoteau, this means selecting cases that may be presumed to have similar mechanisms to compare—either the actual or the real. For instance, she examines Somali communities in Toronto and Minneapolis, each forging health social movements around elevated rates of autism diagnosis. A depth-realist comparative ethnography captures and analytically disentangles the different ways that structures come together in conjunctures, and how agents activate them.

Decoteau focuses on one underlying structural mechanism in each case, namely contrasting forms of racial formation in the United States and Canada. Divergent histories of racism and racialized refugee policy created different structural conditions that communities could then act upon. In Minneapolis, she finds Somali parents were able to leverage available discourses of American racism and health disparities to secure resources and treatment. Ironically, the Canadian ideology of multiculturalism made it harder for the Toronto groups to demonstrate racial disparities and organize around racial discrimination. Rather than isolating or controlling for singular variables, Decoteau carefully shows how varying structural factors come together in complex conjunctions. A key contribution of this depth-realist comparison is the explicit focus on conjunctural mechanistic causality, and showing how agents can use or affect structures, such as communities activating racial formations to exploit differences in health-care systems.

Grounded Theory and Abductive Sequential Comparison

In chapter 7, Tavory and Timmermans address how not only the selection, but also how the timing of a case comparison may impact the directions of a study. Building on their pragmatist reworking of grounded theory (GT), they advocate open-mindedness to the surprises in field research, and reading a range of theories with which to interpret such surprises rather than rigid adherence to a particular theory (as in the extended case method) or comparative design (as in behavioralism) that risks locking practitioners in and preventing creative theorizing. In this volume they offer a suggestion for how to approach comparison—with the sequential addition of another case or site when the study calls for it. This derives in part from an older GT precept, the addition of new cases to see if early theoretical formulations hold. In contrast, Tavory and Timmermans use additional cases more to clarify and better theorize the original case. One could add a similar site but with controlled variation (akin to behavioralism), in another structural location (akin to ECM), to clarify a depth-realist mechanism (Decoteau), or as a thematic lens (akin to DeGloma and Papadantonakis). Tavory and Timmermans's key point is that they believe it is best to add cases *after* gaining a good grasp of the first case, and then seeing which comparison could deepen understanding.

As an example, they offer Gong's study of community mental healthcare. When Gong found public providers to be highly tolerant of the indigent mentally ill's treatment non-compliance or use of illicit substances, he noted the contrast with theoretical accounts of state repression. He suspected that the treatment providers lacked therapeutic capacity for normalizing patients and had come to focus on safety and harm reduction. To hone this point, he sought out a contrasting case of wealthy community-based private services. Here good care was explicitly normalizing, as providers had the resources to try to transform clients, and wealthy families had different classed expectations for the meaning of improvement. For Tavory and Timmermans, the sequential comparison's added value was to avoid foreclosing intriguing findings by prematurely defining the bounds of comparison, and thus enabling a pivot to new literatures and material when justified by findings from the primary case.

Applied Interpretivism: Technological Tools for Scaled Studies of Biomedicine

In chapter 8, Bernstein and Dohan describe how comparative ethnography can inform biomedicine, and how the context of biomedical research can also inform approaches to ethnographic comparison. While medicine has long been dominated by the quantitative gaze, Bernstein and Dohan point to the value of unique ethnographic insights around issues central to health policy—such as patient provider interaction, complex health behaviors, and the implications of the organizational cultures of medicine. They argue that the biomedical field would benefit from integrating these insights, while at the same time, ethnography would benefit from more explicit engagement beyond disciplinary bubbles. As applied ethnographers in the context of

American biomedicine, their goal is not the advancement of abstract methodological or theoretical constructs, but instead solving problems of policy and practice that impact people like cancer or Alzheimer's patients. However, addressing these issues in a way legible to health policy requires revisiting the same quantitative–qualitative divides that dominated social science disciplines in the middle of the twentieth century.

While their work can be characterized as broadly interpretivist in their focus on connecting meaning and behavior in context, Bernstein and Dohan do not use the critical, anti-comparative, and (occasionally) anti-realist approaches of some medical anthropology and sociology. Rather, they describe the utility of importing and fusing techniques used in studies of biomedicine and applied social science. Their goal is not simply adding face validity to ethnography in a field dominated by positivist model of science, but improving the scope, transparency, reliability, and scale of comparative ethnography. While aspects of this mirror the behavioralist emphasis on systematic comparative data for policy, Bernstein and Dohan introduce two specific techniques for addressing issues of scaling ethnography to generate wider data: interactive heat-maps or ethnoarrays and the deployment of geospatial data about ethnographic subjects. Both rely on computer-assisted approaches to enable the production of larger data sets that show both patterns and specifics, facilitating comparisons within and across groups. They conclude by noting how this can inform interventions in clinical settings, community contexts, and health policy.

In chapter 9, Chancer brackets the procedures of comparative methodology to tackle an unspoken dimension: how ethnographers decide what to study. Chancer's contribution is less a prescription for comparison than a meta-commentary on how disciplinary cultures think comparatively. Examining the United States and France, she notes that French sociologists are far more apt to study across the class spectrum, and specifically study elites. American sociologists, on the other hand, devote the majority of their studies to the poor or minority groups. She notes, for instance, that while 40% of the articles in *Qualitative Sociology* focus on the poor or working class, only 1% focuses on the rich. The most common explanation for why there are not more studies of elites is access—in essence, that the privileged don't want to be studied, and have the power to refuse scrutiny. While Chancer does not fully dispute this, she notes both successful American studies of elites and the greater frequency of such studies in France.

Chancer turns points to the utility of a psychosocial and psychoanalytic account of the dispositions of American sociologists. She notes that American sociologists tend to be left leaning politically, and would prefer to be associated with the downtrodden than the oppressor. In effect, spending time and developing relationships with marginalized people can serve as a technique of neutralization to assuage guilt for those academics who are themselves of a higher-class background. Finally, they may believe that since there are substantial social problems to solve, there is no reason to waste time on those who are comfortable. As Chancer notes, this lack of comparative material makes any theory of social class or inequality impossible, since those need to be understood relationally and hierarchically. As a contextualizing piece, it is a call for sociologists to consider not only why they study who they do, but also who they are avoiding—in some cases for privileged academics, that is people like themselves.

Chapter 10 offers Cicourel's reflection on how ethnographic methods, including issues of comparison, have shifted over time. In conversation with Corey Abramson, Cicourel argues for attentiveness to an often-overlooked strength of comparative ethnography—the way cross-site ethnographic comparisons can be used to chart not just variation, but comparatively invariant aspects of human behavior in a way that captures real-time, localized behavior and language use. Cicourel explains how his approach consequently draws upon diverse traditions ranging from cognitive linguistics to behavioral ecology to produce a more integrated form of comparative sociology that encompasses multiple levels of social and physical reality. Cicourel emphasizes the advantage of moving away from the interpretive position that ethnography is thick description, to an approach that uses both language and physical action to develop generalizations about how structural invariance with accountable exceptions constitutes the social world. In the process, Cicourel provides insightful reflections about how his past and present experiences in sociology and cognitive science have led him to this position and what younger generations might learn from his experiences. Cicourel proceeds to voice his current position on topics including approaches to comparison, ecological validity and levels of analysis, language use, the historical connection of his approach to ethnomethodology, team science in contemporary academia, analogical and digital approaches to inquiry, the role of theory, and what he hopes future ethnographers will learn from his career.

Comparing Comparative Approaches: The What, Why, and How of Ethnographic Comparison

Table C.1 is a summary that highlights the differences in approaches to comparison featured in this volume. The columns represent each of the general approaches featured in this volume. The rows represent positions on the following questions: 1) *Why Compare?* Here we summarize what the authors see as the added value of comparison vis-à-vis single site or case studies for each approach. 2) *How do they do it?* Here we sketch key practical aspects of to comparative study design. 3) *What is the end goal*? Here we consider the broader analytical goals and evaluative criteria provided by the authors. 4) *What is a concrete example?* This column highlights exemplary contributions highlighted by the authors.[1]

Themes and Overlaps

For all their differences, the authors' contributions touch on shared themes such as the objects and goals of comparison, the role of mechanisms in comparative ethnographic research, and the contexts in which comparison takes place. We conclude this volume by looking briefly at these themes, differences, and points of overlap.

Objects and Goals of Comparison

The discussions and table here reveal that the contributors are often comparing different objects or units of analysis: people, organizations, class groups, neighborhoods, generative mechanisms, meaning structures, and interactional styles. In practice, many of these are connected. For instance, styles of interaction reflect cultural understandings, which are connected to contexts like neighborhoods, and are ultimately enacted by individuals. All

[1] The table reflects our categorization of our contributors' espoused visions of the traditions in which they are operating. As a caveat, it is important to recognize that such a reduction facilitates interpretation via contrast. Like all ideal types, it helps to clarify but also risks simplifying and understating the points of commonality we discuss in the next section of this conclusion. As we noted in this volume's introduction, there are internal differences between people who we have broadly lumped into a tradition. For instance, Tavory and Timmermans's abductive approach shares procedures with grounded theory, and derives in part from it, but it is also diverges from other strands descendant from the general approach. Similarly, the thematic lens has influences ranging from symbolic interaction to analytical sociology, so we link them here despite considerable variation.

Table C.1 Summarizing Approaches to Ethnographic Comparison

Approach	Why Compare?	How?	End Goal	Examples
Behavioralist participant observation	Understanding variation in real-world behaviors is necessary to charting causal mechanisms	Stratified samples of the population (e.g., people, organizations, neighborhood) being studied	Producing valid generalizable empirical findings about essential social life that other methods fail to capture	How gangs survive as organizations (Sánchez-Jankowski 1991); How prior experiences with inequality shape strategies to aging (Abramson 2015)
The extended case method	Illuminate micro-macro connections, leverage case variance to elaborate theories	Selecting organizations in different structural locations	Extend social theory by connecting local ethnographic findings to macro forces	How national context shapes factory labor practices (Lee 1995), or how differently situated organizations respond to a structural event (Lee 2018)
Formalist/ analytical/ symbolic interactionist	Finding transsituational meaning structures	Selecting very different cases and looking for commonalities	Show formal connections between seemingly divergent empirical phenomena, generates analogies	How people awaken to new identities across a wide variety of life areas (DeGloma 2014)
Abductive analysis/ grounded theory	Additional cases may clarify first case and be useful for theory generation	Start with one case, if necessary look for contrast cases	See connections to aid in theory generation without employing a rigid comparative framework	How resource variation shapes psychiatric case management practices (Gong, 2019)
Cognitive sociology	Understand variation in situations and time to link micro-social structure (cognitive, linguistic) and macro-structure (aggregated history and organization)	Examining variation in time and situation	Identifying both universals and variation in an ecologically valid way that reflects real-world thought, speech, and behavior	How responses to cognitive overload shape clinical medicine (Cicourel, this volume)

Continued

Table C.1 Continued

Approach	Why Compare?	How?	End Goal	Examples
Critical realism	Explain variance to elaborate theory, identify generative mechanisms, show structure-agency connections	Select sites that reveal broader mechanisms	Charting depth mechanisms to connect cases and levels of social reality (e.g., micro, meso, macro)	How communities mobilize around national racial formations (Decoteau, this volume)

the authors recognize the connections between these levels.[2] That said, different approaches generally vary in the extent to which they are most concerned with macro-historical, meso-organizational, or micro-interactional phenomena. Symbolic interactionists and ethnomethodologists often focus on micro-phenomenon like how meanings are negotiated by people in situations. Behavioralists and grounded theorists often focus on middle-range phenomena such as how medical organizations manage the aged or dying and how these people respond in turn. Those who use the extended case method are typically concerned with extending macro-theoretical concepts such as Marxian notions of globalization to organizational and everyday life.

Further, differences in what ethnographers choose to compare, and at what level, reflect different goals and criteria for evaluating comparative research. They compare for different purposes—revealing the causal mechanisms that explain aggregate correlations (Sánchez-Jankowski and Abramson, this volume), mapping empirical variance and invariance (Cicourel, this volume), elaborating depth mechanisms underlying empirical manifestations (Decoteau, this volume), deepening interpretation of an initial study through the addition of alternative cases (Tavory and Timmermans, this volume), extending theories to better incorporate unexpected variance (Lee, this volume), and showing formal links between empirically disconnected phenomena (DeGloma and Papadantonakis, this volume). These approaches judge the value of comparative research

[2] This parallels contemporary theories of social life, which have long recognized and made central the duality and coconstituency of individuals and groups (Breiger 1974), structure and culture (Sewell 1992), agency and constraint (Giddens 1984), and experience and practice (Bourdieu 1984).

relative to these contrasting goals, and in accordance with the methodological principles they have outlined in this volume. Linked to these goals is a procedural question of substantial methodological and analytical importance that we turn to next: when and how ethnographers select their comparative sites.

Case Selection and Timing in the Construction of Comparison

A simultaneously practical and analytical debate threaded throughout the contributions regards how and when ethnographers would select multiple cases. In chapters 1 and 2, Sánchez-Jankowski and Abramson argue that sites should be selected at the outset based on their appropriateness to a scientific question with theoretical and practical implications, such as "How do older Americans from different racial and socioeconomic groups manage the mundane and existential demands of growing older in the context of persistent American inequality?" (Abramson 2015). Such projects use aggregate statistical patterns (e.g., data showing persistent inequality and disparities in health and aging) to (a) frame the problem, (b) identify populations for study and comparative samples that are representative of those categories, in order to (c) examine the plausibility of existing explanations or generate new models of inequality in the process of answering the empirical question. The extended case method (ECM) similarly advocates the initial selection of cases for a comparative design. However, their questions and case selection are more directly driven by a particular theory—for instance, ECM practitioners might seek multiple cases that diverge from the expectations of an existing Marxist theory to help extend or reformulate it.

In contrast, both the abductive and symbolic interactionist contributors advocate an initial investigation and in-depth formulation of the first case before expanding to others. For Tavory and Timmermans, the risk of formulating a comparative case design at the outset is that it may lock researchers into an analytic frame prematurely. Most directly addressing the ECM, they suggest that preselecting a favored theoretical frame is even more problematic with comparison designed in. If the original theoretical framework proves problematic, the second case may no longer make sense as a comparison, and may prevent understanding the data one actually has. DeGloma and Papadantonakis's similarly argue for theorizing an initial case as a thematic lens and then use it to find interesting comparative cases from potentially unlike objects. It would be difficult to select the next cases without a thorough understanding of one's thematic lens to begin with.

How do the extended case method practitioners and behavioralists respond? Lee's contribution, which candidly addresses how her projects actually came together, suggests that ECM practitioners can be flexible in the process of casing. She notes that her study of divergent factories began with an empirical puzzle, rather than a favorite theory she wished to elaborate. Furthermore, her next book actually worked closer to sequential comparison—after an initial investigation of one Chinese protest movement, her addition of a second helped to clarify both. Neither project emerged as a doctrinaire version of the extended case method. Indeed, she notes that Burawoy himself is not dogmatic as a mentor, and encourages students to recursively tack back and forth between theory, data, and potentially new theories. Regarding the need to be open to data far outside of one's original interest, Sánchez-Jankowski and Abramson suggest that researchers remain committed to the original question as it was selected because of its scientific and human relevance. However, they are explicitly open to emergent findings, new sites, and the integration of new theories that advance their analytical tasks. Instead of rethinking the question framework, as Tavory and Timmermans suggest, the researchers would choose another field site that offers the right data for a question or engage with a new theory or model that provides insight. In fact, all of these positions involve flexibility. What differs is what is flexible (e.g., a question, a theoretical frame, a site).

This question of adherence to a question or flexibly recasing reflects a real difference and sticking point. In contrast to the behavioralist vision of conventional scientific method driven by strongly formulated questions, Tavory and Timmermans see fieldwork like "Jeopardy"—one may have the answer in the form of field observations and then reformulate a scientific question around it. They're particularly attuned to surprises in the field, which may change the direction and framing of research entirely. ECM practitioners are ultimately interested in theory extension, and may continually add theories or cases, and recursively "recase" until a project reveals itself. Sánchez-Jankowski and Abramson, however, remain driven by the original question, and posit that over time surprises in the field will either be revealed to be relevant to the original question at hand or tangential findings (which may provide a potential opportunity for a future project).

All note that there are drawbacks to starting one case study and then the other—namely, the introduction of time lag between cases presents problems of whether differences are due to time and new conditions or baseline conditions for most study designs. Lee's third book addresses this with what she calls the eventful comparison of how Chinese state versus private Chinese, Indian, Swiss, and local Zambian mines reacted to the global drop in copper prices. Abramson similarly used a structural shift with austerity measures to see how different neighborhoods respond and would not have been able to observe the immediate and differential effect of austerity measures after the great recession if he observed the neighborhoods in his study sequentially. Thus, the abductive sequential model may offer flexibility but limit certain kinds of claims, and these analytical trade-offs are not easily reconciled. In some cases, ethnographers will find that practical circumstances shape their ability or desire to sample sites simultaneously, and what is most appropriate may vary by project and goals. We next turn to examples and theoretical products of these different approaches to see how the different procedures and conceptualizations actually manifest.

Products: Finding Quasi-Universals and Linking Unlike Cases

Consider first what might appear a stark contrast between ethnographic traditions: the behavioralist approach of Sánchez-Jankowski and Abramson, and the interactionist cultural sociology of DeGloma and Papadantonakis. The former are concerned with causally explaining particular empirical outcomes, such as stratified aggregate health outcomes in later life or urban street gangs' ability to survive continual policy and law enforcement attempts to eradicate them. Operating in what they call the conventional scientific tradition, Abramson and Sánchez-Jankowski articulate a variable logic of similar cases with controlled variation, a concern with statistical generalizability, and the need for strong comparative design at the outset. DeGloma and Papadantonakis, on the other hand, are concerned with meaning structures that travel, what they describe as "situated versions of a formulaic interactive dynamic." They home in on unlike cases with a thematic lens to show how such formulaic dynamics or meanings connect even disparate empirical phenomena. Unlike Sánchez-Jankowski and Abramson's argument for site selection at the outset, they begin thematic lens comparison with an initial case study. "As soon as the formal theme is observed, the single case is put on hold as the primary basis of analysis (permanently or temporarily) and the researcher starts to *see* the world (and other cases) through the lens of the theme itself" (DeGloma and Papadantonakis, this volume).

Yet consider two examples drawn from these contributors own comparative work that have notable similarities alongside differences.

Sánchez-Jankowski's *Islands in the Street* studied gangs across ethnicity and location and identified a psychological disposition that held in all contexts—what he calls "defiant individualism." This category consists of attributes like intensive competitiveness and a social Darwinist world view—a key finding of invariance amidst the wide range of gangs he studied. DeGloma's work on anonymity, on the other hand, examines how seemingly contradictory organizations like the Ku Klux Klan and the Zapatistas use largely similar cultural structures—what DeGloma calls "subversive anonymity." He and Papadantonakis note that these groups might be opposed ideologically and have different histories, yet both use masks to hide identity, raise the possibility that any community member might be involved, and to invoke the spirits of Confederate Soldiers and Zapata, respectively. In their approach, this is prized as a cultural structure that can link phenomena that observers might initially think do not belong together.[3]

Although operating with different vocabularies, background literatures, and even philosophies of science, both Sánchez-Jankowski and DeGloma contribute an analytical category that helps explain key features of nonstate organizations that maintain a capacity for violence. These categories can potentially travel from organization to organization. There are differences, to be sure. Defiant individualism is meant to generalize from a sample of people to a population; that is, it aims to be empirically generalizable. In fact, quantitative researchers later conducted survey research and found support for Sánchez-Jankowski's claim (cf. Jensen 1996). Subversive anonymity may describe a form of cultural practice and meaning-making that goes beyond the types of cases initially outlined. Its generalizability is theoretical, and portable to potentially a vast number of like and unlike cases. Additionally, there is a sense in which categorization and operationalization work differently. For instance, Sánchez-Jankowski operationalizes gangs, and distinguishes them from looser cliques and crews to strengthen claims of representativeness. DeGloma's objects are not strongly operationalized up front, as the researcher may only define the class of cases after considering them through an emergent thematic lens.

Looked at side by side, this comparison shows how these approaches might see a similar object—a nonstate organization with violent capabilities—and offer different routes of comparison and visions of generating knowledge.

[3] This is also similar to Vaughan's work on analogical reasoning, which looks for shared organizational features across sometimes radically different forms of organization (Vaughan 2014).

Both leverage invariance but differ in which invariant element they show is most relevant to their research, namely psychological dispositions or meaning structures. The suitable comparisons necessarily differ as well. Given that they have different goals and criteria (replicable patterns versus transposable concepts), the standards for necessary and sufficient evidence are not easily reconcilable. The key similarity is that both analytically leverage invariance in their approach to comparison, generate categories that can aid in understanding other empirical materials, and make claims that are not possible with single cases. The other major approach addressed in this volume, from ethnomethodologists and Cicourel's cognitive sociology, would similarly leverage comparison to get at even more universal aspects of human reasoning and communication that shape behavior in organizations.

Products: Theory Extension Via Contrasting Cases

Consider also the macro-oriented comparison of the extended case method propounded by Lee, on the one hand, and the interactional and abductive approach advocated by Tavory and Timmermans, on the other. There is, on the face of it, considerable potential for divergence. In doctrinaire form, the ECM would begin with strong theoretical priors to identify cases with theoretical value, and in the comparative approach, the ECM would begin with similar cases in different structural circumstances to help theorize micro–macro connections. In the abductive approach descendent from grounded theory, an ethnographer would engage a field site while reading broadly, and only when the theoretical casing of site one demands a contrast case, move to a second case. While Tavory and Timmermans embrace theoretical pluralism, they work primarily in an interactionist mode. We might expect that the analytical fruits of these different approaches would be quite different.

Here, however, consider some of the strong similarities proffered in the contributions. As an example, Lee describes her work on two factories owned by the same company but on opposite sides of the Hong Kong/Mainland China border. She identifies contrasting styles of management, which she labels "localistic despotism" and "familial hegemony," and shows how different labor markets in the respective regions create different conditions of worker dependence. Theoretically, she complicates Burawoy's existing theory of labor regimes and worker dependence on the state with feminist theoretical sensitivity to women's conditions of dependence in their home communities. Tavory and Timmermans, on the other hand, identify Neil Gong's work on community mental healthcare to illustrate how adding cases can help clarify the initial case. When Gong found public mental health providers working in highly tolerant ways with the homeless or indigent mentally ill, it contradicted accounts of state domination of poor deviants. He observed that the treatment team struggled to normalize patients' behavior and had come to focus primarily on harm reduction rather than behavioral correction. Gong then sought out a contrasting case of wealthy community treatment. Here elite services were in some ways more controlling, as they sought to—and had the resources to—transform their clients and offer respectable futures. He later (Gong 2019) theorized two approaches: a "tolerant containment" public model that eschewed Foucaultian disciplinary power and an elite private "concerted constraint," akin to Lareau's (2011) "concerted cultivation" of privileged children.

In effect, both Lee and Gong engage in a theorization of interactional patterns (how does social control work?) to generate a "why" theoretical puzzle (why do they diverge?) and essentially use empirical cases as ideal types from which to generate theoretical categories. Each engages both structural factors (labor markets, welfare states, class stratification) and interactional dynamics (e.g., the practical problems of management in different settings). Each generates binary theoretical categories in an effort to extend literatures. However, there are some important differences in what they do with these theories related to the goals of comparison and evaluative criteria. Lee's target is not the theorization of interactional styles like familial hegemony, but using their divergence to further understand the nature of contemporary capitalism. She aims to complicate structural accounts of capitalist production, extending Burawoy's largely top down model of state-enterprise to include the way "gender is part and parcel of negotiation between capital and labor" (Lee 1995, 394). For Gong, the description and then interpretation of interactional styles are the theoretical contribution. Concerted constraint, for instance, might help illuminate a variety of socialization projects where the wealthy invest in the control of their members. The category is both *explained by* structural factors like class inequality, and *explanatory itself*, as when differential treatment interactions account for different patient identities and trajectories. The key point is that each leverages the comparison to complicate existing theoretical accounts, and then reformulate social theory.

The Language of Mechanisms and Critical Realist Ontology

Another key point of convergence and difference is in how the authors understand mechanisms and causality. Decoteau's piece is situated in the ECM tradition, but draws on the language of critical realism (CR) to offer a depth-realist approach to comparison. This offers an alternative philosophical vocabulary for the kinds of developments Lee describes in her works. For Decoteau, ethnographers can hone their comparisons by paying attention to what CR calls "ontological stratification," or the distinction between the empirical events we experience and the underlying causal mechanisms that conjuncturally produce them. CR, Decoteau suggests, can offer a cleaner account of causality, structure, and agency than found in much of the current ethnographic literature. She examines Somali communities in Toronto and Minneapolis, each forging health social movements around elevated rates of autism diagnosis. What a depth-realist comparative ethnography captures and analytically disentangles is the different ways that agents can activate and transform structures.

She focuses on one underlying structural mechanism in each case, namely contrasting forms of racial formation in the United States and Canada. Divergent histories of racism and racialized refugee policy created different structural conditions that communities could then act upon. In Minneapolis, she finds that Somali parents were able to leverage available discourses of American racism and health disparities to secure resources and treatment. Ironically, the Canadian ideology of multiculturalism made it harder for the Toronto groups to demonstrate racial disparities and organize around racial discrimination. Rather than isolating or controlling for singular variables, Decoteau carefully shows how varying structural factors come together in complex conjunctions. A key contribution of ethnography to this depth-realist comparison is that explicit focus on conjunctural mechanistic causality, and the way that agents interact with structures, like activating racial formations to exploit differences in healthcare systems.

Sánchez-Jankowski and Abramson also operate in an explicitly realist mode and see identifying causal mechanisms as a central goal. Yet in their focus on empirical generalizability and concrete scientific questions, Sánchez-Jankowski and Abramson would be more likely to focus on directly observable comparisons in bounded contexts and situations, even though they are open to the possibility that observed mechanisms may broaden reach (an empirical question to be determined by future tests). As noted previously, they also diverge from the ECM in terms of how they utilize theory and empirical material; there is shared attention to sequences of causality and conjunction.

Tavory and Timmermans, working in the pragmatist tradition, see mechanisms as chains of human meaning making and subsequent actions at the micro-level. Thus, Decoteau's emphasis on structural mechanisms seems ill-suited to their micro-vision of ethnography. They might ask that Decoteau's emphasis on the agential activation of structural mechanisms be further broken down into more micro-level connections (which may overlap with the sequences Abramson and Sánchez Jankowski advocate for observing). Yet they would not, in principle, be opposed to connecting micro-level meaning-making to institutional manifestations, such as racialized policies. DeGloma and Papadantonakis approach could be compatible with the distinction between the actual and the real, as for them this parallels the difference between an empirical manifestation and an underlying form. This is, again, the point of a thematic lens that sheds light on underlying connections between disparate phenomena. DeGloma and Papadantonakis are not necessarily interested in conjunctural causal explanations, so much as showing how these forms operate in diverse circumstances. Despite differences, all of these traditions are interested in sequencing to understand when and how things happen.

The Dispositional and Disciplinary "Why" Behind Comparison

The final section of the volume emphasizes something often lost in formal discussions of method—that the production and contestation of knowledge occurs in concrete contexts of disciplines, nations, and eras. Several of the authors explain how these contexts shape the practice of comparative ethnography in the past and present, and why taking this into consideration can improve our practice. Chancer, Dohan and Bernstein, and Cicourel take different approaches to examining how and why ethnographers compare, yet in terms beyond the ostensible analytic goals of the various traditions.

Chancer's contribution focuses less on how to do comparative studies than on understanding the available comparative archive in American ethnography. Why, she asks, is there so much in-depth description of the lives of the poor and ethnic minorities, but relatively little on elites? She draws on a psychodynamic and sociological framework to comparatively analyze the ethnographic study of class in the United States and France, and concludes that there are key dispositional reasons for the American emphasis on "studying down." Most notably, she argues, that beyond issues of access, ethnographers choose to study the marginalized out of political identification with the oppressed and dis-identification with the privileged—often the class background of those researchers themselves. For Chancer, the solution is reflexivity—ethnographers must take seriously the social and psychological factors pushing their research agenda. Her aim, ultimately, is for balanced study of different groups so that there is a thorough archive of studies from which to make comparative claims. Her piece suggests the way academic contexts shapes the selection of projects, and the potential costs.

Bernstein and Dohan discuss the importance of another context—health research—and how it shapes the kinds of comparative thinking they engage in. They note the importance of studying how culture shapes biomedicine, and that health policy has increasingly acknowledged the importance of ethnographic research. Yet the culture of biomedicine can also shape ethnography and its packaging. They note that medical anthropologists and sociologists who use qualitative data still need to navigate "epistemological tensions" when they examine biomedicine. Rather than see this as solely a barrier to ethnographic work, they take it as an opportunity. One route that Bernstein and Dohan offer is the adaptation of computational tools more commonly found in biomedicine and computational social science to ethnographic research.[4] This not only broadens ethnographic inquiry, but also allows them to communicate their findings more directly to medical researchers. Borrowed from the visual reduction in genetic micro-arrays, they present ethnoarrays as a way to reduce, filter, and share large amounts of qualitative data. In so doing they can directly address the comparative questions of public health or biomedicine using rich qualitative data—in this case, why and how some people enroll in medical trials compared to others. For Dohan and Bernstein, this transdisciplinary work can in turn aid ethnographers in other contexts. Although not necessarily working within the boundaries of biomedicine, such practitioners may benefit from this alternative way of representing comparisons. In the end, their project shows how stepping outside of disciplinary can benefit ethnographic inquiry, even as it creates other practical challenges.

Finally, Cicourel's interview (as well as his chapter on social structure) shows how ideas reflect the professional contexts in which they are produced, often to the detriment of comparative social science. He provides insights and examples from his career, including his break from Garfinkel and other social scientists of his era. The chapter explains how a narrow disciplinary focus, the current mode of academic production, and the allocation

[4] For more on the logic and utility of computational ethnography and the ethnoarrays approach within sociology, see Abramson and Dohan (2015) and Abramson et al. 2018.

of funding and prestige can generate complacency that runs counter to the goal of improving the theories and methods ethnographers employ. Cicourel urges new generations of ethnographers to be principled and committed, but always critical and self-aware, lest they (paraphrasing Erving Goffman) become taken in by their own act.

Conclusion

The contributors to this volume have offered both rigorous methodological statements and candid explanations of how they use comparison in their own ethnographic research. For the student seeking guidance, or the seasoned researcher looking to add a new comparative dimension to their practice, there is ample material and contrasting perspectives to weigh. Furthermore, the reflections on the institutional context of research, such as national disciplinary cultures or applied health settings, reminds readers to consider how the contexts we inhabit shape our comparative scholarship. In the spirit of pluralism outlined here, we have noted where the chapters conflict, converge, and ultimately make different contributions using comparative research to understand the social world. The wealth of ethnographic traditions represented in this volume show vibrant debate rather than consensus about what constitutes proper ethnographic comparison. But, as Clifford Geertz noted long ago, consensus is often less productive than debate and discussion in refining our models of and for the world. "What gets better," he wrote, "is the precision with which we vex each other" (1973, 29). We similarly hope that with better mutual understanding and respectful engagement, we can both learn from and more precisely challenge each other and improve our research practices.

References

Abramson, Corey M. 2015. *The End Game: How Inequality Shapes Our Final Years.* Cambridge, MA: Harvard University Press.

Abramson Corey M. and Daniel Dohan. 2015. "Beyond Text: Using Arrays to Represent and Analyze Ethnographic Data." *Sociological Methodology* 45[1]: 272–319.

Abramson, Corey M., Jacqueline Joslyn, Katharine A. Rendle, Sarah B. Garrett, and Daniel Dohan. 2018. "The Promises of Computational Ethnography: Improving Transparency, Replicability, and Validity for Realist Approaches to Ethnographic Analysis." *Ethnography* 19, no. 2: 254–284.

Bourdieu, Pierre, and Richard Nice. 1984. *Distinction: A Social Critique of the Judgment of Taste*. Cambridge, MA: Harvard University Press.

Breiger, Ronald L. 1974. "The Duality of Persons and Groups." *Social Forces* 53, no. 2: 181–190.

DeGloma, Thomas. 2014. *Seeing the Light: The Social Logic of Personal Discovery*. Chicago: University of Chicago Press.

Geertz, Clifford. 1973. *The Interpretation of Cultures: Selected Essays*. New York: Basic Books.

Giddens, Anthony. 1984. *The Constitution of Society: Outline of the Theory of Structuration*. Berkeley: University of California Press.

Gong, Neil. 2019. "Between Tolerant Containment and Concerted Constraint: Managing Madness for the City and the Privileged Family." *American Sociological Review* 84, no. 4: 664–689.

Jensen, Gary, F. 1996. "Defiance and Gang Identity: Quantitative Test of Qualitative Hypotheses." *Journal of Gang Research* 3, no. 4: 13–29.

Lareau, Annette. 2011. *Unequal Childhoods: Class, Race, and Family life*. Berkeley: University of California Press.

Lee, Ching Kwan. 1995. "Engendering the Worlds of Labor: Women Workers, Labor Markets, and Production Politics in the South China Economic Miracle." *American Sociological Review* 60, no. 3: 378–397.

Lee, Ching Kwan. 2017. *The Specter of Global China: Politics, Labor, and Foreign Investment in Africa*. Chicago: University of Chicago Press.

Sánchez-Jankowski, Martín. 1991. *Islands in the Street: Gangs and American Urban Society*. Berkeley: University of California Press.

Sewell, William H Jr. 1992. "A Theory of Structure: Duality, Agency, and Transformation." *American Journal of Sociology* 98, no. 1: 1–29.

Steinmetz, George. 2004. "Odious Comparisons: Incommensurability, the Case Study, and 'Small N's' in Sociology." *Sociological Theory* 22, no. 3: 371–400.

Vaughan, Diane. 2014. I"Analogy, Cases, and Comparative Social Organization" *in Theorizing in the Social Sciences*, edited by Richard Swedberg, 61–84. Stanford: Stanford University Press.

Index

Tables, figures and boxes are indicated by *t*, *f* and *b* following the page number
For the benefit of digital users, indexed terms that span two pages (e.g., 52–53) may, on occasion, appear on only one of those pages.

CPSIA information can be obtained
at www.ICGtesting.com
Printed in the USA
LVHW090148111220
673901LV00007B/222

9 780190 608491